Popular S

and the Cris

Constitut

The Constitutional Dress of 1919

Germania: "Well, the old dress made of good German fabric suited

me better!" Reprinted from W. A. Coupe, *German Political Satires from*

the Reformation to the Second World War (White Plains, NY: Kraus

International Publications, 1985), by permission

POPULAR SOVEREIGNTY

and the CRISIS of GERMAN

CONSTITUTIONAL LAW

The Theory & Practice

of Weimar Constitutionalism

Peter C. Caldwell

Duke University Press Durham and London

1997

© 1997 Duke University Press

All rights reserved

Printed in the United States of America on acid-free paper ∞

Typeset in Adobe Caslon with Frutiger display by Tseng Information Systems, Inc.

Library of Congress Cataloging-in-Publication Data appear on

the last printed page of this book.

To

Peter R. Caldwell

&

Susan Havens Caldwell

for their support in

so many ways

CONTENTS

PREFACE

This work examines the debates over the meaning and practice of constitutional law that took place during Germany's first democracy, the Weimar Republic (1919–33). It focuses on the professors of state law who played and continue to play a central role in German constitutional debates: the compilers of manuals of state law, the authors of treatises on the abstract meaning of legal norms, and the scholars who trained and monitored the lawyers and judges of the German judicial system. Under the pressures of the new democracy, these scholars, and to a lesser extent the judges of the high courts, developed approaches to constitutional law that rejected or fundamentally reworked the categories and methods of the legal positivism that had come to dominate the legal profession during the German Empire (1871–1918).

The frontispiece to this book illustrates the way the constitution itself came into question as part of the debate over constitutional theory and method in the Republic. The cartoon, whose title translates as "The Constitutional Dress of 1919," caricatures Hugo Preuss, the author of the Weimar Constitution, as a Jewish tailor fitting Germania with a new dress. The constitutional dress is made up of rags from a number of foreign sources: English parliamentarianism, French constitutionalism, American constitutionalism, and, surreptitiously sewed on behind Germania's back, the ominous Marxism. Germania, looking in the mirror, says, "Well, the old dress made out of good German fabric suited me better!"

The cartoon conveys a number of messages. First, it suggests that the 1871 Imperial Constitution was somehow more "becoming"—more natural and less problematic—than the Weimar Constitution. And in fact, the 1871 Constitution did remain fairly unproblematic during the German Empire. It was in a way an "unpolitical" constitution, a constitution without a list of basic rights, a constitution that merely described the form of the state and the procedure for creating laws. Political controversy took place—but beyond the realm of constitutional law. By contrast, the Weimar Constitution, written in the aftermath of military defeat in the First World War, raised new and difficult—and politically charged—questions. The framers of the 1919 Constitution sought answers to the problems facing a constitutional democracy by examining the functioning of English and French parliamentarianism and the U.S. system of separation of powers. They also sought to accommodate those groups that had been marginalized in the German Empire, most notably the Social Democrats, by including social rights and opening the door to legislation that could have radical or socialist content. The constitution became a matter of political dispute in debates over how the democratic state would function, over the basic rights of German citizens, and over political parties and the president. The cartoon translates those problems into accusations of foreign influence and poor skill in forming the document, with anti-Semitic overtones. It illustrates both the real process of rethinking constitutional law and the ideological condemnation of the constitution itself that characterized antidemocratic thinking during the Republic.

The debates over the theory and practice of Weimar constitutionalism are important, first, because they indicate the possibilities and problems inherent in the concept of constitutional democracy in the context of a weak and defeated central European power in the interwar period. But the debates have also played a major role in the long-term formation of a postmonarchical constitutionalist tradition in Germany—a process that took place within the Federal Republic of Germany between 1949 and 1990—a tradition that emerged victorious, but still conflict-ridden and contentious, in the period after German unification. The main objects of my study, especially Carl Schmitt and Hermann Heller, have once again taken center stage in German constitutional debates during the past half decade as a politically united Germany has begun to discuss the substantive foundations of its unity, the meanings of political democracy, the concept of the German "nation," and the role of the state in times of economic limitations.

With one exception, all translations are my own unless otherwise noted. The exception is to be found in the frequently cited constitutional articles from the Imperial Constitution of 1871 and the Weimar

Constitution, for which I rely on the translations in Elmar M. Hucko, ed., *The Democratic Tradition: Four German Constitutions*, unless otherwise indicated.

Some words describing institutions peculiar to the German political tradition have been left in the original German. The *Rechtsstaat* was, literally, a state that operated within the realm of legality. Historically, the concept of the *Rechtsstaat* was associated as well with an independent judiciary and a neutral and predictable set of procedures for applying the law. But the term is not identical with the English phrase "rule of law." The main noun in *Rechtsstaat* remains the state, conceptualized as a unity, perhaps even a unified will. I have left *Rechtsstaat* in German as a concept specific to the continental tradition of law. During the German Empire, the governments of particular provinces were called states (*Staaten*) as in the United States, enabling a direct translation. By contrast, the Weimar Constitution explicitly referred to these entities as *Länder*, or "lands," to emphasize the states' subordinate place in the constitutional system. I have retained the German *Land* and *Länder* to emphasize the specific meaning of German federalism in the Weimar Republic. The Reichstag is the German popular assembly: something less than a parliament in the English sense before 1919 but more than the U.S. Congress during the Weimar Republic. Similarly, an assembly at the level of the *Land* was called a *Landtag*, a term that I also retain. The assembly of state representatives in the empire was the Bundesrat, or Federal Council; that assembly was considerably weakened and renamed the Reichsrat—literally, Imperial Council, but more accurately Federal Council—in the Weimar Republic. I retain the German names to underline the distinction between the institutions. Finally, the highest court of civil and criminal law in unified Germany was called the Reichsgericht. Substituting "Supreme Court," as a number of authors have done, obscures the important differences between the German and U.S. traditions of judicial review. "Imperial Court" also fails to convey the proper meaning of the institution in the Republic. Therefore I have retained Reichsgericht.

Other words have been given different translations according to the context. I translate *Reich* in the context of the 1871 Constitution as "empire." The 1871 *Reichsverfassung* is therefore translated as "Imperial Constitution." But *Reich* can also mean simply the higher political unity in a federation—the federal state; or it can refer to an organ of the national government, such as the National Economic Council (Reichswirtschaftsrat) of the Weimar Constitution. *Regierung* in German refers to the executive body—the kaiser and his ministers, for example. I have translated the term in different cases as "government" or "executive."

ACKNOWLEDGMENTS

This project was carried out with the generous support of a number of institutions. The Deutscher Akademischer Austauschdienst (DAAD) provided funding for fifteen months of research in Bielefeld and Berlin in 1990 and 1991. The Sage Graduate School of Cornell University supported an additional half year of funding through a Gilmore Fellowship in spring 1992. A Mellon Foundation fellowship provided a full year of funding to finish the dissertation. Rice University funded a research fellowship for the summer of 1995 that enabled me to gather sources in Berlin and Frankfurt. Finally, I was granted the time and resources to complete the manuscript as a postdoctoral research associate at the Center for German and European Studies at Georgetown University in 1995–96. Thanks are due to the librarians who helped me chase down sources at Cornell University, the University of Bielefeld, the University of Michigan Law School, Rice University, and Georgetown University.

Dominick LaCapra, Isabel V. Hull, David Sabean, and Michael Steinberg were excellent and helpful advisers, critics, and readers of my dissertation at Cornell University. Judge Dieter Grimm of the Bundesverfassungsgericht and the University of Bielefeld law faculty was a friendly and helpful host during my year of study at Bielefeld. Christoph Müller of the Berlin Free University's law faculty was a likewise friendly and helpful conversation partner during the 1991–92 school year. In addition, I benefited greatly from discussions with Ingeborg Maus at the University of Frankfurt.

I must also thank all the many individuals who helped me with parts of the project over the years. The members of what has become a kind of "Weimar constitutional theory group" were especially helpful in the final year of my work. David Dyzenhaus and John McCormick generously shared their own impressive works-in-progress and made important criticisms of my work. Stanley L. Paulson provided invaluable aid in comprehending Kelsen in the neo-Kantian context and translating some of his more technical language into English. Bill Scheuerman passed along his own essays and works-in-progress, and made helpful suggestions about my work. In Germany, Bertram Belda, Raphael Gross, and Christoph Schönberger provided useful comments and criticisms. Donald Kommers and an anonymous reader for Duke University Press suggested ways to revise the initial manuscript. Of the many others who helped me, I would like to thank in particular Kathleen Canning, Roger Chickering, Steve Hastings-King, Rainer Horn, Ken Ledford, Mary McGuire, Maria Mitchell, Hubert Rast, Mark Swofford, and Guy Yasko. On a collective level, I thank the Cornell University European History Colloquium, my colleagues at Rice University, and the participants in Roger Chickering's standing seminar in German history at Georgetown University.

Some sections of chapters 1 and 3 appeared previously in "Legal Positivism and Weimar Democracy," *American Journal of Jurisprudence* 39 (1994): 273–301. I thank the *American Journal of Jurisprudence* for permission to use this material. I also thank The Kraus Organization, Limited, for permission to reprint the cartoon entitled "Das Verfassungskleid 1919" from W. A. Coupe, *German Political Satires from the Reformation to the Second World War* (White Plains, N.Y.: Kraus International Publications, 1985).

I owe unrepayable debts to Lora Wildenthal, whose patience, love, and careful criticism helped create this book.

Popular Sovereignty

and the Crisis of German

Constitutional Law

THE POWER OF

THE PEOPLE AND THE RULE OF LAW

The Problem of Constitutional Democracy in

the Weimar Republic

On August 11, 1919, for the first time in the history of the German nation, a constitution based on the principle of popular sovereignty came into effect. The hopes bound up with the proclamation of democracy were quickly undermined by civil strife, inflation, and resentment on both the left and the right against the failures of the new republic. Thirteen years later, the constitutional system lay in shambles, making way for an antidemocratic and anticonstitutional dictatorship. As a final insult to the principles of democratic constitutionalism, Adolf Hitler gave National Socialist rule the gloss of constitutionality through the enabling act approved by the Reichstag on March 24, 1933.[1] At least in appearance, the constitutional democracy had given itself up, legally and peacefully, to its most extreme enemy.[2]

The Weimar Constitution has played a key negative role in German constitutional politics ever since the fall of the Nazi regime. The founders of the 1949 West German Basic Law made a conscious attempt to avoid the "mistakes" of Weimar by limiting the role of plebiscites, restricting the power of the president, eliminating the ability of the parliament to paralyze the government, and asserting the primacy of basic rights over both legislative and executive powers.[3] Less generally recognized is the positive contribution Weimar constitutional lawyers have made to the culture of constitutional debates in the Federal Republic. The ongoing crisis of constitutional democracy in the Weimar Republic provided the backdrop for Weimar lawyers' attempt to break away from the "statutory positivism" that had dominated law schools in the German Empire. Lawyers and courts began to rethink the role of basic rights in a democracy, the way constitutional law could function to integrate antagonistic social groups into the commonwealth, and the limits to constitutional amendment in the basic principles of constitutional democracy. The questions and problems posed by the "postpositivist" theories have continued to dominate German constitutional law up to the present day.[4]

This book examines the development of that new constitutional jurisprudence during the Weimar Republic. The adoption of a democratic constitution raised basic questions about democracy and law that have a familiar ring to observers of debates in the United States. First and foremost came the theoretical problem of what the "foundation" or "source" of the system was. On the one hand, the people allegedly produced all state power. But on the other hand, the production of law took place only through legal procedures. Who was sovereign, the constitutional people or the democratic constitution? That question led directly to debates on the legitimate interpretation and application of constitutional articles in a democracy. At issue was not only the usefulness of natural law and sociology in interpreting law, but also what in the U.S. context has been termed the "countermajoritarian difficulty": Is judicial review of statutes ipso facto antidemocratic, since judges supplant the people's representatives as arbiters of constitutional meaning?[5] A third discussion ensued over constitutional practice itself. High courts of law and political actors struggled over the meaning of the constitution as it appeared in actual adjudication, granting concepts such as "equality before the law" a substantive value where formerly they had possessed a merely formal significance in the realm of practical law. The heated debates over the theory and practice of constitutional democracy took place in the context of a weak postwar republic whose citizens increasingly opposed the values of the Weimar Constitution itself. In 1933, the National Socialists swept aside both constitutionalism and democracy to institute a system that they asserted was based immediately on the racial *Volk* and its obedience to its *Führer*.

As the social and political systems entered into crisis in the Weimar Republic, so did the discipline of "public" or "state" law, defined in the continental tradition in opposition to the "private" law of contracts. But the crisis had deeper roots in the transition from constitutional monarchism to the constitutional democracy of 1919. State law, which encompassed administrative, procedural, and constitutional law,[6] had developed under the stable constitutional system of the German Empire (1871–1918). That stability rested on the putatively unpolitical nature of the 1871 Imperial Constitution. Political debate took place in other arenas: for example, in the development of administrative law, in other areas of social and labor law, and in the Anglo-German naval rivalry. As constitutional law diverged from political practice, constitutional theory became depoliticized. This was the heyday of positivist and organic theories of stability in state law.

Chapter 1 explores the positivist tradition in state law during the German Empire. One must employ the term *positivism* with care because it can signify at least three distinct concepts in legal theory.[7] First, positivism can refer to a theory of law as factual social practice. *Sociological positivism* identifies law with the social practices of a community. The norms that are objectively enforced—whether by state officials or by people in their everyday lives—count as law, regardless of whether those norms are written or unwritten. The task of the legal scholar is to determine which norms are effective. The tools for making this determination are sociological.[8] *Statist positivism*, by contrast, identifies law with those norms positivized by a legal authority, or, to express the point more abstractly, those norms produced according to the correct procedure. This second variety of positivism corresponds to the ideas of H. L. A. Hart and other Anglo-American writers in the analytic tradition.[9] While sociological positivism defines law on the basis of a distinction between effective and ineffective norms, statist positivism distinguishes law from what is not law on the basis of a norm's recognizable validity within the legal system. The distinction between these two approaches is often disciplinary: the sociologist of law observes and records social fact, while the legal statist takes the "internal" point of view (Hart), observing what for the legal actor counts as a binding norm. The distinction also marks a line between a monist view of the world that seeks to reduce law to causal or physical relations, and a dualist view that sees law as an embodiment of spirit or normativity not immediately part of social reality.[10]

The *statutory positivism* associated with state law in the German

Empire was qualitatively different from the other two varieties of legal positivism, although it resembled the statist current more closely. It was a school founded on a specific method of interpreting statutes, understood as the highest expression of the state's will, through concepts such as "dominion" (*Herrschaft*) and "contract." For the central figure of the school, Paul Laband (1838-1918), the articles of the 1871 Constitution and correctly produced statutes comprised the legal system. He excluded all consideration of natural law (i.e., moral or sociological limits to man-made law) and common law to concentrate on the will of the state. The distinction was rooted in a particular historical moment, the creation of a unified German state, rather than in a philosophy. In this respect, Labandian positivism differed from both sociological legal positivism, which took cognizance of social norms, and statist legal positivism, which considered common law to be positive law if the normative rules for recognizing law so allowed it. Laband furthermore refused to grant the constitution as a whole any special authority. In his approach, the state, as a willing sovereign, produced both the constitution and statutory law. The constitution was therefore logically no "higher" or more sacred than statutes.[11]

Laband's school paralleled German liberalism in affirming the existing state. It turned away from questions regarding the nature and status of the constitution. Instead, it analyzed legal norms in a formalist fashion: it sought to clarify the precise rights, duties, and procedures in each legal norm. It then organized these laws into a coherent, logically closed system of norms, compiled in the form of a handbook. But the Labandian approach came into question at the end of the century as changes in society and in the conduct of politics challenged traditional constitutional systems across Europe, from France of the Third Republic, to England during the crisis of liberalism in the years before World War I, to the imperiled tsarist autocracy in Russia. Despite threats to the German constitutional monarchy by parliamentary forces after 1900, however, the 1871 Constitution remained unchanged. But if constitutional laws remained unchanged, the younger generation's approach to them did not.

Chapter 2 examines the works of two constitutional theorists who challenged the foundations of statutory positivism after 1900. In 1911, Hans Kelsen (1881-1973) published a massive *Habilitation* that undertook a systematic investigation of the theory of public law, taking as its starting point the methodological split between "is" and "ought," "fact" and "norm." His radical neo-Kantian skepticism led him to criticize the methods and the ideological, authoritarian implications of Laband's approach to state law.[12] Carl Schmitt (1888–1985) struck at the Laband school from another side. He developed its affirmation of the state into a conservative critique of constitutionalism in general. His work on the "state of siege" during World War I laid the foundations for a theory of dictatorship. Kelsen and Schmitt thus began their attacks on fundamental concepts of nineteenth-century constitutionalism that would bear fruit in reconceptualizations of constitutionalism during the Weimar Republic.

Germany's defeat in the First World War led to the collapse of the monarchy. According to Article 1 of the Weimar Constitution, the state's power emanated from the people. The doctrine of popular sovereignty raised questions about the meaning of minority rights, about limits to the power of the people's representatives (be they political parties, the parliament, or the president), and in general about the relationship between the power of the people and constitutional law. These issues became brutally concrete in the early years of the Republic. The revolutionary right rejected constitutionalism entirely, endorsing instead the quasi-mystical, immediate unity of the *Volk* as symbolized in the "peace of the fortress" (*Burgfrieden*) of World War I. The revolutionary left called into question the constitution's claim to found a "democracy" while leaving untouched property relations and large parts of the military and administrative hierarchies. Rejection of the constitution's claim to legitimacy led to situations approaching civil war in the early years of the Republic. The first president, the Social Democrat Friedrich Ebert, responded with extensive use of the presidential emergency powers granted by Article 48 of the constitution. As Germany entered into hyperinflation and economic crisis in 1922–23, the Reichstag passed enabling laws extending to the president legislative and even budgetary powers.[13] The Republic had barely come into existence, and already the president was undertaking measures that went far beyond what the constitution's founders had expected. The situation was fundamentally new for lawyers trained in the constitutional history and constitutional law of the German Empire. The legitimacy of the Bismarckian constitution, after all, had never been in doubt. Revolution and civil strife put into sharp focus problems of legitimacy for a discipline that had been taught to avoid "political" disputes.

Germany returned to political stability in 1924. But the events of the preceding years had profoundly altered debates about constitutional law. The government had intervened extensively in social and economic relations over the preceding decade, imposing economic and police controls during wartime, regulating the period of demobilization, and revaluing the mark in 1923-24. Under these conditions, lawyers began to rethink their concepts of state law. They asked if the impoverishment of certain social groups by inflation and revaluation amounted to discriminatory and illegal actions by the state that violated citizens' basic right to equality before the law. Some asserted that revaluation had expropriated the middle classes without compensation, against the express wording of the constitution. Underlying these ruminations was the problem of what role the courts should play in the new constitutional system: Did the courts have the right to review the actions of the Reichstag or the president for their constitutionality? The issue of judicial review of statutes and presidential decrees for their constitutionality went to the heart of the political presuppositions of the positivist tradition, which had sought to defer to the sovereign on political questions. The new jurisprudence of constitutional law asked whether the democratic sovereign — as opposed to the sovereign of the monarchical constitution — was limited by constitutional law, adjudicable by the courts.

The debates on currency revaluation were the immediate occasion for rethinking the inherited notions of constitutional law. During the relatively stable years of the Republic between 1924 and 1929, works of the new constitutional jurisprudence began to appear. In 1924, Heinrich Triepel (1868–1946) published a legal brief suggesting the unconstitutionality of revaluation.[14] The influential essay had a profound impact on conservative scholars' approach to the ideas of equality and expropriation. This was soon followed by a dissertation on the subject of equality by Triepel's student Gerhard Leibholz (1902–1982), later a judge on the Constitutional Court in postwar West Germany.[15] Rudolf Smend (1882–1975) released *Constitution and Constitutional Law* in 1928. Smend, a colleague and friend of Triepel, applied an explicitly political standard to constitutional law, asking what would serve to "integrate" society into the political system.[16] In the same year, Carl Schmitt's *Theory of the Constitution* appeared, asking what the fundamental decisions of the constitution were and where limits to legislative activity and constitutional amendment could be found. Schmitt located the limits in "fundamental decisions" of the revolution that stood prior to the constitutional text itself.[17] Finally, over the second half of the 1920s, Hermann Heller (1891-1933) attempted to adapt the antipositivist theories developed by Smend, Triepel, and Schmitt to the needs of Social Democracy.[18]

The development of a new constitutional culture was interrupted by a political crisis that struck at the heart of the constitutional system. In 1928, following victories by the Social Democrats in Reichstag elections, the precarious compromise between unions and industry that had enabled the political parties to cooperate in the Reichstag began to fall apart.[19] The collapse of the international economy the following year contributed to the growing paralysis of the Reichstag. The "great coalition" came under pressure as the number of people on the unemployment lines soared. When the Social Democrats refused to approve a cut in unemployment insurance benefits in early 1930, the coalition collapsed, and President Paul von Hindenburg appointed Heinrich Brüning chancellor. Brüning, from the right wing of the Catholic Center party, had never felt wholly at home in the new democracy. He formed a new cabinet without consulting the Reichstag. In effect, his government excluded the deeply divided Reichstag from state activity. In July 1930, the Reichstag demanded that Brüning's emergency economic decree be repealed. The president responded by dissolving the parliament and reissuing the decree. Over the next two years, Brüning released a string of decrees designed to deal with the "economic emergency" that the major parties of the Reichstag felt compelled to accept; the alternative was elections that threatened to expand Nazi representation in the assembly.[20]

In the short term, much of Brüning's activity, even when it ran counter to basic principles of parliamentary government, seemed necessary for the survival of the constitution. His memoirs (published in 1970) and his papers, however, show that Brüning aimed in the long term to restore the monarch and weaken the Reichstag.[21] Far more open were the antirepublican aims of Franz von Papen and his cabinet of farright aristocrats, who succeeded the Brüning government on May 30,

1932. Papen aimed to create a new authoritarian order based on presidential power and an alliance with the far right. With that aim in mind, he suspended the ban on Nazi storm troopers on June 14, 1932, and on June 28 he forbade *Länder* governments from issuing new bans on wearing uniforms and demonstrating in public. The police of the individual *Länder* had to deal with the dramatic increase in street violence that resulted from lifting the bans. The government in Prussia, dominated by the Social Democrats, openly criticized Papen's course. On July 20, 1932, Papen intervened in Prussia on the basis of Article 48 to remove the Social Democrats from office and insert himself in their place as a commissar responsible only to the president. Article 48 was used to destroy the federalism that the constitution itself claimed to guarantee. The application of Article 48 against the word of the constitution in the name of a legitimacy higher than mere constitutional legality, to paraphrase Carl Schmitt, was the first scene of the final act of the Weimar Republic.[22] By the end of the year, Papen had fallen; the authoritarian-corporatist experiment of General Kurt von Schleicher failed almost immediately; and on January 30, 1933, Adolf Hitler was named chancellor of Germany.

Pinpointing the moment when the Weimar Constitution finally collapsed inevitably raises a theoretical issue for the constitutional historian: What *was* the constitution that collapsed? Precisely this question stood at the heart of the debates over constitutional law that unfolded during the Weimar Republic. And precisely this kind of question was what the tradition of statutory positivism—whatever the value of that tradition's reading of individual legal provisions—neither could nor desired to answer.

Chapter 3 shows how the leading representatives of statutory positivism in the Republic elucidated the new constitution. Richard Thoma (1874–1957) and Gerhard Anschütz (1867–1948) presented a view of the constitution that operated politically to affirm its legitimacy and legally to affirm the validity of all its written provisions. The positivist conceptualization of the constitution came under attack from both conservative lawyers, who decried its lack of "substance," and legal scholars, who argued that the positivists could not address the theoretical and practical problems of constitutional law that faced the new republic.

Chapter 4 returns to Carl Schmitt and Hans Kelsen, who became the most significant philosophers of the constitution during the years of the Weimar Republic. They dealt with the theoretical issue of how to conceive of the constitution as foundation of the state. Kelsen developed a neo-Kantian notion of the constitution as the "basic norm" from which all other norms in the legal system could be logically derived. He conceived of sovereignty as the system's logical unity. Schmitt, however, insisted that sovereignty was not merely a transcendental presupposition (in the Kantian sense of a necessary logical assumption) but rather a transcendent, metaphysical fact. Therefore Schmitt conceived of the constitution as an immutable statement of will posited by the sovereign (the people). Kelsen's nominalism led him to reject claims made by any state organ to represent the will of the sovereign precisely because there was no sovereign will. Schmitt claimed that one state organ immediately represented the sovereign will of the substantively unified people: the president. The debate between the two came to a head in 1931 and 1932.

The theory of legal practice is much messier than that of "pure" theory, because it deals with the way principles, politics, and social pressures enter into decisions.[23] Chapter 5 examines the works of Rudolf Smend and Hermann Heller, whose constitutional theories concentrated on the moment of practice, the point at which a norm becomes a concrete decision. Smend's "theory of integration" started from the assumption that the constitution was a real, living spiritual entity. Legal practice was limited not only by written law, but also by the unwritten law embodied in the state's political needs and the nation's system of values. Smend's theory was important for the interpretation of basic rights. A hierarchy of rights, he argued, could be derived from the basic values of the community in relation to other values, such as political expediency. The theory of integration had conservative implications, especially as it shifted the authority to decide which actions "integrated" society away from the party politics of the Reichstag to the basic values that Smend assumed formed a kind of consensual bedrock for the national community. The conservative Social Democrat Hermann Heller developed a theory of practice that started with the problem of who should determine the content of constitutional norms. The formal organization of the state, Heller argued, was itself based on basic principles of right (*Rechtsgrundsätze*). Like the statutory positivists, Heller viewed the formal procedure of legislation as a source of legitimacy in a constitutional democracy.

Chapter 6 turns from the theory of constitutional practice to the practice of the highest German courts, the Reichsgericht and the State Court (Staatsgerichtshof). Over the course of the Weimar Republic, the high courts began to develop new notions of equality before the law, of property as defined by the constitution, and of judicial review. These notions developed in Reichsgericht and State Court practice would become standard features of the Constitutional Court in the Federal Republic. As the courts grappled with the new problems of the democratic interventionist state, they also invoked the new scholars of constitutional law. The new concepts of jurisprudence began to transform the reality of judicial decision making.

English-language scholarship has begun in recent years to focus on the works of the Weimar lawyers. Carl Schmitt, whose essayistic style and conservative politics are arguably more accessible to U.S. scholars, has been the subject of a number of historical and political science monographs over the past two decades that have explored the context of his antiliberalism in the Weimar Republic and its relevance for the present.[24] By contrast, the scholars who study Kelsen, most of whom are in the legal profession, have concentrated on Kelsen's analytical, abstract thought and paid less attention to historical context.[25] Heller and Smend have received little attention in the English-speaking world, despite their centrality to the development of German constitutional law and the jurisprudence of the Constitutional Court.[26] Yet the debates of the 1920s are still highly relevant for the political and legal culture of the Federal Republic. The amount of German-language literature on the Weimar constitutional debates is overwhelming. The major figures have been examined in detail by legal scholars, sociologists, political scientists, historians, and literary critics. Annually revised handbooks of state law contain summaries of the main figures' arguments. By providing a contextualized account of the Weimar debates on constitutional law, the present volume will contribute to scholars' understanding of the constitutional culture of the Federal Republic.

The issues Weimar constitutional theorists grappled with are not unfamiliar to students of U.S. constitutional history. The problem of popular sovereignty and its relationship to constitutional law, at the heart of the dispute between Schmitt and Kelsen, reappears regularly in debates in the United States over the legitimacy of government actions, court decisions, and the role of the federal government in state politics. "We the People" in U.S. constitutional theory, for example, may be either the "republican" community of citizens or the civil rights and procedures that constitute a "liberal" conception of the Constitution.[27] Likewise, the Weimar period disputes over the theory of constitutional practice resemble developments in the Supreme Court's interpretation of constitutional law. Smend, for example, argued for reformulating rights as values instead of viewing them as absolute negative protections of areas of social life from government interference. Then he sought to balance the values he found in concrete decisions.[28] Smend's arguments parallel U.S. debates over the issue of whether rights, such as the right to own property, are negative in the sense that they exclude state interference, or positive values that must be weighed against the values embodied in other rights.[29]

What may seem foreign to observers in the United States is the abstract level of the German debates. In part, that abstraction reflects German jurists' orientation toward the "state" and the high theory taught at the universities rather than toward concrete aspects of legal practice. To this day, major surveys of German constitutional history contain almost no account of the controversial judicial decisions of high courts.[30] That abstraction reflects something besides a stereotypically "Germanic" orientation toward abstraction and theorizing, however. It reflects the many breaks in legal continuity that punctuate twentieth-century German history: the Revolution of 1918, the Nazi grab for power in 1933, the defeat of Nazism and the elimination of the German state in 1945, and the formation of two new German states in 1949. Constitutional histories of the United States can perhaps all too easily assume a stable, continuous development by examining the decisions of the Supreme Court; in Germany, the highest courts have taken many different institutional structures and carried out many different political functions over the course of this century. Accounts of the major Weimar theorists of constitutional law, not court decisions, provide the continuity between Weimar constitutionalism and that of the Federal Republic.

The concept of constitutional democracy was itself the subject of debate during the Weimar Republic. Indeed, conservative historiography's argument that constitutional democracy was "defenseless" and "gave itself up" hypostatizes what was an unstable entity and not a coherent subject. Further, that historiography obscures the way one conception of constitutional democracy, associated with Carl Schmitt and Chancellor von Papen, undermined other aspects of the Weimar Constitution, and thus laid the groundwork for the Nazi takeover. The debates of the Weimar Republic outlined tensions and contradictions in the theory and practice of constitutional democracy itself. These tensions have not been absent from the constitutional history of the United States; and they have in no way disappeared at the end of the twentieth century.

[1]

THE WILL OF THE STATE AND

THE REDEMPTION OF THE GERMAN NATION

Legal Positivism and Constitutional Monarchism

in the German Empire

In 1871, in the wake of the Wars of Unification, Germany was unified within a constitutional framework. Otto von Bismarck's foreign policy satisfied nationalistic aims. And liberal majorities in the new national assembly, the Reichstag, and in the individual state assemblies ensured that the new system would fulfill some of the constitutional aims of conservative liberals as well.[1] National Liberalism affirmed the new constitutional monarchy. National Liberals worked closely with the government in the early years of the empire to create the laws and institutions of the new state, from the national court system of the 1870s and the Civil Code of 1900 to statutes limiting "ultramontane" and "internationalist" influence in the 1870s and 1880s.[2]

In this context a new, formal approach to law came to dominate constitutional jurisprudence in the German Empire. In the first edition of his commentary on German state law, Paul Laband, the leading representative of the school, declared that the 1871 Imperial Constitution marked the "redemption" of the German people from its division.[3] For Laband, "redemption" meant the fulfillment of a sacred history: Germany's struggle for existence was resolved. Both he (unaffiliated with a party) and the National Liberals found the Bismarckian system open to centralizing and modernizing reforms.[4] Labandian legal positivism took as its task the description of a constitutional system. And what Laband described, he affirmed. His method and his handbook set the standards for work on constitutional law in the empire.

The affirmative approach to the Bismarckian system expressed itself in the "neutral" language of science. Both Laband's legal positivism and its alleged opponent in the empire, the "organic" state theory of Otto von Gierke (1841–1921), were part of a more general trend within the humanities to emulate natural scientific methods in the nineteenth century. Both schools rejected notions that the law had a transcendent origin: the positivist school insofar as it saw all law as posited by the worldly and human state, and the organic school insofar as it derived laws from the worldly "spirit of the nation" (*Volksgeist*) in its natural, historical development. At the same time, both positivist and organic theories—in Germany as in other European states in the nineteenth century—assumed that the law comprised a unified system or even a real subject. The positivists assumed that all statutes and ordinances were the expression of a unified "state's will"; the organic theorists pre-supposed the natural unity of the people or nation (*Volk*) from which law derived.[5] The two opposing theories of law in the empire shared an anthropomorphism of the state.

Perhaps no one offers better evidence of the connection between the organic and positivist traditions than Laband's forerunner, Carl Friedrich von Gerber (1823–1891). Gerber had become famous before 1848 as a compiler and synthesizer of the many systems of private law in the German-speaking lands. Unlike the historical school of legal scholarship, which sought to derive the validity of a law from its historical origins, Gerber built his system on existing law. In order to synthesize the law (contract law, family law, etc.) of the German states, however, he had to assume an underlying, quasi-organic unity of German law. Gerber extended his work to the realm of state law after the Revolution of 1848, when the issue of German unity had been placed on the table. He attempted to describe German state law using the same method of compiling and synthesizing the law of the many German states. Germany had ceased to exist as a public law entity after the fall of the Holy Roman Empire in 1806. Therefore, Gerber had to presuppose an underlying unity of the legal systems. But he excluded that presupposition of organic unity in the dogmatic, systematic exposition of German state law itself.[6]

Paul Laband applied Gerber's approach to law to the new German state coming into being between 1866 and 1871. Like Gerber, he presupposed an organic connection between state and nation. The statutes and ordinances of the empire expressed the "state's will," which he argued was also the will of society. But unlike Gerber, and to the chagrin of scholars in the organic tradition such as Otto von Gierke, Laband never explicitly theorized how the statutes and ordinances he studied related to the social "organism."[7] Prussia's victory over Austria in 1866 had paved the way for the 1867 Constitution of the North German Confederation, the forerunner of the 1871 Imperial Constitution. Laband simply assumed that all laws based on the 1871 Constitution were valid. Because of Bismarck's success in forging a new state, Laband was able to draw a far stricter line than Gerber had between legal scholarship and politics, history, and sociology.[8]

Born in 1838 to a Jewish professional family in Breslau, Laband converted to Protestantism and entered into a professional career in civil law in the 1860s. In 1870 he turned from his earlier work on the history of Roman civil law to address legal aspects of the constitutional crisis that had raged from 1862 to 1866 in Prussia. His essay on the subject quickly earned Laband praise from the most important law journals and jurists of the time.[9] It followed strict, formal rules of exegesis and exposition and excluded all "politics" in approaching the central problem of the new constitutional system: the requirement that the budget be approved by both monarch and popular assembly to become a valid statute. His next major work, the monumental *State Law of the German Empire* (1st ed., 1876–82; 5th ed., 1911–13), set out in systematic fashion the entire system of state law of the German Empire. Already by 1872 Laband had become a professor of public law at Strasbourg and a state adviser on legal matters.[10] His *State Law* was the standard work to which other scholars and even politicians had to refer. Laband was also a cofounder and coeditor of the most important journals of public law in the empire.[11] He died in March 1918, his life as a jurist of state law thus coinciding with the constitutional life of his object, the German Empire.

Laband was not given to long reflections on method, which may help to explain his popularity among practical-minded lawyers, judges, and administrators.[12] His brief statements on method were included in the forewords to the first and second editions of *State Law*. First, he claimed that the jurist had at his disposal a series of superhistorical concepts (such as dominion, property, and contract) with which to order the legal universe. Laband compared these "legal institutes" to logical categories or forces of nature. Next, he argued that the legal scholar's task was to order existing legal norms logically under the individual concepts. All "nonlegal" aspects of the state, such as "historical, political, and philosophical observations," had "no importance for the exegesis [*Dogmatik*] of concrete legal material."[13] Laband hoped that by excluding all "external" material, he could find a value-free, logical method of ordering legal norms and explaining their "positive," true content. His lifelong goal was the exclusion of politics, or "caprice" (words Laband used as synonyms), dilettantism, and political journalism from legal science.[14]

With these brief statements, Laband's discourse on method was at an end. His contribution to imperial legal debates lay only partially in his method, however. Laband's main contribution was in his treatment of the most important structural problems of state law facing the German Empire, beginning with his solution to the Prussian constitutional conflict of 1862–66. At issue in that crisis was the viability of the constitutional structure adopted by the new German Empire in 1871.

The Budget Law and Constitutional Monarchism

Laband's Analysis of the Prussian Constitutional Conflict

Over the half century following Napoleon's invasion, the German states had adopted written constitutions that were with few exceptions based on the so-called monarchical principle, according to which the monarch was the sovereign power. The monarch, however, chose to limit his or her power through a constitution imposed on or "condescended" (*oktroyiert*) to the people.[15] It was, as Ernst-Wolfgang Böckenförde has argued, an inherently unstable system.[16] The monarchical principle found formal expression in the preambles of the constitutions. The preamble to the 1850 Prussian Constitution, for example, declared: "We, Frederick William, King of Prussia by the Grace of God, let it be known and decreed that We . . . have definitively established the Constitution in agreement with both chambers."[17] The monarch was the "willing subject" of the constitution. Formally, the monarch had the power to convene representative bodies, although the constitution determined where and how this convocation should occur; he (or, in principle, she) also had the power of absolute veto against any bill passed by the representative body. Furthermore, the monarch alone controlled the entire sphere of administration. The armed forces also fell under the monarch's sole command, free from the assembly's scrutiny or control (the so-called *Kommandogewalt*).[18] But the constitutions also granted representative bodies the right to vote on laws that would affect the "freedom or property" of citizens, including the yearly budget.[19]

As the state bureaucracies and armies grew in size and expense over the nineteenth century, the possibility of a confrontation over the budget grew as well. But despite the monarchical principle, neither legally nor as a matter of practical politics could the monarch suspend the constitution. In some cases, confrontations over the budget led to a general crisis of the state, as occurred in the Prussian constitutional conflict of 1862–66.

The Revolution of 1848 sought to create a centralized state based on popular sovereignty rather than a constitutional monarchy. The revolution failed, but in its aftermath almost all German states without constitutions adopted one modeled on constitutional monarchism.[20] One such constitution was imposed by Frederick William IV on Prussia in 1850, replacing the more democratic 1848 Prussian Constitution. The 1850 Constitution granted the Landtag, or popular assembly, more powers than the estates-based Prussian assembly of 1847 had possessed.[21] The Prussian king controlled the army and administration, and had the power to make international treaties and declare war and peace.[22] He was also immune to legal prosecution. But the institution of ministerial responsibility transferred legal responsibility for executive actions to the chancellor, in this way enabling the assembly to monitor the executive. The institution of ministerial responsibility remained of limited legal importance, however. The Landtag could not force the king to remove a minister and had legal recourse only in the event of a violation of constitutional law.[23] Nevertheless, an expression of dissatisfaction from the Landtag could have political ramifications whose importance extended far beyond the realm of law, for the Landtag's approval was required for all bills—including the budget presented to it by the monarch each year.[24]

In the early 1860s, the new Prussian monarch William I introduced a series of bills allocating more funds for military expenditures, including an increase in the required military service from two years to three. The liberal majority in the Landtag opposed this proposal for financial and political reasons. As they rightly suspected, the king and his conservative supporters hoped that longer military service would educate citizens to respect the authoritarian state. In March 1862, liberals responded to the king's proposal with the Hague Bill, which would have required a line-item outline of the military budget. In this act the contradiction within the monarchical principle came to the surface. To watch over bills affecting the freedom and property of the citizens, the Landtag logically called for more detailed knowledge of the sphere directly under the monarch's power, the monarchical *Kommandogewalt*. The crisis resulted in a stalemate, and no budget was approved.[25] The king's dissolution of the Landtag resolved nothing; voters returned an even stronger liberal majority to the assembly. William, on the verge of abdicating, decided to appoint Count Otto von Bismarck the new prime minister of Prussia in September 1862, against the advice of his ministers. Bismarck, an extreme reactionary, was to save the crown from embarrassment at the hands of the Landtag.

Bismarck argued that the constitution provided no means for resolving the conflict. As a result, the crown, as an entity "prior" to the constitution itself, had to fill the "gap" in state law. Therefore, he concluded, the monarch was obliged to operate the state even without a budget. Liberals in the Landtag argued in return that the crown had to stand under the constitution.[26] When the Landtag refused to back down, Bismarck put his theory into practice, and the state continued to function—notably, on the basis of the previous year's budget, not the new one. Although Bismarck operated according to a theory of monarchical sovereignty, he did not take the next step and declare the assembly irrelevant to the state.[27]

Bismarck's foreign policy successes ended the conflict. In 1864, Prussian and Austrian troops attacked Denmark to settle a dispute over German-speaking territories held by the Danes. The German victory fulfilled liberal and nationalist hopes that had been dashed in the aftermath of the nationalist Revolution of 1848. In 1866, Prussian troops defeated Austria in a war sparked in part by conflicts over how to govern the new provinces taken from Denmark. In the aftermath of that victory, Bismarck pulled the northern German states into a constitutional system that was ratified in 1867. Conservative liberals, applauding Bismarck's accomplishments, joined conservatives in 1866 to approve the Indemnification Bill, which retroactively ratified the unratified budgets of the previous years and thus legitimized Bismarck's actions during the crisis. But insofar as the Landtag itself approved the bill and, through it, previous budgets, the Indemnification Bill recognized the principle of control by the assembly over the budget law. The conflict between assembly and monarch was resolved for the time being, but it was not permanently laid to rest.[28]

Prussian victories took the edge off liberal critiques of the constitutional monarchy. It was in this context that Laband published his essay on the constitutional conflict—in 1870, directly before German unification. The timing was propitious. Just as conservative liberals sought to reconcile their values with those of the triumphant Bismarck, Laband offered a method of reading constitutions that appeared rationalistic, formal, and scientific, and affirmed the constitutional status quo.[29]

Laband expressly rejected critical or speculative legal thought in his essay. The existing legal system, he argued, was the legitimate and self-sufficient basis for the analysis of all legal disputes. Only by excluding politics and analyzing the positive-legal aspects of the case could one correctly perceive the "legal truth," Laband claimed.[30] Politics had "unintentionally" invaded debates over the budget, he argued, muddying both the legal state of affairs and the different political positions. His own discussion excluded all references to sovereignty, whether popular or monarchical, and to historical precedent.[31] Implicitly, Laband's argument also implicated the popular assembly as the source of political intrigue. Indeed, with one exception, whenever Laband condemned the entry of politics into law in this essay, he referred to the Landtag's activities.[32]

Legally the problem stood as follows: According to Article 62 of the 1850 Prussian Constitution, the highest legislative power—the power to pass statutes (*gesetzgebende Gewalt*)—was to be exercised by the king and representative assembly together. According to Article 99, the budget was a statute (*Gesetz*). Therefore, the budget required the approval of both king and Landtag to be valid. Laband argued that this *formal* definition of the statute was the binding one in a constitutional monarchy. Nevertheless, he continued, the budget was not *substantively* a statute; that is, it was not a "legal rule," a "norm for the regulation or determination of legal relations." While his definition of *substantive statute* was somewhat murky, he seemed to have in mind a legal norm that delimited spheres in which a legal person could exercise its will.[33] The statute in this substantive sense was to be distinguished from an administrative ordinance in a substantive sense, which was not a "legal rule" but rather "legal business." Therefore, although the budget was formally a statute, in terms of its substance or content it was an act of legal business; that is, an administrative ordinance that applied only to the state and its organs.

The 1850 Prussian Constitution made the formal notion of the statute the decisive one.[34] Substantive and formal concepts no longer necessarily coincided. Certain norms that were "substantively" statutes were expressly removed from the control of the representative assembly. Ordinances in a state of emergency, for example, regulated legal relations but were reserved to the monarch. Likewise, not all legal acts to be approved by the Landtag as "statutes" really counted as statutes in a substantive sense. Although international treaties were contracts among states rather than expressions of the state's sovereign will, for example, they required Landtag approval as if they were statutes.[35]

The budget was not a statute in a substantive sense either, in Laband's view. It did not delegate authority; it merely estimated revenues and expenditures for the coming year.[36] The popular assembly, he argued, had the power to oversee administrative actions without actually being able to control the administration. The Landtag had the formal power to approve the budget statute, but that merely amounted to the right to agree with the king that the estimate for the coming year was appropriate.[37] The administration itself was to make the estimates according to its perception of state needs; the Landtag's main power lay in demanding a more or less specific listing of expenditures. Laband viewed even the Landtag's limited power to demand information as capricious.[38]

The budget was thus substantively an administrative ordinance. According to Laband, this formulation limited the significance of the Landtag's failure to approve a budget. According to the basic principle of constitutional monarchism, all administrative acts had to remain within the legal bounds set by the highest expression of the state's will, the statute. Since the budget was a mere ordinance in a substantive sense, it could not suspend any existing statutes. Therefore, existing tax laws and statutes outlining administrative actions remained valid despite nonapproval of the budget. Only another valid statute, approved by both Landtag and king, could alter an existing statute.[39]

Laband's distinctions between statute and ordinance, and between the formal and substantive aspects of each, led to an interpretation of the conflict that differed from those of both the Prussian liberals and Bismarck. Laband argued that the parliamentarians who had seen the budget as a necessary prerequisite for state activity had misrepresented the nature of the budget statute as a legal norm that enabled state activity, rather than a mere preliminary estimation of expenditures. Bismarck's gap theory had been equally incorrect. According to Laband's theory, the Prussian government had acted completely within the law from 1862 to 1866. No theory of legal gaps was necessary. Laband's solution read as follows: "Neither a dissolution of the state and an interruption of all its life functions ensues through the absence of a budget statute, nor does the Crown have the authority to suspend the duty of its ministers to obtain the approval of the Landtag for all state expenditures through unilateral ordinance. Rather, the authority of the regime to supply state expenditures goes on, as does its duty to obtain the approval of the Landtag for these expenditures."[40] Laband provided a nonsolution—which at the same time expressed the internal logic of constitutional monarchism itself. Any decision for ultimate monarchical or parliamentary control would have been inconsistent with the demand for an agreement between the two organs built into the constitution. Laband's reading of the constitution would have permitted the government to continue functioning indefinitely, with or without the Landtag's consent, as long as the existing tax laws were not altered. At best, Laband's solution allowed for the hope that the Landtag would recognize its duty and come to an understanding with the king.

Laband relied on the same assumptions Gerber had used before German unification.[41] The new "statutory positivism" (*Gesetzespositivismus*) presumed that the valid statute expressed the will of the state; the state's will in turn was assumed to express the real will of the nation. As Gerber wrote: "The state's force is the power of an ethical organism's will, conceived as a person."[42] Gerber's state-person was an entity to which sovereignty could be attributed only as a whole. No specific organ within the totality was sovereign. Likewise, in Laband's theory of the state, there was no point of final decision outside the state as a whole.[43] His 1870 analysis of the budget statute in Prussian constitutional law offered a solution that expressed the internal logic not only of the Prussian constitutional system, but also of the new Imperial Constitution. Ironically, in defending a monarchical system, Gerber and Laband undermined the transcendent and metaphysical place of the monarch in the state.[44]

The constitutional monarchy described by Laband was actually achieved, however, through the actions of the National Liberals, who intervened in the 1867 and 1871 constitutional debates to ensure that the new German state would be founded on the dualistic principles of constitutional monarchism embodied in the 1850 Prussian Constitution. Constitutional monarchism presupposed a dualistic division of power within the state, between the monarch and the assembly. Under the Imperial Constitution, the monarch remained subject to state laws through the institution of ministerial responsibility; to become a valid state act, monarchical orders had to be countersigned by a minister who was thereby subject to legal prosecution if those orders violated a law. Bismarck had planned to limit the importance of ministerial responsibility by making it difficult to determine which minister had taken responsibility for an act. In the original draft of the constitution, the Bundesrat, or Federal Council, a sovereign body whose meetings were closed to public scrutiny, was implicitly to act as the cabinet, and the chancellor's role was only to lead Bundesrat business.[45] Liberals reacted strongly to this proposal and demanded that the Praesidium of the Bundesrat create ministerial offices with clear jurisdictions whose exercise would be carried out under the direction of the chancellor. The compromise finally reached erected a limited form of ministerial responsibility under the constitution.[46] Article 17 of the new constitution required the kaiser to publish and execute all statutes and executive ordinances. The chancellor took over all responsibility for monarchical acts. He had to countersign all orders and decrees from the monarch before they could become valid. But it remained an open question to whom this responsibility was due and what the legal ramifications of the article were. For the jurists, this article was a *lex imperfecta*, a norm without clear sanction. In the world of politics, however, Article 17 made the chancellor responsible for policy, answerable to the Reichstag, and subject to critique by the assembly.[47]

The 1871 Constitution thus preserved the dualistic constitutional monarchy. The two organs facing each other in the new system were the Bundesrat and the Reichstag. The Bundesrat, made up of members appointed by state governments, was the "monarch"; the kaiser was only the head of the collective monarch. The Bundesrat, not the kaiser, had veto power over bills passed by the Reichstag. In this sense, the Bundesrat was not a "higher" chamber like the U.S. Senate or the English House of Lords, but rather an executive body with the authority to veto legislative bills. At the same time it was a legislative body whose participation was required to introduce and approve bills.[48] The Bundesrat representatives formed standing committees on imperial affairs that advised the kaiser. These committees were explicitly separated from parliamentary control: no member of the Reichstag was permitted to be simultaneously a member of the Bundesrat (Art. 9). The constitution thereby excluded the Reichstag from exercising direct influence over the state apparatus, unlike the French and English parliaments.[49] The Reichstag had the power to introduce bills, and its approval was necessary for a bill to become a statute, or valid law. Formally, the budget counted as a statute and therefore required Reichstag approval. In effect, the Reichstag had the power to scrutinize all state expenditures every year, and thereby to exercise some control over the domestic and foreign policies of the empire.[50] The Bundesrat's right to dissolve the Reichstag limited the assembly's control of the budget. But even dissolution could not guarantee a political victory for the monarchy in the follow-up elections, as the Prussian constitutional conflict had already shown.

The ideological power of Laband's essay on the Prussian constitutional conflict derived in large part from its timing. It retroactively justified the Indemnification Bill as the only possible *constitutional* solution to the conflict and laid out the logic of constitutional monarchism at a time when liberals were both affirming political unity under Bismarck and fighting for constitutionalist political form. And it set the keystone for a theory of constitutional monarchy in the form of the statute. The statute, in Laband's terms the highest "expression of the state's will," expressed the agreement between the monarch as representative of the state and the assembly as representative of popular interests.[51] The constitution did not determine the content of the statute, but did lay out the formal process by which the state's will could come into being. Just like the English constitution of the nineteenth century, the German constitution created a procedure for lawmaking without setting limits on the power of the lawmaker. In the words of John Austin, the British utilitarian and founder of the analytical tradition in jurisprudence, the sovereign power was "incapable of legal limitation."[52]

Labandian statutory positivism presented an image of unified state authority, of a unified state's will. The subtext of "state sovereignty" was an ongoing struggle for power between monarch and assembly that shaped the German political system of the empire in unanticipated ways. The Bundesrat proved to be an organ of secondary importance in everyday political practice. The kaiser chose the chancellor, and "his" chancellor faced off against the Reichstag. The kaiser, constitutionally merely a representative of the Bundesrat, became a monarch in political life and culture. A central imperial administration, at no point created by the constitution itself, began to grow up around the chancellor, and was extended to other ministers in 1878.[53] The central *political* contradiction of constitutional monarchism developed in the disputes between Reichstag and kaiser.

Nevertheless, from the point of view of Labandian jurisprudence, the German Empire was a remarkably stable period in German history. During the first three decades of the system, both kaiser and Reichstag sought to avoid any constitutional conflict that might have impaired the constitutional system. The ongoing debates about military expenditures were repeatedly put off through complicated multiyear bills. Here smoldered a conflict unresolved since the Prussian constitutional conflict, and perhaps therefore avoided by both parties.[54] Although it remained no easy matter to get approval for the yearly budget statute, Bismarck did manage to gain adequate Reichstag support, through compromise or demagoguery, to ensure its safe passage. After William II dismissed Bismarck in 1890, the task of obtaining a Reichstag majority in favor of government policies became more difficult. Not only had social and economic changes created the need for huge and complicated budgets, but the rise of mass politics meant increasing power for two forces that Bismarck and liberals and conservatives in the Reichstag had already

alienated: the Catholic Center and the Social Democrats. Conflict between kaiser and Reichstag became ever more likely. But despite the
political crises of the time, the kaiser managed to avoid a direct constitutional crisis on all but one occasion.

That occasion was the *Daily Telegraph* affair of 1908. While he was
on vacation, Chancellor von Bülow had authorized a lower official to
countersign the kaiser's public statements. That lower official allowed
the publication of an embarrassing interview with the kaiser in the *Daily
Telegraph*, an English newspaper. A wide spectrum of Reichstag representatives reacted by criticizing the kaiser's capricious "political rule."
Chancellor von Bülow fanned the flames by deemphasizing his own
political and legal responsibility in the affair.[55] Politically, the Reichstag
deputies came perilously close to criticizing the monarchical basis of the
system. Left-liberals tried to rally deputies—from National Liberals to
Social Democrats, "from Bassermann to Bebel"—for a vote of no confidence. And they attempted to insert a clause into the existing Article 17
that would bind the chancellor to the Reichstag's vote of no confidence
but failed to gain the necessary votes for such a measure. Conservatives,
National Liberals, and the left, as it turned out, all had different agen-
das.[56] The principles of constitutional monarchism remained unaltered.

Imperial Sovereignty and State Rule

Laband's Analysis of Federalism

Laband had avoided using the concept of sovereignty in his analysis of
the Prussian constitutional conflict, correctly recognizing that neither
Landtag nor king could claim the right to determine the statute in the
final instance without breaking the constitutional system. He faced a
similar problem in his attempt to reconcile the federalist compromises
necessary to unify Germany with the appearance of unity and power the
empire should present to the outside world. The concept of sovereignty
resurfaced in Laband's discussion of the peculiarities of the new federation.[57]

Prussia's victory over Austria in the war of 1866 made possible the
1867 Constitution of the North German Confederation. The new sys-

tem's military basis lay in Prussian military power and hegemony over the other member states. Indeed, the empire presented a unified army, executive, and legislature to the world, overcoming the legacy of what Samuel Pufendorf called the "monstrosity" of the Holy Roman Empire.[58] But Bismarck's 1867 Constitution also made considerable concessions to the long tradition of state particularism in Germany. The term *Reich* (empire) as used in the 1871 Constitution continued to bear those federalist connotations.[59] As mentioned above, the preambles to the German constitutions of the nineteenth century declared that a monarch had "condescended" a constitution to the people. In this tradition, the 1871 preamble declared: "His Majesty the King of Prussia in the name of [the other royal houses of Germany] conclude an everlasting federation." Neither the united German people nor the people of the individual German states, but rather the individual and implicitly sovereign monarchs had ceremonially called the entity into existence.

The monarchs were represented by deputies appointed by state governments, each required to vote as his state government demanded. Together they composed the Bundesrat, a body that was a kind of collective monarch carrying out the functions normally reserved to the monarch in the German variant of constitutional monarchism.[60] As legislature, the Bundesrat determined which bills would be introduced to the Reichstag. As executive, it issued administrative regulations and was represented on standing administrative committees. Finally, the Bundesrat held judicial powers, such as the power to settle civil disputes between states and the power to mediate constitutional conflicts within states. To emphasize the federal nature of the body, state representatives to it were not granted parliamentary immunity, but rather "the usual diplomatic protection" (Art. 10), as if they were delegates from foreign lands.

The constitution set strict limits to the empire's central authority. Imperial laws took precedence over those of the state but were limited mostly to matters of trade and commerce. State authorities still administered the laws.[61] Furthermore, a number of special powers were "reserved" to individual states—special limits to imperial activity in areas of residency and railroad administration in the case of Bavaria, and postal and telegraph systems in Bavaria and Württemberg, for example. The constitution even left the most important organ for the expression of the new entity's "will," the army, partially decentralized by reserving certain military powers to the state of Bavaria.[62]

Prussia commanded seventeen of the fifty-eight seats within the Bundesrat, although controlling nearly two-thirds of German land and population.[63] The Bundesrat thus remained a strongly federalist organ. But only fourteen votes were required to veto any proposed changes to the constitution (Art. 78), so the Prussian voting bloc could effectively stop any radical change to the system. Furthermore, the Prussian king automatically carried the title of German kaiser.[64] Since the kaiser named the chancellor and the latter served as chair of the Bundesrat, the Prussian king had direct influence over the Bundesrat's order of business. Finally, Prussian representatives served on all Bundesrat committees. In fact, the Bundesrat was created to obstruct any challenges to Prussian hegemony.[65]

As kaiser, the Prussian king formed the Praesidium of the Bundesrat, and in this capacity could declare war, with the Bundesrat's consent (but without the consent of the Reichstag); he represented Germany internationally, and opened and closed sessions of both Bundesrat and Reichstag. The kaiser commanded the entire German military in the event of war. All German armies were to be equipped with the same uniforms and were subject to the same military regulations, which meant a practical extension of the successful Prussian army model across the German states.[66] Regardless of the military powers reserved for Bavaria, the constitution increased the Prussian king's direct military power considerably, especially in a state of emergency.

Prussia exercised a de facto hegemony over the German government as well through an informal system of overlapping offices. While the constitution did not require that the chancellor also serve as the Prussian prime minister, in fact the Prussian prime minister almost always filled both positions. As an imperial bureaucracy separate from the Bundesrat began to develop, ministers were appointed to hold parallel positions in the empire and Prussia, and Prussian ministers often worked out the details of bills to be presented to the Reichstag.[67] The one exception to the parallelism was the Prussian minister of war. There was no imperial War Ministry, and the Prussian War Ministry was separate from the Prussian General Staff, which controlled the army in the event of war. The Bismarckian system ensured that Prussia would dominate the military, and that the Prussian military command would be shielded from the scrutiny of the German Reichstag.[68]

The federalism of the 1871 Constitution thus served not only to integrate non-Prussian states into the new empire but also to limit the Reichstag's control over the government. Laband's method took these limitations as given. It presupposed that the constitution had ceased to be the "object of party conflicts" and had become "the common basis for all parties and their struggles."[69] If the empire was the accepted basis for all legal relations, then judges, politicians, and administrators needed to know exactly what the law and its procedures were. Laband's method addressed that need. At the same time, as a conservative liberal Laband supported the way federalism limited democratic control. His method of describing the system of government without "political" considerations implied that the system was legitimate. Positivist analysis both provided a useful description of the state and implicitly affirmed it.

The affirmative aspect of Laband's analysis lay in his exclusion of politics and history from the concept of federalism. Other jurists in the first years of the empire sought to conceptualize the federal *Reich* in the light of other federal systems, notably that of the United States of America, itself recently shaken by a bloody civil war that had called its constitutional system into question. The Bavarian jurist Max von Seydel cited John Calhoun to reject the very possibility of a federation; the empire could only be a confederation of sovereign states. Justus B. Westerkamp turned to the *Federalist Papers* and cited Lincoln to assert the sovereignty of the empire. The left-liberal Albert Hänel began his critique of Seydel and Westerkamp with a history of the United States.[70] Laband left these historical and comparative methods behind, and with them the political and cultural aspects that gave a sense of depth and urgency to the problem. He sought instead a formal, logical concept of federalism through the correct definition of sovereignty.

Like other "statist" positivists in Europe, Laband defined sovereignty as the highest earthly force.[71] The Bundesrat was the monarch in the sovereign empire, Laband argued. He likened the kaiser to a director of a joint stock company in private law: the representative of states' cooperation in public affairs.[72] The formal concept "sovereignty" differed from the actual content of state activity, however. The latter, which involved the state's right to produce laws and ordinances and to demand obedience from its subjects, fell under the concept of "rule," or "dominion" (*Herrschaft*). As in private law, where the legal person controlled property, in public law the state ruled over people. Unlike private law, however, the public law concept of dominion was modified and limited by a complex set of rights and duties. Like Gerber, Laband compared these controls to the ethical controls placed on the father who ruled in the family, "the prototype of the state and the original source of all public rights."[73] As the father's rights derived from the family as a whole, so did the right of dominion derive from the state *as a whole,* and not from any specific organ within the state such as the monarch. Dominion was an essential attribute of the unity known as the state. The concepts of sovereignty, dominion, and the state combined in Laband's analysis to explain the new federal system. The 1871 Constitution formed a sovereign state, the German Empire, while ensuring that entities like Prussia, although no longer sovereign, remained states by dint of their dominion over people.[74]

Laband thereby solved the critical political question of how the German states related to the empire by distinguishing on a conceptual level between sovereign and nonsovereign states. While his solution to the federalism problem was abstract, it was not useless.[75] Like his solution to the conflict between Landtag and king over the budget, Laband's doctrine of federalism affirmed Bismarck's solution on a formal, abstract level: sovereignty rested with the ruling heads of individual states as they were assembled in the Bundesrat.[76] That solution functioned to oppose challenges to the authority of the German state from two sides. First, by leaving the "monarch" in the form of a collective no single member of which bore final responsibility for political decisions, the Labandian solution militated against a central executive over which the Reichstag could exercise clear control, as the preceding section of this chapter showed. Second, the Labandian solution set a limit to particularist challenges to central authority, as Laband's main challenger, Max von Seydel, recognized. Seydel, while agreeing with much of Laband's analysis (both were, indeed, conservative constitutionalists), rejected the distinction between dominion and sovereignty. Sovereignty, he argued, still resided in the individual states; the empire was an entity created by international treaty.[77] While this view did not prevail, it remained an important challenge to the legal construction of imperial authority throughout the life of the German Empire.

Power and unity were, indeed, central to Laband's construction of the state. His analogy between the dominions of the state and the father implied that the state was a living being, from which emanated commands directed at its subjects. Even as he created a formal or procedural notion of the state in his theory of the statute, Laband had before him the implicit notion of the state as real substance or ruler.[78] A deep-rooted statism was common to other members of his school as well, including left-liberals such as Hänel, Gerhard Anschütz, and Georg Jellinek. Within the dominant approach to state law—as within German National Liberalism—a metaphysics of the state remained, even in Laband's extreme positivism, in his notion of the state, dominion, and sovereignty, as well as in his concept of the statute.[79]

Basic Rights: A Reflection of the Sovereign

The constitutions of the German states at mid-century contained extensive catalogs of basic rights; however, these rights acquired meaning in the legal system only through legal actors' interpretation of them. And the interpretation of rights, like the interpretation of state law in general, came to be dominated by Paul Laband and his statutory positivism.

The immediate influence on Laband's rights doctrine was Gerber. In his post-1848 writings, Gerber conceived of the polity as an "organic popular state" (*organischer Volksstaat*), fusing the nationalist and conservative traditions that had been at odds in the Revolution of 1848. The state encompassed monarch and subjects alike. The rights of the individual, he argued, could never be considered "subjective." They were instead "objective" reflections of the legal order or state organism within which all subjects operated. Rights of the adult male to own property or to express his opinion, for example, were simply negative limits to the state's activity that were posited by the state itself.[80] Gerber limited the practical applicability of rights to the realms of the judiciary and the administration. The statute directly expressed the will of the state— that is, it was the objectified word of the legislature. That will could not be subordinate to rights if it itself represented the organic whole from which those rights emanated.[81] Laband explicitly agreed with Gerber's conceptual and practical approach to basic rights, which he incorporated into his *State Law:* "Rights to liberty [*Freiheitsrechte*] or basic rights are norms for state power, which the state gives itself; they form limits for administrative authority, they secure for the individual his natural freedom of action within a certain parameter, but they do not establish subjective rights of the citizens. They are not rights because they have no objects."[82] By the last statement Laband meant that a right that merely reflected the state's decision to limit its activity at a certain point could not be a true right, insofar as the subject does not rule over the state; by contrast, the private right to property was an authentic right, insofar as it established an owner's dominion over an object.[83] A corollary to this argument was that basic rights did not "stand above" the state's will. In fact, an ordinary statute, as the direct expression of the state's will, could suspend or limit basic rights.

Laband's interpretation corresponded to the actual development of rights practice since 1848. The constitutions of the constitutional monarchies explicitly subordinated the rights they contained to the "will of the state." For example, the 1850 Prussian Constitution contained a wide variety of liberal basic rights. Political and individual rights included the freedom of religion, freedom of scholarship, freedom of the press, and freedom of opinion, and the right to free association and assembly except outdoors. Economic rights included the right to own and dispose of private property. All entailed property was now to be made disposable and divisible, with the exception of property belonging to the royal family and family endowments. Legal privileges granted to large property owners were to be abolished. In fact, such patrimonial rights did not completely disappear until after World War I, but the 1850s constitutions had taken steps toward limiting them.[84] The articles proclaiming the basic rights, however, also contained limits that could subvert the right. For example, while the first sentence of Article 5 of the 1850 Prussian Constitution stated unambiguously, "Personal freedom is guaranteed," the second sentence read, "The conditions and forms under which a limitation of the same, especially an arrest, is permitted, will be defined by statute."[85] Another example of this tendency can be found in Article 33, paragraph 3: "Political groups may be subjected to limitations and temporary prohibitions through legislation."[86] These limitations—standard in the years following 1848 throughout the German states—expressed the principle that the popular assembly had to be consulted before making any change in matters of property or freedom. Statutes could violate rights, but only with the express agreement of males with property and education. Thus, for example, it was common for statutes to deny women the right of free speech, assembly, property, and independent representation in the courts.[87] The principle that rights were limited by formally correct statutes expressed a principle ever more strongly developed by state-theorists after the democratic uprisings of 1848: rights were not to be conceived of as universal, but rather were strictly limited by the legal order itself.[88]

The 1871 German Constitution lacked any bill of rights. In part, that absence reflected the decline of rights theory described above, a decline that was in no way peculiar to Germany. All across Europe, legal scholars were reaching conclusions similar to Gerber's: rights against the sovereign were logically unthinkable and politically questionable. Standard accounts of the English constitution at the end of the century echoed the doctrine, arguing for the principle of parliamentary sovereignty.[89] Similarly, the Third Republic of France incorporated rights into its legal system but left them in the form of statutes capable of being abrogated by parliamentary statute.[90] The practice of rights in Germany differed neither theoretically nor institutionally from that prevailing elsewhere in Europe. Nineteenth-century liberal legal theory, at least on the Continent, tended to view the active citizen not as a source of law, but as an organ of the state.[91]

In any case, Bismarck's immediate concern was to create a strong German Empire that preserved the Prussian constitutional system, not to spend time developing basic rights of questionable application. The new system did not deny basic rights (interpreted through a legal positivist lens) to German subjects because these were already in place in most existing state constitutions. Rights were also guaranteed at the federal level by laws developed in other parts of the legal system and, like the basic rights in the dominant interpretation, taken expressly to apply to the administration but not to the lawmaker.[92] Perhaps the immediate political requirements of the federal system best explain the absence at the federal level of a declaration of basic rights. Such a system of basic rights would have immediately raised the thorny question of how to enforce rights in each state. Any discussion of the empire's right to review state constitutions and statutes had to be avoided in the interest of national unity.[93]

During the parliamentary debates on the constitution in 1867 and 1871, some liberals attempted to tack a series of basic rights onto Article 3, which defined the German citizen. The Reichstag rejected these amendments. Other liberals looked back to the experience of 1848; this time they did not want to waste time formulating rights and thereby lose the chance for national unity. Conservatives opposed limiting the power of the states in the federation. The Social Democratic leader August Bebel condemned the exclusion of rights and complained that the 1871 constitutional debates focused almost entirely on religious rights. His complaint indicates the third reason why liberals did not force the issue: they feared the rise of socialist or Catholic popular forces that might use the rights against them.[94]

Laband's analysis of basic rights became the dominant approach in the German Empire. Again, his success was related to the constitutional structure of the empire itself. The statute, not the basic right, was the linchpin for the entire political system of constitutional monarchism. The statute ensured the assembly's power to participate in controlling the state. The administration was legally permitted to act only on the basis of a statute or constitutional article. The function of basic rights in this system was to indicate where a statute was necessary for administrative activity. In the language of the day, the rights enumerated the private realms of "freedom and property," any violation of which required clear statutory permission. Basic rights performed an important function in the sphere of judicial review of administrative acts, where they ensured that the administration, under the command of the monarch, remained legal.[95] In handbooks of administrative law, rights therefore became objective reflections of the state's will that limited only the administration.[96]

Judicial review of legislative acts for their legality or constitutionality was theoretically possible but unlikely, because review would violate the sovereignty of the state, which itself had made the laws. Judicial review of statutes would furthermore have undermined the federalism of the empire, because adjudication was reserved to the authority of the states. The only exception to this rule involved decisions made by the Bundesrat on constitutional conflicts between states or to arrange "amicable" solutions to constitutional law cases in states that had no high court to resolve the dispute. In 1879, the new Reichsgericht was created to decide civil and criminal cases appealed from the courts of the particular states, and in the following years a common civil code was enacted. Nevertheless, judicial review of statutes for their constitutionality did not ensue. The Reichsgericht explicitly recognized its lack of jurisdiction in matters of constitutional review, and the leading commentators of state law echoed this position.[97] The statute was the highest expression of the state's will, and therefore the legislature (i.e., Bundesrat and Reichstag) could limit rights through a formally correct statute regardless of whether or not the rights were listed in the constitutional document itself. When violations of basic rights occurred (as in the cases of the persecution of Catholics and the Anti-Socialist Laws), it was with the approval of the Reichstag.[98]

The primacy of the statute thus limited the role of rights in the German Empire. But the statutory positivists could not ignore the growing role of new social claims in the expanding German welfare state. While trying to avoid the "fanatical" understanding of rights associated with authoritarian state socialists and Social Democrats,[99] Georg Jellinek (1851–1911) sought to update the Gerber-Laband approach at the end of the century. Jellinek, an Austrian of Jewish descent, had become a professor of public law at the University of Heidelberg in 1890.[100] A renowed left-liberal reformer and intimate member of the intellectual circle around Max Weber, Jellinek followed a strict Labandian method in his legal studies and simultaneously affirmed the importance of sociology as a discipline showing the other, "real" (*faktisch*) side of the state, a theory chapter 2 addresses in more detail. Jellinek approached rights first from the perspective of their history from Hobbes to the U.S. Bill of Rights.[101] Then, after describing French conceptions of rights in the revolutionary period, Jellinek broke off his narrative, stating: "We know today that rights of liberty are not positive but negative in nature, that they do not establish a claim for the state to act, but rather for it to refrain from acting."[102] He took the position that "modern" legal theory, which rejected principles of natural law as archaic, rendered discussion of the historical or political sources of rights irrelevant.[103] Like Laband, Jellinek assumed as his starting point a closed, positive system of laws deriving from a sovereign source (the state).

Jellinek followed Gerber in his basic presuppositions: the legal system was a closed whole, individual rights existed only as part of that closed system, and jurisprudence had to exclude political or historical perspectives to remain a science.[104] Within this framework, Jellinek posed the question of how individual claims on the state—subjective public rights—could exist. Against Laband, Jellinek argued that a legal system without subjective rights was inconceivable. While private rights were founded on the permission granted by the state to the legal person (whether individual or group) to act freely in a sphere delineated by the law, at some point the legal person had to be able to enforce this private right by calling on a state organ such as a court. While the private right was negative, granting permission (*Dürfen*), the subjective public right was a positive right to demand state activity—a legal empowerment (*Können*). Law (*Recht*) presupposed at least two subjects; if the relationship between state and law was to be conceptualized as legal at all, then this was only because the subject had subjective public rights. Indeed, the state as an ideal, nonnatural entity could be concretized only through the procedures of law carried on within it, and thereby by individual legal actors.[105] In this way, Jellinek's theory was capable of incorporating "subjects" of state law such as the new legal persons of the welfare state: public corporations, social groups, and administrative agencies.[106] But Jellinek continued to subscribe to the positivist assumption that rights existed only in and through the legal order. While his theory opened the bureaucratic procedures of the interventionist state to rational review, criticism, and control, he remained within Laband's framework.[107]

Despite Jellinek's original systematic approach to rights, he remained mired in the framework of his country's own legal system when he described general types of legal institutions. Like Laband, Jellinek assumed that the statute was the highest expression of the state's will. Therefore he rejected the notion that courts could review statutes for their correspondence to basic rights. Although he recognized that Switzerland and the United States had systems of judicial review, he took these as negative examples, as states where chaos ruled over law (here referring to the U.S. Supreme Court and labor law) or where the judge failed to recognize his "modern" function as protector, not creator, of law, and as a result produced contradictory judgments (Switzerland).[108] Judicial practice remained for Jellinek the application of the sovereign state's will.[109]

Statutory Positivism and Constitutional Theory

Laband and his followers organized their approach to state law around the statute, conceived as the highest expression of the state's will. The Labandian positions on federalism and rights followed logically from the conception of the statute. Laband asserted the primacy of the state's will over all existing laws, including constitutional laws: "There is no higher will in the state than that of the sovereign, and the binding power both of constitution and of statutes is rooted in this will. The constitution is not a mystical force that floats *over* the state, but like any other statute an act of will by the state and thus changeable according to the state's will."[110] The constitution was subject to change as long as the formal procedure for altering constitutional norms was followed. And once this condition was fulfilled, the legislature did not even need to indicate which constitutional law had been altered; the very act of putting a new norm into effect rendered the old norm invalid.[111] Laband presupposed the primacy of will over norm and assumed that the state as an organized will preceded all norms.

According to this scheme, the judiciary could play no role in judicial review. Judges' duty was only to apply laws, not to review them for their adherence to constitutional norms. Indeed, were the judge allowed to review statutes, he would be raised above the legislature. And if the judge had the power to deny a law's validity, Laband argued, then there was no reason why administrators or even ordinary citizens should not have this right as well. Laband joined Jellinek in rejecting judicial review, which in his eyes would have undermined the state's power of dominion. In fact, Laband argued, a review process already existed. By proclaiming the law, the kaiser acted as guardian and defender of the constitution (*Wächter und Hüter der* Reichsverfassung), and in his proclamation implicitly affirmed the law's formal accordance with the constitution. The chancellor assumed responsibility for the announcement through his countersignature.[112]

Laband's discussion of constitutional review reveals much about his theory. First, he did not problematize the process of judging whether law and constitutional norm coincided. Instead, he left this judgment up to the highest state organs, and furthermore considered only the procedural or formal aspects of the congruence to be of importance for lawyers.[113] Laband rejected judicial review because a constitutional monarchy based on a balance of power between assembly and monarch necessarily assumed that judicial activity would be limited. And in fact, since the dual legislature was deemed the ultimate arbiter of the constitution's content, the Bismarckian system produced virtually no important cases of constitutional law.[114] Second, Laband's theory of review once more reveals his affirmative approach to the Bismarckian state. His theory left the widest possible room for the legislature to operate, even permitting it to effect qualitative changes in state form. All questions were left to the state's will, embodied in the legislature.

Legal positivism remained rigid and formal and therefore could not describe the massive changes to which German politics were subjected at the turn of the century. The German state was in flux, as Laband noted in an 1896 speech in Dresden that echoed the rhetoric of national redemption with which this chapter began. The context of the speech helped determine its content: Laband was addressing the members of an educational forum for those active in the upper echelons of state and economic life.[115] The speech began with an invocation of the constitution as "sacred relic" (*Heiligtum*), "the historical and legal landmark of the redemption of the German people from fragmentation and powerlessness."[116] The bulk of the speech, however, addressed the changes in the practical functioning of the Imperial Constitution that were not registered within the constitution itself.

Three major changes had occurred in the machinery of the state. First, Article 17 had made the chancellor responsible for the kaiser's statements and decrees. Furthermore, it had made politically necessary the creation of an entire bureaucracy under kaiser and chancellor that had not been foreseen in the constitution itself. The requirement that the kaiser sign all laws and decrees de facto made him more than the head of the Bundesrat—it actually transformed him into a monarch.[117] Second, Article 38 gave the empire the right to set up tariffs and taxes that would flow directly into imperial coffers; Article 70 stated that any additional funds that the empire required had to be raised by contributions from the states, as set by the budget. The government attempted to set up a separate source of revenue by imposing tolls and taxes on certain goods in 1879, an act that would have decisively undermined the Reichstag's power. But the Reichstag countered by introducing a clause that permitted the empire to receive only a certain amount of these revenues directly and transferred the rest to the states. As a result, the chancellor was forced to seek Reichstag approval for his requests for state contributions. Article 38, which dictated that all tariffs flowed to the empire, and Article 70, which separated imperial and state finances, had been violated.[118] Third, a national court system came into being. The growing judicial bureaucracy remained unmentioned in the constitution itself.[119]

These changes in political life amounted to a fundamental shift in constitutional structure away from federalism and toward a more centralized state with increased power for kaiser and Reichstag. Laband described this shift as follows:

Just as the foundations and the facade of a building can remain unchanged, while on the inside the essential alterations are undertaken; so also the constitutional construction of the empire shows, on an external examination, the same architectural forms and lines as at the time of its erection. Whoever penetrates to the inside, however, sees that it is no longer the same as it was at the start, that it has been altered and extended according to other needs and view[s], and that in the process much has appeared that does not really fit with the original plan and that does not fully harmonize even with itself.[120]

The facade and the foundation of the building—the constitutional document and the "fundamental" state organization—remained in place, according to Laband's metaphor. Why they should remain was unclear. For Laband as lawyer, there were no basic, no essential constitutional laws that other laws could not undo. But following the logic of the metaphor, there had to be some limits to "renovation" that were inherent in the structure itself. The substantive openness of the constitution to alteration through statute was necessarily accompanied by some idea of formal closure, even if only with respect to the rules regarding production of statutes.[121] Laband begged the question of whether a preexisting legislator created a constitution or the constitution created the will of the state in the first place. In more political terms, he avoided affirming either liberal constitutionalism or conservative statism, but simply assumed that monarchical power could be a functioning part of a constitutional system with a popular assembly. As the next chapter shows, the problem of the will of the state stood at the center of the fin-de-siècle critique of nineteenth-century positivism.

Laband's work on public law spanned the period of the empire and expressed its constitutional system as no other work did. His orientation toward the statute affirmed the power and unity of the state. Statutory positivism was, in that respect, "authoritarian," as its critics claimed and still claim.[122] But at the same time, it was the expression of a kind of right-liberalism, a liberalism that affirmed the rigid system created by Bismarck even as that system began to come under pressure from new social movements—including racist movements—at the turn of the century. In the years before the First World War, other constitutional systems also found themselves exposed to pressure for change. French constitutional culture underwent a major change—from a system oriented toward the primacy of the will of the state as expressed in statutes to a system allowing for autonomous social groups, the development of social law, and a high court able to make value-based decisions regarding the legality of legislative acts. Jurists such as Léon Duguit on the left and Maurice Hauriou on the right began to reformulate the doctrines of state and popular sovereignty.[123] In England, the aging Albert V. Dicey viewed with alarm the transformation of the constitutional system and the threat to liberal rule of law by new parties disrespectful of reigning law: Labour, women, the Irish.[124] German constitutional jurisprudence would face similar issues and pressures only after the collapse of constitutional monarchism itself in 1918.

THE PURITY OF LAW

AND MILITARY DICTATORSHIP

Hans Kelsen and Carl Schmitt in

the Empire

The constitutional stability of Imperial Germany in the two decades before the First World War belied the social and cultural forces that were beginning to destabilize the world of the empire's founding generation. Social Democracy posed a direct challenge to nineteenth-century liberal assumptions about what the state should do in the economic realm. The Catholic Center consolidated its support, asserting the place of a religious minority in the supposedly secular, or at least Protestant, modern world. Racialist and nationalist movements gave conservatism a new way of articulating social problems. Feminism and movements for the reform of everyday life questioned the cultural assumptions of the founding generation. And along with these changes came a new, critical generation in the law schools that began to dismantle the basic assumptions of Labandian statutory positivism.

Although Laband's statutory positivism was the dominant legal method in the empire, it had never been the only, unchallenged school of state law. Older theorists of "organic" jurisprudence, such as Otto von Gierke and Hugo Preuss, were important figures in legal and political thought, and two younger followers of the organic tradition, Erich Kaufmann and Rudolf Smend, would become major figures in the debates of the Republic.[1] Likewise, sociological jurisprudence was gaining popularity among legal scholars. Laband's fellow editor of the *Archiv für öffentliches Recht*, Felix Stoerk, advocated sociological methods in law and criticized the positivists' "juristic alchemy."[2] Individual jurists such as Albert Hänel and Josef Kohler developed politically oriented approaches to the state.[3] But all these approaches remained isolated strands of thought. None could begin to dominate the field of state law as did the Laband school, for none expressed so well the nature of the 1871 Constitution. The real shift away from statutory positivism in the field of state law came only with the fall of the Bismarckian system after the Revolution of 1918.

As long as the Laband school was dominant in the empire, its challengers often seemed marginal, even eccentric figures. But the critics began to grow in number and importance after the turn of the century. "Centrifugal tendencies" arose, to use an expression of the legal historian Michael Stolleis, calling into question the established discipline of state law. Among the younger legal critics, two are of special interest for their effect on later developments of the Weimar Republic: Hans Kelsen and Carl Schmitt. Kelsen presented his first sketch of a pure theory of law in his critique of legal reasoning in 1911. Although his main interlocutors were the leading lawyers of the German Empire, he composed the text in the unstable political climate of the Austro-Hungarian Empire, and in the city of Vienna, then firmly under the rule of the antiliberal Christian Socials. Schmitt began to develop a radical theory of the state as real, existing will while working as a military censor in Munich during the World War. Kelsen and Schmitt, who were to become the antipodes of Weimar constitutional theory, began their careers with surprisingly similar criticisms of the Labandian tradition as developed in Georg Jellinek's theories of law and sovereignty.

Jellinek addressed the philosophical problem of how the state could be at the same time the highest earthly will, prior to law itself, and also bound to law. He dealt with the problem of how to relate "will" and "norm" on the abstract level of the state as a whole. The Free Law movement aimed a similar critique at the positivist theory of applying and adjudicating law. Proponents of that movement examined the complex ways judges made decisions and came to the conclusion that the conception of legal practice as logical and politically neutral had little to do with real legal activity. "Jellinek's Paradox" and the Free Law movement's critique of simplistic notions of legal practice together laid the groundwork for the critical reexaminations of state law undertaken by Kelsen and Schmitt.

Jellinek's Paradox and the Free Law Movement

Laband's *State Law* sought to describe the field of public law in its entirety: its rules for creating new statutes, establishing administrative jurisdictions, issuing ordinances, and so on. His description remained immanent to the existing legal system: he did not question its origin or legitimacy. Nor did he consider the application of legal norms to concrete situations, insofar as the application involved more than the unproblematic subsumption of a factual state of affairs under the higher norm. Both the moment of foundation and the moment of practice became foci in legal theory around the turn of the century. The rising power of Social Democracy as well as the radical right called into question the legitimacy of the system. And new forms of law for the increasingly complex world—such as labor law, social law, and complicated corporate contracts—raised issues of legal practice that undermined the simplistic model of the statutory positivists.

Jellinek dealt with the problem of the state's foundations from within the framework of the Laband school. A paradox lay at the heart of Jellinek's major works: How can the state, conceived as sovereign, be subject to law? In an 1880 work on international treaties, Jellinek argued: "Law [is] possible only on the condition that a directing and coercive force is present."[4] The will of the state as a concrete and factual (*faktisch*) power therefore ensured the continued existence of law. But conceiving of sovereignty as real state power destroyed the very possibility of international law. If every state was free to act as it pleased, then no higher force could exist to guarantee the fulfillment of international treaties and limit state freedom. The problem as Jellinek posed it applied to intrastate law as well. Were the state the highest, sovereign will, then its simultaneous subservience to its own law would be a logical contradiction.[5] The coexistence of law that bound the state and the presumption of the state's sovereignty formed what I will term "Jellinek's Paradox."

Jellinek brought the problem of how power and law related into sharp focus. He "solved" the problem by splitting it into two separate issues in his "two-sided" theory of the state.[6] According to the theory, the state presented two faces to the observer, one factual and the other legal. On the factual side stood the state as real will. In the real world, the state was never utterly free, but rather limited by its concrete needs and by existing economic, military, psychological, and social relations. On the other side, however, the state was a legal person. Viewed legally, the state represented the highest earthly power; it had the power to legislate whatever it wanted. But the sovereign will, viewed legally, voluntarily submitted to the rule of law. The factual reasons for the state's self-obligation to law could be quite varied.[7] The statutory positivist approach to law, however, presupposed the existence of these factors so that it could assume that the state would respect its own legal norms over time. The presupposition of factual validity revealed the limits to the positivist treatment of law in actual, real conditions.[8] Jellinek's *General Theory of the State* (1900) made the two-sided theory the foundation for its consideration of the state as both a system of legal norms and a real entity.

In Jellinek's theory, then, law presupposed the presence of legitimate power; but legal science examined law as an objective system of norms. Understanding constitutional crises required examining both sides of the equation. In a clear strike at Laband, Jellinek argued that a purely legal solution to the Prussian constitutional conflict premised on the closed unity of the legal system represented no more than a "little dialectical artwork" (*dialektisches Kunststückchen*). The conflict could be comprehended only by analyzing concrete political forces.[9] Despite his critique, however, Jellinek remained firmly within the Labandian tradition insofar as he insisted that legal analysis remain strictly separated from, although informed by, political or sociological approaches.[10]

A second critique of statutory positivism took place on the level of civil, procedural, and criminal law around the turn of the century. The Free Law movement, or Free Law school, questioned the possibility, even the desirability, of the positivist model of applying norms.[11] The positivist tradition in private law conceived of law as a closed and unified system of legal norms and assumed that the judge could simply and mechanically apply them to the relevant situation.[12] Hermann Kantorowicz parodied the positivists' conception of the jurist in a 1906 pamphlet:

[A] higher state servant with academic training, he sits in his cell armed only with a thought machine—of the finest variety, of course—the only furniture a green table on which before him the state statute book lies. One presents him with an arbitrary case, real or only invented, and, corresponding to his duty, with the help of purely logical operations and a secret technique comprehensible only to him, he is able to establish with absolute exactitude the decision previously defined by the legislator in the statute book.[13]

Kantorowicz denied that the real process of applying law was predictable or scientific. Rather, a gap existed between concrete case and abstract norm, which the judge had to fill.[14] Conservative jurists such as Max Rumpf turned to ethics, tact, or a "sense for law" (*Rechtsgefühl*) to fill the gap. Kantorowicz and Eugen Ehrlich, who sympathized more with social reform movements, saw sociology as a tool to aid judgment. Yet another group around Phillip Heck thought the gap bridgeable by consideration and balancing of all interests involved.[15] The political significance of the Free Law movement's critique thus remained ambiguous. While some sought to incorporate social considerations into legal decision making, others used the theory of gaps in the law to celebrate the irrational moment of decision, quoting Nietzsche in their arguments.[16] Unlike the Legal Realists of the United States, the Free Law movement lawyers did not call for judges to rule against the word of the law; but they did emphasize the extralegal and often extralogical aspects of a judicial decision.[17]

Transferring these arguments to the realm of constitutional law would have raised several crucial issues for the Laband school. Both Jellinek and the younger positivist lawyer Gerhard Anschütz were prepared to argue that at moments of indecision the will of the state would have to step in to decide a question of constitutional law.[18] But since constitutional conflicts were by and large excluded from actual adjudication, the Laband school was never forced to explain how and why the "will" of the state could fill a gap in law. As opposed to France, where the dynamic and interventionist republican system put questions of gaps in statutes at the center of constitutional theory, in Germany the problem remained on the theoretical level rather than the practical. It was on the level of theory that a new generation of constitutional jurists began to dismantle the assumptions of statutory positivism.

Kelsen's Theory of Legal Normativity

Undermining Laband's Concept of the State's Will

The most significant constitutional theorists of the Weimar Republic— Hans Kelsen, Carl Schmitt, Rudolf Smend, and Hermann Heller— came from a later generation than the founders of the Laband school. All were born in the decade between 1881 and 1891.[19] They were thirty to forty years younger than Jellinek (b. 1851), and separated by half a century from Laband (b. 1838). Laband and Jellinek had helped to create the 1871 system, the former through his "internal" legal method, the latter as a liberal patriot in the Franco-Prussian War.[20] The four younger jurists grew up within the long period of constitutional stability in Central Europe between the 1880s and World War I. A generation gap existed between founders and inheritors: all four younger theorists reacted sharply against the intellectual world of their fathers.[21]

Kelsen, the oldest of the group, undertook a reevaluation of the entire corpus of German and Austrian state theory produced since the 1860s. His massive *Major Problems of State Law, Developed from the Doctrine of the Legal Norm* (1911) comprises more than seven hundred pages of closely written arguments with the leading figures of the old school.[22] Kelsen's systematic and formalistic presentation was deeply influenced by the turn-of-the-century neo-Kantian movement. The neo-Kantians had revived Kantian idealism to show the limits of purely causal or materialist thought, while at the same time providing a theory of knowledge more accommodating to the natural and social sciences in a period of rapid change and industrialization.[23] Just as it sought to clarify the philosophical foundations of the natural sciences, neo-Kantianism posed an imperative to disciplines outside natural science to explain their status as sciences. As Jellinek put it, jurisprudence was still waiting for its Kant to provide a critique of legal judgment.[24] Like other neo-Kantian lawyers, Kelsen took it on himself precisely to "ground" the science of state law. His *Major Problems of State Law* is not a handbook like Laband's *State Law* but rather a critique and refounding of legal theory based on an epistemological definition of law.[25]

A second important context for Kelsen's work was the Austro-Hungarian Empire itself in the politically unstable period before World

War I. Liberalism had lost much of its strength as a political current at the end of the nineteenth century, while authoritarian state socialism and social democracy gained public support with their calls for an interventionist state. Nationalist movements demanding that state borders correspond to lines of ethnicity threatened the existence of the multiethnic Austro-Hungarian Empire. These new currents had to be viewed as alien by the young Kelsen, who, as a Catholic of Jewish descent, could not accept any identification of the abstract state with "nation" or "race." He insisted that the real organization of society or nation did not necessarily correspond to the normative unity of the state. Kelsen's liberal skepticism and criticism of radical nationalist or socialist politics, which compressed state and society into a unity, translated into his radical and total distinction between "is" and "ought," between "causal" and "normative" reality.[26]

Both the neo-Kantian and the neoliberal currents are apparent in *Major Problems of State Law*. Kelsen wrote it as an insider to the positivist legal establishment. He studied with Edmund Bernatzik and Adolf Menzel in Vienna, both of whom participated in the post-1871 debates about state law, and he attended lectures and seminars with Jellinek in Heidelberg and with Anschütz in Berlin. Kelsen's approach remained part of the positivist tradition even as he criticized it from within. In this methodological respect, Kelsen would be one of the most conservative of the four younger jurists of the Weimar Republic.[27]

In *Major Problems of State Law* Kelsen sought to ground legal science on its most basic object of cognition, the *Rechtssatz*, a term Stanley L. Paulson has translated as the "reconstructed legal norm." The *Rechtssatz* was a reconstruction of the statement of law derived from actual statutes, setting out the conditions under which the state "acted"; that is, empowered, denied, required, and so on.[28] Just as Laband had made the statute into the objective, basic statement of the legal system, Kelsen made the reconstructed legal norm into the proper object of legal cognition.

Kelsen's theory of legal cognition sought to identify the a priori categories that permitted perception of law. Like Jellinek and other neo-Kantians, Kelsen began with an absolute distinction between observations expressed in the form of "is" statements (e.g., "the ball is red") and those expressed in the form of "ought" statements (e.g., "the ball should be red"). This distinction between *Sein* and *Sollen*, "is" and "ought," was absolute: "The opposition between 'is' and 'ought' is a formal-logical one, and so long as one adheres to the limits of formal-logical observation, no way leads from one to the other, the two worlds stand opposite each other, separated by an unbridgeable rift."[29] Conceived in a strictly logical sense, there was no way that a statement in the realm of what "is" could have as its foundation or consequence a statement in the realm of what "ought to be." The statement "If X, then Y *is*" was of a different logic than "If X, then Y *should be*." The first set of statements explained the world in terms of causal relations, while the second exposited the world of norms.[30] Concepts and analyses deriving from "causal sciences" (natural science, sociology, and psychology), as important as they might be in their own right, had to be radically excluded if law was to follow its normative logic.[31]

Law had an ideal status, Kelsen argued, as a set of "ought" statements. He rejected attempts to show a necessary connection between the "ought" of law and the "ought" of ethics. While jurisprudence studied valid law, it did not judge which law was right. For Kelsen, attempts to blur this distinction represented not legal science but politics. Kant, for example, erred when he sought to construct law as a rational discipline oriented toward an ethics of autonomy, in which legislator and subject obligated to law were identical.[32] Such a practical-ethical standard for judging law was irrelevant to a science interested in explaining which norms were actually valid, Kelsen argued. In the modern legal system, a law became formally valid through an act of legislation; the norm was now objectively present, even written. The legal norm was not only normative, it was objective in the sense of being heteronomous, or of existing and being valid without necessarily being recognized by the subject either cognitively or ethically. The anarchist who denied the validity of law was still subject to its coercive rule.[33]

In summary, Kelsen distinguished the legal norm, the object of legal science, from two other types of knowledge statements. The legal *norm* expressed a normative, not a causal relationship. The *legal* norm expressed objective validity, and not ethical or moral rightness.[34] Indeed, Kelsen argued that ethical or moral judgment necessarily employed elements of both *Sein* and *Sollen* insofar as a subject legislated morals to itself, and therefore he excluded all discussions of practice from his theoretical science.[35]

Kelsen's notion of the legal norm as normative and objective had profound implications for legal science. For example, the notion of guilt had to have a different sense in law than in ethics, for the legal system could assign guilt even if no moral responsibility could be assigned.[36] Likewise, the psychological concept of guilt, or intention, based on the teleological notion that an individual intended to cause an action, was inadequate for law. The legal system was not concerned with the will as a subcategory of causal logic. Kelsen refuted the intentionalist position with the example of a tort: the owner of a house is held responsible when part of the house falls down on a passerby, even if such an event was not willed. The legal norm, not psychological intention, created the objective responsibility or liability for the event.[37] Kelsen described this process as the "imputation" (*Zurechnung*) of an act to a legally constructed entity, the legal person (*Person*), rather than to a human being (*Mensch*).[38] In other words, even the notion of the individual was split into two separate categories of "is" and "ought." On one side was the human will, which sought to create certain effects through certain causes, and was itself determined by social, psychological, or physical processes analyzable through the causal sciences. On the other side was the legal person, whose "will"—those rights and duties imputed to a person under certain circumstances stipulated by the legal norm—the legal norm itself created. The legal person was an artificial construction, the human a natural one.[39] Compressing the natural or psychological will into the normative or legal will constituted for Kelsen one of the "abominable" fictions that littered the landscape of legal science. It was an ideology to be battled by force of analysis and reason.[40]

Kelsen's alternative conception of the state's will followed logically from his epistemological foundations. First, the state's legal will had to be objective. Law did not have to be popular in order to be valid. Kelsen therefore rejected the organic theorists' assumption that the state was a real organism. Second, the state was understandable only in terms of norms. Causal or teleological analysis of the state's will confused power (a causal relation) with law (a normative relation). Kelsen took the legal theory of the statutory positivists to task for smuggling a causal concept, the psychological state's will, into the formal universe of norms. Constructions of the state's will by both statutory positivists and lawyers of the "organic" tradition represented for Kelsen inadmissible fictions because they blurred fundamentally different conceptions of the will and asserted causal effectiveness and ethical autonomy where none could logically be proven to exist.[41] Kelsen insisted that the state's will should be perceived juridically as the will of a legal person. The state's will was a legal construction or a point of imputation created by the objective norm itself.[42]

The state's will differed from other wills, however, in that all legal norms constructed the state's will, while not every legal norm constituted the will of other legal persons. No part of law was *not* state law; for Kelsen, civil law was just as much state law as was constitutional or administrative law.[43] If no law existed outside of the state, then conversely, the state's will existed only *inside* the law, if the state were conceived juridically: "The 'ought' of the state is always and without exception its 'will' as well . . . , while with other legal subjects a discrepancy between the two may arise, in which something must be imputed to them . . . which can never be imputed to the state, and which may not be considered as the state's will: conflict with ought or duty, illegality [*Unrecht*]."[44] By definition, a violation of the objective legal system by the state was impossible, since the law (*Recht*) made the state in the first place. Such a violation would be equivalent to the state's willing against its own will. According to Kelsen's strict definition, "An illegality [*Unrecht*] of the state must at all events be a contradiction in itself." If a violation of law occurred, even within a state organ, then this violation had to be imputed to a nonstate entity. A state official who violated the law while in a state office therefore committed a deed not imputable to the state, but only to him- or herself as a legal person. Kelsen implicitly viewed state and law as identical, despite his attempt to assert a relative distinction between state as legal person and law as normative system.[45]

Kelsen's "pure" concept of the state as law rejected the Laband school's definition of the state as ruler (*Herrscher*). Dominion, as a moment in the causal world of what "is," destroyed the very possibility of a normative system. Furthermore, it created an ideological fiction according to which the state was a real, causal will.[46] "Relations of domination and power are factual connections, belonging to the world of the 'is,' standing in the causal relationship of psychical motivation, but never juristic relations, not *legal* relations."[47] From the point of view of legal science, the state was a purely normative phenomenon. To conceive of the state as ruler was to elevate the state into a superhuman entity. Kelsen rejected any theory—like Jellinek's—that considered the state a real, effective power modeled on a psychological notion of the will. His critique of statist ideology took on increasing importance in the debates of the Weimar Republic.

But the legal norms making up the system of law were both normative and objective. Kelsen distinguished between the subjective, moral norm and the legal norm, which "indubitably emanates from a power that from the start stands outside the individual and to which the human [*Mensch*] is subordinated through the real, factual authority which it exercises without consideration of his or her agreement, of his or her will: this power is the state." Kelsen then went on to distinguish between a science of effective power and a science of valid norms.[48] Nevertheless, the demand that the legal norm be objective implied a necessary element of causal analysis in the legal scientist's work. Could a positivist science of law really be concerned only with valid laws and leave the question of effectiveness aside? Kelsen's early theory could only lead to a strict split between state and society and a peculiar inability to conceive of their interrelation, which would in turn lead to theoretical difficulties at the points where law was created and applied.

First, his theory could not explain legislation. *Major Problems of State Law* is essentially an epistemological treatise on how to read a unified body of written legal statements. For such a static system, the dynamic process of creating law appeared an inexplicable miracle.[49] Kelsen argued that the state, as a purely normative phenomenon, had no ability to regulate its own creation: "Ich kann *wollen* sollen, aber ich kann nicht *sollen* sollen, was logisch ebenso unsinnig wäre wie: *wollen* wollen." In other words, the state, that point to which all positive legal norms impute a will, could not logically impute to itself the right of imputation, and therefore could not call itself into existence.[50] The creation of law occurred in the realm of society—a fractured, dynamic, unstable realm in which ethics and morals, social movements and psychological drives, biology and environment intermingled and occasionally created the correct preconditions for a valid legal norm (e.g., agreement of representative assembly and monarch). Jurisprudence could not examine *how* law was created, only the created norm.[51]

Kelsen used the term *Mysterium* to describe the creation of a new law. By making a total distinction between law and society, however, his theory abdicated before the task of judging which norms were legal and which were not. The destruction of a legal norm by open refusal to enforce it was just as "metalegal" a change in law as a revolution or a procedurally correct product of legislation.[52] In this early work Kelsen had not yet developed the criteria necessary for a legal scholar to discuss what was inside the legal system and what outside, unless the standard was a mere appeal to fact or effectiveness.

At the same time, Kelsen refused to "solve" the problem of legal change by resorting to a fixed core of the state such as the monarch. For example, Laband had asserted that only the monarch's proclamation of a statute conferred on it binding authority. Kelsen argued that all conditions for its proclamation, including agreement by the assembly, were of equal value.[53] In refusing to view the monarch as the substantial core of the state, however, Kelsen ran up against the very logic of constitutional monarchism.[54] According to that system, the monarch, although head of the state administration, was nevertheless not subject to law; he was in a way "outside" the "state organism."[55] As Kelsen put it, the monarch in the monarchical system was something like God in deism. Viewed legally, the monarch was a kind of unmoved mover who submitted voluntarily to the rule of law.[56]

Neither a return to Jellinek's Paradox nor Gerber's and Laband's constructions of the monarch as the head of a family were acceptable to Kelsen.[57] He turned instead to the institution of ministerial responsibility to describe the monarch's legal duty. Since both minister and monarch had to sign every monarchical decree, the two were of equal rank in the process, Kelsen argued. And since the minister was subject to the law, the administration had to remain lawful. But Kelsen showed only that the minister was subject to the law; the main issue of the monarch's power remained untouched.[58] The problem of the monarch remained unresolved in Kelsen's work because he refused to view the monarch as the sacred center of the state, as the embodiment of the state's self-binding sovereignty. Kelsen's theory represented a radical rejection of Laband's theory of monarchical sovereignty and the system of constitutional monarchism, which was founded on the metaphysical monarchical principle.[59]

The "ground" of the legal system was thus a blind spot unapproachable by Kelsen's theory of law for reasons that were internal to Kelsen's system and corresponded to his neoliberal critique of ideological fictions. His theory of judicial practice, however, did not even bear the marks of a critique of ideology. He simply set the problem of interpretation or judgment aside: application fell outside the realm of theory.[60] This dismissal was all the more questionable given the centrality of courts in Kelsen's theory of the state. They, not the monarch, were the sites at which law's validity and effectiveness were simultaneously displayed; in fact, Kelsen argued, one could discuss a legal norm (*Rechtsnorm*) only if one spoke at the same time of a norm proclaimed by a court, the objective symbol of the legal system (*Gerichtsnorm*).[61] This passage in particular came perilously close to providing a theory of law based on concrete institutions, not on the strict distinction between "is" and "ought."

The court, like legislation and the institution of monarchy, posed a problem for Kelsen's theory because it lay on the borderline between the valid legal norm and its effective existence. But even when Kelsen's theoretical approach reached the limits of its effectiveness, it nevertheless served an important purpose: it indicated ideological and political aspects of the statutory positivist tradition itself.

Schmitt's Early Work on Dictatorship

Sublation of the Constitution?

Schmitt agreed with Kelsen about the need to rethink the foundations of Labandian positivism. Like Kelsen, he began his critique of statutory positivism by examining the relationship between "is" and "ought."[62] But Schmitt took the critique in a very different direction. While Kelsen had sought to demystify legal science, Schmitt sought to affirm the myth of the state as an autonomous will capable of extraordinary action in an emergency.

From the very beginning of his career, Schmitt was fascinated by the role of the decision in the state. His 1912 dissertation, *Statute and Judgment*, examines the notion of the judicial decision using the same absolute distinction between theory and practice that characterized Kelsen's work. Schmitt pushed the Free Law movement's critique of legal reasoning to the limit. He rejected all attempts to "ground" the judge's decision, whether legal or extralegal. References to abstract "norms drawn from the sky," whether based on society, natural law, or legislative will, could never fully explain how a concrete decision might be judged correct in its concrete situation, Schmitt argued.[63] He shifted attention away from the precise reasons for a legal decision and insisted that the decision's importance lay in its mere existence. Legal security was based on the assumption that law would culminate in a definite decision, he argued; the content of the decision need not be predictable.[64] The only prerequisite for a correct decision was that it be founded on reasons: "It must explain why it is correct in the present legal situation in which it is made."[65] And in the final analysis, the only guide to choosing reasons was the ideal community of jurists: "Today a judicial decision is correct, then, if it is to be assumed that another judge would have decided similarly. 'Another judge' signifies here the empirical type of the modern, legally educated jurist."[66] The solution begged the question. Each judge still had to construct an average, empirical judge, and if no consensus existed among judges as to which sources might be valid, a judge's construction could be nothing other than subjective or capricious.[67] Schmitt problematized the moment of decision but still failed to explain how a decision might be objectively justified.

That justification lay, for Schmitt, in the existence of the state. Legal security, Schmitt argued with reference to Hegel's state theory, was realized when the state became a substantial force realizing law in the world.[68] Schmitt solved the problem of objectivity by assuming that the judge or administrator was part of a real, worldly state. In *The Worth of the State and the Significance of the Individual* (1914), Schmitt developed the argument further. The realm of what "ought to be" (law) and what "is" would be completely separated, he argued, were it not for the presence of the state, which "realized" law in the world even as law (*Recht*) "created" the state.[69] Schmitt conceived of the state as an entity both worldly and divine, bridging the gap between law and fact. By "law" Schmitt meant a "natural law without naturalism" that was "originary" and outside the state; it was the "element" on which positive legal norms rested. The state realized law (*Recht*) by producing positive laws or measures (*Staatsrecht*). As such, every state was a *Rechtsstaat*.[70] Schmitt asserted the metaphysical role of the state as a real, ethical unity of fact and norm. Before the "superpersonal dignity" of the state, the concrete individual disappeared; it existed only as recognized by the state.[71] He ignored the role of negation, of disintegration, of fractures in society and social conflict, to assert the ideal origin of the state; as such, he seemed poised between neo-Kantian idealism and a neo-Hegelian position mythifying the state.[72]

The model for Schmitt's idea of the state seems to have been his conception of the Catholic church. In *The Worth of the State* as well as in other works published during and after the war, Schmitt made the church his leading example of a concrete governing form in the world. The church embodied God's law on earth.[73] Like Schmitt's state, the church realized abstract law under concrete circumstances.[74] The content of Schmitt's "Catholic" jurisprudence was scarcely different from the statist approach to law of some conservative Lutheran political thinkers.[75]

Elements from the Free Law movement, neo-Hegelianism, and authoritarian statism (in Catholic guise) came together in Schmitt's theory of the state as a strong substance or core of form and order. His concept seemed to become reality with World War I and the kaiser's pronouncement of a "state of siege" (*Belagerungszustand*) on July 31, 1914. The kaiser transferred special powers to the military authorities for the duration of the war, and as the war progressed, the military intervened in ever broader areas of social life. After the fall of General Erich von Falkenhayn from his position as chief of the General Staff and the appointment of Generals Paul von Hindenburg and Erich Ludendorff in his stead, the Military High Command became more and more a "silent dictatorship" that claimed the right to intervene in and control society while at the same time standing outside legal and political controls.[76] The dictatorship transformed the federalist principles of the empire through the centralization of political life and intervention into state administration.[77] The traditional legal interpretation of the state of siege could not explain the extent of this military activity. Schmitt's analysis went beyond the traditional interpretation of the state of siege to present a theory of military dictatorship without legal bounds during a state of war.

Laband provided the standard analysis of the state of siege in prewar German law.[78] Article 68 of the Imperial Constitution granted the kaiser, and only the kaiser, the right to declare a state of war in the event of either internal disturbances or war.[79] The dictatorship was part of the kaiser's *Kommandogewalt*, and therefore not subject to parliamentary control. Furthermore, military actions during the state of siege were limited only by the military commander's personal judgment.[80] The central provisions regulating the state of siege lay in the Prussian statute of June 4, 1851, passed in the period of reaction following the Revolution of 1848. According to the 1851 law, the military commander gained direct control of the administration in his geographical area of jurisdiction, as well as the right to issue directives that the administration was to execute. Although the military as executive organ was subordinate to the law, it had the right to suspend the basic rights listed in the Prussian constitution during a state of siege.[81] For a series of crimes, the military had the right to create special courts. Among the crimes to be tried by special court were those defined according to Article 9, section b, of the 1851 law, which stated that whoever violated a "prohibition" issued under the state of siege was liable to imprisonment for up to one year. Laband developed no precise definition of what such a prohibition was, nor did he explain how a military decree could take the place of existing statutes if the military was subordinate to the latter. The organic school's analysis of the law evinced few differences. Wilhelm Haldy argued that in pursuit of the substantial aim of maintaining the state, the military could issue orders suspending all citizens' rights, not just those explicitly mentioned in the law. But he also failed to explain what it meant for the military to remain "under law" in the state of emergency; he suggested it meant that the military should not interfere in private law matters and should respect the "spirit of the constitution," or that the kaiser should recognize his responsibility "before God."[82] Neither theory specified the limits to military control through Article 9, section b.

World War I made the theoretical problem of limits to military decrees a practical problem. The Reichsgericht provided a series of exceptionally wide interpretations of Article 9, section b, in 1915, maintaining that the only condition necessary for valid military decrees under the Prussian law was that they protect public security. Determining the existence of such a condition was left to the military commander and was not subject to civilian review.[83] In effect, the military was to have an unlimited right to issue directives. One of the strongest critiques of the military's unlimited power came from Werner Rosenberg, a leading lawyer of German procedural law, in 1916. He made two basic arguments: First, the wide interpretation of the 1851 law did not square with the "original intent" of its creators; second, Article 5 of the law, which explicitly listed the constitutional articles that the military could suspend, implicitly excluded all other constitutional norms from violation, as well as all subconstitutional laws that did not explicitly rely on basic rights. The military had no right to issue orders with the status of a formal statute. It could not abrogate previous law, nor did it have an unconditional right to issue orders, especially not in the realm of economic activity.[84] Rosenberg's legalistic interpretation argued against those who sought to remove legal barriers to military action in defense of the state by claiming that "necessity knows no law."[85] Schmitt's article attacked Rosenberg's critique.

Schmitt framed his article as a conceptual argument with Rosenberg over how to define dictatorship, denying its connection to the state of siege then in effect.[86] Schmitt insisted that dictatorship and state of siege were different things. The two concepts had come to be falsely identified, he argued, in the period from 1793 to 1848, when the state focused its attention ever more on internal disturbances to be suppressed within the existing constitutional framework. A state of siege empowered the military to carry out measures necessary to fulfill a limited, concrete task. The military commander was granted control over the entire administrative apparatus and the right to suspend certain rights. But the military commander's authority was delegated by the legislator in the case of the state of siege. A military dictatorship suspended the separation between legislative and executive: the institution of dictatorship granted the executive or military legislative authority. "Under the state of siege," Schmitt summarized, "a concentration takes place within the executive while the separation of legislation and execution is maintained; under dictatorship the difference between legislation and execution continues to exist, but the separation is removed insofar as the same authority [*Stelle*] has control of both decree and execution of laws."[87] Commentators on Schmitt's early work have by and large taken the above statement at face value.[88] In so doing, they have missed the subtler aspects of Schmitt's conception of the executive and his historical examples.

The first paragraph of Schmitt's essay calls for uncoupling the "heterogenous" concepts lumped together (*vermengt*) under "state of siege." Next, Schmitt asserted that since the German laws regulating the state of siege were drawn up under the influence of French legislation, one had to examine French constitutional history to explain the underlying concepts. This play of themes becomes even more apparent as the paragraph progresses: "To be sure, the influence of French ideas on the reform of Prussia's internal *administration* and *army system* is not so great as [is] often supposed. But the *constitutions* of the German states have nevertheless adopted their terminology, which cannot be permanently detached from the concepts[,] and the history of the Prussian state of siege is not to be separated from the history of the Prussian constitution."[89] The "to be sure" that begins the passage precedes a basic split in the tradition of constitutional monarchism, between the administration and army (the realm of the monarch) and the legislative authority.[90] While the administration fulfilled substantive goals and engaged in "legal business," the legislative issued abstract legal norms or legal rules. Schmitt made the distinction between legislative and executive central to his analysis, and furthermore he "nationalized" it. The administration remained Prussian, while the formal system of norms regulating the further production of norms—the constitution with its formal concept of law—was inseparable from the terminology, and thus the essence, of the French conceptual system.[91] Schmitt suggested an essential connection between nationality and legal concepts or legal culture.

Schmitt argued that the dominant concept of the state of siege derived from its interpretation in France between 1789 and 1848. The guiding principle behind this concept was the theory of the separation of powers, which had its roots in Locke (an Englishman) and Montesquieu (a Frenchman). The idea of balancing state powers in the interest of the individual played into a relativistic state theory, out of which the French Revolution had made "an absolute axiom" in which it believed "with doctrinaire pathos."[92] That theory could only conceptualize the actions of the military and administration during the state of siege as delegated by the constitution or by the legislator. To be sure, the process of reaching a concrete, factual goal might require that some constitutional rights be suspended. "The old question of the suspension of constitutional rules was therefore always the salient point of the affair,"

Schmitt argued with reference to the 1848 Revolution in France.[93] But even in 1848 General Cavaignac recognized his place in the constitutional system, and as a "correct soldier" he "gave back all powers to the delegating authority after the task was finished."[94] In a state of siege, whether for reasons of foreign war or internal disturbance, the military remained within the system even while suspending part of the system. Thus the French had a mechanical conception of the military: "The French conception always emphasized the nature of the military as a merely executive organ; it viewed the military as the executive organ par excellence, as a state power complex [*staatlicher Machtkomplex*] that merges so utterly with the executive that in principle it does not start functioning without an impulse from outside."[95] Article 9, section b, of the Prussian state of siege law belonged completely within this system based on the delegation of all executive power, no matter how widely the article itself might be interpreted.[96]

The concept of military dictatorship, Schmitt argued, was totally different from the state of siege. It arose out of the concrete situation facing France in 1793, when the nation was encircled by a host of invading enemy powers threatening the very existence of the French state.[97] Faced with these dangers, the Committee of Public Safety turned to a different conceptual system, one based on Rousseau's philosophy. The relativism in the tripartite separation-of-power doctrine was to be overcome through a conception of the state based on the dualism of legislative and executive powers.[98] But Rousseau maintained a conceptual system that privileged the legislative over the executive: "The true expression of popular sovereignty lies in the legislative: it is the brain, the executive is only the arm—comparisons from which the Convention drew practical consequences."[99] Rousseau did not escape "the terminology of this mechanical opposition of Law and Execution."[100] The 1793 dictatorship remained conceptually within the same rationalistic *French* system that Schmitt had criticized in *Statute and Judgment*. It assumed that the concrete actions of the administration might be derived from a set of abstract norms—that is, the constitution.[101]

Up to this point Schmitt had discussed the state of siege and the dictatorship, both of which involved either legislative delegation of powers to the military or the direct assumption of administrative powers by the legislative. Now Schmitt suddenly shifted to the perspective of the administration. From that perspective, the statute seemed no more than "the framework inside of which the administration's creative activity takes precedence." According to Schmitt, the framework within which the administration acted was not closed, because the positive norm could never encompass all the concrete goals the administration (creatively) realized.[102] Quoting Kelsen and Hugo Preuss,[103] Schmitt distinguished between theory and practice. In fact, practice overwhelmed theory. It was not reducible to rationalist principles or to constitutional norms. In fact, the administration had an originary status; it preceded the legislative's production of abstract norms. The administrative decision was foundational, Schmitt argued, not just philosophically but also historically: "The originary condition [*Urzustand*], if one is permitted to use this word, remains the *administration*."[104] The originary realm was "outside" abstract law because it was the realm of the concrete, of concrete measures undertaken for concrete goals. The state of siege was a kind of mythical return to origins. It suspended the French constitutional rationalism that restrained the military in normal times: "Within the space [of positive law], a return to the originary condition [*Urzustand*] takes place, so to speak, the military commander acts [within it] like the administrating state prior to the separation of powers: he decides on concrete measures as means to a concrete goal, without being hindered by statutory [*gesetzlich*] limits."[105] Schmitt was discussing the state of siege, not military dictatorship. But he turned the tables on the legal concept. By shifting to a logic of practice, he undermined the notion of delegated authority so carefully developed in the essay's first part. From the executive-military point of view, the state of siege had already suspended the separation-of-powers principle.[106] Article 9, section b, played no role in this part of Schmitt's argument, presumably because it was irrelevant whether or not executive orders were "legal" if they were part of an unlimited realm of concrete practice.[107]

Schmitt's concept of dictatorship went one step further. It identified legislative and executive totally. All concrete measures now became immediately valid law or statute. The concrete conquered the realm of abstraction or mere understanding—or *Räsonieren*, to use Hegel's term.[108] When Schmitt discussed the concepts from the executive point of view, he turned to eschatological Hegelian language: "If Hegelian formulations are still allowed, the distinction would be grasped in this way: the earlier, undifferentiated unity of state functioning was the position; the separation of powers is its negation; the state of siege signifies (for a certain space) a return to the position, while the dictatorship is the negation of the negation, i.e., the separation of powers is suspended, to be sure, but also taken over and presupposed."[109] The military dictatorship signified the return of the concrete totality now raised to a higher level. Or, to return to the historical example: encirclement by the enemy, endangering the state's very existence, justified immediate, concrete measures in all areas of state life, regardless of supposed legal limits to such actions. The logic of total war realized the originary unity of the state in a new, ideally higher, form.[110]

Schmitt's essay ends ambiguously, arguing that the concept of dictatorship remains the same, whether legislative takes over executive or vice versa.[111] If this descriptive argument were the only point of the essay, then one would have to consider the essay a failure. It neither clearly develops the relevant constitutional norms nor explains how the historical examples relate to the specific situation. But understood in terms of its possible or probable reception, the essay provides a rather different reading. In particular, a look at the concrete constitutional development of Germany during the war casts a different light on the essay. The careful balance of forces in the Imperial Constitution was being threatened from two sides. The Reichstag demanded with increasing effectiveness a basic reform in the form of a transition to parliamentary rule, while the General Staff under Hindenburg and Ludendorff took on increasingly more power, manipulating or ignoring the kaiser to develop a caesarist, or "dictatorial," system. Given these alternatives, Schmitt's indifference with regard to the question of parliamentary or executive control becomes unbelievable.

But the essay allows one to draw several different conclusions. From one angle Schmitt's implicit argument might run: the military dictatorship was necessary in 1917, as Germany faced enemies on all sides, threatening the nation's very existence. But his model for the dictatorship was the democratic Terror of 1793—hardly a favorable example for traditional conservatives or liberals. If one takes Schmitt's example seriously, then, one might read the essay as a conservative critique of the military dictatorship. If one takes the distinction with which Schmitt began his essay seriously, between an administration and military from

Prussia and a constitution from France, then a different reading appears. Perhaps Schmitt was developing a radical and conservative critique of constitutionalism, rationalism, and parliamentarianism. What if the dictatorship represented the triumph of the administration, of the Prussian army, over the democratic rationalistic-mechanistic French conceptual system, and therefore over Jacobin terror? The choice implied in Schmitt's essay would then become parliamentary absolutism and the Terror of 1793, or caesarism and a return to the Prussian administration, outside constitutional logic entirely.[112]

Schmitt employed an almost apocalyptic style, especially in his reversal of French constitutional logic to reach a moment of redemptive rediscovery of the *Urzustand*. His style brought the problem to a head. During the war, the normal legal situation was suspended so that the state could act quickly and directly to preserve its unity and existence. The alternatives for Germany during the crisis were caesarism or parliamentarianism, Prussia or France, Schmitt seemed to argue. He led the reader up to the point of crisis without resolving the issue. Assuming, however, that Schmitt's reader in 1917 already accepted the war's legitimacy as a battle of German *Kultur* against French *Zivilisation,* as intellectuals from Mann to Scheler and Simmel to Kohler did, then French examples would not be read as scholarly and value-free, but as proof that the German constitution was based on non-German concepts and represented a type of logic against which Germany was fighting. Schmitt's article viewed from this perspective is a radical rejection of "western" constitutionalism. The constitutional historian Hans Boldt puts Schmitt's Weimar-era works in the same category as Josef Kohler's writings on war unrestrained by the bounds of law; as this chapter has argued, Schmitt's wartime writings seem already to fit with Kohler's approach.[113]

Schmitt's essay played havoc with the positivist style of legal interpretation. He pushed the opposition between theory and practice, between validity and effectiveness, constitution and administration, to a head. In this respect he left the realm of traditional legal scholarship behind, just as Kelsen had shifted away from the moderating style of the Gerber-Laband position by demanding "purity" of legal science. But Schmitt continued to separate law and politics as Laband had, both on the level of institutional actions and on the level of epistemology; Schmitt rendered positive norms completely "unpolitical" and inessential before the needs faced by the state in a concrete situation. For Schmitt, as for Kelsen, the ambiguous concept of the state in the Gerber-Laband tradition—both norm and will, both law and order— afforded the opportunity to undermine the entire tradition, just as that tradition's basis, constitutional monarchism, was collapsing.

[3]

THE RADICALISM OF

CONSTITUTIONAL REVOLUTION

Legal Positivism and the Weimar

Constitution

From the point of view of Germany's ruling elites, the First World War had begun propitiously. Social Democrats joined with conservatives and liberals to approve war credits and to transfer extensive powers to the executive in the Enabling Act of August 4, 1914. The people appeared united behind the kaiser and his government. But the long war accentuated the dualistic tendency of constitutional monarchism and exposed its rigid separation between the monarchy and military, on the one side, and the political and social groups represented in the Reichstag, on the other. The demands of total war compelled the government to rely on social groups for purposes of regulating the war economy. Private entrepreneurs and managers such as Walter Rathenau coordinated raw material allocations; trade unions and employers cooperated to ensure production of war materials; social groups exercised de facto state authority. Nevertheless, the monarchy, government, and military elite resisted calls for constitutional reform in 1917 that would have formalized political control through a parliamentary system. Finally, in the face of military defeat, the government agreed to open the way to a parliamentary monarchy in October 1918. The revolution that took place one month later rendered the reforms irrelevant.[1]

On November 9, 1918, the monarchy fell. The first basic decision of the revolution had been made: the new state would be a republic. From December 16 to December 20, the Berlin Congress of Soldiers' and Workers' Councils convened to discuss the future of the revolution. The representatives of the local revolutionary organs voted to elect a national assembly to draft a new constitution for Germany. That vote expressed the councils' support for a parliamentary rather than a council-based system. The new Germany would be a parliamentary republic.[2]

Friedrich Ebert, chancellor of the interim regime and chair of the Social Democrats, appointed Hugo Preuss to draft the new constitution. Preuss was one of the few left-liberal constitutional lawyers in the empire. He was furthermore a convinced democrat who had actively cooperated with the Social Democrats in local Berlin politics. On the morning of his appointment, he published an extended attack on workers' councils, calling them the authoritarian flip side of an authoritarian state.[3] From December 9 through December 12, 1918, Preuss chaired a meeting of twelve experts, including Max Weber, representing the left-liberal German Democratic party (DDP), the Catholic Center, and the Social Democrats.[4] The first draft of the constitution, composed by Preuss and dated January 3, 1919, set down the main principles of the new constitution and decided for a strong parliamentary regime balanced by a strong president. It also sharply reduced the power of the state and enumerated no basic rights, in both cases expanding federal power. On January 19, 1919, the German electorate chose the National Assembly. The assembly met in Weimar not only to escape the street violence in Berlin but also to avoid being linked with the tradition of Prussian hegemony in the old regime. While still holding to the principle of parliamentary democracy, the National Assembly added stronger elements of federalism and basic rights to what became known as the Weimar Constitution.[5]

Even with the concessions to federalism and the adoption of basic rights, the new constitution, if interpreted according to the dominant notions of statutory positivism, would affirm the revolutionary principle of parliamentary democracy. The primacy of the statute would now lead to a doctrine of parliamentary sovereignty, and the positivist interpretation of rights would underline the lack of legal limitation on the sovereign legislature. When a democratically elected parliament took the place of kaiser and Reichstag as the producer of statutes, the highest expression of the state's will, then the political function of Labandian positivism changed as well: it now affirmed the democratic principles of the new constitution.

A reading of the Weimar Constitution that affirmed parliamentary democracy flowed from the pens of the leading representatives of statutory positivism in the Weimar Republic, Richard Thoma and Gerhard Anschütz. Born in 1874, the son of a factory owner in Baden, Thoma was an early adherent to principles of statutory positivism.[6] After Georg Jellinek's death in 1911, Thoma took over the chair in public law at Heidelberg. He soon became an intimate member of the circle around Marianne and Max Weber.[7] Anschütz was born in 1867 in Halle, where his father was a law professor. A follower of Labandian principles already in his dissertation, which he defended at the age of twenty-three, Anschütz also affirmed the constitutional monarchism of the empire. His prerevolution work viewed the Reichstag and excessive parliamentarization as a threat to the German constitution.[8] During World War I, Anschütz returned to the position at Heidelberg, which he had given up a few years before. Brought into the left-liberal milieu of the school, he began to call for reforms that would better integrate the German people into the government and overcome the chronic dualism of the Bismarckian system.[9] After the revolution, Anschütz, as one of the left-liberals like Preuss and Weber who had advocated reform in the war years, was invited to participate in drafting the new constitution.[10]

Thoma and Anschütz played central roles in the constitutional debates of the Republic. Anschütz wrote the standard commentary on Weimar constitutional law; it went through fourteen editions. The two also edited and contributed extensively to the *Handbuch des Deutschen Staatsrechts,* the most important manual of Weimar state law.[11] When the National Liberals dissolved at the end of the war, both men opted to join the left-liberal DDP and not the antirepublican liberals in the German People's party (DVP).[12] Neither renounced his commitment to republicanism after 1933. Anschütz refused to work with the new regime in 1933 and retired from public life.[13] Thoma kept a low profile during the dictatorship and returned to public life after 1948.[14] As an examination of the work of these two lawyers shows, statutory positivist methods of interpretation affirmed the democratic principles of the Weimar Constitution.

Popular Sovereignty and Parliamentary Democracy

The preamble to the Weimar Constitution stated, "The German people, united in every branch . . . , has given itself this Constitution." As Anschütz noted, the preamble clearly distinguished the Republic from the monarchical empire, which was, according to the preamble, a federation of state monarchs. The Weimar Republic was "the state community of the German nation. . . . We [the people] are the empire [*Reich*]." [15] Democracy meant the unity of the entire German nation, irrespective of the particular *Land* in which an individual resided. All actions by the German state presumed a source in the German nation. As Article 1 stated: "The German *Reich* is a Republic. All state authority emanates from the people." [16]

The basic decision for democracy colored all of Anschütz's work during the Weimar Republic. He emphasized the political side of his decision in his 1922 speech at the University of Heidelberg, "The Three Main Ideas of the Weimar Constitution." Ignoring protests from the antidemocratic student body, he affirmed democracy as the foundation of the German system. [17] The specific meaning he imputed to the term *democracy* crystallized in the final lines of his speech: "And just as no love is without a hatred of the mortal enemy of what one loves, so also love of the fatherland. Just as it is holy, so also is the hate which it demands. Do not turn your hate against your national comrade [*Volksgenosse*] and fellow citizen, turn it where it belongs. The enemy is not on the left or right, he is on the Rhine." [18] Democracy, for Anschütz, meant national unity for the common good, best illustrated by national unity in wartime. With this notion of an overarching "national good," Anschütz placed himself in the National Liberal tradition. Following from the principle of unity, he condemned the unions and the employers' organizations that sought to realize their special interests over the supposed general interests of the democratic state. [19]

As a statutory positivist, Anschütz distinguished his political considerations from the formal meaning of individual constitutional statutes. From the point of view of formal law, popular sovereignty meant that the active citizenry, which enjoyed general and equal voting rights, was the source of all state power. [20] Formal analysis of the constitution, while it presupposed national unity, examined the procedures by which individual voters could create law: normally through the Reichstag and the president, and occasionally through carefully delimited forms of direct democracy.

The system of representation eventually created by the National Assembly was a product of the political conflicts that raged at the end of the war. When left-liberals and Social Democrats had called for a parliamentary government in 1916 and 1917, they had presupposed the continued existence of the monarchy as a counterweight to the Reichstag. With the collapse of the monarchy, liberals and conservatives alike expressed fears of "parliamentary absolutism." Max Weber explicitly called for a strong leader to balance the power of parliament.[21] The Preuss committee rejected Weber's more extreme call for granting the president power of command (*Kommandogewalt*) over the army, free from parliamentary control, but agreed on the need for a president, elected by popular vote and armed with the power to dissolve the Reichstag, to provide a counterweight to the strong Reichstag.[22] The requirement of Reichstag confidence in government ministers, including the chancellor, would guarantee the unity of the system and serve to limit the president's power. The general proposal produced by the Preuss committee remained largely intact during the debates in the National Assembly.[23] All the other parties rejected attempts by the Independent Social Democrats to abandon the presidential system. The more moderate Social Democrats' attempts to limit presidential power were likewise defeated. The majority of the delegates to the assembly were more concerned with limiting the possibility of parliamentary absolutism than a powerful president. The article granting the president emergency powers (later Art. 48) was hardly discussed at all and was seen merely as a carryover from the 1871 Imperial Constitution and the 1850 Prussian Constitution.[24] The result was a parliament with one chamber balanced against a strong presidential system, both based on the principle of popular sovereignty.

The Reichstag assumed the central place in the new constitution. In contrast with the 1871 Constitution, the Weimar Constitution granted the Reichstag the power to pass laws as well as the right to conduct its own business. Although the Reichsrat, the assembly of the *Länder* (as the individual states were now termed), could reject laws passed by the Reichstag, the latter could overrule the former.[25] The Reichstag had the right to demand the presence of ministers, who were compelled to answer questions put to them by the deputies and who kept their positions subject to Reichstag confidence.[26] Finally, the Reichstag could demand a recall vote for the president. The president, elected for a seven-year term, served as the head of state and administration and as commander in chief of the armed forces.[27] He named the ministers and chancellor and determined the main lines of national policy within the limits of parliamentary confidence. The president had the power to dissolve the Reichstag and call a new election—but not twice for the same reason, as the constitution ambiguously stated (Art. 25).[28] The president, unlike a monarch, was expressly subject to the rule of law. One hundred Reichstag deputies could call the president before the new State Court on charges of violating the law.[29] Finally, the president was empowered by Article 48 to use the armed forces to ensure execution of a law in a *Land* (par. 1) or to restore "public security and order" (par. 2); in the latter case he was also empowered to suspend certain individual rights. The president's emergency power was limited by the right of the Reichstag to abrogate his measures, of which the president was required to inform the Reichstag. Article 48 balanced the Reichstag and president against each other so that the president could respond to the immediate dangers facing the Republic, while the Reichstag could still limit the president's actions.[30]

The united German nation was the source of the constitution. It elected Reichstag and president, and it acted as the last resort in conflicts between top organs. When the president dissolved the Reichstag, he called on the people to vote in a new set of representatives. Likewise, if the Reichstag were to approve by a two-thirds vote a resolution to remove the president, it would do so by calling for a new popular vote. If the Reichsrat, in which individual *Länder* were represented, expressed opposition to a Reichstag bill, the president could expose the bill to a popular referendum. He could do the same with an already approved bill and with the annual budget. Finally, if 10 percent of the voters so demanded, a bill would have to be considered by the Reichstag, and if not passed, then sent before the people (Art. 73). Thus, all laws and orders were subject, directly or indirectly, to popular control.[31]

In the positivist tradition, the sovereign was legally unlimited. Anschütz and Thoma took that principle to its logical conclusion in their analysis of the Weimar Constitution. Article 76 created rules for altering the constitution: a revision was valid when at least two-thirds of the Reichstag was present, and, of this number, two-thirds voted for the constitution-altering statute. In the event of an objection by the Reichsrat, the president would deliver the bill to popular referendum. Aside from these formal rules, there was no substantive limit to the authority of the people and their representatives to alter the constitution. Echoing Laband's assertions about the 1871 Constitution, Anschütz stated: "The constitution does not stand above the legislature, but rather at its disposition."[32] And Thoma argued that through Article 76 the people had the right to determine their own political form according to their own interests following a positive, constitutionally defined procedure.[33] While the constitutional system had to presuppose the democratic conviction and willingness of citizens to work within the bounds of parliamentary democracy, it could not outline the substantive unity of the cultural whole in advance.[34]

For the Weimar statutory positivists, parliamentary democracy was closely connected to popular sovereignty. The sovereign was ever present, a potential *pouvoir constituant* capable of taking the polity in whatever direction the nation deemed best.[35] Conceptualizing the *demos* in *democracy* as the preexisting unity on which the new state's power was based, Anschütz took a strong stand against the advocates of states' rights.

Popular Sovereignty and the Rights of the *Länder*

Anschütz's Offensive against Federalism

In his memorandum regarding the first draft of the Weimar Constitution, Hugo Preuss argued that the transition to popular sovereignty would necessarily eliminate the old "collective monarch," the Bundesrat. He suggested replacing the Bundesrat with a *Staatenhaus*, a popularly elected higher assembly resembling the U.S. Senate. The draft also broke Prussia into a number of smaller administrative regions. Preuss's proposal was leaked to the press, occasioning a surge of opposition from the *Länder*, many of which had just been refounded by popular force after successful revolutions. The proposal was quashed, and the Reichs-rat, a watered-down version of the old Bundesrat, was created instead.[36]

On the surface, the *Länder* preserved federal representation at the highest level in the Reichsrat. As in the Bundesrat, representatives to the Reichsrat were appointed by the governments of the individual *Länder*. By not explicitly granting a representative the right to vote according to his or her conscience, the Weimar Constitution implicitly bound representatives to the instructions of their *Land* governments. Prussia remained undivided. To mitigate against a solid bloc from Berlin, the new constitution demanded that a portion of the Prussian representatives be appointed from the provinces.[37] Unlike the Bundesrat, the Reichsrat had no judicial powers. The power to decide constitutional conflicts between lands was shifted to the new State Court (Art. 19), while other conflicts on the constitutional level became the purview of the Reichsgericht (Art. 13).[38] The Reichsrat's legislative functions were reduced to the right to reject laws passed by the Reichstag, a suspensive veto that could be overridden by a two-thirds vote of the Reichstag or by German citizens in the form of a plebiscite. Otherwise, the Reichs-rat's powers were almost exclusively in the area of administration, such as advising the government on bills and forming oversight committees on matters clearly related to *Land* affairs (e.g., railroad administration).

The Weimar Constitution weakened German federalism. Anschütz applauded the process as part of his defense of democracy, which he conceived as a unity of people and state. His 1919 critique of the Prussian state matched Preuss's in its forcefulness: "[The Prussian problem], as things stand, can be solved only in the sense of dissolution, of breaking the Prussian state into those of its parts which as closer historical-organic (regional, ethnic, or economic) units are suited for becoming politically independent."[39] Anschütz later turned away from that extreme position and even admitted that Prussia's "mission" of forging state unity had not yet been fully realized in the Republic. But he never ceased to question the wisdom of allowing an entity covering two-thirds of the Republic to exist as a state.[40]

Anschütz's "unitarist" politics connected with Labandian method in his 1922 speech "The Three Leading Ideas of the Weimar Constitution." For Anschütz, the Weimar Constitution settled once and for all the empire-era debate about whether Germany was a state. It was definitely a state, "a people united under a highest power." And the Republic dictated to the *Länder* the basic principles of parliamentary democracy. Article 17 stated that the popular assembly of each *Land* had to be elected by a general, equal, direct, and secret vote according to the principles of proportional representation, and that all *Land* ministers required confidence from the popular assembly. Through Article 17, the Republic asserted its right to keep *Länder* from returning to monarchical rule or from adopting some form of voting by class or council. For Anschütz, the Weimar Constitution resolved the old imperial debates over the site of sovereignty: it lay, without question, at the level of the Republic.[41]

The political argument for unity guided Anschütz's legal interpretation of the constitution as well. Laband had insisted that the Bundesrat as a whole was the sovereign source of the 1871 Constitution, and that individual states retained only a limited power of dominion. Anschütz applied the same theory to Article 18 of the Weimar Constitution to show that the new German state was unitary. Article 18, paragraph 1, gave the Reichstag the power to change any *Land* borders with a two-thirds majority. The article also potentially limited such legislative activity. The first line demanded "due consideration for the will of the population concerned." Some scholars assumed that this sentence set an absolute limit to legislative activity: the federalist system was itself inviolable, even if small-scale changes were made. Others interpreted the article as providing *Länder* with a way to demand substantive judicial review of a Reichstag act, in order to see if the affected population had been adequately taken into consideration.[42] But Anschütz read this norm only as a "guiding principle": "If the legislator, i.e., the Reichstag, does not keep to it, no one can . . . call it to account."[43]

Hans Nawiasky, a Bavarian democrat who followed the legal positivist method developed by the conservative Bavarian particularist Max von Seydel, argued that Article 18 was invalid because the constitutional assembly of 1919 lacked the authority to issue legislation involving the borders of a *Land* in the first place.[44] Anschütz rejected that argument: the sovereign act of revolution, enunciated in the constitution's preamble, made the federal government the highest ruling power in the political system; furthermore, all aspects of the constitution were subject to potential alteration by statute (although some required special

conditions, such as a two-thirds vote), and no judicial instance interpreting the "substantive" constitution stood above the Reichstag.[45]

The subordination of *Land* to Republic also marked Anschütz's reading of Article 48, paragraph 1, which permitted the president to employ
force to ensure that the *Land* executed federal laws. The only requirement for such an action, Anschütz argued, was the president's judgment
that the *Land* had failed to carry out its legal duty.[46] Nawiasky, continu-
ing the federalist argument, pointed out that *Länder* also had the right
to question the president's interpretation through an appeal to the State
Court.[47] Anschütz agreed. But the intervention itself, he argued, could
occur without a decision from the courts; it was a decision to be made
by the democratically elected president, not the judiciary. And furthermore, he argued, an intervention could take place even when a decision
was pending before the courts.[48] Thus in fact, the *Land* had to accept
immediate subordination under the president without prior legal mediation. In his interpretation of Article 48, paragraph 1, just as in his earlier
conception of the "unitary" state, Anschütz provided a theory of direct,
hierarchical control, rejecting a conception of federalism that put *Land*
and federal state on an equal footing as entities with mutual rights and
duties regulated by law.[49]

Anschütz's interpretation of the relationship between the law of the
Länder and federal law laid out in Article 13 illustrates once again his
decision against federalism. The article consisted of two paragraphs that
seemed to provide contradictory interpretations. Article 13, paragraph 1,
read simply, "Federal law breaks *Land* law." Article 13, paragraph 2, gave
Länder the right to appeal to the new highest court, the State Court,
to decide conflicts with the federal government. Anschütz argued for
the primacy of the first paragraph, which proved that the Republic was
sovereign. Federal law was the "higher, legally stronger will" standing
above *Land* law.[50]

Like Laband, Anschütz had a metaphysical notion of the state as a
real, willing entity standing prior to law itself. In this respect, he was
subject to the same criticism that Kelsen had leveled at Laband during
the days of the empire. In 1929, Kelsen criticized Anschütz's interpretation of federalism on these lines, arguing that simply asserting the
primacy of federal law over *Land* law destroyed the specifically legal relationship on which federalism was based.[51] Anschütz responded sharply,

arguing that a federation, as opposed to a confederacy, subordinated the particular state to the federal state.[52] In the years that followed, Anschütz would revise his opinions and call for substantially more judicial review of presidential intervention into state affairs in the face of Chancellor von Papen's blatant "coordination" of the Prussian polity in 1932. But up to 1929, Anschütz's position, in affirming the constitution, also affirmed the existing strong, unitary state.

The Basic Rights of the Weimar Constitution

Worldview and Guidelines for Legislation

The 1871 Constitution enumerated no basic rights; such rights as existed were embodied elsewhere in the legal system. By contrast, the rights section in the Weimar Constitution consisted of fifty-seven articles, each of which detailed one or more specific rights. Neither Preuss nor Weber had wanted this development. They opposed wasting valuable time on rights that, according to pre-1918 legal scholarship, had little concrete significance. Nevertheless, pressure from the political parties induced the Preuss committee to include basic rights in the constitution, and twelve traditional "liberal" rights—such as freedom of speech, privacy, property, and assembly—were included in the second draft.[53] In a speech before the National Assembly, the social liberal Friedrich Naumann attacked these "old," "liberal" rights as mere "museum pieces" that failed to express the new cultural unity embodied in the constitution in a way understandable to the people. In their place, he called for a set of rights expressing values conducive to national and social development. The rights he proposed included phrases like "order and freedom are siblings" and "*Deutschland, Deutschland, über alles, über alles in der Welt.*"[54] A committee appointed by the National Assembly in March 1919, headed by the Catholic Center representative Konrad Beyerle, developed from Naumann's suggestions a new system of legally relevant individual and social rights, which it presented to the National Assembly for debate in June.[55]

Naumann had hoped that the new rights catalog would express a German cultural worldview distinct from Russian Bolshevism and U.S.

capitalism. The set of rights eventually ratified did, in fact, seem to describe all aspects of German life. They encompassed a range of rights-bearers, from the individual (sec. 1), to the family and community (sec. 2), to public institutions like schools (sec. 3) and churches (sec. 4), and, finally, to economic institutions and the welfare of the whole nation (sec. 5). A representative from the far-right German National People's party (DNVP) approvingly described the catalog as a spiritual totality that recognized the deep-rooted Christianity of the German people.[56] His interpretation went too far. Much less than a coherent totality, the catalog of rights codified compromises protecting the basic interests of the groups that put the constitution together.

The National Assembly approved the long catalog of rights but did not address the issue of how the new social and cultural rights were to be applied.[57] The statutory positivists therefore approached rights in the traditional way. In his interpretation of the Weimar basic rights, Anschütz employed the same phrases he had used almost ten years before in his commentary to the 1850 Prussian Constitution. He divided rights into three formal categories. First, there were programmatic norms devoid of legal significance. These were directed at the legislature, which had the task of making the vague norms into applicable law. Phrases such as "Details shall be determined by special laws of the *Reich*," modifying the right to unemployment benefits in Article 163, made this intent clear. Thus a whole series of basic rights became for Anschütz juristically meaningless.[58] The second group consisted of norms properly not rights at all, but rather duties or orders that reflected the state's claim on the individual.[59] The third group gave the individual citizen recourse against administrative or judicial infringement on an area of freedom (negatively defined against the state). These rights were subjective in that they recognized an area of activity outside of the state itself.[60] Following the interpretation of rights within the German legal positivist tradition, Anschütz argued that rights were invocable against the formal process of execution and adjudication of statutes but not against the statutes themselves, whose content the Reichstag was to decide.

In Anschütz's view, the first section of individual rights, which echoed the "liberal" rights included in nineteenth-century German constitutions, fulfilled the third function of protecting citizens against the administration. Rights to equality, personal freedom, privacy, and free expression were subjective rights subject to limitation on the basis of a formally correct statute, just as in the Prussian Constitution of 1850. The right to privacy, for example, could be limited by a statute specifying certain conditions under which privacy could be violated.[61] Similarly, Article 109, paragraph 1, guaranteed equality before the law as applied and adjudicated, but not equality with regard to the "substantive" or "nonformal" content of the law.[62] The legislature could determine the meaning of equality as its majority chose.

The "communal life" section of the rights catalog dealt with family life, the rights of civil servants, and the right to public assembly. The articles on family life provide some insight into the complex compromises the constitution undertook. Article 119, paragraph 1, recognized marriage as "the foundation of family life" and placed the institution under the constitution's special protection, adding that marriage "rests on the equal rights of both sexes." Article 119, paragraph 3, granted motherhood a "claim on the protection and care of the State." Article 120 declared the right of parents to educate children as they saw fit. And Article 121 read: "By means of legislation, opportunity shall be provided for the physical, mental and social nurture of illegitimate children, equal to that of legitimate children." Anschütz argued that these articles preserved the institution of monogamous marriage as the basis of family law, against "certain communistic teachings,"[63] echoing a position strongly defended by the Catholic Center in the negotiations over the constitution. As Eduard Burlage had stated before the National Assembly, "Marriage is the pillar on which human society rests . . . and therefore we want to protect it from all dangers." Quoting Bible verses, he agreed that illegitimate children deserved adequate care but insisted that adulterers be publicly castigated.[64] Anschütz agreed with this interpretation, as did other lawyers who viewed family rights as an extension of patriarchal marriage defined in the Civil Code.[65] But at the same time, he affirmed the open nature of the constitution. The Reichstag could alter this foundation if it had a two-thirds majority, he asserted.

Anschütz also took seriously the article calling for the protection of illegitimate children, an article brought in by the left despite Catholic Center and conservative concern that it would undermine the family.[66] Luise Zietz of the Independent Socialists demanded that paragraphs of the Civil Code regulating rights of illegitimate children be reviewed according to Article 121, that illegitimate children be granted the right to inherit from their fathers, and that a woman have the right to leave a marriage without losing the financial security necessary for raising a child. Anything less, she argued, would make the institution of marriage little more than legally sanctioned prostitution.[67] Anschütz rejected Zietz's claim that these rights possessed derogatory force. But he agreed that they set the legislature the political task of improving the economic and social situation of illegitimate children.[68] Once more, the positivist interpretation asserted the primacy of the Reichstag in determining the content of a right.

But by recognizing that abrogation of the rights required a two-thirds majority, the positivist position recognized the importance of compromise to social peace. Such compromises stood at the heart of political life. For example, in the area of education and religious rights, a difficult compromise was reached that, though controversial, remains in effect to the present day. On the one hand, the new state expressed the "establishment clause": there was to be no state church (Art. 137), and all schools would be overseen by public authorities. On the other hand, established churches would have the rights to collect taxes with state authority as public law corporations and to create public, confession-based schools at the primary level.[69]

The fifth area of basic rights, "economic life," reflected agreements and compromises between labor and capital that had crystallized between 1916 and 1919. Article 151 guaranteed freedom of trade and industry, and Article 152 granted freedom of contract, within the bounds of federal statute; likewise, Article 153 guaranteed private property, although its extent and the restrictions that could be placed on it were to be determined by statute. The basic economic institutions of capitalism were explicitly guaranteed, as Anschütz noted.[70] But as the constitution also stated that "property obligates" and should be directed toward the common good, socialist values had thus also entered into the constitution, Anschütz stated.[71] His analysis showed that both capitalist and socialist principles were embodied in the basic rights. To the Reichstag was reserved the task of working out a compromise between left and right for the future.

Antipositivist legal scholars on the right and the left sought to overcome Anschütz's restraint and deference to the legislature. Carl Schmitt and his students, for example, rejected the idea that a coherent system could be founded on a compromise of basic values, arguing instead for a clear decision; for example, either for capitalism or for socialism.[72] Richard Thoma rejected that interpretation from a republican and positivist viewpoint. Only the rights catalog as a whole, with its many contradictions, had unified the majority necessary for approval of the document and acceptance of the Republic. The contradictions, seen in this light, represented not a failure to decide but a compromise enabling integration of opposed groups into the state and an opening for future decisions within the framework of parliamentary democracy.[73]

To argue against a substantive interpretation of basic rights was to argue for the right of the democratically elected legislature, and not other state organs, to determine the content of those basic rights. Thoma made the political arguments behind the positivists' restraint explicit. Like Anschütz, he argued that at a certain point, state law ceased and interpretation became political argument about legislation.[74] Precisely here, lawyers needed to be aware of the political aspect of their arguments. Thoma illustrated his point with the example of judicial review of legislation for its constitutionality. The constitution, he argued, provided no clear legal solution to the problem.[75] The question, Thoma claimed, had to be radically rephrased: "Can German jurisprudence continue to adhere to the basic principle of the nonreviewability of statutes, which has been quite satisfactory in legal politics, or is it compelled to give it up to rush to the aid of the threatened new constitutions?"[76] Thoma answered that formal guarantees of the constitution already existed in the constitution itself, from periodic elections to possible plebiscites, and in the political world of competing political parties and the critical press. Judicial review of the substantive correspondence between statute and constitutional law was therefore unnecessary.[77]

In a similar vein, Thoma provided political arguments to support the positivist interpretation of the equality clause. Equality before the law was merely a formal principle: from a legal standpoint, "a statute is a statute." A law was a law because it fulfilled the formal or procedural requirements necessary for it to become a law, not because it corresponded to some a priori notion of what a law's content should be.[78] Basic rights, Thoma argued, could never be absolute if they were part of a legal order: "The collective majesty of the power of the people formed into the state excludes any absoluteness of the freedoms and rights of those subject to the state."[79] The key word in the above quote is "majesty." The "state" was the organized power of the unity of the people. And in a parliamentary democracy, the formation of a unified decision arose through the formal parliamentary process of decisionmaking.

Critics of the statutory positivists accused them of advocating "parliamentary absolutism" unlimited by the rule of law.[80] Thoma rejected these critiques. All political systems, he argued, involved some moment of political decision, and each decision was bound to harm some group in society and help some other.[81] The body best able to make such a decision, he argued further, was the one that allowed all social groups, including women and the proletariat, a chance to express and vote on their interests: the parliament.[82] He advocated proportional voting as the best method for electing representatives because it allowed the widest possible inclusion of interests from across the nation.[83]

Thoma's approach to basic rights leads back to the main function of statutory positivism in the Weimar legal system. It affirmed the power of the Reichstag to work out compromises and thereby to integrate social groups into the state. The multiparty system with all its forced compromises provided the only alternative to "a splitting of the nation into a socialist and a 'bourgeois' block." It provided, in Thoma's view, the alternative to civil war, which at the time seemed a distinct possibility.[84]

Antipositivism and the Crisis of Constitutional Law

The first years of the Republic (1918-23) were marked by social unrest approaching civil war. To deal with the problems of demobilization, the transformation to a peacetime economy, and civil strife, the National Assembly approved enabling laws that allowed the government to take extraordinary measures and even to issue decrees with statutory force. President Ebert and his ministers made extensive use of these laws and Article 48 as well in those critical years, not only to respond to concrete emergencies but also to approve new statutory law. In practice, the president and his ministers had exercised the power reserved to the Reichstag in the constitution. From the point of view of the statutory positivists, the executive's actions were legal.[85] But the positivist picture of the normal polity scarcely corresponded to the realities of crisis.

The early crises gave evidence as well of many lawyers' alienation from the new republic, expressed from the start in terms of a rejection of the positivist tradition. Even Anschütz swerved for a moment from his Labandian roots when, in 1919, he called for judges to transform the principle of equality before the law into a substantive ethical principle that would guard the institution of private property against a parliamentary "dictatorship of the proletariat." Anschütz eventually regained confidence in the parliamentary system and returned to the methods of statutory positivism. But his momentary turn to substantive rights against "individual caprice" foreshadowed jurists' turn en masse to natural law during the upheavals of inflation and monetary revaluation in 1923–24.[86]

By 1923, both working-class and bourgeois Germans were expecting a return to "normal" conditions, by which they meant the prosperity and stability of the empire. But stabilization at the prewar level was impossible. Not only were the devastation wreaked by the war on the German infrastructure and means of production massive and the reparations demanded by the victors huge, the mode of financing the war and the ensuing demobilization had destabilized the monetary system itself. In 1922–23, inflation became hyperinflation, German attempts to avoid reparations led to French intervention in the Ruhr, and once more the Republic found itself at the brink of the abyss.[87]

In fall 1923, passive resistance to the French occupation collapsed. The German government faced revolts from both left and right and a currency that had essentially lost its value. The government's drastic plans for currency stabilization, begun in the summer, were on the verge of failing. The government requested and received an enabling law, approved on October 13, 1923, that transferred legislative power to the cabinet for necessary social and economic measures. The act explicitly permitted the government to violate constitutionally guaranteed basic rights.[88] After the collapse of the Great Coalition on November 2, a new, less far-reaching enabling law was approved on December 8. On the basis of Article 48, paragraph 2, and the enabling laws, three different governments managed to revalue and stabilize the currency. The Reichstag played no direct part in these measures.[89]

As part of its stabilization plan, the government banned further currency revaluation, countering a decision by the Reichsgericht of November 28, 1923, that would have potentially brought millions of cases before the courts. Banning revaluation made debts incurred at an earlier time repayable in devalued marks. The ban would have been ruinous for some members of the middle class whose savings remained at the preinflation level or who were creditors. The Reichsgericht had already expressed its opposition to the law on a number of grounds, but as yet the German judiciary had no power to review a statute for its conformity with constitutional law, so long as it had been produced according to the correct legislative procedure. Nevertheless, the court issued a letter on January 8, 1924, that threatened to invalidate any statute or decree banning or limiting revaluation. Such a law, it argued, would violate the principles of equity and good faith as well as property rights. The government was forced to back down and reconsider the regulation.[90]

The Reichsgericht's actions opened a floodgate in the legal community. New arguments about the theory and practice of the Weimar Constitution quickly engulfed the discipline of state law, threatening to wash away methods and concepts accepted by the discipline for decades. Hans Kelsen and Carl Schmitt developed opposing views of the theoretical and political foundations of constitutional systems. Rudolf Smend and Hermann Heller developed extensive theories of constitutional practice. And following the 1923–24 breakthrough, the high courts began altering their practice of adjudication. These central problems of constitutional law (discussed in chapters 4, 5, and 6) attacked statutory positivism, producing new countercurrents in legal thought.[91]

Paradoxically, the crisis of constitutional law found its expression in a new organization designed to promote the profession's integration. Heinrich Triepel, a professor of state law in Berlin, helped found the Association of German Scholars of State Law (Vereinigung der deutschen Staatsrechtslehrer) in the early 1920s. Officially, the association offered a forum where legal scholars could discuss problems of constitutional law despite their scholarly and political differences.[92] Rudolf Smend later recalled a more political aim: "to hinder fellow specialists from breaking up into contrary political groups, and thereby [to hinder] the public loss of credibility of German scholarship of state law."[93]

The conference reports of the association painted a picture of unity in difference.[94] The publications of the association told a different story. The "fragments" of arguments that came forward in the debates revealed a growing number of fissures within the discipline,[95] political as well as methodological. And they had already become unbridgeable by the mid-1920s, as a 1928 exchange between Triepel and Kelsen illustrates. The panel dealt with the essence and development of judicial review in public law, and the two scholars presented utterly different approaches to the problem. Triepel's essay dealt with the historical development of judicial review, while Kelsen's was an abstract examination of the legal basis for a highest court and technical arguments for its development.[96] Richard Thoma tried to smooth over the differences with a metaphor: the two had entered the same forest, he said, but from different sides.[97] Triepel countered, "Kelsen and I speak with different tongues because we see things with different eyes." Kelsen agreed: "We haven't met each other today, and presumably will never meet." The problem lay, Kelsen continued, in differing definitions of the constitution itself.[98]

Herein lay the discipline's crisis: it had become unclear exactly what constitutional jurisprudence was supposed to investigate. Nowhere was the crisis of the discipline more apparent than in the shift in style and genre of constitutional analysis during the Republic. The Laband school had produced dry and reasoned interpretations of statutes, such as Laband's *Budget Law,* and an analytical approach to problems of legal theory, exemplified by the work of Jellinek. Now authors developed new, often extreme styles of legal analysis. Hans Kelsen sought a purely theoretical description of law that gave his works an abstract and logical style, setting them apart from both the Labandian tradition and most German scholarship of the time. The shift was especially apparent in Kelsen's extremely sparing use of footnotes; the aim was no longer to summarize and incorporate all relevant scholarship, but to develop an intensive argument. Carl Schmitt expressed the separation between normal and exceptional situations through a "dual" style. He would develop a "normal" argument, then suddenly crush it with a statement asserting a deeper, existential reality.[99] Both Kelsen and Schmitt developed personal essay styles that were not those of standard textbooks.

New styles of approaching law opened new insights into assumptions about law and state. But they could also impede communication, heightening the sense of a disciplinary crisis. In 1928, for example, the republican administrative lawyer Walter Jellinek noted his difficulty in understanding Ernst von Hippel's presentation on supervision of administrative acts because of Hippel's many confusing metaphors. Hippel, a conservative and antirepublican administrative lawyer who integrated ideas of natural law into his work, responded that his opposition to positivism required a "new face" to scholarship involving a "baroque type of humor."[100] Indeed, Hippel's return to natural law was accompanied by a language and a set of metaphors that left the liberal world of Labandian positivism behind. In a review of a work on Kelsen, Hippel labeled Kelsen's work "intellectualistic," "lacking substance," and, most important considering the rising force of anti-Semitism, "un-German."[101] Freiherr Marschall von Bieberstein, another conservative state lawyer, stated in a poem commemorating the fifty-fourth anniversary of the empire's foundation that the actors in the Revolution of 1918, including Ebert, were usurpers who had committed high treason from the point of view of the Imperial Constitution of 1871.[102]

Changes in the content and genre of legal analysis accompanied changes in style. In 1928, Schmitt's *Theory of the Constitution* and Smend's *Constitution and Constitutional Law* appeared. They represented a significant shift in juristic literature on the constitution, as contemporaries realized.[103] Previous monographs on the constitution had emulated Laband's *State Law*, which organized existing state laws according to a set of abstract concepts, or Anschütz's commentaries, which enumerated and interpreted individual constitutional laws.[104] Schmitt's long monograph, by contrast, began by asking what a constitution is. Schmitt argued that constitutional theory had to examine the state as a real, existential unity. Therefore he rejected "mere" analysis of positive law. His book resembled less a systematic treatment of the constitution than a series of essays on the concrete political situation of the Weimar Constitution.[105] Smend's monograph likewise rejected positivist analysis. It began by conceiving of the constitution as the continual self-integration of the state community. His dense prose did as much to convey the notion of an immanent totality as did his subject matter.

The crisis in state law jurisprudence called into question the discipline's methodological identity and its dominant genre and style of presentation. The new approaches were unified by a common enemy: the Labandian tradition of statutory positivism and liberalism. A chorus of voices accused the Laband school of having emptied the content from legal theory. Positivism had made the state into "just another" legal person, the same as a business or a corporation. By attempting to distinguish strictly between jurisprudence and politics, the antipositivists claimed, the Laband school had failed to recognize that the very essence of state law *was* politics.[106] Kelsen, the final executor of the positivist tradition, was the antipositivists' main enemy.[107]

The critique of positivism led into a parallel critique of "liberalism." The papers and discussions of the Association of German Scholars of State Law were strewn with attacks on liberal thought. Some scholars considered liberalism already dead, others thought it had become irrelevant in the new social or political system, while still others considered it a source of untold damage to the "state." The most important accusation leveled against liberalism was that it was "individualist."[108] By implication, liberals were thought to view the state negatively and to see rights only as protection against the state.[109] Hans Gerber, an administrative lawyer on the far right, declared liberalism a "danger for the state's continued existence."[110] Hermann Heller argued that Laband was a liberal theorist of absolutism who had no relevance for a strong democratic state.[111] Since liberalism was relativistic, Smend and Erich Kaufmann argued, it could not defend basic values such as property, marriage, and academic freedom. The latter now appeared to be nonliberal values, just as Kant's philosophy became "miles removed" from liberalism.[112] Similarly, lawyers denied that liberalism could deal with the social demands of the twentieth century. When Walter Jellinek objected that liberalism *could* have a "social" side, referring to Friedrich Naumann, his critique went unanswered.[113]

The crisis of constitutional law often reflected a lack of faith in German democracy. The conservative statist Carl Bilfinger, for example, raised the specter of an unlimited power of the political parties to alter the constitution by having a two-thirds majority in the Reichstag. Bilfinger, Schmitt, and other conservatives openly attacked the "majesty" of the democratic sovereign, calling for setting absolute limits to legislative action.[114] Freiherr Marschall von Bieberstein compared the doctrine of statutory positivism to rule by the Cheka or the Catholic Inquisition.[115] It was another question entirely, of course, whether judges should be the ones to monitor the legislature. Schmitt argued that the president should take the kaiser's place as "guardian of the constitution."[116]

The terms *statutory positivism* and *liberalism* lacked a clear definition in the debates. But the debates were not really about the "correct" definition of the terms. Instead, they expressed the sense after 1923 that there would be no return to the world of "normalcy" before 1914. No longer could Bismarck's dictum that the Germans were saturated and satisfied be accepted.[117] No longer were lawyers willing to have faith in their constitutional system, now based on the primacy of a democratic parliament and political parties. The widely proclaimed crisis of state law reflected a reexamination of the fundamental assumptions regarding the theory and practice of democratic constitutionalism.[118]

4

THE PARADOXICAL FOUNDATIONS OF

CONSTITUTIONAL DEMOCRACY

Hans Kelsen and Carl Schmitt in the Weimar Republic

The constitutional debates of the 1920s revolved around the relationship between popular sovereignty and law. The sovereign source of law was the people, stated the constitution. But constitutional articles defined who "the people" was and how its will was to be expressed. The foundation of the constitutional system, "the people," seemed to be created by the system.

As Jacques Derrida notes in his analysis of the U.S. Constitution, the foundation of constitutional democracy seems to be paradoxical. The "subject" of the democratic constitution, "We the People," is both a constative utterance—it states that "We" are the "People"—and a performative utterance—it states that from this point on there shall be a "We the People." But, to quote Derrida, "this people does not exist. They do *not* exist as an entity, it *does not* exist, *before* this declaration, *as such*. . . . The signature invents the signer." Derrida asserts that the "subject" of constitutional democracy is created by a kind of "fabulous retroactivity"; sovereignty is the effect of textuality. He offers a second reading of the paradox as well, however, one that might be called "decisionistic": "The coup of force makes right, founds right or the law, gives right, *brings the law to the light of day*."[1]

In this space between "fabulous retroactivity" and "coup of force" took place one of the most important debates of constitutional law in the Weimar Republic. Hans Kelsen and Carl Schmitt both examined the paradox of constitutional democracy. The way each man worked through its paradoxical foundations and conceptualized sovereignty, the people, and law corresponded to radically different political understandings of the new postwar republics in central Europe. In Kelsen's case, a formalist theory of the constitution led to his affirming the role of political parties and interest groups in the creation and application of law: the "will" of the people was a retroactive construct determined by the procedures of constitutional law. For Schmitt, the party system was illegitimate insofar as it divided the will of the people, which he presupposed as a unified, existential basis of the system.

Kelsen and Schmitt continued to pursue the problems they had set for themselves in the period before 1919. Kelsen continued his project of "purifying" legal science and thereby indicating the limits to its subject matter on the model of Kantian critical philosophy. Schmitt developed further his notion of "radical practice," seeking to establish the point at which an exceptional state of affairs (e.g., a state of emergency) created a rupture in the "normal world" of the "bourgeois *Rechtsstaat.*" The stylistic continuities of each author are striking. Kelsen's language remained analytical, careful, restrained, and "dialogical" as he developed his theory through extended critiques of the works of other legal scholars. Schmitt perfected his technique of combining "normal" analysis with the hint of a radical rejection of that normality. The implication arising from his style was that something real, substantial, and existential—something extraordinary—lay beneath the surface of normal discourse.[2] But despite the continuities in style and subject matter, both authors' theories underwent major changes in the light of the new postwar constitutional democracies.

Kelsen was directly involved in creating the postwar order. The Social Democratic lawyer Karl Renner, who had become chancellor of the interim Austrian government in 1918, gave his friend Kelsen the assignment of writing a draft of the new republican constitution of Austria. Although he had only limited influence on the content of the final constitution, Kelsen played a major role in shaping its basic form, including the important section "Guarantees of the Constitution and Administration," which developed the system of high courts that were to review statutes and administrative orders for their legality or constitutionality.[3] Kelsen himself served as a judge on the highest court in Austria, the

Verfassungsgerichtshof (Constitutional Court), from 1921 until 1930. The conservative constitutional reform of 1929 forced him to leave that post.[4] Along with his legal scholarship he published a series of openly political articles and pamphlets that defended a tolerant, party-based parliamentary system open to the proposals of Social Democracy.[5] As a left-liberal of Jewish descent with personal connections to the Austrian Social Democrats, Kelsen faced threats from right-radicals and anti-Semites as well as harsh attacks from fellow professors during the late 1920s. He left Austria in 1930 to take a position as professor of public law in Cologne, where he remained until he was pushed into exile in 1933. The Austrian constitution he had written was suspended by authoritarian forces in 1934.

Following World War I, Schmitt retreated from his wartime administrative duties into the security of academic life. He became a full professor of public law at Greifswald in 1922, moved to Bonn in the same year, and finally, in 1928, went to the Handelshochschule in Berlin, an independent business academy run by the left-liberal political scientist Moritz Julius Bonn, where he took over Hugo Preuss's chair in constitutional law.[6] Schmitt's fame derived from his essays. His work in the early years of the Republic on romanticism and liberal indecisiveness, on dictatorship, and on the notion of political theology laid the groundwork for his later constitutional theory.[7] His career took a practical turn during the political crisis at the end of the Republic, when his theory of dictatorship was used to legitimize the president's repeated use of extraordinary powers. In 1932, with the support of Hans Kelsen, he was called to a professorship at Cologne. In the same year, the Papen government appointed Schmitt its legal representative to defend the government's intervention in Prussia before the State Court. At the end of 1932, Schmitt conspired with Kurt von Schleicher and other generals to set up an authoritarian state excluding the Nazis.[8] After Hitler took control, Schmitt joined the Nazi party and participated in constructing the new system. He refused to sign a petition circulated by the Cologne faculty to keep Kelsen from being removed from his post. Schmitt quickly rose as a star of the Nazi legal profession during the early years of the dictatorship, and he was able to place his own students in positions made available by Nazi political and racial purges. His personal prominence lasted until 1936.[9]

Kelsen's Basic Norm

The Presumption of Foundations

The problem of positivity, already developed in Kelsen's *Major Problems of State Law,* remained at the center of his work during the interwar period. *Positivity* referred to the status of the legal system as both a set of norms expressing "ought" propositions and a set of norms whose validity was "objective" and therefore not identical with subjective morality, ethics, or individual preference. By understanding law as an objective system of norms, Kelsen excluded from legal science both subjective ethics and the "real" world understood by means of natural or causal-oriented sciences. During the interwar years, Kelsen sought to work out the implications of this notion of positivity for a strict, neo-Kantian theory of law.[10] In 1920, he published *The Problem of Sovereignty and the Theory of International Law,* in which he argued that "sovereignty" referred solely to the objective system of legal norms. Two years later, he presented an extended critique of nonnormative, sociological concepts of order in *The Sociological and Legal Concept of the State* (1922). In 1925, he published the *General Theory of the State,* in which he elaborated a normative state theory. The emphasis on normativity contrasted starkly with Georg Jellinek's *General Theory of the State* from twenty-five years before, which had conceived of the state as both norm and factual will. After taking on natural law theories and publishing several short extensions of his Pure Theory of Law, Kelsen was prepared to offer an abstract synthesis of his work in his 1934 book *Pure Theory of Law.*[11]

The point of departure for Kelsen's theory was the *Rechtssatz,* or "reconstructed legal norm" (hereafter referred to as "legal norm"),[12] which he defined in neo-Kantian terms as a *"hypothetical judgment,* which attaches a definite result to a definite state of affairs as condition, in the declarative form of an 'ought.'"[13] According to Kant, causality was an a priori category of human cognition that enabled the mind to sort out empirical intuitions and create synthetic judgments of the causal world (empirical cognition). A similar category for law, Kelsen argued, would enable synthetic judgments or cognition in the realm of the "ought," and specifically in the "objective" realm of positive legal science. Kelsen termed the category of legal or normative cognition "imputation" (*Zurechnung*). While causality linked the condition and the consequent in "is" statements in order to show a causally necessary relationship, imputation linked the condition and the consequent of legal norms in order to express the "specific existence of law, its validity." Causality made possible judgments in the realm of causal necessity (*Müssen*); imputation made possible judgments about what ought to be (*Sollen*).[14] Kelsen stressed the constitutive role of the a priori category: the a priori category of imputation did not merely make possible cognition of certain facts but actually created a certain kind of knowledge, based specifically and exclusively on an "ought" of the norm.[15] Accordingly, any attempt by a science to establish a necessary connection between these two types of knowledge—or, in Kelsen's words, the two "worlds" of *Sollen* and *Sein*, "ought" and "is"—had to be a fiction or an ideological assertion rather than pure knowledge.

The neo-Kantian manner of posing the problem of normativity was undialectical insofar as it totally separated the two worlds of normativity and causality.[16] Emphasizing the strictly scientific study of law excluded careful consideration of human practice, which always took place in the space mediating the factual and the normative. But Kelsen's conscious refusal to enter into the problem of praxis served a practical purpose by emphasizing that the legal system was not reducible to social and natural reality. The dualistic conception of norm and fact, ideal and nature, reflected Kelsen's insistence on the existence of human freedom to issue ethical judgments regarding the contingent realm of necessity.[17]

While Kelsen's Pure Theory of Law was a theory of the normative, it was also a theory of positive law. Kelsen rejected the idea that positive law could be derived from a transcendent, normative order such as God's revealed law. Such arguments were political or ethical, not scientific, he argued; they permitted the legal scholar to disguise his or her opinions as absolute truths, and to cloak prescriptions in phrases that claimed to be merely descriptive.[18] According to Kelsen, natural law could be used to justify the status quo and to make existing legal norms such as those guaranteeing marriage, slavery, or property appear "natural";[19] or it could justify anarchy, denying law altogether in the name of an authentic natural order.[20] Against both positions, Kelsen argued that the legal system consisted of objective, positive law and was therefore not identical with the ideal world of "justice." Conversely, all positive law was subject to moral, ethical, and political criticism. Kelsen's positivism placed the responsibility for judging positive law in the hands of humans. As a purely theoretical science, however, it presented no standards for such practical judgment.

Law was thus both *Sollen* and *Sein,* both "ought" and "is," in Kelsen's theory; it was both normatively valid and effective.[21] The normatively and objectively valid legal norm formed the basis of his theory of the state. Legal norms attached legal conditions to legal consequences; the consequences were in turn "ought" statements that enabled, permitted, ordered, or denied certain persons to carry out certain coercive acts. This set of legal norms *was* the state, according to Kelsen; law and state were identical. With this claim he struck at the very heart of the Labandian positivist tradition, which had maintained that the state existed in some sense as a nonlegal or prelegal will. Georg Jellinek, for example, had argued that the state had two sides, one normative and the other factual. Against Jellinek, Kelsen argued that there was no third term mediating between the state and the supposed "other side." The method one used to comprehend an object was itself constitutive of that object.[22] A legal approach to the state yielded only legal results. If one viewed the state "normatively," then one saw only norms. "For a positivist examination, which does not absolutize law in natural law," Kelsen argued, "the state is a King Midas: all he touches turns to law."[23] Pure theory insisted that law and state had to be identical as long as the state was to be considered a normative system at all.[24] Kelsen attacked Ferdinand Lassalle, a founder of German Social Democracy, for asserting that the real constitution lay in power, not norms. By itself, he argued, a bayonet was simply a bayonet. It became state power only when an empowering legal norm of an objective legal system granted it legal significance.[25] And the essence of the state lay precisely in the ideal, objective order of norms constituting the legal system.[26]

By rejecting the statutory positivists' assumption that the state was a real, existing, willing entity, Kelsen focused attention on the state as normative system.[27] He defined sovereignty as the legal system's absolute character of not being derivable from a higher norm.[28] "Sovereignty" became simply another expression for "legal system"; it expressed the sense that the state was a unified normative order. With that argument Kelsen set aside the entire statist tradition that had linked sovereignty to a real state will.

In one respect, Hermann Heller was correct when he accused Kelsen of having turned the legal scientist into the source of sovereignty, since it was the jurist who had the task of producing legal unity.[29] But far from raising the legal scientist to kingmaker, Kelsen's theory of sovereignty served to emphasize the limits to the ideology of state sovereignty. If, as so often happened in constitutional jurisprudence in Germany and elsewhere, sovereignty was equated with a highest worldly will, then one had to consider the sovereign, or state, as the actual causal source of the system itself, and not merely the imputed source of a system's laws. The state would become a first cause preceding and creating its own rules, an indivisible and uncaused primary substance—a worldly God. But as Kelsen noted, reversing Spinoza, "substance *is*, however, divisible." A worldly will can never claim to be uncaused without raising itself above the world.[30]

The legal theory explicated so far closely resembles Kelsen's work before 1918. A major change appeared, however, in Kelsen's shift from a "static" to a "dynamic" theory of law around 1917–18.[31] The doctrine, borrowed from his colleague Adolf Merkl, conceived of the legal system as a hierarchical set of stages of authority. Each level derived the authority to issue norms from a higher level; and each level was capable of issuing norms that would enable a lower level to exercise authority.[32] The new doctrine (termed the *Stufenbaulehre*) allowed Kelsen to examine how a normative system "produced" itself, or regulated its own development. The theory provided the legal scholar with a way of "recognizing" lower-level legal norms as part of a more general legal system. A given norm was to be judged legal only if it was in accord with all higher-level legal norms, up to and including what Kelsen termed the "originary norm" (*Ursprungsnorm*) of the entire legal system.[33] A city ordinance, for example, was legally valid only if it was issued pursuant to an enabling statute from a higher authority such as the state. The statute, in turn, was valid only if it had been enacted according to the constitutional rules regulating the production of statutes. And finally, the constitution was valid only if it presupposed a hypothetical basic norm granting its validity. The validity of each individual norm could therefore be explicated in terms of its conformity to the unified whole; that is, its ultimate "derivability" (in the sense of being authorized) from the originary norm.

The dynamic theory placed the issue of the legal system's foundation at the center of discussion. Although the issue had already appeared in his 1911 work, it was perhaps not coincidental that Kelsen's theory of the basic norm developed while he was actively involved in creating the constitutional foundations of the Austrian republic. Indeed, another term for constitution (*Verfassung*) in the German constitutionalist tradition is "basic law" (*Grundgesetz*).[34] For Kelsen, the constitution in a "positive-legal" sense consisted of the fundamental norms that prescribed the highest level of legislation; for example, the parliamentary or monarchical forms of government.[35] Kelsen used "constitution" in this sense to isolate five distinct constitutions, or procedures for issuing laws, in Austria between autumn 1918 and midsummer 1920, when the new federal constitution was adopted.[36] But these founding rules themselves often derived their validity from some previous norm, Kelsen pointed out. The 1920 Austrian Constitution, for example, was created according to the norm regulating the formation of a constitutive national assembly in 1918. When a legal scientist followed the rules for creating a new constitution back to the rules creating those rules, eventually a break appeared in the continuity of legal development. Viewed in terms of legal norms, the Austro-Hungarian emperor's agreement in 1918 to recognize any decision by the National Council on the state's form was illegal according to existing law, since it was not approved by the Austro-Hungarian Imperial Council (Reichsrat).[37] That revolutionary break in legal continuity raised the question of how to explain why a constitution was valid.

One possible solution could be found in the theory of the revolution as a social contract made by the citizens to decide how they wanted to be ruled. Legality would then be derived from a prelegal will, thereby resolving the tension between "is" and "ought" in an autonomous, foundational act. Kelsen rejected that solution. One could only view an attempt to bridge the "is-ought" gap by means of the all-encompassing general will as a fiction in the troubled years after World War I in Austria and Germany.[38] The connection between "is" and "ought," between real people and the normative legal system, could not be proven true; the connection could only be indicated through the concept of the basic norm.

The basic norm was the presupposition that a given legal system was objectively valid. It had the function of establishing and maintaining the normative system. Kelsen had described it already in 1920:

This presupposition for law, this starting point, this originary norm, which I also term constitution in a juridico-logical sense, since it sets in place the "highest" organs of the state, the highest sources of law, has the function throughout of a fundamental hypothesis. When it was maintained above that the whole legal order is "derived" from it, this naturally cannot be so understood as though all positive statements of law were presupposed to be *a priori already* determined *in content*. The hypothetical originary norm is only the highest *rule for production*.[39]

In later works Kelsen renamed the "originary norm" the "basic norm." Nevertheless, the doctrine of the basic norm as a presupposed rule "founding the unity of the legal order in its auto-motion [*Selbstbewegung*]" remained central in Kelsen's work throughout the period of the Weimar Republic.[40] The basic norm represented Kelsen's attempt to come to terms with the fundamental problem of how legal norms could be simultaneously valid (i.e., normative "ought" propositions) and objectively effective: the act of presupposition took both validity and effectiveness into account.[41]

The basic norm was, as Kelsen explicitly recognized, a borderline concept in his Pure Theory of Law. It marked a limit to the realm of positive law, a point at the limit of legal science where law began.[42] The fundamental presupposition that the legal system as a whole was valid could not itself derive from that system: "For to want to determine the choice of juristic starting point juristically would be tantamount to standing on one's own shoulders, [and] would be equivalent to Münchhausen's attempt to pull himself out of the swamp by his own pigtail."[43] The phenomenon of state coercion puts the problem more concretely. Kelsen's theory as a positivist theory of law treated the legal order as a heteronomous, coercive order, not necessarily identical with the subjective wishes of those subject to that order. From the point of view of jurisprudence itself, however, coercion can be conceived of only as normative. That act of coercion which expresses the system's objective validity can itself be deemed valid—and not merely capricious—only if it is rendered normative; or, in other words, if it is expressed by an "ought" that is derived from the normative system itself. A logical circle appears. The legal system is objective because coercive; the coercion is legally valid insofar as it originates in an objective normative system. What, then, is the jurist's basis for recognizing a certain legal system as an objectively valid system of coercion? Normative jurisprudence can give no answer. "Certainly," Kelsen wrote, "it is not inconsequential whether and to what extent this 'ought'-validity [*Soll-Geltung*] becomes an 'is'-effect [*Seins-Wirkung*], the state system becomes the motif [*Motiv*] for human behavior, the content of its 'ought' becomes the content of an 'is.' But this connection to being, as decisive as it can be and in fact is in a certain respect, is of no consequence for the essence of the state."[44] Kelsen set aside the practical problem of the relationship between state (law) and society in order to inquire into the nature of the state itself. The state came to be "recognized as an ideal system, as a system of coercive norms, in whose *validity* its specific existence rests."[45] Once more, Kelsen remained within a logical circle.

The theory of the basic norm seems to confirm yet again Heller's accusation that, in Kelsen's view, only the jurist decided which legal system was effective or "in force." Heller misunderstood, however, the nature of Kelsen's theory. For Kelsen, law itself, as an objective system, was ideal. But in order for it to be positive or objective, it had to have some relationship to the world of causal relations. At the least, Kelsen argued, the legal system had to correspond at some level to real psychological processes of the people themselves, given that "a state order can be presupposed as valid only when it—more precisely, when the fact that it is imagined by people—is also effective." This reality, he noted, was precisely what the "positivity" of law meant.[46] Even while a complete identification of legal norm and fact was impossible, the content of an "ought" grounded by the originary norm nevertheless had to correspond to a certain extent with the world of the "is": "In this determination normativity and facticity are connected in a peculiar way to a characteristic parallel of validity and effectiveness."[47] Without this parallel (not identity) between "is" and "ought," legal science would be meaningless. A study of Russian law based on the tsarist legal system, for example, would be absurd in 1922 given the reality of Bolshevik rule.[48]

Some basic minimum of correspondence had to exist between legal systems and the "real" world as a prerequisite for positivist jurisprudence, according to the Pure Theory of Law.[49] The central question at this point, which Kelsen's critics had already raised in the Weimar Republic, was whether the call for a "correspondence" meant the failure of Kelsen's attempt to separate "is" and "ought"—whether Kelsen's doctrine of the basic norm really meant that law and power were identical, from which the collapse of Kelsen's entire theoretical enterprise must follow.[50]

Such a perspective neglects Kelsen's starting point in neo-Kantian philosophy. The key to Kelsen's theory of the legal norm is its hypothetical formulation: if certain conditions are present, then certain consequences should follow. The legal norm is constructed according to the transcendental category of imputation. While the category of causality assigns causal agency to a subject and effect to an object, imputation assigns legal liability to legal persons. Kelsen's theory of the origin of law carried a similarly transcendental and hypothetical character: "The basic norm confers on the act of the first legislator—and thus on all other acts of the legal system resting on this first act—the sense of 'ought,' that specific sense in which legal condition is linked with legal consequence in the reconstructed legal norm." Presupposing the reality or effectiveness of a certain coercive system, the jurist can assume that those legal norms making up the system are objectively valid, and positive, in spite of the many individual violations of the legal system that occur in reality.[51] Only this presupposition of effectiveness permits the jurist to perceive the legal system as a coherent and unified whole. The basic norm according to Kelsen was the expression of a necessary transcendental presupposition which every positivist had to make in order to practice positivist jurisprudence.[52]

The basic norm, then, was a *transcendental* presupposition, and not a *transcendent* unity; the legal system's unified foundation was a necessary principle for the legal theorist, but not necessarily a real, preexisting will. The ontological assumption contained in contract theory, that the state was the combined popular will, became the epistemological presupposition of the legal scientist. Kelsen used a logical distinction to stress this difference between epistemological presupposition and ontological assertion: "a certain effectiveness of the state order is to be sure the *conditio sine qua non,* but not the *conditio per quam* for the validity of this order."[53] Real existence was merely a precondition, not part of the order's validity itself.

Both Jellinek's Paradox, discussed in chapter 2, and the paradoxical foundations of constitutional democracy outlined at the start of the present chapter pointed to an "undecidable" moment in the legal system when law and power each seemed to be the foundation of the other. Kelsen responded by radically excluding the paradox from consideration, by pushing it into the overdetermined basic norm in order to guarantee the purity of legal science and the unity of the normative and objective legal system. His doctrine had come under fire before 1933 when Hermann Heller accused him of smuggling facticity and even the "will-theory" of the state back into his system under the guise of the basic norm.[54] Later, even some of his closest students turned toward a "realistic" jurisprudence, essentially stating that the search for a purely normative science of law had failed.[55]

But simply turning back to the "is" is not a sufficient answer to the problems posed by Kelsen. As long as one assumes that the legal system is not identical with social practice but indeed constitutes something else known as the "state," then one assumes a tension between law and fact, between state and society. An identity of law and society in the form of institutional or organic conceptions of law would make the problem of legal science superfluous. In the end, as Kelsen noted, the basic norm of positivism had to assume "a certain connection" between validity and effectiveness that was neither below a certain minimum, in which case the legal system would lose its objective quality and become the "*Wünschenrecht*" of the jurist, nor above a certain maximum, in which the tension between "is" and "ought," only within which a legal system can make sense, would be dissolved and replaced by some unnamed substantial unity or anarchic disunity.[56] The dilemma Kelsen presented is one inherent in the positivist notion of law, law grounded not in the transcendental will of God but in the immanent and relative realm of human life: "The problem of the *positivity* of law consists precisely in this, that it figures simultaneously as both 'ought' and 'is,' although these two categories logically exclude one another."[57]

Constitutional Fundamentalism

Carl Schmitt

Kelsen's abstract theory of the basic norm illuminated the paradoxical foundation of the legal system. Schmitt approached the same problem, but in a radically different way. His starting point was the concrete history of the German state and European, especially French, constitutionalism. He made no attempt to separate politics from law, historical origins from social present, or theology from philosophy. As his student Leo Strauss remarked, Schmitt's work was intended to provide a critique of the "liberal" principle of dividing life up into a series of autonomous spheres such as ethics or law or art.[58] Schmitt's style revolted against the sharp distinctions and "purity" of theory in Kelsen's legal science.

Schmitt's history of constitutionalism was the history of the modern technological age. He described an age dominated by two "worldly" powers, capitalism and communism, "American financiers and Russian Bolshevists," with the common goal of furthering economic rationality and a common enemy in political or institutional "form." No matter which antagonist won the worldly battle over the technical-rational distribution of goods, he argued, the jesuitical church and the jurists of public law would survive, for only those two groups comprehended the true essence of politics: its existence as institutional form in the world.[59] For Schmitt, the Catholic church expressed in its unalloyed form the principle of representation. The church was a "concrete" representation of Christ in the world; its legal person was the Person of Christ himself. Whereas Judaism, according to Schmitt, could conceive of God only as absolute transcendence, and Protestantism turned on a purely worldly existence, the Catholic church mediated between spirit and matter as the actual, institutional embodiment of Christ on earth.[60] Schmitt presupposed that a political form, like the church, was a real, living entity, and as such neither purely ideal nor merely a technical-rational organization of power. His theoretical point of departure was thus diametrically opposed to Kelsen's critique of such "fictions."[61]

The notion of the state as substance created an undercurrent in Schmitt's work, a moment of pure, real will that threatened to break through the surface of "normal" legal discourse. This was the moment of the exception, the moment of real life, politics, or war that was the system's authentic base.[62] He expressed the moment through his dual style, which pointed out the limits to everyday, normal procedure: "In the exception the power of real life breaks through the crust of a mechanism that has become torpid through repetition," Schmitt proclaimed in his *Political Theology*.[63] Romanticism, liberalism, and anarchism, he thought, denied the moment of exception or transcendence in favor of human immanence. Romanticism promoted a solipsistic and voyeuristic "subjectified occasionalism." Liberalism, which he cast in effeminate terms, was indecisive and passive. Atheism and anarchism were the militant wings of modernity, setting out to destroy all things claiming transcendent value.[64] The history of liberalism, romanticism, and anarchism coincided with the history of constitutionalism in Schmitt's two major books of constitutional law published during the 1920s, *Dictatorship* and *Theory of the Constitution*.

Dictatorship appeared in 1921. More than an intellectual history of the concept of dictatorship, the book traces the emergence of the modern written constitution. For Schmitt, the concept of dictatorship had nothing to do with authoritarianism, as "bourgeois political literature" might suggest.[65] Instead, as he had already argued in 1917, dictatorship was the specific situation in which the sovereign granted a commissar the power to suspend laws and take "concrete measures" in order to protect or reinstate the "normal" situation under which laws could operate. Schmitt's concept of dictatorship formed the keystone for his concept of sovereignty, which he defined as the right to decide whether an exceptional situation existed that would require the suspension of laws.[66]

Dictatorship remained an unproblematic concept in Schmitt's narrative as long as the sovereign retained unquestioned, traditional legitimacy. According to Schmitt, in the Middle Ages "God, the final source of all earthly force" operated "by means of the Church, a firmly constituted organism."[67] Even the Reformation and the rise of "pious Protestantism" did not bring about an "immanent" theory of sovereignty or the "dissolution of all social form." At most, Protestantism granted pious individuals outside the church hierarchy the right to appeal directly to God in a protest against the existing order. As Schmitt pointed out, even Cromwell avoided basing his "mission" on principles of popular sovereignty, and saw the source of his power instead in God.[68] God's transcendent, anchoring power remained the basis for theories of sovereignty and dictatorship, Schmitt suggested, until the French, represented by Rousseau and the French Revolution, turned to an immanent and creative notion of popular sovereignty.[69] With popular sovereignty arose the concept of a sovereign dictatorship that "does not refer to an existing constitution but to one which is to be brought about [*herbeizuführend*]."[70]

The conceptual distinction lay between commissarial and sovereign dictatorship, between the dictatorship seeking to restore the "normal" state of affairs and the dictatorship trying to create a new state of affairs that would be the basis for a new constitution.[71] The key to Schmitt's concept of the dictatorship does not lie in this abstract conceptual definition, however, but rather in the historical narrative that accompanied it. The "sovereign dictatorship" appeared with the French Revolution in Schmitt's narrative — and with the first revolutionary constitution in Europe. A prerequisite for the sovereign dictatorship was the belief that a people could freely and consciously constitute itself into its own form of government without appeal to a higher, transcendent legitimacy — a belief, in other words, that people could apply technical rationality to society itself. The earthly power itself, the people, became in Schmitt's narrative the constitutive power, and earthly institutions thus became relative and subject to criticism or change. The language Schmitt used to describe the turn to democratic ideals implies a loss of stability, a plunge into chaotic nothingness: "The people, the nation, the original power of all state essence, constitutes ever new organs. From the infinite, inconceivable abyss of its power arise ever new forms, which it can smash at any time and in which its power is never definitively delimited."[72]

The "constituting force" (*pouvoir constituant*) invoked by Abbé Sieyès in his theoretical defense of the French Revolution was an ever-formless former, the people were *natura naturans*. Organs created by the sovereign act of the people, however, were strictly limited to the powers defined in the original act, since constitutional power was subordinate to the sovereign.[73] The problem for the French revolutionaries as well as for Schmitt was how to relate these two extreme positions, the "constitutionally constituent" and "constitutionally constituted" powers. Somehow one had to theorize the creation of static norms by an ever-changing and completely immanent political "substance," namely, the "will of the people."

The most radical elements of Sieyès's theory of popular sovereignty formed the foundation for Schmitt's theory of democracy. According to Sieyès, there remained a gap between the people (*pouvoir constituant*) and the state or constitution (*pouvoir constitué*). The latter could be constructed in all its details only by some mediating organ. A moment of representation was necessary to mediate between general will and constitution, namely, a commission acting in the name of the people. At its most extreme, Schmitt argued, the commission became a revolutionary "dictatorial action commission," which no longer appealed to God, but rather "to the ever-present people, which can enter into action at any time and thereby have legally immediate significance." The examples Schmitt had in mind were the revolutionary French National Convention and the Bolshevik party.[74] Schmitt's analysis went beyond a theory of totalitarianism.[75] If it was a critique, it was a critique of "constitutionalism," of the presumptuous belief of mere humans that they could consciously organize themselves into a state. According to Schmitt, even the Weimar National Assembly was a sovereign dictatorship. The assembly acted on the orders of the formless "people" to produce "its" constitution. As such, the Weimar National Assembly, like the Catholic church, was based on the principle of representation; it was not identical with the will of the people. But this representation had lost its stable foundation in a transcendent God. It was limited only by the vague political desires of the masses, or "public opinion."[76]

Schmitt's theory of dictatorship began and ended with the problem of the foundations of a constitutional system. The modern world reflected a shift away from theological, undiscussed foundations in a sacred, traditional authority to popular sovereignty, to an immanent and unlimited "foundation"—to an abyss. The theory of sovereignty developed in *Dictatorship* became the basis for Schmitt's *Theory of the Constitution* (1928).

In the 1928 work, Schmitt distinguished between the constitution in a broad and overarching sense (*Verfassung*) and the individual written laws (*Verfassungsgesetze*) of the constitution itself.[77] Schmitt rejected the statutory positivist approach to the constitution, which focused on the constitutional document.[78] Like Kelsen, Schmitt examined the moment "before" the constitution that justified looking at the constitution itself as a unified legal order. But where Kelsen founded a science of law on the hypothetical basic norm, Schmitt presupposed an immanent people that fulfilled the same task, in creating a real legal system, as the transcendent God. The immanent will of the people had a transcendent character; it could never be encompassed or regulated by the written constitution.[79]

"The People," Schmitt argued, "must be present [*vorhanden*] and presupposed [*vorausgesetzt*] as a political unit if it is to be the subject of a constitution-granting power."[80] Stated somewhat more abstractly, only a subject with a unified will could confer the power to create (itself as) a unified subject, to constitute itself. Kelsen's normative purism would have added: the legal scientist must presuppose such a unity. But Schmitt argued that by framing the problem in terms of a "metaphysical presupposition," one lost sight of the actual basis of the system. For Schmitt, this unity had to be real as well; it had to be a living will. The curious formulation in the passage cited, "present and presupposed," reflects the ambivalence in Schmitt's entire manner of posing the question. On the one hand, the "people" was a presupposition that a will existed prior to the constitution; on the other, Schmitt *asserted* the will's actual presence or prior existence. Turning to a metaphysics of existence was Schmitt's answer to the logical or epistemological problem of the grounds of the constitutional system. It was an assertion, not an argument.

The word Schmitt used to express this primary unity was *political*. The "political" being was presupposed; "political" unity was present prior to the constitution. In his essay "The Concept of the Political," also written in 1928, Schmitt argued that "the political" was a fundamental distinction between the self and an other who posed a potential existential threat to the self. The distinction between Friend and Enemy became political, or a part of "life," only if it involved the possibility of war: the precondition for political unity was an external threat. The polity therefore existed only if it was a fighting unity.[81]

Schmitt's arguments about the foundations of the state amounted to a logical circle: the people constitute a unified will if they have the will to constitute themselves as a unified will in the face of an enemy that poses a mortal threat to that (not yet formed) unified will.[82] As Kelsen pointed out elsewhere, individuals have many different empirical reasons for accepting a given legal system as legitimate, ranging from psychological to social, from intellectual to aesthetic.[83] Schmitt's shift from presupposing state unity to asserting its real existence immediately connected the ideal normative unity of law with the social world, obscuring the complex workings of the latter and creating precisely the kind of "juristic fiction" Kelsen had been battling since 1911.

Yet Schmitt's work clearly expressed the presupposition of the German positivist tradition — *including Kelsen* — that some unified will stood at the basis of the legal system. Schmitt turned from a *transcendental* (hypothetical) to a *transcendent* or existential logic of the constitution, from the basic norm to the basic will. Kelsen had excluded this will from positivist legal science.[84] He had reduced the Rousseauian problem of the general will to a transcendental hypothesis, a presupposition for cognition. Kelsen found himself on a razor's edge. On the one hand, he denied that the legal system was an individual, solipsistic construction emanating from the mind of the solitary jurist. Against Heller's assertion that he had made the jurist into the sovereign, Kelsen consistently argued that coercion was a part of the legal system, that law was *objective*.[85] At the same time, Kelsen denied that law was identical with power.[86] Schmitt's internal critique of the positivist tradition hinged precisely on Kelsen's basic problem of positivity. But Kelsen's theory of the basic hypothesis, by resisting an immediate identification of "is" and "ought," left room for investigating the concrete problem of minimum and maximum correspondence between society and legal system. By contrast, Schmitt's absolute will closed off investigations of the relation between fractured society and unified state by bluntly asserting the unity of life and law. While Kelsen's theory could encompass a multitude of reasons for different social groups to accept a state's legitimacy, Schmitt insisted that some single, homogeneous element had to exist that unified the entire nation, be it religion, class — or race.[87]

By formulating an autonomous, existential notion of the political, Schmitt created a tension in his account of constitutional law. Originating in the French Revolution, the modern constitution, including the Weimar Constitution, consisted of two parts: an existential, political part, and the unpolitical principles of the "bourgeois *Rechtsstaat*."[88] The second, "*rechtsstaatlich*" element was the source of no political form whatsoever, Schmitt asserted. It was neither a part of the state's real life nor its essence. The *Rechtsstaat* merely "relativized" state power. The "real" constitution of the state was based on authentic principles of political form that could distinguish between friend and enemy, the existential foundation of a state. These principles were either the organic "integration" of people into a solidary will or their "representation" as a solidary will through monarch or leader.[89]

The key to Schmitt's notion of the bourgeois *Rechtsstaat* is to be found as much in the adjective "bourgeois" as in the term "*Rechtsstaat*" itself. The bourgeoisie was, for Schmitt, more a moral and political stance than a social group. Its essential characteristics were individualism, liberalism, and support for government by parliament. It yearned for the "eternal conversation" of parliamentary debates rather than concrete decision.[90] It was indecisive and unable to act. It avoided the "real" world of politics in favor of "political romanticism."[91] Schmitt saw an intrinsic connection between the effeminate and indecisive bourgeoisie and the *Rechtsstaat*. That connection lay in the utterly individualistic basic principle of the bourgeois *Rechtsstaat*: "The freedom of the individual is *in principle unlimited,* while the authority of the state to intervene in this sphere is *in principle limited.*"[92] Basic rights and the separation of powers guaranteed the private realm of the individual.

The conception of basic rights being proposed by Schmitt was essentially bourgeois and liberal. Property rights, the right to free speech, and the right to assembly all set limits to state activity, preserving individual freedom. Social rights, such as the right to work, had no real place in Schmitt's *Theory of the Constitution.*[93] To ensure the limited nature of the state in the bourgeois *Rechtsstaat,* the principle of the separation of powers divided state functions among separate organs of the state.[94] In practice, each organ could act only within its jurisdiction as outlined by the written constitution. The constitution was thus sovereign over the state organs, and the crucial issue became whether or not a specific act could be subsumed either under the general constitutional norm or under some norm itself subsumable under the general norm.[95] The idea of the bourgeois *Rechtsstaat* thus culminated "in a *general shaping* of the entire state life *like the judiciary* [*Justizförmigkeit*]." All state activity was to be modeled after the rational judicial proceeding.[96]

The tension between the bourgeois *Rechtsstaat* and the existential foundations of politics permeated *The Theory of the Constitution.* Schmitt continually interrupted himself in the course of his argument to proclaim that a written constitution could *not* be sovereign, or that the state was *not* a merely judicial organization.[97] He contradicted the relativistic and legalistic logic he was developing regarding the bourgeois *Rechtsstaat* to insist on a separate notion of political decision. The parliament, however, remained within the normal *Rechtsstaat,* as Schmitt's doctrine of the statute showed.

Despite many differences between his theory and Laband's, Schmitt made a similar distinction between the abstract general statute and the concrete administrative ordinance. But he asserted that Laband's distinction between form and content of the statute made sense only in the context of the Bismarckian constitution; when monarchical, bourgeois, and democratic interests all entered into the creation of a statute, then faith in the formal validity of the statute was warranted. Once the monarch disappeared, only two elements remained: the democratic, political principle of unity, based on an act of original decision prior to the written constitution; and the bourgeois institutions created by the prior decision: the merely legal Reichstag. The Reichstag was no longer limited by the political force of the monarch; now it had to be viewed as limited by the originary, political force of the constitutional decision. The "legislative officials" (*Gesetzgebungsbehörden*) were constituted by the constitution, not sovereign lawgivers. A formal theory of the statute that took no account of substantive limits to legislative activity would grant the Reichstag the right to stand above the sovereign that granted it power in the first place.[98]

Raising the problem of the substantive definition of the statute meant, in effect, finding limits to legislative activity. Schmitt's strategy became clear in a legal brief of 1926 in which he questioned the legality of an attempt by liberals, Social Democrats, and Communists to expropriate property belonging to the former monarchs of German *Länder*. Such a statute would be a "substantive" administrative act, an individual order (*Einzelbefehl*), insofar as it intervened against a specific group, he argued; by such an action the Reichstag would take over the functions of another branch, making itself the absolute power.[99] The statute would not be "general" in that it would not provide the grounds according to which the administration could make a concrete decision, but would itself carry out a certain "measure." In this way, Schmitt argued, the "measure" would violate the basic right to property, which allowed expropriation only "on the basis of a statute"; that is, according to a general rule.[100] To intervene directly against a specific target instead of promulgating a rule applicable to all would also violate the principle of equality before the law (Art. 109). By not requiring a substantive degree of equality in the statute itself, argued Schmitt, the approach of the statutory positivists opened the way to parliamentary absolutism.[101] Schmitt made similar arguments against the Reichstag's "unlimited" right to use Article 76 to change the constitution. He argued that a constituted body could have no right to change fundamental principles of its own constitution.[102] With regard both to expropriation through legislative act and to amendment of the constitution, Schmitt applied his theory of the prior constitutional will to derive results in direct contradiction to the constitution's explicit wording.

Schmitt's theory thus limited the power of the Reichstag to issue legislation and transferred specific decisions, such as those involving expropriation or socialization of property, to the administration.[103] The value of conceptualizing the statute as a legal norm that was in its essence general and abstract was, however, of limited value, as an example produced by Hermann Heller shows: "The legal norm which forbids the emperor to return to the Republic would have to be valid for ten emperors." The generality of form regulated the abstract construction of a legal norm; it did not regulate its content, at least not unless it were transformed into a principle of substantive justice.[104] Schmitt's theory of generality, furthermore, could not explain the points in the constitution where the Reichstag was given the power to pass statutes that were in no way "general" in Schmitt's sense. The most important of these was the Reichstag's exclusive right to determine the budget for the forthcoming year. As Laband had shown in 1871, the budget amounted to a series of specific allocations of money and predictions of expenditures, not merely to "general" norms. Schmitt evaded the issue, reducing such moments to "a simple dodge [*Kunstgriff*] of linguistic technique."[105]

Schmitt claimed that his argument took the constitution seriously, both legally and politically.[106] By "constitution," however, he meant something specific: the decision by the unified will to constitute itself as a state. In the German case, that decision, Schmitt argued, had fallen against the Soviet model of socialism. The nation had decided against workers' councils and for parliamentary democracy, against expropriation of the capitalist class and for bourgeois property rights and marriage. Therefore, as he argued ever more strongly in the final years of the Republic, the general will had decided for a bourgeois-liberal state.[107] The constitution protected existing social relations against the Reichstag. Were the Reichstag to pass statutes against the "basic decision," and were these to be respected as valid law by the statutory positivists, Schmitt argued, the Reichstag would have committed illegitimate "apocryphal acts of sovereignty."[108] Precisely the assumption made by Social Democracy on entering the Weimar Republic—that it could use the Reichstag to engineer an evolutionary rather than revolutionary transition to socialism—came under attack. In fact, Schmitt's Manichaean approach to politics could make no sense of reformist Social Democracy, which hovered between liberal constitutionalism and Jacobin revolution.[109]

While Schmitt turned to a history of ideas to develop a legal concept of constitutionalism, Kelsen consciously avoided political, ethical, or historical theories of the modern constitutional state.[110] Most important, he refused to develop a substantive concept of the statute that would limit legislative authority as Schmitt had done. Kelsen developed a strictly formalistic conception of the legislature as one law-creating organ in a dynamic, self-creating legal system. The legislator, for Kelsen, was no different from an administrator or a judge. All were state organs with a certain legally designated realm in which to act.[111] Higher-level norms determined the degree of freedom in the creation of new norms or new powers for "lower" officials; constitutional norms, for example, set the rules for legislative activity. Each level of the legal system, except for the basic norm at the very top and the final moment of practice at the very bottom (what Kelsen referred to as the moments of "pure word" and "pure deed"), contained a moment of determination as well as a moment of will. Kelsen explicitly adopted the Free Law movement's theory, which had rejected absolute determinism in the process of making abstract norms concrete, while at the same time stressing the role of norms in setting jurisdictional limits to organs' actions.[112] His positivist theory of law did not consider the problem of how state organs were limited by ethics, morality, or politics. As a "pure" theory, it considered only the formal aspects of a legal norm, the way a statute enabled a lower official to make certain decisions under certain conditions, for example.

Kelsen's theory thus did not provide the means for criticizing Schmitt's specific historical conception of the bourgeois *Rechtsstaat*. But it did provide arguments showing that Schmitt's arguments were not compelling from the point of view of the legal system viewed formally, and that they were therefore necessarily subject to dispute. Kelsen's central tenet in his critique of substantive theories like Schmitt's was: "So muss es nicht sein" (It doesn't have to be like that). His skeptical theory undermined all arguments seeking to find a priori limits to legislative activity, whether in natural law, sociological positivism, or a history of ideas.[113] Kelsen's critique served as a means to criticize Schmitt's substantive theory of politics in the final years of the Republic.

Schmitt, Kelsen, and the Guardian of the Constitution

Kelsen and Schmitt took vastly different approaches to constitutional democracy, but both addressed the same paradox of constitutional foundations: the way factual will and normative legal order each seemed to "ground" the other. Kelsen employed the metaphor of the basic norm to isolate and exclude the paradox from legal science. Schmitt, making reference to classic texts of the French Revolution, asserted that the foundation existed in a real substance: the people united in opposition to an enemy. The two approaches became politically significant as the Weimar Republic entered into crisis after 1929 and the problem arose as to who "really" represented the fractured German nation.

Central to the debate was the place of the president and his control over emergency powers according to Article 48. The concept of dictatorship changed in the bourgeois *Rechtsstaat*, Schmitt argued in 1924. Dictatorship no longer described the total suspension of the constitution or the authentic "state of exception," but merely the "state of siege." Under a state of siege, the written constitution remained in force instead of being suspended; it delegated and delimited even extraordinary authority.[114] Unlike the monarch, who received his authority directly from God, the republican president received his authority from the constitution. Unlike the monarch, who was able to tap into a residue of sovereignty to exercise "extraordinary state power, which is never capable of being totally grasped through constitutional regulation," the president was constituted by and within the constitution.[115] Dictatorship according to Article 48 was itself subordinate to the sovereign constitution.

Schmitt's own arguments therefore suggested that the commissarial dictatorship, which suspended the constitution to preserve it, was impossible in the bourgeois *Rechtsstaat*. But he nevertheless asserted that the dictatorship according to Article 48 was commissarial. President Ebert had made extensive use of emergency powers in the early years of the Republic. And the legal scholarship of the time generally took the view that Ebert had operated constitutionally when he exceeded the limited authority explicitly granted by Article 48—proclaiming legislation, making financial decisions, and in fact, as Schmitt pointed out, deciding on the life or death of German citizens under martial law.[116] The president's ability to go beyond the boundaries of the written constitution to deal with an emergency situation had somehow to be explained.

The problem lay in the concept of the constitution, Schmitt said. Rather than being "a multitude of individual statutes,"[117] Schmitt argued, the constitution had a substantive meaning. It was an "inviolable minimum of organization." The basic organization of the Republic—president, cabinet, and Reichstag—could not be infringed on or suspended through use of Article 48.[118] Schmitt's conceptual solution deviated from the actual text of Article 48, which merely listed several basic rights that the president was permitted to violate in an emergency. In fact, Ebert had violated other rights and procedures of the constitution—with the express agreement of the Reichstag. Schmitt's argument gave the president the right to act against "nonessential" elements of the constitutional system created by the National Assembly. Until the president's rights were specifically laid out by legislative statute, which Article 48, paragraph 5, of the constitution demanded, Schmitt argued, the presidential dictatorship would work "like the residue of a sovereign dictatorship of the National Assembly."[119] Indeed, Schmitt queried whether the Reichstag had violated the constitution by not passing the required clarifying statute.[120]

The eventual solution on which Schmitt settled in 1924 appeared to limit the power of the president, restricting him to actions that would neither usurp the Reichstag's legislative power nor eliminate the role of ministers, who by countersigning presidential orders ensured parliamentary control over the president. But, as so often, Schmitt wrote in a dual style. He clearly distinguished at one point between the state of siege according to Article 48, paragraph 2, and the emergency laws of a state confronted by an authentically political, existential threat.[121] In *Political Theology*, published in 1922, Schmitt developed an approach to Article 48 that took into account that existential threat. He proclaimed that the power of the Reichstag to regulate emergency decrees (Art. 48, par. 3) was an attempt to defer and divide sovereignty. But the content of Article 48 led back toward an undivided sovereign: it granted "an unlimited fullness of power" in the moment of the true exception, a moment that norms could not predict.[122] Schmitt then argued that the "existence of the state is undoubted proof of its superiority over the validity of the legal norm. The decision frees itself from all normative constraint and becomes in an authentic [*eigentlich*] sense absolute. The state suspends the law in the exception on the basis of its right of self-preservation."[123] In *Political Theology*, the content of Article 48, paragraph 2, was said to correspond to the notion of the commissarial dictatorship in a monarchical regime that the legal "form" denied. Schmitt's dual style allowed him to argue both that a limited state of siege corresponded to the demands of constitutionalism and that a moment of existential peril opened the way to a suspension of constitutionalism.

Schmitt's theory of extraordinary presidential authority created what Karl Dietrich Bracher has described as a second constitution that potentially undermined the written one.[124] Schmitt played down the implications of his theory in *The Theory of the Constitution*. At that time of political stability, when the Reichstag was functioning relatively smoothly, Schmitt was more concerned with developing limits to "normal" legislative power than "extraordinary" executive power. His attention turned back to presidential emergency powers during the political crisis that arose after 1929.

In the light of the inability (or unwillingness) of parties to form a stable majority in the Reichstag in 1930, the Brüning government turned to rule by emergency decree. When the Reichstag voted to annul the emergency measures, Brüning responded by dissolving the Reichstag and reimplementing the measures. For practical reasons, even the Social Democrats agreed to tolerate this questionable rule by decree until the Reichstag was again able to function. As republicans such as Thoma and Walter Jellinek reasoned, if the Reichstag was not able to act, then the second half of the democratic constitutional system, the president and the cabinet, had to assume wider powers until the crisis was overcome. Since the measures in great part dealt with economic matters, the question arose as to whether Brüning was acting in violation of the constitution, especially of Articles 85 and 87, which gave the Reichstag the power to determine budgetary and financial decisions.

Jellinek, Thoma, Anschütz, and other statutory positivists argued that legally Article 48, paragraph 2, empowered the president to issue decrees with the force of law, and politically there was no alternative to such actions as long as the Reichstag was unable to act.[125]

As the crisis continued, some on the left began arguing for increasing the government's independence from shifting Reichstag majorities while still maintaining the Reichstag's right to reject government decrees.[126] Conservatives who opposed rule by parties on principle went further. The Federation for the Renewal of the Empire (Bund zur Erneuerung des Reiches) called for transferring more authority to the president (a policy it claimed was already implied in the constitution itself). The proposals the Federation presented amounted to a surreptitious return to the Bismarckian system: separating the president from parliamentary pressures, relieving him of the responsibility of finding party-political support for his ministers, and separating the administration from "party politics." Further, the proposals corresponded to the long-range plans of Papen and perhaps Brüning as well.[127] Schmitt's 1931 work, *The Guardian of the Constitution,* contains a political and legal defense of the authoritarian position, going beyond the pragmatic defense of the Republic advocated by the statutory positivists, and even the arguments of the conservatives for a stronger president, to criticize the party-political system in general.

Key to Schmitt's argument was the concept of the constitution itself. If the constitution consisted of a set of highest legal norms, then it could be protected by courts that considered the legality of the actions of lower state organs. Administrative courts might guard against bureaucratic violations of rights, procedures, or statutes; a court system might be given the task of determining whether a parliamentary statute conformed to constitutional norms. In a 1929 article Schmitt had conceded that these complex problems of judicial review could be seen as questions of protecting the constitution.[128] In the 1931 polemic, however, Schmitt rejected the argument that the judiciary was the guardian of the basic order. The arguments Schmitt mustered against judicial review of state acts can be left aside at this point. (In any event, neither history nor logic has accorded most of them lasting validity.)[129] Schmitt's main argument concerned the proper place the judiciary should occupy in a bourgeois *Rechtsstaat.* In that system the judiciary was confronted with "natural" limits, he said; in particular, courts could apply only general norms. In such circumstances, judges should "subsume" a certain situation under a more general norm, thereby applying a higher decision without themselves acting "politically" to produce norms of their own.[130]

Schmitt knew full well that this mechanical concept of "subsumption" made little sense after the critique of the Free Law school; indeed, he had helped to take the notion apart in his 1912 dissertation.[131] As Kelsen noted, judicial decisions involving redefinitions of unclear laws took place constantly. In fact, he argued, disagreement over the meaning of laws was what triggered most judicial action in the first place.[132] The act of subsumption, Kelsen noted, was not defined so much as invoked by Schmitt. Schmitt sought to deny that the judiciary could review a statute for its correspondence with a constitutional norm, because only a situation, not a norm, could be subsumed under another norm. Schmitt, Kelsen said, had failed to note that the lower-level norm was the "situation" to be subsumed under a higher-level norm. In the end, the judge, like the legislator, exercised power within certain bounds. "There exists," wrote Kelsen, "only a quantitative, not a qualitative difference between the political character of the legislator and that of the judiciary."[133]

Kelsen's critique did not yet touch on the strategic point of Schmitt's argument, which lay in his distinction between political and unpolitical organs. In *The Guardian of the Constitution* Schmitt attempted to isolate the representative of the substantial political will that, as he had asserted in *The Theory of the Constitution,* lay at the basis of the constitutional system. His argument paralleled those of two classic works in the pantheon of German state theory: Pufendorf's *Constitution of the German Reich* (1667), and *The Constitution of Germany* (1799–1802), one of Hegel's early works. In the one-page foreword, Schmitt even termed his work "*de Statu Imperii Germanici,*" the Latin title of Pufendorf's work.[134] All three works reject "positivistic" jurisprudence, in the deprecatory sense of it as legal scholarship that merely collects and orders legal norms regulating rights and duties of organs or legal persons within the state without dealing with the larger issue of a polity's existence. They turn instead to Pufendorf's question: "Who decides?"[135] For Pufendorf, the Holy Roman Empire of the German nation did not provide a coherent answer to the question of who was sovereign and could therefore command the full power of the state. The Holy Roman Empire was not a state but a "*Monstrum*," a multiplicity of positive legal rights enjoyed by competing estates and factions which denied the full expression of the state's unity.[136] For Hegel, writing after the ignominious defeat of the German states at the hands of Napoleon, the Holy Roman Empire was little more than a collection of subjective rights, a massive system of private law without any central power. If the Holy Roman Empire could be viewed as a state, then "its political state would have to be viewed as a legal anarchy, its state law as a legal system [acting] against the state." A state that could not fulfill its highest duty to exist could not be a state. And if the state could not subordinate private rights to the needs of the whole, there could be no state.[137]

Schmitt claimed that the Weimar system was transforming public law into a procedural system analogous to that of private law, with "subjective public rights" sanctioning the "pluralistic dissolution of the state."[138] Labor law conflicts were being decided according to the merely arithmetic principle of equal representation, by an "*itio in partes,* like that of the Catholics and Protestants since the 16th century in the old German Empire."[139] New demands from municipal and *Länder* governments threatened the unity of public policy. The splintering of the state would lead back to a state of estates (*Ständestaat*), "under which the German state has already once perished."[140] Schmitt presented a picture of the German *Reich* on the verge of repeating its old disasters and falling back into feudal, corporate systems of representation—for lack of a strong state.

This argument illuminates the grounds for Schmitt's rejection of a constitutional court. The adjudication of political disputes would permit individual parties to act as though their own subjective rights raised them above the "real" interest of the state. Under such conditions, the constitution would come to appear a mere contract among nations or private individuals.[141] Schmitt's concept of the unpolitical bourgeois *Rechtsstaat* sought to theorize the refeudalized, "judicial" state that lacked a strong center.

The single greatest danger to the state, Schmitt asserted, was "pluralism," a multiplicity of "*social* power complexes, which take possession of state will-formation for themselves as such, without ceasing to be social (nonstate) creatures [*Gebilde*]."[142] According to Schmitt, the pluralization of the state was part of a more general historical development from the nineteenth-century "neutral" liberal state, which did not intervene in society, to the "total state" of the twentieth century. The interventionist state blurred the distinction between state and society.[143] Social groups had become "political." They formed the modern political party, a "social complex" with "a standing army of paid functionaries and a whole system of aid and support organizations, in which a spiritually, socially and economically cohesive clientele is bound." Through the proportional voting system, Schmitt argued, a new feudal system had been created that was based on the proportional representation of individual or party "estates."[144] Schmitt's critique of pluralism became a critique of the "pluralistic party state," a concept already fully developed by the 1923 edition of his *Crisis of Parliamentary Democracy*.[145] Parliament had lost its function of transforming individual wills into a "will above parties [*überparteiischen Willen*]," and had instead become an "arena [*Schauplatz*] of pluralistic distribution of the organized social powers." Once more Schmitt noted the "numerous parallels" between the dissolution of the Holy Roman Empire into estates' interests and the parties in the Weimar Republic.[146] Since he conceived of the constitution as an originary, unified will, Schmitt saw pluralism as unconstitutional.[147]

To halt the pluralist threat, Schmitt sought a political "substance" in the modern state that would represent the state's true unity.[148] And to find this substance Schmitt turned back to the problem of the dictatorship: "The state of exception unveils . . . the core of the state in its concrete singularity."[149]

The pragmatic arguments that Schmitt used to defend the Brüning government's use of Article 48 were accepted by other lawyers, as has been shown above. Many agreed that the only means to correct presidential misuse of Article 48, paragraph 2, lay in the Reichstag's control function, and agreed further that if the Reichstag was unable to act, then it had no moral or legal right to cripple the one organ that *was* able to act. But Schmitt went further. He argued that the Weimar Constitution was democratic, and therefore opposed to liberalism, since "democracy" meant a unity of nation (*Volk*) and State; the Reichstag was the threat against which the constitution had to be guarded.[150] As long as parliament reflected the fragmentation of social reality and allowed a multiplicity of groups access to state power, it imperiled the real constitution — the unified will of the people.

The parliamentary component of the constitutional system, which

Schmitt identified as part of the bourgeois *Rechtsstaat,* had failed to provide a unified political system. Therefore Schmitt turned to the democratic, form-giving elements of the constitution to find the political basis for state unity. The head of state in the Weimar constitution, he announced, "above and beyond the competences allocated it, represents [*darstellt*] the *continuity* and *permanence* of the state unity and its unified functioning."[151] And in the Weimar system, it was the president who could claim to represent the whole: "The president stands at the center of a whole system of party-political neutrality and independence constructed on a plebiscitary groundwork. To him is assigned the state order of the present-day German Empire in the same measure as the tendencies of the pluralistic system make a normal functioning of the legislative state more difficult or even impossible." The president was the "summoned [*berufen*] watcher and guardian of the constitutional condition [*Zustand*]" according to the "positive content of the Weimar Constitution," Schmitt claimed.[152] The president played the role of the "neutral third." He would decide in the interest of the whole which groups to promote and which to repress, which "neutral" decisions were necessary for security, and which economic measures should be undertaken to preserve the economy. The president was the head of neutral economic institutions not controlled by the pluralistic parliament: the central bank (*Reichsbank*) and the railway network (*Reichsbahn*). Quoting Johannes Popitz, Schmitt asserted that some form of centralized economic control, some "unified guiding principles," were necessary for the modern economy. "Pluralistic parliamentarianism" was naturally unable to provide such leadership. The president was, for Schmitt, the correct source of such central economic decisions.[153] The economic aspect of Schmitt's argument became clearer in his next major work, *Legality and Legitimacy* (1932). In it, he contrasted the "strong total state," in which the state would intervene to control society, with the "weak total state" of the Weimar Republic, which was controlled by interest groups. The strong total state would recognize the administration as its real "core."[154]

Schmitt's argument for a strong executive in the modern interventionist state paralleled arguments from other democratic countries; Harold Laski, for example, developed a similar conception of the U.S. president, and the technocrat movement focused on an ostensibly scientific and superpolitical administration.[155] What distinguishes Schmitt's work is the metaphysical tone that entered into it. The president would be the direct expression of the "positive" constitution, the unified will of the people:

[The Weimar Constitution] presupposes the entire German nation as a unity, which is immediately ready for action, and not first mediated through social group organizations; [as a unity] that can express its will and at the decisive moment over and beyond pluralistic divisions find its way back to unity and bring its influence to bear [*Geltung verschaffen*]. The constitution seeks in particular to give the authority of the president the possibility of binding itself immediately with this political total will of the German nation and precisely thereby to act as guardian and protector of the constitutional unity and totality of the German nation.[156]

In these sentences lies the essence of Schmitt's constitutional theory: the assertion that there is a unified will, the assertion that the unified will is "represented" by the head of state, and the assertion that this sovereign organ[157] takes measures responding to concrete political needs of the entire state. Article 48, paragraph 2, enabled the return of the state as substance in the form of the unbound executive, which would be able to act apart from the pernicious influence of interest groups in the Reichstag.

Schmitt's theory of the positive constitution asserted that the president was the representative of a collective will and the embodiment of the nation. That assertion, Kelsen stated, was an unexplained mystery, an article of faith.[158] After all, the president was elected in a procedure carried out under the pressure of party politics. A minority almost always remained dissatisfied. The president was not neutral and above party conflicts, despite Schmitt's assertions to the contrary. Furthermore, Kelsen argued, the Weimar system was based on the principle of pluralistic representation through the Reichstag. Although some might consider the system "pernicious" from the viewpoint of "some political ideal," it was not unconstitutional.[159]

As Kelsen recognized, Schmitt's argument was based on a certain notion of the constitution as "a condition, the condition of the *unity* of the German people. What this *unity* consists of, which has a substantive, not some merely formal character, is not defined any more closely. It cannot be anything but a condition desired only from a definite politi-

cal point of view. *Unity* as a wished-for ideal of natural law thrusts itself
into the place of the positive-legal concept of the constitution."[160] It was
this wish that led Schmitt to ignore the possibility that the president
might violate the substantive constitution. And it was apparently this
wish that led Schmitt to misquote one of the most important articles
of the constitution. According to Article 42, the president pledged his
allegiance to the constitution and statutes of the German republic. And
statutes, according to Article 85, were those legal norms passed by the
Reichstag. Therefore the president had a constitutional duty to obey
parliamentary statutes. Schmitt, however, asserted that Article 42 required the president to pledge his allegiance to the constitution; the
reference to statutes was left out. Schmitt's affirmation of the president
as "guardian of the constitution" took place only at the cost of ignoring
the central role of the Reichstag in the constitution. Here, as before,
Schmitt's critique was at root not a legal argument at all, but rather one
based on antiparliamentary political assumptions.[161]

Kelsen's legal argument took the form of a skeptical critique of
Schmitt's attempt to jump from law to reality. The logic of Kelsen's critique was devastating, but its political impact was limited. In the end,
Schmitt was able to use his *political* theory of the plebiscitary dictatorship, in which the president embodied the popular will, to legitimize
the Papen regime's coup d'état against the Prussian government and
General Schleicher's attempt to institute a kind of corporatist fascism
at the end of 1932. The deed ended the discussion. Schmitt never both-
ered to respond to Kelsen's critical article. But Kelsen's theory implied
a political criticism whose importance extended beyond the immediate
problem of presidential authority.

Conclusion

This chapter began with a paradox of constitutional democracy: the
sovereign creator of the constitution appears to be created by the constitution itself. Kelsen restated the paradox through his theory of the basic
norm. Schmitt solved the paradox by asserting the immediate presence
of a sovereign people: a people substantially homogeneous and united
in some basic aspect, such as race or religion, that became "political"

in response to an external, existential threat to their unity. The enemy constituted the friend.

Schmitt's fundamentalist solution to the paradox culminated in the affirmation of the president's immediate and legitimating connection to the sovereign. The argument followed an important conservative tradition of German state theory, represented by Pufendorf and the early Hegel, which asserted that the state possessed a substantial "kernel," or core. Constitutional monarchism presumed as well that the monarch exercised a power that existed prior to the constitution itself and resided in the administrative apparatus.[162] Kelsen argued that positivists in the tradition of Laband had made this legal "theory of surplus value" (*Mehrwertstheorie*) serve the political purpose, conscious or unconscious, of transferring more power to the monarch.[163] Laband himself had argued that the kaiser was "guardian and protector of the constitution."[164] Schmitt, echoing Laband's phrase and arguments, revealed his roots in the constitutionalist system that the Revolution of 1918 had overthrown.

Kelsen's Pure Theory of Law provided no means for disputing the existence of a "primary" legal system based on executive commands. One needed only to presuppose a hypothetical basic norm (deviating, of course, from the mere written text of the constitution) according to which the executive's orders were the sole source of legislation. Kelsen's theory provided no means for depriving Papen's or Hitler's robber band of its claim to promulgate valid law.[165] But the Pure Theory of Law did not lose all critical potential because it lacked an ethical moment. Criticism could begin as soon as a jurist asserted that the state represented a real substance in the world, an existential and real unity that was somehow beyond law or norms. Precisely that assertion underlay Schmitt's arguments and connected his 1917 work on dictatorship (administration as *Urzustand,* or originary state of affairs), to his 1931–32 search for the state's substance in authoritarian executive control free from pluralistic party influence, to his 1933–36 theoretical and historical work on the "concrete order" of the Nazi state. Schmitt employed an article of faith to "solve" the paradox of the constitutional foundation. He asserted the identity of the state's will with authoritarian, institutional representation: the power of the military, or the president, or the *Führer.* The authentic representative in Schmitt's theory was the real, worldly substance forming the general will over against the "will of all" of the "pluralistic party system."[166] Kelsen rejected from the start this metaphysics of the state. The authoritarian or even the fascist state could not escape the basic *normative* problem of how an act performed by a lower-level official could be attributed to the state as a whole and declared a state act.[167] And the problem of attribution involved, necessarily and irrevocably, the possibility of nonattribution, of the failure of a human act to correspond to the enabling norm within the borders of which a state act could be assumed. Kelsen showed how the presupposed state substance, the supposed source of the positive legal order, was itself subject to the logic of the legal order and therefore to the paradoxes of positivity.

The philosophical positions on constitutionalism led to radically different conceptions of the way state and society interacted in the postwar world. Schmitt separated the two terms *state* and *society*. Democracy, for him, was rule by a leader representing the nation as a unified whole. The democratic state was a political form, a will free from contradiction and unified in a single representative speaking with the voice of the hidden God, the People. Society, by contrast, was the site of disunity. Here, private rather than public interest reigned, channeled only by the disinterested, general norms of the bourgeois *Rechtsstaat*. For Schmitt, a monstrous state of affairs ensued when society presumed to enter the state, dictate the state's will, and thereby alter the abstract norms regulating society itself: "When the 'earthly God' tumbles from his throne and the Realm [*Reich*] of objective reason and ethics [*Sittlichkeit*] becomes a *magnum latrocinium* [great band of robbers], then the parties butcher the mighty Leviathan and cut their respective piece of flesh from its body."[168] Schmitt's metaphor of the public body being devoured by social groups illuminates the central logic of his theory. The Leviathan was separate from and above society. The state, or "earthly God," had an existence autonomous from that over which it ruled. The basic political assumption of the democratic welfare state, that social groups can determine state policy for their own good, became more than merely a problem of organization; it became a sacrilegious act of devouring the Father. The coherent subject "state," which Schmitt considered "present and presupposed," now seemed to be in constant flux. The result, he implied, was a state theory that had lost the ability to differentiate between legitimate states and robber bands.[169]

By contrast, Kelsen blurred the boundaries between state and society that Schmitt had assumed. He considered constructions of either state or *Volk* as coherent, willing subjects to be primitive, totemistic fictions.[170] By "purifying" legal theory of all nonlegal elements, the Pure Theory of Law brought into focus the complicated relationship between law and society at all levels of the legal system, from the constitution to legislation to administration and adjudication. Kelsen's theory paradoxically tried to ground a purely normative science while at the same time denying the possibility of separating will and norms, society and state. Unlike Schmitt, who sought a solution to the social conflicts of industrial society through a mythical leader, Kelsen argued that social groups had to regulate themselves. Indeed, he argued, the problem of negotiating social tensions had become the "fateful question" of all modern democracies.[171]

Kelsen's voice was not heard in Germany. With *Legality and Legitimacy,* Schmitt provided intellectual support for Papen's attempt to alter the constitution on authoritarian lines. The work radicalized the critique of parliament and the affirmation of the presidency already present in *Guardian of the Constitution.* Schmitt advised Papen on how legally to justify his July 20, 1932, coup against the Prussian *Land,* an act that signaled the final defeat of the republican forces. But the authority and legitimacy of the presidency, which Schmitt's theory presupposed, did not carry over to the chancellor. The Schmittian theory provided no solution. It merely opened the gate for the eventual Nazi takeover.

5

CONSTITUTIONAL PRACTICE AND THE

IMMANENCE OF DEMOCRATIC SOVEREIGNTY

Rudolf Smend, Hermann Heller, and the Basic

Principles of the Constitution

Despite their many differences, Kelsen and Schmitt both evinced an un-dialectical, "Hobbesian" model of the sovereign state. For Kelsen, the state was identical with law; it could be apprehended only through a pure theory of law that excluded "impure," practical considerations. For Schmitt, the state was a real, existing substance threatened by inter-est groups. Both men sought in different ways to separate the moment of sovereignty from everyday political practice—the "Hobbesian" mo-ment—in order to come to terms with the paradoxical foundations of constitutional democracy.[1]

A different conception of constitutional law emerges if one focuses on the process of making and applying law in concrete situations. In the Anglo-American context, Lon L. Fuller and Ronald Dworkin have each shifted attention to the complex interaction among legal norms, values, and facts in law. Their approaches counter the Austinian tradition of H. L. A. Hart and British analytical jurisprudence, with its search for a body of formal, positive law.[2] Many decades before the critiques by Fuller and Dworkin were published, a similar attack on "undialectical" conceptions of constitutional law appeared in the Weimar Republic, in the writings of Rudolf Smend and Hermann Heller.

The way Smend and Heller conceptualized popular sovereignty illuminates the difference between their notion of constitutional law and that of Kelsen and Schmitt. Smend and Heller turned away from the objective conception of sovereignty, invoking instead Ernest Renan's image of the "plebiscite of every day" to describe a dynamic and continuously unfolding popular sovereignty.[3] The sovereign was implicated at all times in practical politics; it had a place immanent to a functioning democracy.

Both Smend and Heller supported the Weimar Republic by 1930 (Smend somewhat grudgingly), and both argued that in politics as well as in law, affirming democracy meant breaking with the assumptions of the statutory positivists as well as with Schmittian statism. The two followed very different paths to this position. Smend's conservative sociology of politics contrasted sharply with Heller's explicitly political arguments for the primacy of the statute. Both, however, explicitly reposed questions of constitutional law from a point of view immanent to the system, as interested participants within a republican community.

If law involves consideration of values and social context, then the practical lawyer will find himself or herself forced to grapple with influences and arguments that, in retrospect, may seem ethically and politically suspect. Without a doubt, both Smend and Heller fell victim to questionable views. But their arguments, including those that were authoritarian or even protofascist, were part of a radical reorientation of constitutional law toward a theory of ethical and political practice; and that theory laid the foundation for the democratically oriented constitutional jurisprudence of the post-1949 West German state.

Smend

The State as Integration

Smend was born in 1882 to an established family of the academic elite. His father, Rudolf Smend (1851–1913), was a renowned Calvinist scholar of the Old Testament. The younger Smend was also active in the reformed Protestant church, and after 1945 dedicated himself to questions of church law.[4] Calvinism combines the doctrine of predestination and the immanence of humans to the world of necessity with a vision of the church congregation as an organic group of believers, each of whom fulfills his or her duty to the whole. As Smend stated many years later, an individual cannot be understood apart from the "spiritual-social world" in which he or she participates as a "member of a community."[5] Smend's religious background set the tone for his legal theory, particularly his 1928 theory of integration. The preconceptions with which Smend approached constitutional law can have conservative consequences if they lead to asserting the primacy of the community and the duty of the individual to conform. But they can also have an "iconoclastic" effect not unlike Kelsen's skeptical critique of Schmitt's "substance." Smend rejected the idea that a stable "point of rest" (*ruhender Pol*) was possible in the human world and criticized Carl Schmitt's search for a transcendent organ that truly "represented" the state.[6]

The political ambiguity of Smend's theory reflects ambiguities within the "organic" approach to constitutional law in the empire, which shaped his legal training. While the older representatives of that tradition—Otto von Gierke, Albert Hänel, and Hugo Preuss—had associations with the liberal tradition, younger representatives, such as Smend and Erich Kaufmann, took the notion of the state as organism in a conservative direction. The organic theory of law in the late empire defended the existing system as an authentic expression of the historically formed German nation.[7] Smend and Kaufmann repudiated what Smend later termed Laband's "colorless representations."[8] Kaufmann sought instead to describe the philosophical, historical, and political aspects of constitutional monarchism in his 1906 dissertation. Similarly, in his 1904 dissertation, Smend turned his back on Laband's prescriptions for scientific legal analysis and showed how historical conditions specific to Prussia had determined the meaning of the term *statute* in the 1850 Prussian Constitution.[9]

The politics of the young "organic" lawyers translated into a blind defense of the status quo during the First World War. In 1916, Smend published an essay that traced the federalism of the 1871 Constitution to an "unwritten law" of trust and friendship among the heads of the member states. Since the Reichstag in the German Empire insisted on formal, enumerated rights and duties, Smend claimed, its parliamentary representatives were unable to comprehend the organic functioning of the Bundesrat.[10] The 1916 defense of the unwritten laws of German federalism appeared just as the chaos and inefficiency of the Bismarckian system were becoming evident for all to see. Yet Smend asserted that any reforms of the political structure would destroy its legitimacy. Reforming the Prussian three-class voting system, for example, would destroy the federalist basis of the German constitution; rationalizing the administration would undermine the key organ of the system, the Bundesrat.[11]

It took at least ten years for Smend to become reconciled to the Weimar Republic. In 1916, he criticized the Reichstag for being a "rationalistic" body incapable of comprehending organic aspects of the 1871 Constitution. When the Reichstag took on far greater significance after 1918, Smend argued that the parliament was merely composed of different, conflicting interest groups and was incapable of substantially integrating the nation.[12] As late as 1928, he described the 1871 Constitution as the "consummate example of an integrating constitution" and compared Bismarck's "political art of the constitution" (*verfassungspolitische Kunst*), "unreflectedness" (*Unreflektiertheit*), and "intuitive clarity" with the "constitutional politics" (*Verfassungspolitik*) of the framers of the Weimar Constitution.[13] Smend belonged to the antirepublican, far-right DNVP (German National People's party) until 1930.[14]

Over the course of the 1920s Smend began to reconcile himself to the new system and to examine constitutional law in the new constitutional democracy. The fruits of his labor appeared in his path-breaking treatise of 1928, *Constitution and Constitutional Law*, in which he argued that the state was a social totality constantly in the process of integrating and reintegrating citizens into the community. Smend's immanent approach to the "living" constitution posed problems that constitutional scholars had avoided under the influence of Labandian positivism, in particular the problem of how a scholar could claim to be "objective" and "scientific," to stand outside politics in constitutional analysis. Smend composed this text over the space of only a few months. His haste combined with the fundamentally new set of problems for constitutional law that he was considering resulted in a text that is convoluted and at times virtually unreadable.[15]

Smend's style lent itself to confusion or even "false" interpretations.[16] Kelsen took him to task for his internal inconsistencies and the "oscillation" of his main concepts.[17] But Kelsen's sarcasm could not obscure

Smend's importance for Weimar constitutional theory. Not only Kelsen but also other leading jurists such as Fritz Stier-Somlo and Otto Koellreutter devoted lengthy reviews to Smend's book.[18] One critical reviewer stated that "the book belongs among those one must know."[19] Despite its imprecise and even contradictory nature, *Constitution and Constitutional Law* provided an important and original point of departure for constitutional jurisprudence: the concept of "integration," a term that resonated in the dis-integrated political culture of the Weimar Republic.

Smend viewed the process of integration as the essence of the constitution, as a "unifying fusion" (*einigender Zusammenschluss*), the "core process" and the "core substance" of "state life."[20] More than a system for technically organizing social interests toward a goal, the state was a real, integrated "association of wills,"[21] a "meaningful unity of real, spiritual life, of spiritual acts" (*Sinneinheit reellen geistigen Lebens, geistiger Akte*). Smend asserted that his organic approach overcame the pure "normativism" of Kelsen's positivism and brought the state as a real organism back into state theory.[22]

The organic theory of integration blurred the distinctions on which the Labandian positivist tradition and conservative liberalism in the German Empire had been built: private and public law, state and society, individual and whole.[23] If the state was viewed as a total "spiritual life-community" (*geistige Lebensgemeinschaft*),[24] any absolute distinction between state and society became meaningless. Smend's organic theory likewise led to an immediate identification of individual and society. His "dialectical understanding" of the relationship between individual and collective, between ego and state, proved to be an unmediated "total lived experience" (*Gesamterlebnis*) of the state, in which individuals participated even while sleeping.[25] Smend readily admitted that antagonisms and disagreements played an important role in politics, but he reduced conflict to a function that ensured the community's cohesion. He described the struggle to determine the aims of the state as a "cathartic" affirmation of the state, regardless of concrete results.[26] Voting and balloting, for example, were "purely spiritual means of integration." But by turning from a static, "anatomical" notion of the state to a dynamic, "physiological" one, Smend granted individual actions significance only insofar as they were part of the state's "self-formation."[27]

The examples Smend used to describe integration best illustrate the conservative, totalizing nature of his theory. "Personal integration" took place through leaders (*Führer*), who were the "life-form of that which is socially and spiritually unfolding in [those being led]."[28] The monarch, for example, was "in [his] own person the embodiment, the integration of the whole of the *Volk*." He ought not to engage in merely technical or practical activities and in so doing prove himself a dilettante, as William II had done; instead, he should act to renew the "self-perception" of the nation. He was supposed not only to "enliven" (*beleben*) but also to "shape" his individual subjects through his own "creative personality."[29] After the collapse of the monarchy in 1918, Smend argued that others should take the monarch's place. But not every person could. "There are persons who by their nature [*ihrem Wesen nach*] are unfit for integrating functions," he stated, and in a footnote remarked that Max Weber "evidently" viewed the "*Ostjuden*" as "impossible leaders of German state life, even in the revolution."[30] In fact, Smend believed that only one of his contemporaries possessed the ability to unite Germany through his personality: General Paul von Hindenburg, who had recently been elected president of the Republic to succeed Friedrich Ebert.[31] At no point did Smend discuss the concrete policies or goals that sections of the population might wish to realize through a given leader. Integration through the leader appeared to be a total, self-determining process devoid of concrete content.

In Smend's view, "functional integration," or integration through procedures, was similarly oriented toward an organic "social synthesis." His examples of functional integration included voting, organized dance, gymnastics, and marching. Smend was especially interested in the relationship between work and rhythm, and in the effort of labor psychology to create a spiritual unity between the worker and his or her work to raise individual output.[32] Reconciliation of worker and work was to occur through purely spiritual means rather than through concrete negotiation and compromise. The "formal procedures of integration" were "as such without goal."[33] Smend turned to Italian fascism for examples of "unmediated integration." Fascism, he argued, was more relevant to conditions of mass democracy than liberalism or parliamentarianism was. He claimed that fascism had the "paradoxical insight" and that "corporatism, militarism, [and] myth" were the techniques that the "mass citizenry of present-day democracies" needed.[34]

"Concrete" integration consisted of values that realized and were realized by the state community.[35] The state's "unified lived experience" (*einheitliches Erlebnis*) was the experience of a "value totality" (*Werttotalität*): ideals and the community were inseparable. Through symbols such as "flags, state emblems, heads of state (especially monarchs), political ceremonies, and national celebrations," the individual both created and was created by the totality. Symbols allowed citizens to experience the "fullness" of the symbolized content with a "special intensity." Smend described the process as follows: "Everyone can experience a symbolized value-content [*Wertgehalt*] 'as I understand it,' without the tension or contradiction that formulation and rule [*Satzung*] inevitably call forth, and at the same time everyone experiences it as a total fullness, in a manner unreachable in any other way."[36] Rationalists, he argued, viewed speech as a "technical invention with the goal of understanding . . . , therefore as a technical artifact instead of an elementary, essentially necessary life-form of the human spirit."[37] Smend's "antirationalist" theory of symbol and speech was devoid of concrete content; for example, of the contradictions and struggles for position in a politically fragmented society. Symbols and speech instead acted to unify a nation on the basis of myth. As an example Smend referred to the mythical importance of Mussolini's March on Rome for the legitimization of fascism.[38]

It is not surprising that Smend turned to Mussolini's Italy for examples. Italian fascism was an important phenomenon in the Europe of the 1920s; it provided "a rich yield . . . that would be valuable independent of the value and future of the fascist movement itself."[39] Smend implicitly asserted that fascism's empirical existence did not necessarily coincide with its moral value. But at the same time, Smend's theory of integration seemed to derive ethical or political value from the actual fact of existence. The fascist state fulfilled its function of being a living national community. How could it not be affirmed by Smend's theory? Although Smend attempted, over the last five years of the Republic, to develop arguments for the validity of the Weimar Constitution, his theory often pointed in a distinctly anticonstitutional, total, and repressive conception of the "integrated state."

Heller

The State as Organization

Hermann Heller was born in 1891 to a Jewish family in the Austro-Silesian town of Teschen. His father, a lawyer, died when Heller was young, and he was raised by relatives in Vienna. According to his friend Fritz Borinski, Heller was deeply involved in the Austrian *Wandervogel* movement before World War I.[40] He volunteered for the Austrian army in 1914 and was wounded at the front in early 1915. His injuries left him with a weak heart, which contributed to his early death in 1933. After the war, he played an instrumental role in developing youth centers and vocational schools in Leipzig, and he worked with the right wing of the Young Socialists, the youth organization of the Social Democrats, during the years of the Republic. Heller was marginalized in the discipline of state law in the Republic. His Jewish ancestry and open support for the Social Democratic Party (SPD) ensured his exclusion from most university careers. Only in 1928 was he called to a university chair, in a controversial appointment Smend later called political.[41]

The cult of youth of the *Wandervogel* and the direct experience of the nation at war were reflected in Heller's work. His *Socialism and Nation* (1925), a call for Social Democracy openly to embrace patriotism, begins: "The present work appeals to all that is young and strong in socialism and in the German nation [*Volk*]." [42] The notion of socialism in that book and elsewhere in Heller's works has more in common with Johann Gottlieb Fichte than with Marx. It implies a national community based on a sense of duty and mutual respect among national comrades—not "merely" economic innovation.[43] When Heller joined the SPD on March 10, 1920, one day before defending his *Habilitation* on Hegel's concept of the state, he did so under two conditions: he recognized the theoretical validity of neither historical materialism nor proletarian internationalism.[44]

The reservations enunciated by Heller corresponded to his larger project: to fill a gap in the intellectual tradition of Social Democracy by putting the movement on a constitutionalist, and therefore also nationalist, footing. His contribution has proven to be important and lasting; indeed, he was the most important Social Democratic theorist of constitutional law in the Weimar Republic. The political and constitutional arguments he made for a regulatory state of law, a "social *Rechtsstaat*," corresponded to the political trajectory taken by Social Democracy in practice during the Weimar Republic and in theory since the Bad Godesberg program of 1959. Heller's argument fused nationalism and socialism, an undertaking shared by the right-wing Young Socialists of the Hofgeismar Circle in the Weimar Republic. That project seemed to left-wing Social Democrats who remained in the internationalist tradition dangerous if not outright reactionary—with good reason.[45] Heller's critique of the "shameful" Treaty of Versailles and defense of the ostensibly "defenseless and plundered German people," "overpopulated to bursting" but deprived of both "national" land to the east and colonies, echoed the rhetoric of the right. But Heller sought to place ethical and political limits on the right-wing strategies. He called for a strong German nationalism, for example, but also for an integrated, socialist European community (excluding the "Asian" parts of Russia) to limit the possibility of war and defend Europe against U.S. capital.[46]

Heller joined the conservatives Schmitt and Smend in the mid-1920s in attacking Kelsen's Pure Theory of Law,[47] which he labeled "rationalistic," "demo-liberal," "Marxist," "anarchistic," "abstract," and "subjectless." It was, he argued, the final result of Labandian analysis, a state theory without the state.[48] And indeed, it was Kelsen's skeptical analysis of the state as a hierarchical system of simultaneously limiting and empowering norms that infuriated the two conservatives and Heller. Like Schmitt, Heller conceptualized the state as a concrete institution unifying "is" and "ought" and emphasized the centrality of absolutism, centralized bureaucracy, and the military in its historical development.[49]

The "statist" tradition played a major role in Heller's early work as part of his critique of pacifist and internationalist tendencies in the SPD. In 1920, he wrote the introduction for a new edition of Hegel's 1799–1802 work on the constitution, a work that was central to Carl Schmitt's political argumentation after 1928. Heller followed the tradition of the conservative, neo-Hegelian state theorists in praising Hegel's work for replacing the idealistic, moral-based conception of politics with the notion of national interest, or reason of state.[50] In an article published a few years later, Heller repeated Hegel's "quite significant" argument that the survival of a nation required a strong state for its self-assertion and self-defense.[51] To be sure, Heller questioned the intrinsic value of *Realpolitik* and criticized the right-wing, neo-Hegelian vision of war as social ideal proposed by Erich Kaufmann. But in the end he presented a theory of international relations that was strikingly in line with the conservative position.[52] His 1927 book on sovereignty defends the primacy of the "will" of nation-states and justifies state actions against existing international or national law on the basis of the state's right to self-preservation. From the perspective of foreign affairs, Heller conceived of the state as a living, willing entity standing above law—hardly any differently, in other words, than did Carl Schmitt.[53]

The *realpolitisch* approach to international relations, however, played a strategic role in Heller's work. He sought to counter trends in Social Democracy that refused to take responsibility for foreign policy, such as the idealistic pacifism of Leonard Nelsen and the proletarian internationalism of Max Adler.[54] Heller hoped that by appropriating conservative views of international politics he would force socialists to develop a coherent foreign policy that would take account of existing power relations even while striving to fulfill socialist goals such as peace and regulation of international markets.[55] Heller believed that conservative statism could and should be adapted to socialist or left-liberal goals. But one might ask why he turned to the far right for his theories of power politics, and not to liberal theorists such as Max Weber, Hugo Preuss, or Alfred Weber, who asked where the limits to responsible state power lay. Heller, always temperamental, may have hoped to stir up controversy among his intended audience on the left; if so, the strategy misfired. His use of questionable theorists made his theory vulnerable to attacks from left and center socialists.[56]

Just as Heller's discussion of the state in international relations tried to connect conservative theory with socialist politics, his turn to the "nation" as the source of the state's will also relied on conservative theories. Once again, his defense of the nation was part of a strategy to develop a Social Democratic politics of nationalism. The nation, he argued, formed the real, collective basis for socialism: the worker, through the socialist party, had to fight his way into the national community.[57] Heller defined the national community itself according to certain "national characteristics" common to the entire people. These characteristics, he argued, were of natural origin: in "soil" (*Boden;* i.e., geography) and in "blood" (*Blut*), by which Heller meant the biological similarities that developed through a people's mutual interaction with the soil and with each other, through marriage and reproduction. He described blood not as a purely biological fact, but as a social process by which a "solidifying of the blood" (*Blutverfestigung*) created characteristics common to the entire community.[58] To be sure, Heller continually undermined these moments of biological determinism. His 1925 work on nationalism shows a well-developed critique of right-wing racialism; in that work and later ones he consistently defined blood in terms of common cultural developments.[59] Indeed, Heller's language reflected in part his conception—much like Smend's—of democratic politics as an immanent reality, in opposition to Kelsen's notion of the state as pure law and Schmitt's concept of the state as transcendent substance.[60] Nevertheless, Heller's constant invocation of the right-wing phrase "blood and soil," his criticism of internationalist "Esperanto culture," and his insistence that the essential differences among nations appeared during the First World War seemed to repeat right-wing or populist themes with little criticism rather than to develop a strategic, Social Democratic affirmation of the German nation.[61]

Heller's use of right-wing rhetoric began to fade in the late 1920s. After visiting fascist Italy in 1928, he produced a lengthy critique of the allegedly "integral" state. His main enemy was shifting from Kelsenian liberalism to fascism.[62] With the shift in polemical focus came a less *realpolitisch* characterization of the state and a calmer and more measured rhetoric—indeed, one far more compatible with the liberal or the Social Democratic welfare state. Talk of "blood and soil," for example, became a critique of monocausal analyses of state and nation.[63] Although still interested in the national foundations of political democracy, he now described the nation in terms of a sense of belonging among its citizens. The sense of being in a collective (*Wirbewusstsein*) was the substantive prerequisite for the legitimacy of the rules governing state activity, and in particular legislation. The precise connection between "being and consciousness" could not be determined in general, Heller now argued, but depended on the conditions of a specific time and place. He found an abstract solution to the problem of how to relate state and nation in the skeptical formulation that all political systems require "a certain degree" of social homogeneity.[64]

At the heart of Heller's shift in focus was a new conception of the state, first elaborated in his 1927 work on sovereignty. In place of Smend's totalizing, dynamic concept of integration and Schmitt's hypostatization of the state's will in a single organ, Heller argued that state and nation, unified will and dynamic, national (re)generation, were dialectically related through a complicated process of organization. While Heller adopted the conservative conception of the state in international affairs as a sovereign will, he defined the state "directed inward" as the "universal, necessarily unique, and sovereign decisionary unit [*Entscheidungseinheit*] in a certain territory." The state as sovereign will stood above all social forces and was potentially capable of making decisions regarding any social conflict.[65] Like Schmitt, Heller developed a Hobbesian notion of the state as a separate and higher force guaranteeing social peace;[66] but unlike Schmitt, he rejected the identification of sovereignty with any particular state organ. Sovereignty, or "majesty," he argued, was neither "localizable" in an individual organ (against Schmitt) nor (against Kelsen) "dissolvable into positive law." It was rather a symbol for the dialectical unity of will and norm in a state act. The state as "subject" or "ego" existed neither as a mere "bundle of human actions" nor as an "ideal order" but as an "effective unity" (*Wirkungseinheit*) of norm and will.[67] Only an action undertaken within the normative framework of the state could be an expression of the state's will, and similarly, only the legal norm that was effective and actually applied by some state organ was part of the state's will. The dialectical combination of Gierke's organicism and Laband's statism, as Heller put it, underlay his theory of organization.[68]

The term *organization* as used in Heller's late work referred to an "ordered structure for acting" (*geordnetes Handlungsgefüge*) that allowed "cooperation through the super-, sub-, and coordination of individuals and groups involved in the whole." Citing the nineteenth-century Social Democrat Ferdinand Lassalle, Heller asserted that the organization consisted of "existing, factual power relations."[69] From the viewpoint of political science, which Heller termed a "science of practical reality" (*Wirklichkeitswissenschaft*), the organization existed only as long as real, living wills gave its individual norms a concrete significance.[70]

At the point where will and norm came into contact, Heller introduced a "Smendian" moment. The will of the organ, he argued, was limited not only formally by its legal jurisdiction (set by a "higher" organ), but also by extralegal, ethical, and sociological considerations. The ethical considerations in particular, Heller argued, served as basic, unwritten norms shared by a community.[71] These "basic principles of right" (*Rechtsgrundsätze*) made up a real, not merely constructed, will of the people. But as soon as Heller developed a kind of Rousseauian "general will," he denied its *immediate* presence. While the state was more than merely a system of norms, it could not be reduced to a will of the people, since every "people" represented a multiplicity of opposed wills. "The specific task of politics," he argued, "always remains the organization of opposing wills on the basis of a community of wills."[72] While a nation might share certain notions of what was right, these notions were not as yet complete. It was the job of the legislature and others in the organization to transform "basic principles of right" into legal norms (*Rechtssätze*); that is, positive law.[73]

With this argument Heller relativized his opposition to legal positivism. He admitted that Labandian analysis, which took positive law as an objectified order of norms, had a place in his wider theory of law and the state.[74] With his theory of political organization and his argument that law could be viewed as objective and differentiated from social reality, Heller distinguished between his theory and the conservative theories he had earlier emulated. Where Smend had identified life and law, successful political integration and legal norms, Heller insisted that the two sides were related but not necessarily identical: only the process of legislation gave the basic principles of right a concrete significance, and only these concretized legal norms could resolve social conflicts. Where Schmitt had asserted that the bourgeois *Rechtsstaat* had a definite, fixed content prior to the written constitution itself, Heller argued that an additional process of concretizing the basic principles of right was necessary as well. The substantive idea of the *Rechtsstaat* therefore did not deprive the legislature of all will, but it did set limits within which the legislature could act. Smend and Schmitt sought a "primary" constitution that could override the written set of rules that constituted the Weimar Constitution; Heller, by contrast, insisted that written, positive constitutional norms provided the form within which political power or will operated, just as will was necessary to elevate mere form to the level of political organization.[75] It was this dialectical theory of organization that separated Heller's notion of the state from more conservative, state-affirming theories.

Indeed, Heller's reformist, Social Democratic leanings required such a theory of organization. Social Democracy was faced with the apparently contradictory task of defending the basic law of the German state while at the same time condemning the basic economic order of German society. Heller's reformist socialism made the strategic presupposition that a formal-democratic, parliamentary state was "relatively autonomous" and had its own internal laws (*Eigengesetzlichkeit*) that could be used to alter society.[76] Whether Heller admitted it or not, his theory of law corresponded better to that of left-liberals like Kelsen and Thoma than to the conservative theories of Schmitt and Smend that he had earlier sought to emulate.

A Jurisprudence of Values

Smend

The political differences between Smend and Heller should not obscure their methodological similarities. By conceiving of the state as an ongoing social process, they reoriented constitutional law toward concrete problems of legal interpretation that took account of values, politics, and the social context of decisions.

Smend's theory of constitutional jurisprudence presupposed the notion of the constitution developed in *Constitution and Constitutional Law*. But even Smend's basic concept of the constitution contained contradictions.[77] Smend simultaneously defined the constitution as part of the legal system and as distinct from law. By considering the constitution a "statutory governing" (*gesetzliche Normierung*) of the process of integration,[78] Smend seemed to reconstruct the positivist separation between law and politics or ethics. Elsewhere, however, Smend denied outright the identity of constitution and law: "legal life" (*Rechtsleben*) was "a foreign body [*Fremdkörper*] in the constitution," even if at the same time the judiciary and the administration were "state life-forms as well."[79] At times, Smend sought to provide both definitions at once, stating, for example: "As positive law, the constitution is not only norm, but also reality; as constitution, it is an integrating reality."[80] As these examples indicate, Smend's *theory* seemed to fluctuate between conceptualizing the constitution as a set of rules and as real political life. His description of constitutional *practice,* however, emphasized the inseparability of formal and substantive elements in actual interpretation.

Constitutional interpretation, Smend argued, required that one move beyond the level of individual norms to the "physiological" process of collective will formation. This sense of the constitution "not only allow[ed], but even demand[ed]" an "elastic, supplementary exposition": the meaning of a constitutional law could not be derived from the constitutional document alone, but only from the social practices that made use of the article, giving it new meanings in concrete contexts.[81] The most important constitutional articles were Article 1, which asserted that "all state power emanates from the people," and Article 3, which determined the colors of the state flag. They expressed, as Smend put it, a "rule" for interpreting all other constitutional norms, in the interest of integrating citizens into the Republic. These articles formed an "authentic commentary" on the basic rights, which filled in the content of the "cultural system" of the Republic. The basic rights of contract, property, marriage, and inheritance reflected the "bourgeois" nature of the nation, Smend argued, while universal and proportional voting rights reflected the influence of the "proletarian revolution."[82] These examples echoed the summary of the basic rights system presented by Adalbert Düringer to the National Assembly on March 3, 1919 (see chapter 3); even Anschütz appeared to be in agreement with this portrayal of the German system of values. The difference lay in the consequences that Smend was willing to derive for constitutional jurisprudence.

Smend illustrated how the nonformal method of interpretation should work in a paper on the right to free speech presented to the Association of German Scholars of State Law in 1927. Against the understanding of the statutory positivists, Smend argued that rights should be viewed as basic values of the national community. Like the national flag, rights took the place of the monarch in symbolizing the substantial unity of national cultural values.[83] Article 118 proclaimed the right of every German to express his or her opinion "within the limits of the general statutes."[84] From a formalist point of view, the latter phrase reflected the customary argument that the only valid limits to free expression were those approved according to the procedurally correct statute.[85] The word *general* was either redundant (given that all statutes are "general") or at best a vague injunction against passing laws that singled out a specific group for persecution. Smend argued that formalists misunderstood the historical sense of the term *generality,* which had its origin in the Enlightenment. Generality in this context signified the "more general" social values preceding and guaranteeing free and open discussion, namely "morality [*Sittlichkeit*], public order, state security." "General" statutes were those that took precedence before Article 118 "because the value [*Gut*] protected by them is more important than freedom of opinion."[86] The precise content and ranking of these values, Smend argued, could be obtained only by examining a nation's cultural history.[87]

For the positivists, Smend claimed, Article 142 (guaranteeing freedom of art, scholarship, and teaching) was little more than a repetition of Article 118.[88] In fact, he continued, Article 142 had originated in the first half of the nineteenth century and reflected the demands of German idealism for a space of free discussion in the atmosphere of repression produced by the Carlsbad Decrees.[89] Article 142, he argued, guaranteed one part of society, the universities, a special right to free expression and demanded that the legal system respect the internal laws specific to academic life.[90] Smend hereby claimed to derive the value or rank of a basic right in the legal system from the history of the German nation.

The "true" content of the constitution, according to Smend, was to be found in real, "living" values and institutions, not in mere formal, written norms. The values he identified as vital were conservative and bourgeois. His defense of the university, for example, was an argument for the special legal status of an elite and generally conservative social group, the professorate.[91] By linking Article 142 with one specific institution, Smend implicitly rejected the claims of extrauniversity cultural productions to be the "scholarship" or "art" protected by the article. His institutional interpretation of Article 142 complemented Schmitt's institutional interpretation of Article 153 (private property) in its defense of conservative values.[92] And by reinterpreting the term *general,* he was able to avoid the reservation of limits to the institutions by statute expressed in Articles 118 and 142, as well as in the articles defending freedom of contract, marriage, property, and inheritance—limitations that would have extended considerable power to the Reichstag to shape social relations.[93]

Smend's analysis presumed that the judge could locate one coherent system of values and one coherent cultural tradition in a nation. He avoided considering the potential for real conflicts and contradictions.[94] The assumption seemed like wishful thinking in the context of the Weimar Republic, which, especially in its final years, lacked an underlying consensus.[95]

Although Smend's guidelines for interpreting basic rights were conservative, they were not in themselves antidemocratic if one accepted the "organic" definition of democracy Smend offered, in which no state organ was sovereign. More politically problematic were his assumptions about who had the right to interpret basic values of the nation. Implicitly, Smend argued that the Reichstag did not represent the real, collective will. The parliament lacked the authority to judge the content of a legal good.[96] The question was, which part of the state could recognize the authentic national community of values?

Smend had apparently already excluded the ordinary judiciary, whose activity served the "value" of law, not living integration. A more likely possibility was the government (*Regierung*), whose role lay in "integrating" (i.e., politically unifying) the nation.[97] Unfortunately, Smend did not directly address this question. While he focused on juristic method and on "filling" the constitutional norms with content derived from the "real" process of "constitution," he neglected the important procedural and technical problem of which organ was actually to carry out interpretation and review.

Smend's failure to address this problem reflects a more general dilemma of organic conceptions of law. By concentrating on the immanent and total process of a nation's self-formation, the theory of integration tended to ignore—or repress—the moment of actual decision in politics and law.[98] While basic rights had the general political function in the Republic of "integrating" social forces under one common legal and political system, rights on a concrete level were present in the constitution precisely to help resolve disputes between citizens and the state or among citizens. Legal cases with arguments based on rights-oriented claims did not concern the basic agreement of the parties involved, but rather their basic disagreement over the meaning of the law. By presupposing a national community of values, Smend neglected the important practical role that law played in distinguishing permissible and impermissible acts, resolving disputes over contracts, and otherwise ruling on conflicts of human will.[99]

In more theoretical terms, Smend avoided entirely the central point of dispute between Schmitt and Kelsen: the problem of sovereignty.[100] Schmitt had sought to locate the source of "objective" decisions—those "above" parties—in a specific organ, and Kelsen had identified sovereignty as the objectified legal system itself. Smend rejected both positions, just as he had rejected the notion of an objectified constitution. The political significance of Smend's radical anti-Hobbesianism may be interpreted in two ways. From one point of view, Smend provided an essentially antiabsolutist argument in his denial of sovereignty. Perhaps, then, Smend actually was laying the groundwork for a democratic system open to reformist alternatives and receptive to changes in public opinion, as his supporters after 1945 argued. From another point of view, however, the organic theory, with its naturalist assumptions, deformalized constitution, and rejection of "liberal" skepticism, may lead to unrestrained terror. If a state of noncontradiction—the popular community—is presupposed as the normal and natural state of affairs, then what differs from the social norm, what is not part of the public "organism," may be in need of radical excision and elimination. The deformalized constitution may "naturalize" the right of certain social groups (perhaps judges, perhaps the executive) to enforce the totality without regard for legal parameters or formal process.

A Jurisprudence of Political Restraint

Heller

The assumption of homogeneous and adjudicable community values lay at the heart of Smend's problematic definition of the constitution as a real, living process. By failing to distinguish between the constitution as formal law and the constitution as real process, the theory of integration at times slipped into authoritarian rhetoric. Heller sought to develop a clearer and more analytical conception of the constitution in his final book, *The Theory of the State*, in part to deal with the danger inherent in Smend's approach.[101] Heller distinguished between two basic epistemological approaches to the constitution. First, the constitution could be viewed sociologically, either as a "life totality" (Smend's notion) or, in a narrower sense, as the relatively stable rules and procedures that lent a state unity over time. The latter "basic structure" seems to correspond to Heller's notion of "organization." Second, viewed legally, the constitution consisted either of all legal norms regulating state activity (something like Laband's notion of state law) or, in a narrower sense, of all fundamental legal aspects of a state's "basic order."[102]

Heller's arguments remained fragmentary. Clearly, though, he viewed the four categories as dialectically interdependent. Sociological analysis of the "state" could not exist without some knowledge of legal structure, and vice versa. When a lawyer described the basic law of a state, for example, that description presupposed that the lawyer could distinguish essential from nonessential, or trivial, norms, a distinction to be drawn from observation of social practice. Similarly, sociological description of the state's "basic structure" relied on knowledge of what legal norms directed "ought" to be done. The central methodological problem of how to relate social fact and legal norm, *Sein* and *Sollen*, appears in the final chapter of the *Theory of the State*. Heller argued for a dialectical understanding of the difference between political totality and organization, between an institution's effective reality and its normative order.[103]

To these notions of the constitution Heller added a fifth: the so-called formal, or written, constitution itself. At first glance, the formal constitution might seem an irrelevant "foreign body" (Smend) in Heller's political analysis of the state. Indeed, Heller pointed out that a total correspondence between formal and substantial constitution could never exist because the constitution as real organization was always developing and changing.[104] But he argued against resolving the distinction between "normalcy" (*Normalität*) and "normativity" (*Normativität*) in favor of real, existing being. The distinction between "is" and "ought" could only be conceived of dialectically. While a norm required some sort of regularity and effective application in order to be valid, nevertheless as a norm it was also capable of being violated and therefore of *not* being in conformity with actual behavior. The legal norm was both connected to being (*seinsbezogen*) and transcended being (*seinstranszendent*).[105] Heller argued that the formal, written constitution had played a key political role in the development of the modern democratic state. It had arisen as part of the general process by which fundamental rules constituting the state became differentiated from other parts of law and ethics. Economically and politically, the differentiation of the basic law from other laws made state activity predictable and controllable.[106]

Heller asserted that these historical and political considerations, rather than prior notions of what positive law ought to be, made the "juristic method" in the tradition of Laband important for legal scholarship. For political reasons, the lawyer was justified in hypothesizing a closed legal order that determined the jurisdiction of state organs in order to grant consistency and predictability to institutional and organizational reality. But analysis based on legal dogmatics was not sufficient in itself, Heller argued; the practical act of reaching a judicial decision involved expanding or "concretizing" positive law as well. Law was "gapless" only for the writer of handbooks. In practice it required legal actors to adjust the norm to reality.[107] Like Kelsen and Thoma, Heller pointed out where the authority of the lawyer shaded into the ethical and political reasoning of the citizen, where jurisprudence became "worldly knowledge." But knowledge of the political world provided at the same time the dialectical justification for the jurisprudence of statutory positivism.

Heller's substantive defense of formalist methods of interpretation emerged in the 1927 paper he presented to the Association of German Scholars of State Law. He began by affirming Smend's method of interpretation and philosophy of law, which had been presented to the association at the same meeting, "in all its essential points."[108] But he used the "cultural-historical" approach to justify a formal understanding of the statute in the Weimar Constitution. The absolutist tradition had centralized state authority by constructing the statute as the direct expression of the state's will and the foundation of state law.[109] Heller insisted that the absolutist notion of the state as a "decisionary unit" remained fundamental to the modern state, in which decisions were the product of organized procedures. The "bourgeois revolution" had established both the power of the popular assembly to participate in determining monarchical statutes and the subordination of the judiciary and the administration to legislative acts. Heller argued that the formal or procedural prerequisite for a valid statute constituted its political and historical legitimacy: the constitutional procedure for creating a statute guaranteed society's self-determination in creating the state's will.[110] The substantive side of the statute, its "generality," was embedded in the statute's formality. It was therefore not defined by substantive criteria such as generality of application or duration. Heller rejected the distinction between formal and substantive aspects of the statute, which had been central to Laband's jurisprudence in the empire and to Schmitt's theory of the statute—theories that firmly opposed the power of the legislature.[111]

By rejecting the notion that a statute had some substantive essence such as generality or duration prior to its formal or procedural qualities, Heller stepped outside the Labandian tradition. Like Kelsen, Heller argued that all legal acts, from statute to ordinance to contract, took the form of a legal norm. Considered from a purely formal angle, the legislature could grant the statute any content, whether that of a general norm or of an individual order.[112] Unlike Schmitt, who sought to deduce rigid limits to the statute from his ideal system of the bourgeois *Rechtsstaat*, Heller insisted that the limits to legislative activity fluctuated as the political and social conditions of a nation changed. Like Kelsen, he left the content of the statute up to existing power relations and political needs. Unlike Kelsen, however, Heller based his concept of the statute on political arguments.

Heller's arguments in favor of statutory supremacy were both formal and substantive. Formal analysis of the written constitution showed no more and no less than that the statute was the foundation of the entire state system, and that the administration and the judiciary were to operate within the framework of constitutional norms and statutes. As Heller pointed out, the constitution invoked only a few exceptions to this rule, such as the president's right to issue pardons (Art. 49, par. 1), and then did so explicitly.[113] The political and historical tradition of German constitutionalism stressed the role of parliament in organizing and representing social interests, promoting social peace by providing a forum for discussion and compromise, and translating multiple social interests into a unified decision through the process of organization that created the statute. The procedural and formal predominance of the

Reichstag in the written constitution found its source in its political and historical place as representative of the people. As Heller put it, "Form and content of the statute are inseparable."[114] And therefore, he argued, the parliamentary system was based on the presumption that the legislature had made a correct decision.[115]

Heller's hierarchical theory of interpretation was based on his theory of organization. The judiciary had the right to apply laws only within the bounds of existing statutes. If the Reichstag had the right to make statutes, then it was only within the formal and procedural limits set out by the constitution, which ensured adequate representation of social groups. Finally, the legislature—and indeed all legal actors—was limited by an unwritten set of general ethical principles (*Rechtsgrundsätze*), which it had to concretize and preserve. The boundaries set by these "basic principles of right" varied over time and could not be determined without reference to actual political practices. In making these basic principles concrete, the democratic legislature could regulate society— and perhaps even move beyond existing social relations to a qualitatively new social system, the social *Rechtsstaat*.[116] Put slightly differently, the constitution both determined a certain area of set "form" that provided for the state's continuity and allowed for extensive development or "freedom" in shaping the state's goals.[117] Heller conceptualized the mediation between formal law and social content in the same way as did his supposed opponents, left-liberal positivists and supporters of parliamentary democracy such as Kelsen and Thoma.[118]

Conclusion

Toward a New Constitutional Jurisprudence

Smend and Heller did not develop antithetical theories of constitutional interpretation. Rather, their theories were complementary. Smend's stressed the necessity of considering values in interpretation; Heller's pointed out that the formal organization of the constitution itself contained substantive values. Heller would have drawn the line between legislative and judicial activity at a point granting more power to the democratic legislature; Smend probably would have drawn a line more favorable to conservative judges and the administration. It is in the field of practice outlined by these two legal thinkers that the active process of interpretation, evaluation, and line drawing characteristic of judicial politics in West Germany after 1949 has taken place. Indeed, Heller and Smend framed the issues that postwar West German jurisprudence would face in the complex theories of interpretation developed by Martin Kriele, Friedrich Müller, and Robert Alexy.[119] And in a way, the issues Smend and Heller raised frame contemporary U.S. debates about constitutional law as well. Like Smend, for example, Ronald Dworkin argues that constitutional jurisprudence should treat basic rights as flowing from principles that require judges to engage in complex moral argumentation as part of the legal process. Like Heller, John Hart Ely on the left and Robert Bork on the right argue for a more limited, procedural interpretation of rights that reserves power to the legislature.[120] Oddly, the political poles in the Weimar debates have been reversed in the U.S. debates, where the substantivist position has become associated with leftist, activist judges, and the formalist or originalist position with judges on the right.[121] Many of the issues, however, remain the same.

Smend's and Heller's theories of constitutional practice presupposed a stable constitutional system in which integration actually took place and the people viewed the state organization as legitimate. That stability began to disappear after 1928, and with it the immediate political relevance of the theory of constitutional practice.

Smend left the far-right D N V P in 1930, after media baron Alfred Hugenberg took over the party and openly proclaimed authoritarian ideals. Smend's decision to affirm the Republic had become clear the year before in his introduction to a paperback edition of the Weimar Constitution. The constitution, he stated, had the difficult task of integrating citizens into a Republic that was poor and defeated in war. Both the primacy of the Reichstag—that is, the principle of representative democracy—and basic rights would contribute to integration. Echoing Heller, Smend referred to the new social rights as "objective basic principles of right" that contained necessary compromises between capitalism and socialism and between religious and secular forces. Against Schmitt, Smend asserted that these compromises were a part of the process of making the nation one and creating a "living unity."[122] He echoed these sentiments in a speech given just days before the fall of the Republic, on

January 18, 1933. In a thinly veiled attack on Schmitt, Smend rejected the notion that the pluralism of the parliamentary system rendered it ipso facto illegitimate. Instead, he affirmed the right of social groups to organize and participate in determining state policy in a democracy. Both trade unions and private property, he argued, were guaranteed by the constitution. That guarantee permitted both classes to overcome their "bourgeois" orientation toward individual interests and turn their attention as citizens (*Bürger*) to the interests of the whole community. Much like Heller, Smend argued that there were social prerequisites to integration. And also much like Heller, Smend argued for a communitarian notion of the state while rejecting the Schmittian solution of the authoritarian president and the Nazi revolution that Schmitt openly supported a few months later.[123] While it is true that even at this late stage Smend did not affirm the role of the political parties, his writings from the late Republic nevertheless show that he had adopted some republican values.[124]

Heller had a chance to put his substantive defense of formal law into practice in fall 1932. That summer, Chancellor von Papen had convinced President von Hindenburg to issue a decree replacing the Prussian caretaker government, composed of Social Democratic and Catholic Center ministers, with Papen himself as commissar of the *Reich*. The deposed Prussian ministers, the Prussian Social Democrats represented by Heller, the Catholic Center party, and several other *Länder* took the case to the State Court, arguing that the federal government had exceeded the limits of its authority. Chapter 6 deals with that case more fully from a legal standpoint. Important in the present context is the way Heller rejected Carl Schmitt's assertion that the president was a neutral power with the right to undertake emergency acts at his own discretion.[125] For the first time, Heller argued, the federal government had intervened in a *Land* with the intent of violating rather than preserving the constitution; the court should therefore rule against the political executive and annul the action.[126] In making the argument and turning against his earlier support for the Schmittian position, Heller found himself allied with representatives of the positivist traditions, including Gerhard Anschütz and Friedrich Giese in the Labandian tradition, and Hans Nawiasky, who was close to Kelsen. Soon after the trial, Heller went to Britain on a lecture tour. Unable to return to Germany after

Hitler seized power, he took a position in Madrid, where he succumbed to a heart attack on November 5, 1933.

Neither Smend nor Heller avoided entertaining politically dangerous notions. Both were cited positively by early defenders of the new Nazi system, which also attempted, after all, to unify nationalism and socialism in a system aimed at integrating the national community.[127] But as I suggested at the outset, entering into practical matters necessarily exposes a scholar to political dangers. Neither man succumbed to the lure of fascism in 1933. Heller openly defended Social Democracy and the Weimar Constitution. Smend did not produce pro-Nazi propaganda during the dictatorship; his defense of federalism was furthermore unquestioned, which made him suspect in the eyes of the centralizing Nazi regime. He was forced out of the school of law at the University of Berlin (Schmitt took over his position) and spent the war years working on church law and administrative law at the politically less relevant University of Göttingen. Both men reflected on the way a nationalistic civic republicanism can slide into fascism. Heller did so before 1933, in his analyses and criticisms of fascism, and Smend did so after 1945.[128] Both nevertheless argued that some variant of a postpositivist civic republican or communitarian legal theory was necessary for a constitutional democracy to function.

Smend returned to the public sphere with a seminar on constitutional law in 1945. The students who went through that seminar became some of the most important constitutional theorists in Germany. Peter Häberle, for example, used Smend's work together with Heller's to develop a substantive defense of the role of parties and social groups in the democratic public sphere.[129] Horst Ehmke examined the limits to constitutional revision inherent in objective principles embodied in the constitution, and argued as well for a new jurisprudence of social values, one that unified Smend's ideas of balancing values with Heller's call for a social *Rechtsstaat*.[130] Through these scholars and others, Smend's and Heller's conceptions of constitutional democracy made an important contribution to West German constitutional law after 1949.

[6]

EQUALITY, PROPERTY, EMERGENCY

The Constitutional Jurisprudence of the

High Courts in the Republic

The previous chapters have shown the close connection between constitutional theory and constitutional politics in the Weimar Republic. The German high courts likewise confronted the new demands of constitutional democracy and the new theoretical approaches to constitutional law being developed in the academy. But their response to these challenges was indirect, halting, and gradual. Their restrained response was in large part due to the ideals of institutional continuity and stability that the courts were supposed to embody in the continental tradition of the *Rechtsstaat* as it developed over the nineteenth century. Courts were supposed to apply statutes and ordinances without deviating from their written sense and without interference from other state actors. Concrete decisions were supposed to express the objective content of the abstract norm in the interest of security and predictability. Courts in the German Empire were institutions whose duty was to apply the will of the state as it was expressed through procedurally correct statutes.[1]

There can be little doubt that the mechanical model of judicial practice outlined here had become untenable by the mid-1920s. Criticism had come not only from the Free Law movement in private law but also from the most important new theorists of constitutional law: Kelsen, Schmitt, Smend, and Heller. Legal theory and practical politics required a reconsideration of the role of high courts in constitutional law. Some leading lawyers looked for examples to follow in two other federalist democracies, the United States and Switzerland. In a confidential letter of May 30, 1925, to the Ministry of Justice, for example, President of the Reichsgericht Walter Simons argued that the U.S. and Swiss examples showed that a strong court was the "necessary counterweight" to popular sovereignty. Granting a high court powers like those enjoyed by the U.S. Supreme Court would be useful for Germany, he continued.[2] But such comparative arguments quickly ran up against institutional and political obstacles to reform.

First and foremost, arguments for simple emulation of foreign examples overlooked the major historical and institutional differences between the national systems being compared. The applicability of the U.S. system of constitutional review to German conditions was questionable. The U.S. Supreme Court had secured its power of judicial review over the course of many decades; indeed, the first major case of judicial review in the United States, *Marbury* v. *Madison,* took place in 1803, sixteen years after the U.S. Constitution was approved. A comprehensive constitutional jurisprudence developed over the many decades that followed.[3] The Weimar Republic, by contrast, lasted only fourteen years, and its legislature was paralyzed in the final three years of its existence. Institutionally, too, the differences were vast. The U.S. Constitution constructed the Supreme Court as the highest court of the land. The German court system, by contrast, remained fragmented, split up among criminal courts, civil courts, and administrative courts. The Reichsgericht had been constructed in the early years of the empire to rule in cases of high treason and to act as a final court of appeal in cases of civil and criminal law that were decided by the "ordinary" courts of the individual states (as opposed to courts of administrative law). But it was not intended to unify the entire legal system, including administrative law, since that would have undermined the federalist principles of the empire.[4] Nor was it intended to decide matters of "high politics." Under constitutional monarchism, in which the formally correct statute was considered the direct expression of the state's will, there was no room for a higher judicial guardian of the law.

Closer examination of the institutional structure of the high courts indicates another important limit to developing a substantive practice of constitutional law at that level. In 1929, the Reichsgericht consisted of some one hundred judges spread among thirteen different courts seated in Leipzig: eight civil senates, four criminal senates, and the National Labor Court (Reichsarbeitsgericht). Decisions were issued collectively, without an indication of which judge wrote the decision and without official dissents. The Reichsgericht decided thousands of cases a year; a few hundred deemed of importance for the judiciary made their way into a semiofficial but privately published collection of decisions. And these published decisions often gave only sketchy details of the case at hand, seeking instead to provide answers to abstractly posed questions of law. The sheer volume of decisions, the limited number of published decisions, and the lack of clear authorship or clear statements of dissent set objective limits to the coherence of constitutional law. Indeed, the Reichsgericht's structure militated against the ability of individual judges to develop a personal approach to constitutional law as well as the ability of contemporaries (and later historians) to observe the personalities and ideas behind specific rulings.[5]

Alongside the Reichsgericht the Weimar Constitution created a specially organized State Court (Staatsgerichtshof), which was intended to have a different function in the judicial system. While the Reichsgericht decided "ordinary" cases of civil and criminal law, the State Court was supposed to decide matters of constitutional law. Its function was to address "political" issues and to review decisions by the highest state organs related to the points of friction in the constitutional system. In cases of "authentic" constitutional controversies involving conflicts over jurisdictions or between a *Land* and the federal government, the president of the Reichsgericht presided over a panel of seven judges, including the heads of the highest courts of administrative law in Prussia, Bavaria, and Saxony and their aides. In cases that involved state enterprises such as railways and postal services, the State Court also included legal professionals named by the Reichstag and Reichsrat. In cases of ministerial impeachment, finally, a fifteen-person panel was erected, named in part directly by the parties in the Reichstag. In the early 1930s, for example, both Nazi and Communist representatives served on the court for these cases.[6] The separate and special organization of this constitutional court prefigured that of the West German Constitutional Court after 1949.[7]

A history of the jurisprudence of the Weimar Constitution by the high courts must remain rather modest, given the complexity of the institutions and the many individuals empowered to make decisions in them. Nevertheless, an examination of the decisions made by the Reichsgericht and the special State Court after the revaluation crisis of 1923–24 reveals some important characteristics. First, the high courts became steadily more activist as they attempted to respond to new problems of constitutional law such as the meaning of equality before the law, property rights, and presidential powers. Second, these shifts often corresponded to a conservative political position, which is not surprising in the light of the sociological profile of the judges. Many of the justices seemed to want to limit the power of the democratic legislature, against the intentions of the constitution's founders. Third, the changes in constitutional jurisprudence reflected at the same time a response to objective problems of an increasingly complex industrial democracy.[8]

Heinrich Triepel and the Constitutionality of Revaluation

In its letter of January 8, 1924, the seven-member directorate of the Judges' Association of the Reichsgericht threatened to nullify on substantive grounds aspects of the laws and measures regulating currency revaluation.[9] Soon thereafter, Heinrich Triepel prepared a legal brief questioning whether executive actions in conformity with the Enabling Law of December 8, 1923, had been constitutional. That essay, written by one of the discipline's most respected and established scholars of state law, developed a new set of terms and guidelines for courts to use in applying constitutional law. In his critique of the government's handling of the revaluation crisis, Triepel examined the interpretation of the equality clause, property rights, and emergency powers of the executive, three of the most controversial areas of judicial activity during the Republic.

Triepel's analysis of equality before the law differed sharply from that of the statutory positivists. In his standard commentary, Anschütz asserted that Article 109, proclaiming equality before the law, stated merely that all Germans were equal before the formally correct statute. Equality before the law thus became a solely formal principle that stated: what is law, is law. Differential—that is, nonequal—treatment of different social groups was permitted as long as such treatment was embodied in the form of a statute. As Anschütz argued, Article 109, paragraph 1, ordered "equality *before* the law, not equality *of* the law."[10]

Against Anschütz, Triepel argued that the basic right was more than an "empty declaration." Article 109, paragraph 1, limited the "absolutism of the statute" (*Gesetzesabsolutismus*) that threatened "to free the legislator from all legal bounds."[11] The equality clause, he argued, was an "immanent principle" of the constitution that required the legislature to make reasonable distinctions among types of social groups. He summarized his position as follows:

All subjective arbitrariness is a sin against the holy spirit of the law [*Recht*]. The basic principle of equality before the law signifies the demand that individual legal norms are to treat everything as equal, [and] to treat something unequally would signify arbitrariness, that is, be based on the lack of a serious consideration. The principle of equality before the law is injured by distinctions for which no reason, or at least none but one that would confuse [*verfangen*] a reasonably and justly [*gerecht*] thinking person, can be cited.[12]

Triepel shifted attention to the substantive or ethical requirements of legislative activity, thereby opening the way both to judicial review (modeled after the U.S. Supreme Court)[13] and to theories of natural law. A conservative logic appeared in the way Triepel described the problem. He presented the parliament as a capricious, unpredictable institution. The "reasonably and justly thinking" individual stood outside the parliament and judged its actions in terms of their substantive justice and reasonableness.[14]

The logic of Triepel's essay led to an evaluation of legislative actions on the basis of higher law, and therefore to theories of natural law that the legal profession had by and large rejected in the empire. These implications became clear in a paper presented by Erich Kaufmann at the 1926 Congress of the Association of German Professors of State Law.[15] Kaufmann argued that the principle of equality before the law expressed a fundamental conception of justice in a political system. For Enlightenment thinkers, "equality" meant the demand for abstract rules of law that applied equally to all individuals. For Germany in the 1920s, he continued, unaltered "liberal" principles were no longer adequate; the "national community" had altered its sense of equality. The concept of equality was no longer based on "commutative" justice—equal access to markets, for example—but on "distributive" and "institutional" justice. Now equality under the law meant taking cognizance of inequalities, he argued, either to rectify them or to preserve them in the interest of social institutions such as marriage and property. The demand for equality before the law required those who made or applied laws to take into account the substantive notion of justice, of *Recht,* that prevailed in the national community.[16] Kaufmann's language implies a radical attack on the political principles of democracy. *Recht,* for example, he described as a "superpositive order" that positive law "may not injure."[17] Justice became not something about which individuals may argue (a conception of justice that Kaufmann termed "relativistic"), but a "substantive order, which it is our duty to realize."[18] The legal actor became, in Kaufmann's words, the agent of higher law: he had to be a "pure vessel," allowing the higher law to pour into his actions. "He who is pure of heart is just, as one who acts or as one who sets right, and only he."[19] And statutory positivism became a sin: "Merely technical legal scholarship is a whore, who is to be had by all, for all [things]."[20]

Those were fighting words, and discussion at the 1926 meeting revolved around the dispute between positivism and natural law. The debate over the meaning of "equality before the law" reflected a more general debate over the legitimacy of constitutional democracy. Advocates of the positivist interpretation of the equality clause such as Anschütz, Thoma, and Heller, as previous chapters have shown, tended as well to affirm the new democracy and to accept as legitimate the role of political parties in creating law; Triepel, Kaufmann, Schmitt, and other anti-positivist conservatives had grave reservations about the viability and desirability of a pluralistic, party-oriented democracy.[21]

Equality before the law, on Triepel's account, guarded against the arbitrariness of the Reichstag. He provided a similar account of the right to private property. Triepel questioned whether a government ordinance regulating revaluation that had been released on March 28, 1924, respected the right to property set out in Article 153. That ordinance derived its authority from an ordinance of December 28, 1923, which was in turn based on the Reichstag's Enabling Law of December 8, 1923. According to the ordinance of March 28, with the transition to the gold mark, holders of preferred stocks, issued during the inflation to guarantee German stockholders more voting rights than foreigners in German firms, would lose more in revaluation than holders of ordinary stocks.[22] Following the logic developed by the conservative civil lawyer Martin Wolff in an essay published the previous year, Triepel argued that the ordinance in effect expropriated a group of stockholders and thereby violated Article 153, which guaranteed private property and set out guidelines for legal expropriation. The arguments he and Wolff used amounted to a radical restructuring of property rights.[23]

First, Triepel expanded the concept of property itself. According to the Civil Code of 1900, property consisted of movable and immovable things over which a person had absolute control. For Triepel and Wolff, the constitution's concept of property was broader: it extended to rights to use or gain from property, such as the special rights of holders of preferred stock to a portion of company profits. If these rights were property, Triepel reasoned, then the March 28, 1924, ordinance had been an act of expropriation. To use the language of the property rights movement in the United States in the 1980s, property was reconceived as a "bundle of rights," the disturbance of any one of which could constitute a government "taking" requiring compensation.[24] And expropriations were regulated by Article 153, paragraph 2, which bound the legislature as well as the government.[25]

Second, Triepel argued that Article 153, paragraph 2, set substantive as well as formal requirements for legal expropriation. The act of expropriation had to be in the interest of the "general welfare" and not merely a response to the immediate needs of a social group or the financial interests of the state. And the act of expropriation had to be objectively necessary.[26] The logical conclusion of Triepel's argument was that the constitution banned the state from carrying out capricious expropriations. While the legislature and the government were free to exercise discretion in their decisions, those decisions could not be left entirely to the "moods of a sovereign people," any more than the king could have unlimited power under constitutional monarchism. The legitimate realm of "discretionary judgment" did not cover capricious actions against property.[27]

While Triepel's theory of the equality clause opened up law to natural law judgments in the abstract, his discussion of property rights posed a concrete challenge to the doctrines of parliamentary sovereignty associated with statutory positivism. Reworking the clauses of Article 153 that reserved determination of the shape and content of property to the legislature (par. 1, sec. 2), the new doctrine exposed legislative and administrative acts that affected property to review by the courts. And it potentially dissolved limits to the concept of property. Most state actions affect use of property or personal rights in some way. The problem implicitly posed by Triepel and Wolff and developed in the courts over the course of the Republic was how to draw lines between expropriation and normal state regulation in an era of quickly expanding state regulatory power.[28]

Triepel's 1924 essay examines the regulatory power not of the legislature, but of the president and his ministers—the government (*Regierung*). The Enabling Law of December 10, 1923, had granted the government the power to take measures necessary to deal with the hyperinflation and civil unrest then taking place. Triepel argued that this realm of executive discretionary judgment should be subjected to strict judicial examination. First, he questioned whether on the basis of an enabling statute the government could delegate to itself more discretionary powers. Such an act of subdelegation, he stated, overstepped the formal bounds of the initial enabling law. At least one of the decrees issued by the government to deal with revaluation was therefore illegal.[29] Triepel next called for substantive judicial review of executive ordinances to ensure that they were necessary and reasonable. Admitting that substantive review was neither accepted by other legal scholars nor practiced by the highest courts, he nevertheless insisted that the courts could distinguish the realm of free discretion (*freies Ermessen*) from that of arbitrariness (*Willkür*), and that the courts had the power to review executive actions just as they should review actions by the police or the legislature for their reasonableness.[30]

Triepel's call for judicial review of governmental acts (as opposed to actions taken at the lower levels of the administration) remained isolated during the first half of the Republic. Democratic republicans such as Thoma and Anschütz argued that control over executive actions should be reserved to the legislature and that the judiciary should play a secondary role. Conservatives such as Carl Schmitt and Carl Bilfinger, who called for limiting the democratic legislature, opposed review of presidential and executive acts for reasons of state. But Triepel not only favored judicial review of normal executive orders, he wanted to limit presidential powers according to Article 48, paragraph 1, which permitted the president to take emergency actions to "execute" federal laws not properly executed by the *Länder*. Standing virtually alone among the scholars of state law, he argued in a 1923 essay that presidential intervention to "execute" laws was permitted only on the basis of a decision by the State Court. Once again, he stated: "Discretion does not mean the same thing as arbitrariness. Not only the discretion of the administration, but also that of the government [*Regierung*] and the legislature, which stands under the law, has its limits."[31] But even Triepel erased these limits to presidential power in the event of a national emergency. He explicitly argued against substantive review of presidential emergency actions carried out on the basis of Article 48, paragraph 2, which extended extraordinary power to the president to respond to a severe disturbance of "public security and order." True emergency actions were "highly political," he said, and therefore out of bounds for the courts.[32] As an examination of the high courts' jurisprudence of Article 48, paragraph 2, shows, this conservative deference to the president had disastrous effects at the end of the Republic.

The Equality Clause

After the critical year 1923, the Reichsgericht began, cautiously and selectively, to address the issue of how to limit legislative and executive excesses without unduly limiting political decisions. Two points were at stake: whether or not the court could review statutes for their conformity to the constitution, and on what basis constitutionality could be argued.

The first point was addressed in a case of November 4, 1925.[33] The case concerned a debt incurred in 1909 and revised after 1914. The creditor stood to lose a great deal of money in 1923 if the debtor were to repay the debt in devalued notes. The court decided that the Revaluation Law of July 16, 1925, provided adequate grounds for the creditor to demand more money from the debtor even though that law treated different types of debts according to different, or "unequal," rates of revaluation. The Reichsgericht upheld the constitutionality of a statute that reorganized — but did not eliminate — private property in the interests of the entire economy. But at the same time it asserted that it had the authority to hear the case in the first place: "Since the constitution itself contains no norm according to which the decision on the constitutionality of a *Reich* statute should be removed from the courts and transferred to another authority, the power and duty of the judge to review the constitutionality of *Reich* statutes must be recognized."[34] The court resolved that in this case it could not reasonably say that equals had been treated unequally and unequals treated equally; the standards presented by Triepel had not been violated; thus the occasion for making a decision did not appear.[35] The court had reviewed the Revaluation Law for its reasonableness, then used the fact that the law could be taken as "reasonable" to say that it did not need to review for reasonableness.

The Reichsgericht turned to such hypothetical argumentation increasingly during the Weimar Republic. A decision of December 3, 1929, illustrates the point.[36] The case involved several Westphalian noble families that claimed compensations annually paid them for landed property lost in the Napoleonic invasions. During the inflation, the Prussian province of Westphalia had fallen into arrears on these payments, and a lower court had granted a compromise giving the families 60 percent of the normal amount. Westphalia appealed on the basis of a 1929 *Reich* law that suspended cases involving older pensions granted by the individual states. The noble families argued that this law had treated them unfairly. The court rejected this argument and refused to reexamine the Revaluation Law.

The decision in the case was less important than the reason given for the decision:

Even if one takes the stricter approach [to the problem of Art. 109, par. 1] and sees in the rule a binding [norm] for the legislator as well, one can attribute to it, according to previous rulings of the Reichsgericht, only the meaning that the law should treat such cases equally [when] treating such cases unequally would be arbitrariness, which could not be justified on the basis of reasonable considerations. . . . One can argue about the necessity, efficacy, and fairness of the measures taken; but it cannot be asserted that the reason for them was unreasonable.[37]

Noteworthy in the above decision is the court's explicit attempt to preserve a "discretionary realm" within which policy could be elaborated by democratically elected or appointed officials. In a number of other cases as well, the Reichsgericht stated that *if* the courts had the power to make a decision as to whether or not the principle of equality had been violated, *then* the question would be whether or not the legislature's act was arbitrary, *but* it was not so in this case.[38] Again and again, the court actually made a decision while stating that it did not know if it could make a decision.

The Reichsgericht did not, then, act on the power of review that it had begun to exercise in hypothetical judgments. In part, its judges were probably waiting for the Reichstag to deal with proposals for judicial reform coming from the scholarly debate, including a final decision on the admissibility of judicial review.[39] The Reichstag's paralysis after 1929 brought those reform efforts to a halt. One could read these decisions in two different ways. Gerhard Leibholz, a student of Triepel and Smend, saw them as developing a new constitutional jurisprudence that took into account the need to reserve to legislative and governmental authorities discretion over political questions while at the same time setting certain limits to state action based on the idea that distinctions among groups could not be "unreasonable."[40] Following Leibholz's interpretation, the court's actions resembled those of the U.S. Supreme Court in *Marbury* v. *Madison*, which opened the way to judicial review in the United States while avoiding direct confrontation over the issue at hand. Against Leibholz, Anschütz argued that the Reichsgericht actually had not made any controversial decision or specified with precision what "reasonableness" meant.[41]

The debates over the significance of the Reichsgericht's rulings on Article 109 indicate a deeper dispute over the role of judicial institutions in a mass democracy. Anschütz argued for the primacy of the democratic legislature in such a system. Leibholz, though supportive of some democratic principles, argued for a stronger judiciary. The political dispute was not resolved during the Republic. The Reichsgericht's jurisprudence of the equality clause was brought to a halt by the collapse of legislative power after 1930. A decision on judicial review was only made in the vastly different West Germany following the Nazi dictatorship. Leibholz's approach to the equality clause was appropriated at that time, almost word for word, by the new Federal Constitutional Court (Bundesverfassungsgericht), on which Leibholz himself served as one of the first judges.[42]

Restructuring Property Rights

The arguments about property and expropriation developed by Triepel and Wolff likewise found an echo in the Reichsgericht's decisions during the Weimar Republic. Indeed, the courts entered into a dialogue with the two scholars, seeking in some cases to limit and in others to apply the new notion that property was a bundle of rights, that interference in those rights constituted expropriation, and that the court had the power to review regulations affecting property for their constitutionality.[43]

The transformation of property rights in the Reichsgericht's jurisprudence began as a reaction to the Revolution of 1918 and the rise of the left within individual German *Länder*. On November 18, 1921, the Reichsgericht decided a case that established the precedent for later decisions on property rights.[44] Following the revolution, the *Land* of Lippe, dominated by a leftist government, ceased payments agreed on in 1762 to the descendants of a collateral line of the Lippe royal family. Those descendants brought suit, and the Reichsgericht, upholding the decision of lower courts, struck down the Lippe law as a violation of Article 153, paragraphs 1 (guarantee of property) and 2 (requirement of compensation for expropriation). Much of the decision was uncontroversial. The court certainly had the power to review *Land* law for its conformity to the federal constitution, and Article 153, paragraph 2, certainly reserved the power to expropriate without compensation to the federal legislature alone, implicitly depriving the *Länder* of that authority.[45] The controversial part of the decision was its assumption that ending a yearly income constituted the "expropriation of a vested private right" that required compensation.[46]

The 1921 decision altered the terms of discussion by vastly expanding the notion of property covered by Article 153. A decision of December 13, 1924, provides more details about the new approach.[47] In anticipation of superprofits in the coal industry following the war, in 1920 the government of Anhalt increased taxation on the coal industry; furthermore, it provided that profits above a certain amount would flow into the coffers of the *Land*. The Reichsgericht ruled that the new regulations constituted an expropriation of property, defined as "all subjective private rights, including rights of financial claims [*Forderungsrechte*]." "Subjective rights" of "economic value," it argued, ought to be viewed as property protected by Article 153 of the constitution.[48] Later decisions echoed the language of the 1921 and 1924 decisions without, however, developing further criteria for drawing a line between property rights and any other subjective private rights with economic significance.[49]

The threat to the *Länder* and municipalities posed by this new concept of property became clear in a controversial decision of March 11, 1927.[50] The owner of land bordering on the Galgenberg in Hamburg, which was listed as a monument according to the Hamburg Law for the Protection of Historical Monuments and Nature, attempted to remove sand and gravel from his property on April 26, 1924. City officials intervened and stopped the activity. They registered his property as being "in the area of a monument" and therefore under land use restrictions. The landowner took the case to court, demanding compensation for lost property rights. Overruling both lower courts, the Reichsgericht ruled that the landowner deserved appropriate compensation for the "expropriation," that is, the limitation on the owner's right to use his property.

The implications of the 1927 decision were immense, as commentators realized.[51] The court essentially mandated that regulations limiting property use required compensation for lost use rights. Since only a federal statute (*Reichsgesetz*) could annul the demand for compensation, the Reichsgericht decision potentially imposed huge financial obligations on local efforts to plan, zone, and regulate. The issue came to a head in a series of rulings on construction ordinances in 1930 and 1931. The leading decision of February 28, 1930, concerned the owner of a plot of land in Wannsee on the outskirts of Berlin.[52] His plans to build an apartment house on that site were thwarted by a new set of rules regulating the placement and construction of new buildings in that area. The owner took the city of Berlin to court, demanding 100,000 marks plus interest in compensation, a huge amount. The Reichsgericht decided in his favor. It was "indubitable" that Article 153 applied to "burdens on landed property" and that such imposed burdens required adequate compensation, the court ruled.[53] The decisions on municipal regulation opened the way to potentially unlimited claims against the *Länder* and local governments for infringing on property. The explosion of cases threatened the finances of the *Länder* and local governments and halted reforms of regulatory laws such as Prussian environmental legislation just as the Great Depression hit.[54]

Up to this point, this chapter has considered Reichsgericht decisions concerning either *Länder* and local law or the administration of federal laws. In the published cases that dealt with the constitutionality of federal legislation, the court drew back from extensive review, much as it had in its jurisprudence of the equality clause.[55] One case threatened to engulf the Reichsgericht in controversy, however: the 1926 Reichstag proposal to expropriate without compensation all former royal families in Germany. Decisions from the early 1920s had stopped Saxony-Gotha (later Thuringia) and Lippe from eliminating costly payments to royal families and expropriating their royal domains. These decisions occasioned outbursts of criticism, not only from the left but also from conservative lawyers such as Otto Koellreutter, later a leading Nazi legal scholar.[56] The families had in many cases altered the legal status of their domain to accord with the rules of private law, ensuring that elimination of royal wealth would necessarily constitute expropriation in the legal sense.[57] Representatives in the Reichstag, including Democrats (DDP), Communists (KPD), and Social Democrats, called for banning royal families' access to the courts in expropriation cases. The KPD brought a bill before the Reichstag in late 1925 that would have completely expropriated the royal families. The bill, which required a two-thirds majority to pass because it altered the constitutional right to a judicial proceeding, was voted down, as was a less radical bill presented by the Democrats that would have transferred authority to decide the issue to the *Länder*, to the exclusion of legal appeal. A popular referendum supported by the SPD and the KPD brought the bill before the Reichstag once more in April and May 1926, when it was once again defeated by the nonsocialist parties, now galvanized in their opposition to the specter of Socialist and Communist cooperation. Liberals and conservatives alike now expressed fears that expropriating a specific group without compensation and banning legal appeal would violate the basic principles of the *Rechtsstaat*.[58]

Carl Schmitt took the expropriation bill as an occasion to emphasize another concept important to the developing debate about property and expropriation. The 1926 referendum, he argued, would have resulted in a statute affecting a single group, thereby violating the "substantive" notion of the statute that Schmitt defended—that a statute should be general in its application—and would therefore have been unconstitutional. As chapter 4 showed, Schmitt's argument was part of a more general strategy to limit parliamentary power, in direct contrast to the theories of parliamentary sovereignty developed by the statutory positivists.[59] Because the Reichstag did not approve the bill to expropriate the royal houses, the Reichsgericht was not forced to confront the problem of how to review Reichstag legislation according to Article 153. In later decisions it deferred to the federal legislature, asserting that it was a "self-ruling" body (*selbstherrlich;* the word also implies "tyrannical") bound only by the constitution and its own statutes.[60] The Reichsgericht did not expressly say how the constitution limited the legislature, but it adopted the language suggested by Schmitt and others according to which an "individual intervention" was an "expropriation" and thereby set a limit to the normal legislative power of the Reichstag.[61]

The new opposition between individual and general statutes was of limited usefulness, however, as the Reichsgericht's decision of May 27, 1930, shows.[62] A natural healer who had been employed at a hospital to treat female victims of venereal disease lost his position after the Reichstag passed the 1927 Law for Fighting Venereal Diseases, which reserved treatment of such cases to state-approved physicians.[63] He took the German state to court, alleging that his skills constituted a "subjective property right" (*subjektives Vermögensrecht*) that required compensation. The Reichsgericht felt compelled to respect the argument as legitimate according to its conception of property as a bundle of rights, but rejected the plaintiff's call for compensation for different reasons: the statute was not an expropriation of a specific social group, but rather forbade anyone to practice natural healing of venereal diseases; the law was a general rule rather than an individual intervention. In fact, the new law affected specific people, much as zoning and other municipal ordinances would. The highest judges of Germany had by no means found a way to draw the line between expropriating and nonexpropriating regulations.[64]

In its attempt to guard against leftist democratic elements at the local, *Land,* and federal levels, the Reichsgericht had developed an extensive understanding of property as a bundle of rights, the removal or limitation of which would potentially constitute a taking requiring compensation. Portions of the new doctrine would be reclaimed in West Germany after 1949; indeed, strong arguments have been made, both in the Weimar Republic and in the Federal Republic, that careful scrutiny of regulations and a more complex understanding of property is necessary in an increasingly complex social system.[65] But in the context of the Weimar Republic, the Reichsgericht's decisions were disastrous. According to Minister of Labor Adam Stegerwald, a leader of the Catholic trade union movement, the new doctrine threatened to cost Berlin alone "many hundreds of millions of marks."[66] Stegerwald advocated a new law that would undo the rulings in the interest of the municipalities, which were already pushed to the wall by demands for social services in the depression years. His proposed law banned all claims for compensation for expropriation on the basis of a construction code (*Fluchtlinienplan*). The law was enacted by the presidential emergency decree of June 5, 1931.[67] In a ruling on that decree released on July 2, 1932, the Reichsgericht itself admitted the negative effects of its doctrine of property rights. Citing the financial burdens imposed on municipalities by its rulings, the court upheld the decree of June 5, 1931.[68]

As contemporary commentators noted, the Reichsgericht's new doctrinal positions seemed to be based more on its fear of the democratic legislature than on the juridical logic that had heretofore marked the German *Rechtsstaat*.[69] While the Reichsgericht had struggled to limit local and *Länder* authorities and the caprice of the parliamentary majority, it chose not to review the content of the presidential emergency decree. It declared that the president was bound only by Article 48, paragraph 2, and granted him the power to suspend basic rights with or without expressly stating that fact.[70] The contrast between the court's distrust of the democratic legislature and its faith in the president could not have been more apparent.

Presidential Emergency Powers and Federalism

Throughout the years of the Republic, the court held back from reviewing presidential emergency decrees, arguing that Article 48, paragraph 2, granted the president virtually unlimited power. The courts' approach reflected the exceptionally wide conception of dictatorial powers that it had developed during the First World War (discussed in chapter 2).[71]

Challenges to presidential emergency decrees usually involved controversies in constitutional law, such as the relationship between the federal government and a *Land*, disputes among *Länder*, the constitutionality of ministerial actions, and impeachment proceedings against the president or ministers. The Reichsgericht, as the highest of the "ordinary" courts, refused to decide these "political" issues. Because they involved controversies in constitutional law, the cases fell under the jurisdiction of the State Court in the form of a seven-judge panel.[72] That form of the State Court began to develop a jurisprudence of emergency decrees during the mid-1920s in its rulings on actions by the governments of the *Länder*.

On November 21, 1925, the State Court issued its first major ruling.[73] The case concerned a series of emergency decrees issued by the Prussian government during a week-long recess of the Prussian Landtag in March 1925. The conservative D N V P fraction in the Landtag challenged the legality of the actions. The State Court upheld the constitutionality of the decrees, and in the process made clear the fact that it considered controversies over such decrees to fall under its jurisdiction. In these cases, the decision stated, the court should ascertain whether an emergency ordinance was "urgent" and "necessary"; but adequate room should also be reserved for the government of the *Land* to exercise discretionary judgment in responding to emergencies. Indeed, the court should view *Länder* governments' emergency decrees as justified "so long as the opposite is not established beyond a shadow of a doubt [*einwandfrei*]."[74] Several years later, the State Court struck down an emergency decree by the Prussian government. The decision of March 23, 1929, concerned a decree extending Prussia's monopoly over coal and oil exploration and exploitation rights to a part of the *Land* previously not covered by the ordinance after new fields were reported in the area.[75] While it restated the principle that governments should have freedom of action in the state of emergency, the State Court also argued that the content of the emergency ordinance should stand in a proper (*zweckmässig*) relationship with the aims of the action. Extending a rule to a new jurisdiction amounted to something more than an appropriate decree of limited duration. Instead, the new ordinance was intended to be a lasting legal norm. It entered into the area proper to legislation.[76] Therefore the State Court ruled the emergency ordinance invalid.

Presidential emergency decrees issued with the authority of Article 48 were another matter, however. Until 1931, the State Court avoided addressing the issue of whether and how to review presidential emergency decrees. When a flurry of wide-ranging decrees began issuing from the Brüning government in 1930, the State Court found itself forced to confront the issue. It initially did so in two decisions released on December 5, 1931, both of which concerned the way presidential emergency decrees delegated to the *Länder* the power to issue their own emergency decrees.

In the first case, the president issued the so-called Dietramzeller Decree (named after the place he was vacationing) on August 24, 1931, which permitted. *Länder* governments to take necessary measures to settle *Land* and community finances during the depression. The *Länder* governments were permitted to deviate from their own constitutional laws under these measures.[77] The government of Mecklenburg-Strelitz used the delegation of power to incorporate a small, ailing municipality into a larger one. The small municipality and the DNVP fraction in the Prussian Landtag called the case before the State Court, arguing that both the *Land* government and the president had overstepped their legal authority. The plaintiffs charged that the president had violated Article 17 of the Weimar Constitution, which stated that all *Länder* should be democratic and constitutional, by permitting the governments of the *Länder* to deviate from their *Land* constitutions. The State Court rejected the argument. Article 48, paragraph 2, it argued, was an "independent norm of jurisdiction" (*selbständige Zuständigkeitsvorschrift*) in the sense that it was not derived from other constitutionally defined jurisdictions such as the normal powers of the president or Reichstag. It permitted presidential emergency ordinances in realms reserved to the *Länder* by the Weimar Constitution in normal periods.[78] Furthermore, the court argued, decisions about whether or not conditions justified the use of Article 48, paragraph 2, as well as the measures used to restore order should "in principle" (*grundsätzlich*) be left to the president.[79]

The case of December 5, 1931, concerned a similar controversy. The Brüning government, appointed after the beginning of the economic depression and the breakup of the Great Coalition in early 1930, had sought to circumvent Reichstag opposition to its social and economic activity by releasing two far-reaching presidential emergency decrees on July 16, 1930. On July 18, the Reichstag voted to suspend the emergency decrees, at which point the president dissolved the assembly. On July 26, the Brüning government reissued the decrees. The relevant portion of the decrees for the case at hand authorized *Länder* governments to issue emergency decrees that allowed them to raise communal taxes. The government of Saxony responded by imposing higher taxes on beer and other beverages. The Party of the German Middle Class (Reichspartei des Deutschen Mittelstandes) charged that the Saxon government had exceeded its legal authority by issuing tax regulations.[80] In its decision, the State Court asserted that an emergency decree had to fulfill three conditions. First, there had to be a significant disturbance or threat to public security and order, which included economic perils. That condition was clearly satisfied by the depression. Second, the measures taken should be appropriate to the aim of restoring security and order. Stabilizing municipal finances constituted an appropriate tool for restoring economic order. Finally, the measures should be temporary. The court noted that it had applied these three criteria in assessing the emergency decrees issued by *Länder* governments. It stated further: "One can be of the opinion that corresponding [considerations] apply here [to presidential emergency decrees] as well." But such considerations, it continued, were pointless, since clearly disturbances did exist, the government was taking measures to deal with them, and in any case Article 48, paragraph 2, granted an "independent jurisdiction" to the president to act even in areas reserved to the *Länder*.[81] Just as the Reichsgericht had avoided a ticklish situation by couching its review of legislation on the basis of the equality clause in hypothetical language, so the State Court claimed it need not review a presidential emergency decree since the preconditions necessary for its employment were clearly fulfilled.

As the Weimar Republic entered into its final year of existence, the State Court's jurisprudence of presidential emergency decrees remained vague. It had not stated clearly whether it had the power to review; nor had it indicated limits to the president's "independent jurisdiction" by Article 48, paragraph 2; nor was it clear where "discretionary judgment" ended and illegal activity or arbitrariness began. The doctrine of a presidential independent norm of jurisdiction allowed the president to go far beyond even normal legislation. And in the case of Mecklenburg-Strelitz, the court had essentially permitted an action with permanent effects—the incorporation of one community into another—which undermined the requirement that emergency decrees be temporary. Such was the state of its jurisprudence of presidential emergency powers when the State Court was called on to rule in a case that sealed the fate of the Republic: the actions taken by presidential emergency decree on July 20, 1932, against the Prussian *Land*.

The Presidential Intervention in Prussia of July 20, 1932

Elections to the Prussian Landtag on April 24, 1932, had made the National Socialists the strongest Landtag fraction and had given Communists and Nazis together an absolute majority of the delegates. A prorepublican coalition in Prussia had become impossible. Because of a change in the Landtag bylaws enacted on April 12, however, the former Prussian ministers, who were from the SPD and the Catholic Center, remained as a caretaker government until a majority could elect a new government. The old government thereby stopped the Nazis from taking power in the largest German *Land*. The hard line against Nazi incursions into the government seemed to correspond to federal policy. On April 13, President Hindenburg and Chancellor Brüning had issued a decree banning the Nazi storm troopers (Sturmabteilung: SA) and the Blackshirts (Schutzstaffel: SS). An abrupt change of course ensued at the end of May, however. A conspiracy led by General von Schleicher convinced Hindenburg that Brüning was not trustworthy. In his place Hindenburg appointed Franz von Papen, an aristocrat who stood at the far right of the Center party and had strong ties to monarchists and antirepublican reactionaries. Papen and Schleicher sought to placate the Nazis and to gain their support in the Reichstag by promising to hold new Reichstag elections and lift the ban on the SA. The Reichstag was dissolved on June 4, following a vote of no confidence. Ten days later, a presidential decree lifted the ban on the SA. Soon thereafter, the federal government deprived the *Länder* of the authority to ban the wearing of paramilitary uniforms on the streets.[82]

The result was a two-month period of street violence. Only a few months after they were told to halt SA assemblies, the Prussian police were ordered to allow the SA to march unhindered through the streets. (The Communist paramilitary organization, the *Rotkämpferbund*, by contrast, had been banned since 1929.) A bloody street fight on July 17 in the working-class neighborhoods of Altona, north of Hamburg, where the SA had staged a march, produced scores of casualties and seventeen dead. On July 18, the Prussian police acted with more force to contain a Nazi rally in Königsberg, eliciting complaints by Nazi leaders to Papen. Accusing the Prussian government of being unable to halt conditions of civil war in the *Land*, of being "dependent" on the Communists, and of lacking the support of the Landtag, on July 20 the government issued an emergency decree that had been signed by Hindenburg a week before. Papen became the *Reich* commissar for Prussia, replacing the head of the Berlin police Praesidium, and SPD members were purged from the top level of the government. The Prussian government, a coalition between the SPD and the Catholic Center, was essentially overthrown.[83]

During the weeks that followed, Papen took more actions within Prussia, claiming to represent the *Land* as the presidential commissar. He fired civil servants and appointed representatives to the Reichsrat, the assembly of the *Länder*. The Prussian ministers suspended by the decree, the SPD and Center delegations to the Prussian Landtag, and the *Länder* of Bavaria and Baden appealed to the State Court. First, the plaintiffs denied that the objective conditions that would permit application of Article 48 to the Prussian government were present. Second, they asserted that the commissar's interference with the basic structures of federalism, including representation in the Reichsrat, was unconstitutional. Finally, they accused the Papen government of using the emergency action to further its own political intrigues with the Nazis.[84]

After six long days of arguments from the leading scholars of German constitutional law, including Anschütz, Nawiasky, Heller, Schmitt, and Bilfinger, the State Court rendered a verdict on October 25.[85] The Conclusion looks at the arguments presented during the trial in more detail. Of interest in the present context is the decision itself, which shows both continuities and discontinuities with the State Court's earlier decisions.

The Papen government had justified the July 20 presidential decree on the basis of paragraphs 1 and 2 of Article 48. Paragraph 1 gave the president the right to intervene if a *Land* failed to carry out its duties to the federal government; paragraph 2 gave the president the power to take extraordinary measures in the event of a serious disturbance of or threat to public security and order. The State Court considered the validity of each claim separately. In so doing, it rejected the Papen government's claim that the two paragraphs granted the president an unreviewable and virtually indistinguishable independent norm of jurisdiction when political relations between the federal government and the *Länder* were in crisis.[86]

The federal government had not satisfied the conditions necessary for intervening in a *Land* on the basis of Article 48, paragraph 1, the court stated. Carefully reviewing the facts presented by all sides, it found no evidence that the government of the *Land* had violated its duty to carry out federal laws. Furthermore, although individual Social Democrat officials had talked to individual Communists, there was no evidence that the SPD was dependent on the KPD. Finally, the court rejected the assertion that changing Prussian Landtag bylaws while still permitting a Landtag majority to elect a new Prussian government marked a break with the principles of parliamentary democracy required by Article 17 of the constitution.[87] The State Court had taken the plunge, reviewing a presidential emergency decree enacted by the authority of Article 48, paragraph 1, to see if it satisfied the prerequisites for constitutionality: an objective violation of duties to the federal state imputable to the *Land* or a turn away from the principles of parliamentary democracy. It declared these preconditions absent.[88]

With one hand, the State Court offered Prussia a victory. With the other, however, it took the victory away. In its ruling on the dictatorship clause (Art. 48, par. 2), the court all but gave the president a free hand in his use of emergency decrees. There were, however, undertones to the decision that suggested the possibility of future delimitations. First, the court addressed the question whether it was permitted to review the preconditions for an emergency decree. It declined to do so in this case, stating that it was "evident" (*offenkundig*) that a state of emergency existed, and that the president had reasonably concluded that a concentration of Prussian and federal power in one hand would help to alleviate the state of emergency.[89] Just as the Reichsgericht had done in its hypothetical review of legislation according to the equality clause, the State Court in effect reviewed the preconditions for Article 48, paragraph 2, affirmed the president's judgment, and then refused to declare whether it had the power to review.[90]

The State Court next examined the president's use of his discretionary powers. First, it asked whether the discretionary realm had been misused as part of a secret agreement between Papen and Hitler. It rejected that claim, citing lack of proof of such an agreement.[91] Notably, the court did not ask whether Papen intended to use presidential emergency powers to alter the constitution in an authoritarian direction, a point that could have been supported by Papen's radio addresses. However, the plaintiffs had also failed to make that argument, relying instead on the accusation of conspiracy.[92] Second, the court examined whether the president had gone beyond the actions necessary to reach his goal. It argued that the appointment of a commissar for Prussia did not overstep reasonable limitations to presidential emergency power, and that only the president, and certainly not the State Court, was empowered to review his commissar's specific actions.[93] Indeed, the court echoed its earlier argument that Article 48, paragraph 2, constituted an independent norm of jurisdiction that permitted the president (or his commissar) to take over areas that normal constitutional law placed under the jurisdiction of the *Länder*.[94]

But the State Court also declared an absolute limit to presidential authority in the institutions created by the Weimar Constitution. Article 17 stated that each *Land* should have a government elected according to democratic procedures within the *Land* itself. The federal commissar therefore could not designate himself as the government of the *Land*. Articles 60 and 63 provided for a Reichsrat in which the *Länder* would be represented and which would vote on certain legislation, including reform of the federalist system. Since he was not an authentic representative of the *Land*, the federal commissar could not appoint representatives to the Reichsrat.[95] For the first time, a high court had made a binding decision setting absolute limits to presidential authority according to Article 48, paragraph 2.

Prussia thus celebrated a Pyrrhic victory: the State Court had announced that the Papen government could not dismantle Prussia's representative institutions completely, but at the same time it gave the commissarial government the authority to take whatever concrete and temporary actions it deemed necessary. The Papen government found itself in an embarrassing situation. The court had created a dual regime in which Papen could act but without the authority of the *Land*, and the *Land* could exercise authority but not take concrete actions. Papen refused to return the old ministers to their offices. The legal actions against the commissarial regime came to an abrupt end a few months later when Hitler assumed power.[96]

The presidential emergency decree of July 20, 1932, gutted the federalist system of the Republic, undermined the bulwark of parliamentary democracy in Prussia, and amounted to a coup d'état by Papen. But it would have been surprising had the State Court gone further in its ruling. That would have required heroism on the part of the judges and a willingness suddenly to alter the traditional refusal of the high courts to review discretionary actions by the executive. Not only was such a break unlikely in the light of the history of the high courts in the Weimar Republic, it is furthermore hard to imagine the conservative judges of the State Court, including Chief Justice Erwin Bumke, who would serve as president of the Reichsgericht throughout the Nazi period, granting a victory to the Social Democrats of Red Prussia.[97]

Conclusion

The decision of October 25, 1932, has gone down in history as a grand failure of the judiciary to halt the dissolution of the Republic—in Karl Dietrich Bracher's words, it was a "tragedy of the theory of the State Court."[98] Contemporary reactions were much different. Indeed, those who defended the Republic initially welcomed the decision, while the supporters of Papen and the authoritarian attempt to alter the constitution were outraged by it.[99]

Hans Nawiasky, representing Bavaria, and Arnold Brecht, the chief lawyer for the deposed Prussian government, greeted the decision as a victory.[100] Thirty-five years later, Brecht still defended the decision of the State Court, arguing that the ruling both permitted the federal government to carry out emergency actions that were necessary and urgent and required it to respect the federal structure of Germany and preserve Prussia.[101] Anschütz welcomed this part of the decision as well.[102]

Heinrich Triepel's reaction to the decision indicates how little conservatives, even those ostensibly in favor of expanding the role of courts, were willing to countenance State Court–imposed limitations on presidential emergency actions. Triepel condemned the decision as "to a great extent incorrect." It was up to the president to examine the concrete question whether Prussia had violated its obligation to be faithful to the federal government, and the court should not put its own value judgment in place of the president's. Furthermore, Triepel rejected the idea that *Länder* representative institutions were off-limits for the president. The dictatorship, he stated, was a "constitutional anomaly." Using language to describe the institution reminiscent of Schmitt's Triepel argued: "It is the peculiar dialectic of the institution that it *must* attack what it should protect, precisely to protect it."[103] Triepel's defense of the power of a unified executive organ contrasted sharply with his call for limiting the party-political parliament, which he viewed as part of an "atomistic, individualistic" mass party state. Even before 1929 Triepel had issued a plea for replacing the "mechanized society of the present" with an organic sociopolitical system.[104] Although he was not a Nazi, Triepel was certainly no defender of parliamentary democracy and federalism when these interfered with the unity and strength of the German state.

In fact, the conservative critique of the State Court's decision grew into a general appeal to ban judicial activity in "political" arenas.[105] That call was answered soon after Hitler assumed power. In his pamphlet *State, Movement, Nation* (1933), Carl Schmitt, now solidly in support of the Nazi revolution, stated that the institution of the State Court in the Weimar Constitution had annihilated the political idea of the *Führer* and given power to forces that intended to destroy the state.[106] Otto Koellreutter, who was an open supporter of the Nazis even before 1932, attacked the State Court for engaging in "political justice" by making *Land* and federal governments into equal parties in the trial.[107] Both official representatives of Nazi state law viewed the decision of October 25, 1932, as the last dying gasp of the liberal-democratic state rather than as a ruling opening the door for authoritarian rule. Both welcomed the coming of the new, "responsible" leadership of Adolf Hitler.

The criticisms made by Schmitt and Koellreutter indicate the complexities involved in tracing judicial politics in the Weimar Republic. The high courts' constitutional jurisprudence conveyed at least two messages. First, it delivered a conservative message in its immediate political context. Court decisions expressed a distrust of the democratic legislature and a desire to limit its activities.[108] Second, the courts' actions reflected an attempt to deal with new kinds of challenges to social and political life. By claiming the right—however hypothetically—to review legislative statutes for their substantive fairness according to Article 109, the Reichsgericht may have substituted its conservative worldview for the views of the democratic legislature. But it also opened the possibility of heightened protection of minorities against legislative majorities. If the Reichsgericht's all-too-undefined "takings" doctrine had more deleterious than positive consequences in the Republic, it also showed that the Reichsgericht was trying to adjust its rulings to the different world of the regulatory state and regulated society. And the State Court's review of presidential emergency ordinances, while not halting the antidemocratic practices of Chancellor von Papen, made clear that review was possible and that even the executive had to explain its actions thoroughly and rationally to the high courts. The Reichsgericht and the State Court provided no definitive resolution of the proper role that high courts should play in a constitutional democracy. But they did begin to stake out the terrain on which future struggles for the meaning of constitutional democracy would take place, and in the process to rethink the relationship between judicial institutions and the *Rechtsstaat* in a constitutional democracy.

CONCLUSION

The Crisis of Constitutional Democracy

This book began by invoking the image of constitutional democracy giving itself up to its enemies. The final chapter ended with an account of the 1932 trial at which the federal government's intervention into Prussia was debated. The trial qualifies the image of constitutional democracy's surrender in two ways. First, "constitutional democracy" did not "give itself up." Individual actors, claiming to operate in the interest of "constitutional democracy," took steps to defend or destroy specific provisions of the Weimar Constitution. The second, more abstract reason that the image of constitutional democracy's surrender is problematic is that the concept "constitutional democracy" itself was then under debate. Indeed, at least as interesting as the State Court's ruling of October 25, 1932, is the range of conceptions of constitutional democracy presented by the lawyers at the trial.

The radical, existential conception of constitutional democracy in Carl Schmitt's thought came through in his opening statement for the Papen government.[1] As he had since 1917, Schmitt invoked a superlegal logic of the emergency situation: under conditions of civil war someone had to make a sovereign decision distinguishing between legal and illegal parties. In the state of emergency, "illegal" meant not merely the lack of correspondence to positive legal norms, but the factual condition of being an enemy of the state. The concrete decision about who was a friend and who was an enemy was reserved to the president and his government, who were, Schmitt asserted, "independent" and "above the parties."[2] Article 48 functioned in Schmitt's analysis as the "real" basis of democracy. According to Schmitt, neither the judiciary nor constitutional articles designed to govern under normal conditions should limit presidential emergency power: "What one does in a concrete situation with respect to a concrete question is an affair of the president according to Article 48." The president could not be limited by pluralistic or federalistic interests since he himself immediately expressed the unified, "democratic" foundation of the system. As Schmitt said, "precisely democratic organization tends to foreground the idea of national democracy, national homogeneity, and the national political unity that follows from them."[3] The conception of constitutional democracy defended by Schmitt at the trial amounted to substantial political unity guaranteed by the singular representative of the state—the president— against interests that would divide the sovereign state or the united nation. Pluralism was on this account unconstitutional and would lead to the end of the political entity, Schmitt argued. He concluded a speech at the trial with Abraham Lincoln's words: "A house divided against itself cannot stand."[4]

Hans Nawiasky, a professor of public law in Munich, developed a legal-positivist approach to constitutional law that corresponded in many respects to Hans Kelsen's. Nawiasky pointed out that in Schmitt's interpretation, Article 48 created a second constitution for extraordinary times that could take precedence over all the other "ordinary" constitutional articles.[5] Put in Kelsen's terms, there were two "basic norms" in Schmitt's constitutional theory. One presumed the validity of the written constitution in normal times; the other presumed the validity of presidential emergency acts as higher acts of state in abnormal times. As Nawiasky noted, Schmitt viewed the president as responsible to no other state organ during the state of emergency: Schmitt presented a theory of presidential absolutism.[6] By contrast, Nawiasky presumed the validity of the positive Weimar Constitution, and therefore presumed that the rights and duties of both federal government and *Länder* were legally defined by those positive norms. Creating a parliamentary legislature inevitably meant creating a system that allowed multiple interests to be represented; similarly, creating a system of *Länder*, each with its own system of representation, necessarily meant that politics would emanate from both national and local sites of authority.[7] While Schmitt had emphasized the unified *demos* of constitutional democracy, Nawiasky viewed the constitution as the legal "creator" of democracy. The president, the Reichstag, the Landtags, the *Länder* governments, and the courts all stood under the "comprehensive state" (*Gesamtstaat*).[8] Therefore he felt "a stab in [his] jurist's heart" on hearing arguments like Schmitt's and Schmitt's colleague on the defense, Carl Bilfinger, that "merely" positive norms should be shaped or ignored in accord with political expedience.[9]

Nawiasky's position was strictly bound to positive law, perhaps because he was representing Bavaria. Bavaria claimed a right to plead at the trial because Papen's appointment of Prussian representatives to the Reichsrat had undermined the most important organ for representing *Länder* interests. The *Länder* had much to lose from the legitimation of federal interventions into state affairs. By contrast, Gerhard Anschütz's statutory positivism and Hermann Heller's theory of the constitution as "organization" were part of political projects that affirmed national unity and the power of the Reichstag. Both were willing to concede to the president more powers under Article 48 than was Nawiasky. Both argued, for example, that a prior decision by the State Court was not necessary for presidential action under Article 48, paragraph 1, and that the violation of a duty by a *Land,* the prerequisite for presidential intervention, could also be a violation of unwritten norms.[10] But for both Anschütz and Heller, the sovereignty of the unitary nation was constructed through the positive constitution itself. Both therefore rejected Schmitt's "situational" interpretation of constitutional law, which permitted "mere" written rules to be suspended by the one true representative of the German people, the president.[11] As Anschütz argued: "The constitution *wants* a federal state and *wants* a . . . parliamentary democracy."[12]

The statutory positivism to which Anschütz adhered thus evinced substantial similarities to Heller's theory of the state. But overshadowing these similarities were basic differences in temperament. In his first statement to the court, Anschütz responded to members of the audience who had shouted "Louder!": "I am not speaking to the audience, but to the court and to the expert representatives of the opposing party."[13] Later in the case, he condemned the "raised volume" and politics of the proceedings. He attempted instead to lay out the relative and absolute limits to presidential emergency powers, abstractly and without direct connection to the case at hand.[14] The value of Anschütz's style of argumentation, so reminiscent of Laband's, lay in the way it legitimized court actions on ostensibly unpolitical, logical grounds. His testimony was probably central to the State Court's decision to review the presidential emergency act of July 20 and to strike down some parts of it. But Anschütz could not address Schmitt's political arguments, which suggested that the state faced an existential crisis that went beyond the situations addressed by positive constitutional law.

Heller, representing the Social Democratic party, addressed Schmitt's political arguments head-on. He denied that Papen had acted to preserve the constitution. Papen's aims, Heller asserted, were rather to undermine and to alter the constitution—to eliminate the formal parts of constitutional law that were, according to Heller's theory of the state, an intrinsic part of the constitution's substance.[15] Other lawyers in the trial referred, jokingly or disparagingly, to Heller's "temper," and at one point Judge Bumke warned Heller to lower his voice.[16] But Heller's raised tones and political remarks, which he combined with a positivist analysis of constitutional law,[17] may have reflected his attempt to expand legal argumentation by foregrounding "basic principles of right." More than the relative and absolute limits to presidential authority were at stake in the case, after all. Also at issue were the political institutions and rules that granted form to the will of the popular sovereign, that created state power. The "organization" of the Weimar Constitution integrated workers into the state, Heller had argued in his Weimar writings. As he argued at the trial, Schmitt's demand for presidential dictatorship would destabilize and destroy the legitimacy of the first political system to allow Socialist participation in government.[18]

Heller was right. The experiment with presidential authority under the chancellorships of Papen and Schleicher was a failure. Papen's radical intervention in basic constitutional institutions laid the groundwork for Hitler's later destruction of the constitutional system as a whole. First, the arguments put forward by Schmitt reserved legally unlimited power to the president and his government if the president—in this case a senile old Junker unable to judge his surroundings—could be convinced to declare a state of emergency. The Hitler regime made extensive use of this power in its first months, culminating in the "Emergency Ordinance for the Protection of Nation [*Volk*] and State" suspending basic rights, which was issued on February 28 following the Reichstag fire. The enabling act approved by the Reichstag on March 23, 1933, implemented a permanent state of emergency and extended direct dictatorial powers to Hitler. The permanent state of emergency was—paradoxically—institutionalized.[19] Second, Papen had taken actions in Prussia to "cleanse" the "body of the civil service" (*Säuberung des Beamtenkörpers*),[20] which included, as was expressly stated in the trial, removing officials because of their affiliation with the SPD.[21] The Nazi Law for the Restoration of the Civil Service of April 7, 1933, formalized the earlier purges, extending them to other political organizations and to "non-Aryans."[22] Finally, the Papen government's lawyers had argued that the *Länder* could not contradict national policies and that in the event of an emergency the federal government had the right to appoint a commissar to take over all functions of a *Land*, including representative functions; indeed, Schmitt argued that the intervention in Prussia was only a minimal, restrained example of presidential executive power.[23] The Hitler regime began to "coordinate" (*gleichschalten*) *Länder* and national policies with a series of decrees beginning in March 1933. The Law for the Reconstruction of the Reich of January 30, 1934, formally abolished *Länder* parliaments and governmental independence.[24] In his early Nazi-era writings, Carl Schmitt strongly supported these measures. They would, he argued, protect the state from the State Court and from federalism.[25]

Papen's coup d'état against Prussia thus marked the beginning of institutional processes that culminated in the consolidation of power by the National Socialists. The events of June 30, 1934, made Hitler the highest judge of the land as well. On that day, he ordered the execution of political opponents within the Nazi party. The murders of Ernst Röhm, Kurt von Schleicher, and dozens of others were only the final stage of a development that, viewed in terms of its constitutional logic, was already present in the Papen government's arguments before the State Court in October 1932 for a judicially free realm of presidential discretion in the case of emergency.[26]

Schmitt's conception of constitutional democracy won out in the final weeks of the Republic—ultimately to be replaced by the far more radical and far less formal rule of National Socialism, which Schmitt himself helped to develop.[27] The factual end of the debate should not, however, obscure the lasting importance of the philosophical and legal issues it raised. These issues remain central constitutional problems of the West German Basic Law, and they mirror contemporary debates in the United States. The yearning for a "substantial" foundation of the constitution, for a patriotism that is something more than "constitutional patriotism," can be found in assertions made in both the United States and Germany that the constitution's foundations lie in a prelegal homogeneity of the citizenry, a set of common morals and values, or the Christian religion. Other politicians and liberal political theorists argue in contrast that the constitution itself provides the organization that creates the unified people of a constitutional democracy. The role of the high courts in "political" matters also remains controversial. Debate ensues whenever the U.S. Supreme Court or the Federal Constitutional Court in Germany acts to limit majority rule to protect minorities. Political commentators on both the left and the right ask whether hard decisions about policy and the meaning of rights might be better left to democratically elected organs. Finally, the politics of federalism continues to rouse tempers, especially in the United States since federal courts and Congress implemented civil rights reforms. Defenders of states' rights have argued for strictly limiting federal intervention into state governments, even when state governments act to exclude certain groups from participating in the political system (e.g., the Jim Crow laws), from having access to public institutions, or from having their rights protected.

What counts as "left" and "right" in constitutional law varies with the political context. To point out parallels in constitutional arguments is therefore not to assert an identity of the political meaning of those arguments. A defense of federalism, for example, was the rallying cry of the republican left in Germany in 1932, and is also the focal point of much right-wing, antiliberal politics in the contemporary United States. The first task of this book has been to show the political stakes of constitutional debates in the specific context of the Weimar Republic. The second has been to analyze the transformation of constitutional law and constitutional debate with the coming of constitutional democracy. The guiding principles of the statutory positivism that developed under the stable constitutional system of the German Empire came under attack with the arrival of constitutional democracy. The presumption that the "people" was sovereign opened up discussion about the substantive foundations of the Weimar Constitution, developed most radically by the debate between Kelsen and Schmitt over who was the "guardian of the constitution." The different yet related approaches of Heller and Smend brought out the ramifications of the democratic constitution for the politics and practice of constitutional interpretation. Finally, the beginnings of a constitutional jurisprudence of the German high courts indicated the problems to be faced in seriously addressing the substantive or "political" content of constitutional law in concrete cases.

This book has traced the opening of a new constitutional culture in Germany. "Culture" in this context refers not to a stable set of accepted social norms guiding legal practice, but instead to a set of contradictions and conflicts that are immanent to "constitutional democracy" itself, and which take on different political significations in different contexts. The various ways in which constitutional democracy may be articulated are, however, generally limited in any given constitutional system. In the United States at present, for example, approaches to constitutional democracy that affirm racist conceptions of the national subject or socialist conceptions of the primacy of popular sovereignty over property rights are marginalized, although elements of each radical position may appear embedded in more moderate political programs. What was notable about the constitutional culture of the Weimar Republic was the failure of a particular conception of constitutional democracy to gain hegemony over political life.

A different story can be told of the Federal Republic of Germany. The trauma of National Socialist dictatorship and war, revelations of atrocities and the Holocaust, and the division of the country into East and West contributed to the development of a constitution and constitutional culture distrustful of both the power of the people and the power of the state. Postwar West German constitutionalism, as it crystallized in the 1950s, emphasized federalism, a strongly institutionalist conception of democracy that favored established political parties and interest groups, and substantive judicial review by the Constitutional Court, an institution modeled in part on the Weimar State Court. Despite the challenges from the left during the 1970s and 1980s, the West German model of constitutional democracy remained stable.

Nor has the collapse of the "People's Democracies" of Eastern Europe and the unification of East and West Germany in 1990 significantly altered the character of German constitutionalism, at least at the time of the present writing.[28] Following the East German Revolution, however, the problems of constitutional democracy outlined in the present work reappeared. Some leading representatives of the East German opposition allied with leftists in the West to call for a more radical democratic conception of constitutional democracy through direct means such as popular initiatives and referenda.[29] The far right, now gaining intellectual respectability with the fact of national unification, has introduced the themes it developed during the 1980s on the need for strong institutions, ethnic homogeneity, and patriotism into the center of public discussion.[30] And criticisms of the Constitutional Court's role in evaluating the constitutionality of legislative decisions, epitomized in the 1993 abortion ruling and the 1995 ruling on crucifixes in Bavarian classrooms, have aroused new and more strident opposition to judicial review.[31] The fact that these critiques of constitutional democracy have reappeared indicates the continued relevance of the dilemmas of constitutional democracy in the present day.

NOTES

Abbreviations Used in the Notes

VVDSRL   *Veröffentlichungen der Vereinigung der deutschen Staatsrechtslehrer.* Vols.
1-7. Berlin: Walter de Gruyter, 1924-32.
RGZ   *Entscheidungen des Reichsgerichts in Zivilsachen.* 172 vols. Berlin: Walter de Gruyter, 1880-1945.

Introduction

1. The enabling act was approved under the threat of the storm troopers. See Karl Dietrich Bracher, *The German Dictatorship: The Origins, Structure, and Effects of National Socialism,* trans. Jean Steinberg (New York: Praeger, 1970), 199-211; and the collection of documents assembled by Rudolf Morsey, *Das Ermächtigungsgesetz vom 24. März 1933* (Dusseldorf: Droste, 1968).

2. On the "defenselessness" of the Republic, see Hagen Schulze, *Weimar. Deutschland 1917–1933,* 4th ed. (Berlin: Severin und Siedler, 1994), 102-5, where reference is made to "the Social Democrat Hans Kelsen's" relativism and the constitution's "liberality without foundation" (*bodenlose Liberalität*). Schulze's language echoes that of the radical right during the Republic: Kelsen, a Jew, is asserted to be a Social Democrat (he was, in fact, a member of no party) associated with liberalism, and that liberalism is asserted to lack "foundation," or "soil" (*Boden*).

3. See Schulze, *Weimar,* xii; and, in more detail, Friedrich Karl Fromme, *Von der Weimarer Verfassung zum Bonner Grundgesetz. Die verfassungspolitischen Folgerungen des Parlamentarischen Rates aus Weimarer Republik und nationalsozialistischer Diktatur* (Tübingen: J. C. B. Mohr [Paul Siebeck], 1960).

4. Handbooks of constitutional law of the Federal Republic are replete with references to the Weimar debates. See, e.g., Konrad Hesse, *Grundzüge des Verfassungsrechts der Bundesrepublik Deutschland,* 18th ed. (Heidelberg: C. F. Müller, 1991), which includes discussions of the Weimar figures throughout; Peter Badura, *Staatsrecht. Systematische Erläuterung des Grundgesetzes für die Bundesrepublik Deutschland* (Munich: C. H. Beck, 1986), 11-13 on Kelsen, Schmitt, and Smend;

and the centrality of Smend in Ekkehard Stein, *Staatsrecht*, 9th ed. (Tübingen: J. C. B. Mohr [Paul Siebeck], 1984), 97, 253, 268; and on Heller, 268–69.

5. See, esp., Alexander Bickel, *The Least Dangerous Branch: The Supreme Court at the Bar of Politics*, 2d ed. (New Haven: Yale University Press, 1986), 16–23.

6. More specifically, "state law in a narrower sense," i.e., constitutional law and laws regulating the operation of top state organs. See B. Erwin Grueber, *Einführung in die Rechtswissenschaft. Eine juristische Enzyklopädie und Methodologie* (Berlin: O. Häring, 1908), 91–108; Friedrich Giese, *Einführung in die Rechtswissenschaft*, 2d ed. (Berlin: Spaeth und Linde, 1932), 62–65.

7. See Walter Ott, *Der Rechtspositivismus. Kritische Würdigung auf der Grundlage eines juristischen Pragmatismus* (Berlin: Duncker und Humblot, 1976); I have simplified his analysis somewhat.

8. In the German context, see Eugen Ehrlich, *Fundamental Principles of the Sociology of Law* (1913), trans. Walter L. Moll (Cambridge: Harvard University Press, 1936). Lawrence M. Friedmann explicitly makes the description of authoritative public rules the object of sociology of law in *Law and Society: An Introduction* (Englewood Cliffs, N.J.: Prentice-Hall, 1977), 3–5. Niklas Luhmann presents the "classical" positions on the sociology of law in *Rechtssoziologie*, 3d ed. (Opladen: Westdeutscher, 1987), 23.

9. See Hart's now classic work: *The Concept of Law* (London: Oxford University Press, 1961).

10. This distinction was brought out in the famous exchange in 1916 and 1917 between Hans Kelsen and Eugen Ehrlich in the *Archiv für Sozialwissenschaft und Sozialpolitik*, repr. as *Hans Kelsen und die Rechtssoziologie. Auseinandersetzungen mit Hermann U. Kantorowicz, Eugen Ehrlich und Max Weber*, ed. Stanley Paulson (Aalen: Scientia, 1992). Notably excluded from the category of "legal positivism" is the approach to law that concentrates on communication, practice, and interaction, a kind of legal anthropology. See the polemic by Lon L. Fuller, *The Morality of Law*, rev. ed. (New Haven: Yale University Press, 1969), esp. 106–8, 145, 237–42.

11. See the explicit statements to this effect in Laband, *Das Staatsrecht des Deutschen Reiches*, 4 vols., 5th ed. (1911–13; repr., Aalen: Scientia, 1964), 2:39–40.

12. Kelsen, *Hauptprobleme der Staatsrechtslehre, entwickelt aus der Lehre vom Rechtssatze* (Tübingen: J. C. B. Mohr [Paul Siebeck], 1911).

13. Ebert produced more than 130 decrees and ordinances based on emergency law between 1919 and 1924, most of them in response to civil strife. See Ulrich Scheuner, "Die Anwendung des Art. 48 der Weimarer Reichsverfassung unter den Präsidentschaften von Ebert und Hindenburg," in *Staat, Wirtschaft und Politik in der Weimarer Republik. Festschrift für Heinrich Brüning*, ed. Ferdinand A. Hermens and Theodor Schieder (Berlin: Duncker und Humblot, 1964), 249–86;

Harlow James Heneman, *The Growth of Executive Power in Germany: A Study of the German Presidency* (Minneapolis: Voyageur, 1934), 180-81, 183-86; Ernst Rudolf Huber, *Deutsche Verfassungsgeschichte seit 1789*, vol. 7: *Ausbau, Schutz und Untergang der Weimarer Republik* (Stuttgart: W. Kohlhammer, 1984), 363-64, 422-25. A list of presidential acts by emergency decree in English can be found in Lindsay Rogers, Sanford Schwarz, and Nicholas S. Kaltchas, "German Political Institutions II. Article 48," *Political Science Quarterly* 47 (1932): 583-94; see also Clinton L. Rossiter, *Constitutional Dictatorship: Crisis Government in the Modern Democracies* (Princeton: Princeton University Press, 1948), 31-73.

14. Triepel, *Goldbilanzenverordnung und Vorzugsaktien. Zur Frage der Rechtsgültigkeit der über sogenannte schuldverschreibungsähnliche Aktien in den Durchführungsbestimmungen zur Goldbilanzen-Verordnung enthaltenen Vorschriften* (Berlin: Walter de Gruyter, 1924). On Triepel, see Alexander Hollerbach, "Zu Leben und Werk Heinrich Triepels," *Archiv des öffentlichen Rechts* 91 (1966): 417-41.

15. Leibholz, *Die Gleichheit vor dem Gesetz. Eine Studie auf rechtsvergleichender und rechtsphilosophischer Grundlage* (Berlin: Otto Liebmann, 1925). On Leibholz, see Manfred H. Wiegandt, *Norm und Wirklichkeit. Gerhard Leibholz (1901–1982). Leben, Werk und Richteramt* (Baden-Baden: Nomos, 1995).

16. Smend, *Verfassung und Verfassungsrecht* (1928), repr. in *Staatsrechtliche Abhandlungen und andere Aufsätze,* 3d ed. (Berlin: Duncker und Humblot, 1994), 119-276. On Smend, see Axel Freiherr von Campenhausen, "Rudolf Smend (1882–1975). Integration in zerrissener Zeit," in *Rechtswissenschaft in Göttingen. Göttinger Juristen aus 250 Jahren,* ed. Fritz Loos (Göttingen: Vandenhoeck und Ruprecht, 1987), 510-27.

17. Carl Schmitt, *Verfassungslehre,* 6th ed. (repr. of 1st, 1928, ed.; Berlin: Duncker und Humblot, 1983). On Schmitt, see Reinhard Mehring, *Carl Schmitt: Eine Einführung* (Hamburg: Junius, 1992).

18. Heller's work is collected as *Gesammelte Schriften,* 3 vols., 2d ed., ed. Fritz Borinski, Martin Drath, Gerhart Niemeyer, and Otto Stammer (Tübingen: J. C. B. Mohr [Paul Siebeck], 1992); for an introduction to his work, see Christoph Müller, "Hermann Heller: Leben, Werk, Wirkung."

19. See Ernst Fraenkel, "Der Ruhreisenstreik 1928-1929 in historisch-politischer Sicht," in Hermens and Schieder, eds., *Staat, Wirtschaft und Politik in der Weimarer Republik,* 97-117; on the context of the Social Democratic offensive for "economic democracy," see Heinrich August Winkler, "Unternehmer und Wirtschaftsdemokratie in der Weimarer Republik," in *Probleme der Demokratie Heute,* Sonderheft 2 of *Politische Vierteljahrsschrift* (1970): 308-22.

20. A general account of the events is in Bracher, *Die Auflösung der Weimarer Republik: Eine Studie zum Problem des Machtverfalls in der Demokratie,* 5th ed. (1971; repr., Dusseldorf: Droste, 1984). Detlev Peukert, *The Weimar Republic: The*

Crisis of Classical Modernity, trans. Richard Deveson (New York: Hill and Wang, 1992), puts the crisis into a wider cultural, economic, and social context.

21. A defense of Brüning is in Scheuner, "Die Anwendung des Art. 48," 279–80; also Heinrich August Winkler, *Weimar 1919–1933. Die Geschichte der ersten deutschen Demokratie* (Munich: C. H. Beck, 1993), 376. On the content of the memoirs regarding constitutional politics, see Karl Otmar Freiherr von Aretin, "Brünings ganz andere Rolle," *Frankfurter Hefte* 26 (1971): 931–39. On the reception of the memoirs and the state of the question of Brüning's orientation toward constitutional democracy, see Frank Müller, *Die "Brüning Papers." Der letzte Zentrumskanzler im Spiegel seiner Selbstzeugnisse* (Frankfurt am Main: Peter Lang, 1993), esp. 12–13, 72–80.

22. On the events of summer 1932, see Bracher, *Die Auflösung der Weimarer Republic,* 503–18; Scheuner, "Die Anwendung des Art. 48," 282–85. Schmitt's position is in *Legalität und Legitimität* (1932), repr. in *Verfassungsrechtliche Aufsätze aus den Jahren 1924–1954. Materialien zu einer Verfassungslehre,* 2d ed. (Berlin: Duncker und Humblot, 1973), 262–350.

23. See the full discussion of the theoretical problem in works by two lawyers deeply influenced by the Weimar debates: Friedrich Müller, *Juristische Methodik,* 3d ed. (Berlin: Duncker und Humblot, 1989); and Martin Kriele, *Theorie der Rechtsgewinnung entwickelt am Problem der Verfassungsinterpretation,* 2d ed. (Berlin: Duncker und Humblot, 1976).

24. Older English-language works on Schmitt have tended toward the apologetic: Joseph W. Bendersky, *Carl Schmitt: Theorist for the Reich* (Princeton: Princeton University Press, 1983); George Schwab, *The Challenge of the Exception: An Introduction to the Political Ideas of Carl Schmitt between 1921 and 1936* (Berlin: Duncker und Humblot, 1970); Paul Edward Gottfried, *Carl Schmitt: Politics and Theory* (New York: Greenwood, 1990). More recently, political scientists have attempted to reappropriate some of Schmitt's arguments in an attempt to refashion pluralist democracy. See, e.g., Chantal Mouffe, "Pluralism and Modern Democracy: Around Carl Schmitt," *New Formations* 14 (1991): 1–16; and the more critical approach of John McCormick, "Fear, Technology and the State: Carl Schmitt, Leo Strauss and the Revival of Hobbes in Weimar and National Socialist Germany," *Political Theory* 22 (1994): 619–52, and *Against Politics as Technology: Carl Schmitt's Critique of Liberalism* (New York: Cambridge University Press, 1997). More critical responses have also been forthcoming. To mention a few: Richard Wolin, "Carl Schmitt: The Conservative Revolutionary Habitus and the Aesthetics of Horror," *Political Theory* 20 (1992): 424–47; William P. Scheuerman, *Between the Norm and the Exception: The Frankfurt School and the Rule of Law* (Cambridge: MIT Press, 1994); Stephen Holmes, *The Anatomy of Antiliberalism* (Cambridge: Harvard University Press, 1993), 37–60.

25. See, e.g., the following excellent theoretical works: Stanley L. Paulson, "Introduction" to Hans Kelsen, *Introduction to the Problems of Legal Theory. A Translation of the First Edition of the Reine Rechtslehre or Pure Theory of Law,* trans. Bonnie Litschewski Paulson and Stanley L. Paulson (Oxford: Clarendon, 1992), v–xlii, with further bibliography, 145–53; Hans Aufricht, "The Theory of Pure Law in Historical Perspective," in *Law, State, and International Legal Order. Essays in Honor of Hans Kelsen,* ed. S. Engel (Knoxville: University of Tennessee Press, 1964), 29–41; and Ronald Moore, *Legal Norms and Legal Science. A Critical Study of Kelsen's Pure Theory of Law* (Honolulu: University of Hawaii Press, 1978). Exceptions do, however, exist; see, e.g., Paul Silverman, "Law and Economics in Interwar Vienna. Kelsen, Mises, and the Regeneration of Austrian Liberalism" (Ph.D. diss., University of Chicago, 1984). The new investigation by Stanley Paulson into the stages of Kelsen's Pure Theory of Law is leading toward a more historical analysis. See the summary of his research: "Toward a Periodization of the Pure Theory of Law," in *Hans Kelsen's Legal Theory: A Diachronic Point of View,* ed. Letizia Gianformaggio (Turin: G. Giappichelli, 1990), 11–48.

26. On Heller, see Ellen Kennedy, "The Politics of Toleration in Late Weimar: Hermann Heller's Analysis of Fascism and Political Culture," *History of Political Thought* 5 (1984): 109–25; and the forthcoming work by David Dyzenhaus: *Truth's Revenge: Carl Schmitt, Hans Kelsen and Hermann Heller in Weimar* (New York: Clarendon, 1997). The only works in English to date that deal with Smend come from sociology and political science. See Werner S. Landecker, "Smend's Theory of Integration," *Social Forces* 29 (1950): 39–48; Otto Butz, *Modern German Political Theory* (Garden City, N.Y.: Doubleday, 1955), 44–46.

27. This problem is addressed in Bruce Ackerman's attempt to mediate republicanism and liberalism: *We the People,* vol. 1: *Foundations* (Cambridge: Harvard University Press, 1991); the full range of issues is brought out in the symposium on Ackerman printed in *Ethics* 104 (1994): 446–535.

28. Smend, "Das Recht der freien Meinungsäusserung," *Veröffentlichungen der Vereinigung der deutschen Staatsrechtslehrer* [hereafter abbreviated VVDSRL], vols. 1–7 (Berlin: Walter de Gruyter, 1928), 4:44–74.

29. On "balancing" in U.S. law, see Edward S. Corwin, *The Constitution and What It Means Today,* 14th ed., rev. Harold W. Chase and Craig R. Ducat (Princeton: Princeton University Press, 1978), 307–9; for a general critique of values-based jurisprudence and "balancing" in property rights, see Richard A. Epstein, "Property, Speech, and the Politics of Distrust," in *The Bill of Rights in the Modern State,* ed. Geoffrey R. Stone, Richard A. Epstein, and Cass Sunstein (Chicago: University of Chicago Press, 1992), 41–89.

30. See, e.g., Hans Boldt, *Deutsche Verfassungsgeschichte,* 2 vols. (Munich: DTV, 1984, 1990); and Boldt's defense of the structuralist method in *Einführung in die*

Verfassungsgeschichte. Zwei Abhandlungen zu ihrer Methode und Geschichte (Dusseldorf: Droste, 1984).

1 The Will of the State and the Redemption of the German Nation

1. Wolfgang J. Mommsen, "Die Verfassung des Deutschen Reiches von 1871 als dilatorischer Herrschaftskompromiss" (1983), repr. in *Der autoritäre Nationalstaat. Verfassung, Gesellschaft und Kultur im deutschen Kaiserreich* (Frankfurt am Main: Fischer, 1990), 39–65.

2. Hans-Ulrich Wehler reduces this system to an "autocratic, semi-absolutist sham constitutionalism" (*The German Empire 1871–1918,* trans. Kim Traynor [Leamington Spa: Berg, 1985], 55), an analysis that obscures liberal aspects of the system; in general, see Helga Grebing, *Der deutsche Sonderweg in Europa 1806–1945. Eine Kritik* (Stuttgart: W. Kohlhammer, 1986), 96–101. Wolfram Siemann presents reasons for the National Liberals' acceptance of the 1871 compromise in *Gesellschaft im Aufbruch. Deutschland 1849–1871* (Frankfurt am Main: Suhrkamp, 1990), 218–231. The centrality of constitutionalism in liberal thought is stressed especially well by Thomas Nipperdey in *Deutsche Geschichte 1800–1866: Bürgerwelt und starker Staat* (Munich: C. H. Beck, 1983), 290–98; see also Nipperdey, *Deutsche Geschichte 1866–1918,* vol. 2: *Machtstaat vor der Demokratie* (Munich: C. H. Beck, 1990), 37–39, 314–17, on liberalism and unification. On the Civil Code, see Michael John, *Politics and the Law in Late Nineteenth-Century Germany. The Origins of the Civil Code* (Oxford: Clarendon, 1989). On the Anti-Socialist Laws, see Ernst Rudolf Huber, *Deutsche Verfassungsgeschichte seit 1789,* vol. 3: *Bismarck und das Reich,* 3d ed. (Stuttgart: W. Kohlhammer, 1988), 1021–22; vol. 4: *Struktur und Krisen des Kaiserreichs* (Stuttgart: W. Kohlhammer, 1969), 1157–60; and "Grundrechte im Bismarckschen Rechtssystem," in *Festschrift für Ulrich Scheuner* (Berlin: Duncker und Humblot, 1973), 175–76. On the creation of the court system, see Ken Ledford, "Lawyers, Liberalism, and Procedure: The German Imperial Justice Laws of 1877–1879," *Central European History* 26 (1993): 165–93.

3. Paul Laband, *Das Staatsrecht des Deutschen Reiches,* 3 vols. (Tübingen: H. Laupp, 1876), 1:10.

4. Laband himself was not officially a member of the National Liberal party. In a speech to the Reichstag on January 11, 1887, Bismarck told the liberals to read "the books of law friendly to your convictions" by von Rönne and Laband: Bismarck, *Werke im Auswahl,* 9 vols., ed. Gustav Adolf Rein et al. (Stuttgart: W. Kohlhammer, 1981), 7:450; see also the report by Wilhelm Raimund Beyer, "Paul Laband: ein Pionier des öffentlichen Rechts," *Neue Juristische Wochenheft* 41 (1988): 2227.

5. Ernst-Wolfgang Böckenförde comments on the implicit agreement between

historicism and positivism regarding the unity of the state in "The School of Historical Jurisprudence and the Problem of the Historicity of Law" (1965), repr. in *State, Society and Liberty. Studies in Political Theory and Constitutional Law*, trans. J. A. Underwood (New York: Berg, 1991), 1–25. Rupert Emerson describes the "organic school" in detail in his *State and Sovereignty in Modern Germany* (New Haven: Yale University Press, 1928), 126–54. Gierke's assumption of the unity of the German *Volk* is in "Labands Staatsrecht und die deutsche Rechtswissenschaft," *Schmollers Jahrbuch für Gesetzgebung, Verwaltung und Volkswirthschaft im Deutschen Reich* 7 (1883): 31–32. On positivism and the state in Europe, see W. A. Tumanov, *Contemporary Bourgeois Legal Thought: A Marxist Evaluation of the Basic Concepts* (Moscow: Progress, 1974), 112–24.

6. Carl Friedrich von Gerber, *Über öffentliche Rechte* (1852; repr., Tübingen: J. C. B. Mohr [Paul Siebeck], 1913), 16ff.; idem, *Grundzüge des deutschen Staatsrechts*, 3d ed. (1880; repr., Aalen: Scientia, 1969), 217–25; Walter Pauly, *Der Methodenwandel im deutschen Spätkonstitutionalismus. Ein Beitrag zu Entwicklung und Gestalt der Wissenschaft vom öffentlichen Recht in 19. Jahrhundert* (Tübingen: J. C. B. Mohr [Paul Siebeck], 1993), 92–167; Walter Wilhelm, *Zur juristischen Methodenlehre im 19. Jahrhundert. Die Herkunft der Methode Paul Labands aus der Privatrechtswissenschaft* (Frankfurt am Main: Vittorio Klostermann, 1958); Peter von Oertzen, *Die politische Funktion des staatsrechtlichen Positivismus. Eine wissenssoziologische Studie über die Entstehung des formalistischen Positivismus in der deutschen Staatsrechtswissenschaft*, ed. Dieter Sterzel (Frankfurt am Main: Suhrkamp, 1974); Michael Stolleis, *Geschichte des öffentlichen Rechts in Deutschland*, vol. 2: *Staatsrechtslehre und Verwaltungswissenschaft 1800–1914* (Munich: C. H. Beck, 1992), 331–37; Emerson, *State and Sovereignty*, 48–56.

7. Gierke's critique is in "Labands Staatsrecht," 17–22, 34–35, 39–41.

8. On the difference between Gerber and Laband, see Pauly, *Methodenwandel*, 13–14; and Ingeborg Maus, "Plädoyer für eine rechtsgebietsspezifische Methodologie oder: wider den Imperialismus in der juristischen Methodendiskussion," *Kritische Vierteljahresschrift für Gesetzgebung und Rechtswissenschaft* 74 (1991): 114–15.

9. See Laband's *Lebenserinnerungen* (printed privately, 1918), repr. in *Abhandlungen, Beiträge, Reden und Rezensionen*, vol. 1 (Leipzig: Zentralantiquariat der DDR, 1980–83), 63. For examples of positive response to the work, see Rudolf von Gneist, *Gesetz und Budget. Constitutionelle Streitfragen aus der preussischen Ministerkrisis vom März 1878* (Berlin: Julius Springer, 1879); Joseph von Pözl, review in *Kritische Vierteljahresschrift für Gesetzgebung und Rechtswissenschaft* 13 (1871): 567–75; and more references in Michael Stolleis, *Geschichte des öffentlichen Rechts*, 2:341–42.

10. On Laband's political activity, see Bernhard Schlink, "Laband als Politiker," *Der Staat* 31 (1992): 553–69.

11. Laband helped start the *Archiv für öffentliches Recht* in 1886, the *Deutsche*

Juristen-Zeitung in 1896, and the *Jahrbuch für öffentliches Recht* in 1907. On the *Archiv,* see Erk Volkmar Heyen, "Die Anfangsjahre des 'Archivs für öffentliches Recht.' Programmatischer Anspruch und redaktioneller Alltag im Wettbewerb," in *Wissenschaft und Recht der Verwaltung seit dem Ancien Regime. Europäische Ansichten,* ed. Heyen (Frankfurt am Main: Vittorio Klostermann, 1984), 347–73. On the importance of Laband in German state law, see the remarks by Ernst Landsberg, *Geschichte der Deutschen Rechtswissenschaft,* vol. 2, pt. 3 (Munich: R. Oldenbourg, 1910), 833; Heinrich Triepel, *Staatsrecht und Politik* (Berlin: Walter de Gruyter, 1927), 8–9; Walter Mallmann, "Laband," in *Staatslexikon. Recht-Wirtschaft-Gesellschaft,* 6th ed., vol. 5 (Freiburg: Herder, 1960), 203–7; Manfred Friedrich, "Paul Laband und die Staatsrechtswissenschaft seiner Zeit," *Archiv des öffentlichen Rechts* 111 (1986): 199–201; and Stolleis, *Geschichte des öffentlichen Rechts,* 2:343–44.

12. As Dieter Grimm notes, in "Methode als Machtfaktor" (1982), repr. in *Recht und Staat der bürgerlichen Gesellschaft* (Frankfurt am Main: Suhrkamp, 1987), 365.

13. Laband, *Das Staatsrecht des Deutschen Reiches,* 5th ed., 1:ix. Unless otherwise noted, all further references to the *Staatsrecht* are to this edition. Claus-Ekkehard Bärsch, "Der Gerber-Laband'sche Positivismus," in *Staat und Recht. Die deutsche Staatslehre im 19. und 20. Jahrhundert,* ed. Martin J. Sattler (Munich: List, 1972), 43–71, examines the methodological precepts; more attention to practice is given in Maximilian Herberger, "Logik und Dogmatik bei Paul Laband. Zur Praxis der sog. juristischen Methode im 'Staatsrecht des Deutschen Reiches,'" in Heyen, ed., *Wissenschaft und Recht der Verwaltung,* 91–104.

14. Laband, *Das Staatsrecht des Deutschen Reiches,* 1:vii, x. See also Emerson, *State and Sovereignty,* 57: "In brief, it was not, according to Laband, for the jurist to reason why, but merely to accept the forms of the given and build up a conceptual construction of it."

15. Translation of *octroyée* by "condescended" suggested in R. K. Gooch, *Parliamentary Government in France: Revolutionary Origins, 1789–1791* (Ithaca: Cornell University Press, 1960).

16. Ernst-Wolfgang Böckenförde, "The German Type of Constitutional Monarchy in the Nineteenth Century" (1967), repr. in his *State, Society, and Liberty,* 87–114; Dieter Grimm, *Deutsche Verfassungsgeschichte, 1789–1866* (Frankfurt am Main: Suhrkamp, 1987), 116–19. The origins of this argument are in Carl Schmitt's militaristic and authoritarian work, *Staatsgefüge und Zusammenbruch des Zweiten Reiches. Der Sieg des Bürgers über den Soldaten* (Hamburg: Hanseatisch, 1934). Against Schmitt, Ernst Rudolf Huber argued that constitutional monarchism represented a coherent and stable system of government: "Bismarck und der Verfassungsstaat" (1964), repr. in *Nationalstaat und Verfassungsstaat. Studien zur Geschichte der modernen Staatsidee* (Stuttgart: W. Kohlhammer, 1965), 188–223. On

the debate, see Hasso Hofmann, "Das Problem der cäsaristischen Legitimität im Bismarckreich" (1977), repr. in *Recht-Politik-Verfassung. Studien zur Geschichte der politischen Philosophie* (Frankfurt am Main: Alfred Metzner, 1986), 181–205, esp. 181–82, n. 1; and Elisabeth Fehrenbach, *Verfassungsstaat und Nationsbildung 1815– 1871* (Munich: Oldenbourg, 1992), 71–72.

17. Unless otherwise noted, all constitutional references are to *Deutsche Verfassungen*, 20th ed., ed. Rudolf Schuster (Munich: Wilhelm Goldmann, 1992).

18. On the monarchical principle and German constitutionalism, see Otto Hintze, "Das monarchische Prinzip und die konstitutionelle Verfassung" (1911), in *Gesammelte Abhandlungen,* vol. 1: *Staat und Verfassung. Gesammelte Abhandlungen zur allgemeinen Verfassungsgeschichte,* 2d ed., ed. Gerhard Oestreich (Göttingen: Vandenhoeck und Ruprecht, 1962), 359–89; Georg Jellinek, *Regierung und Parlament in Deutschland. Geschichtliche Entwickelung ihres Verhältnisses* (Leipzig: B. G. Teubner, 1909).

19. Dieter Grimm, "Der Wandel der Staatsaufgaben und die Krise des Rechtsstaats" (1990), in *Zukunft der Verfassung* (Frankfurt am Main: Suhrkamp, 1991), 161–63.

20. Boldt, *Deutsche Verfassungsgeschichte,* 2:103–5.

21. Huber, *Deutsche Verfassungsgeschichte seit 1789,* vol. 2: *Der Kampf um Einheit und Freiheit 1830 bis 1850,* 3d ed. (Stuttgart: W. Kohlhammer, 1988), 492–98, 582– 86.

22. The king's right to make and break treaties was limited only by the assembly's right to deal with matters affecting the property of citizens: commerce or debts (Art. 48).

23. Huber, *Deutsche Verfassungsgeschichte,* 3:55–57, 65–68; Grimm, *Deutsche Verfassungsgeschichte,* 216. Boldt, *Deutsche Verfassungsgeschichte,* 2:198, discusses the way conservatives and liberals differed over the principle of ministerial responsibility.

24. Böckenförde, "The German Type of Constitutional Monarchy," 109; Ludwig von Rönne, *Das Staats-Recht der preussischen Monarchie,* vol. 1, pt. 2 (Leipzig: Brockhaus, 1870), 597–601. Legal and political arguments related to this kind of dispute had already developed before 1850; see Hans-Christof Kraus, "Ursprung und Genese der 'Lückentheorie' im preussischen Verfassungskonflikt," *Der Staat* 14 (1990): 209–34.

25. Otto Pflanze, *Bismarck and the Development of Germany. The Period of Unification, 1815–1871* (Princeton: Princeton University Press, 1963), 156–67; Gordon Craig, *The Politics of the Prussian Army, 1640–1945* (London: Oxford University Press, 1955), 136–79; Dieter Grimm, *Deutsche Verfassungsgeschichte 1776–1866. Vom Beginn des modernen Verfassungsstaats bis zur Auflösung des Deutschen Bundes* (Frankfurt am Main: Suhrkamp, 1988), 231–37; Boldt, *Deutsche Verfassungsgeschichte,* 2:106–23.

26. The two positions are best represented by the Landtag's resolutions of October 7 and 13, 1862, repr. in *Dokumente zur deutschen Verfassungsgeschichte*, vol. 2, ed. Ernst Rudolf Huber (Stuttgart: W. Kohlhammer, 1961), 45–46; and Bismarck's speech before the representatives on January 27, 1863 (in ibid., 49–53); see also Lothar Gall, *Bismarck: The White Revolutionary*, vol. 1: *1851–1871*, trans. J. A. Underwood (London: Allen and Unwin, 1986), 223–25.

27. Huber claims that this was a conflict between two opposing and *mutually exclusive* notions of sovereignty—monarchical and popular; only Bismarck, not the liberals, operated within the "value system" of the constitution (*Deutsche Verfassungsgeschichte*, 3:333–38; "Bismarck und der Verfassungsstaat," 198–201). However, the liberals seemed willing to accept constitutional monarchism with a relatively stronger place for the assembly, just as Bismarck continued using the budget from the year before, both implicitly recognizing the necessity of eventual compromise. See Hans Boldt, "Verfassungskonflikt und Verfassungshistorie. Eine Auseinandersetzung mit Ernst Rudolf Huber," in *Probleme des Konstitutionalismus im 19. Jahrhundert, Der Staat*, Beiheft 1, ed. Ernst-Wolfgang Böckenförde (Berlin: Duncker und Humblot, 1975), 75–102.

28. Böckenförde, "The German Type of Constitutional Monarchy," 105–9; Huber, *Dokumente*, 2:88–89; Nipperdey, *Deutsche Geschichte 1866–1918*, 2:35–36.

29. The context of Laband's work is in Thomas Nipperdey, *Deutsche Geschichte 1866–1918*, vol. 1: *Arbeitswelt und Bürgergeist* (Munich: C. H. Beck, 1990), 658–62; and Stolleis, *Geschichte des öffentlichen Rechts*, 2:339–41, 347–48, and ch. 8, passim.

30. *Das Budgetrecht nach den Bestimmungen der Preussischen Verfassungs-Urkunde unter Berücksichtigung der Verfassung des Norddeutschen Bundes* (Berlin: J. Guttentag, 1871), 1–2.

31. The 1850 Prussian Constitution was borrowed in large part from the 1831 Belgian Constitution, which introduced a system of constitutional monarchism; see John Gilissen, "La constitution belge de 1831: ses sources, son influence," *Res Publica* 10 (1968): 107–41, esp. 140.

32. *Budgetrecht*, 61–62, 63–64, 79. The one exception (49) concerns the Bundesrat's right to review constitutional conflicts in states.

33. *Budgetrecht*, 3. Laband did not define the concept through any concrete characteristics (such as duration or generality) that might have aided clarity (see ibid., 3–4, 11–12). Laband's clearest definition (ibid., 12) is taken from Gerber, *Grundzüge*, 220–22; Ernst-Wolfgang Böckenförde, *Gesetz und gesetzgebende Gewalt. Von den Anfängen der deutschen Staatsrechtslehre bis zur Höhe des staatsrechtlichen Positivismus* (Berlin: Duncker und Humblot, 1958), 233–34.

34. *Budgetrecht*, 5–6.

35. Ibid., 8–9.

36. Ibid., 12–13.

37. Ibid., 61.

38. Ibid., 61–62; precisely this right was at stake when the assembly demanded specific estimates of military expenditures in the Hague Bill.

39. Ibid., 12–13.

40. Ibid., 81–82.

41. See Gerber, *Über öffentliche Rechte*, 16ff.

42. *Grundzüge*, 19–22. See also Oertzen, *Die politische Funktion des staatsrechtlichen Positivismus*, 170–74, on the term *organischer Volksstaat*.

43. See, esp., *Staatsrecht*, 1:64–75, 90–91; Ortrun Fröhling, *Labands Staatsbegriff. Die anorganische Staatsperson als Konstruktionsmittel der deutschen konstitutionellen Staatslehre* (Ph.D. diss., Universität Marburg, 1967), 26–40, 120ff.

44. Oertzen, *Die politische Funktion des staatsrechtlichen Positivismus*, 200–211.

45. Gall, *Bismarck*, 316–19; Bismarck, *Werke im Auswahl*, 4:31–50.

46. Albert Hänel, *Studien zum Deutschen Staatsrechte*, vol. 2, bk. 1: *Die organische Entwicklung der deutschen Reichsverfassung* (Leipzig: Haessel, 1888), 7–96; Carl Betzold, ed., *Materialien der Deutschen Reichs-Verfassung*, vol. 1 (Berlin: Carl Habel, 1871–73), 725–71.

47. Huber, *Deutsche Verfassungsgeschichte*, 3:658–61, 898–900; Mommsen, "Die Verfassung des Deutschen Reichs," 51–56; Hugo Preuss, building on the work of Hänel, "Die organische Bedeutung der Art. 15 und 17 der Reichsverfassung," *Zeitschrift für die gesamte Staatswissenschaft* 45 (1889): 420–49; substantially in agreement with Preuss is Laband, *Staatsrecht*, 1:382, n. 2.

48. The kaiser himself was constitutionally barred from introducing bills.

49. Huber, *Deutsche Verfassungsgeschichte*, 3:850; Max Weber, "Parliament and Government in Germany" (1918), repr. in *Political Writings*, ed. Peter Lassman and Ronald Speirs (Cambridge: Cambridge University Press, 1994), 168–70.

50. Huber, *Deutsche Verfassungsgeschichte*, 3:956–57.

51. *Budgetrecht*, 3.

52. Austin, *The Province of Jurisprudence Determined*, ed. Wilfrid E. Rumble (Cambridge: Cambridge University Press, 1995), 212. See also A. V. Dicey, *Introduction to the Law of the Constitution*, 8th ed. (London: Macmillan, 1915), 1–36, on the doctrine of parliamentary supremacy.

53. Elisabeth Fehrenbach, *Wandlungen des deutschen Kaisergedankens 1871–1918* (Munich: Oldenbourg, 1969). The duty to countersign was extended to other ministers and subordinates by a decree of January 15, 1878, repr. in Huber, *Dokumente*, 2:312–14; see also Hänel, *Die organische Entwicklung*, 21–22; Laband, "Der Bundesrat" (1911), repr. in *Der Bundesrat. Die staatsrechtliche Entwicklung des föderalen Verfassungsorgans*, ed. Dieter Wilke and Bernd Schwelte (Darmstadt: Wissenschaftliche Buchgesellschaft, 1990), 40–50.

54. Böckenförde, "The German Type of Constitutional Monarchy," 107–9; Craig, *Politics of the Prussian Army*, 219–32, 238–51.

55. Bülow declared himself responsible in his speech to the Reichstag, as a tactic to make the kaiser appear irresponsible. The speech is reproduced in Huber, *Dokumente*, 2:440–41; Nipperdey, *Deutsche Geschichte 1866–1918*, 2:734–37.

56. Beverly Heckart, *From Bassermann to Bebel: The Grand Bloc's Quest for Reform in the Kaiserreich, 1900–1914* (New Haven: Yale University Press, 1974), 73–76; Huber, *Deutsche Verfassungsgeschichte*, 3:302–9. The concrete reforms, as presented by Georg Jellinek in 1908, fell far short of introducing a parliamentary system: "Die Verantwortlichkeit des Reichskanzlers" (1908), in *Ausgewählte Schriften und Reden*, vol. 2 (Berlin: O. Häring, 1911), 431–38. Jellinek was far from advocating parliamentarianism; he thought it could destroy the federalist foundations of the Reich; see "Bundesstaat und parlamentarische Regierung," in ibid., 2:439–47.

57. Nipperdey, *Deutsche Geschichte 1866–1918*, 2:85–98.

58. Samuel Pufendorf, *Die Verfassung des deutschen Reiches*, ed. and trans. Horst Denzer (Stuttgart: Reclam, 1985), 96–107.

59. Huber, *Deutsche Verfassungsgeschichte*, 3:767; Elisabeth Fehrenbach, "Reich," in *Geschichtliche Grundbegriffe. Historisches Lexikon zur politisch-sozialen Sprache in Deutschland*, vol. 5 (Stuttgart: Klett-Cotta, 1984), 504–5.

60. Boldt, *Deutsche Verfassungsgeschichte*, 2:179; Otto Heinrich Meisner, "Bundesrat, Bundeskanzler und Bundeskanzleramt (1867–1871)" (1943), repr. in *Moderne deutsche Verfassungsgeschichte (1815–1918)*, ed. Ernst-Wolfgang Böckenförde (Cologne: Kiepenheuer und Witsch, 1972), 76–77. The phrase "collective monarch" I borrow from Dieter Grimm. See Paul Laband, *Staatsrecht*, 1:97–98. See the summary of points in English in Woodrow Wilson, *The State. Elements of Historical and Practical Politics*, 2d ed. (Boston: D. C. Heath, 1903), 258–64.

61. Boldt, *Deutsche Verfassungsgeschichte*, 2:172–73; Reinhard Mussgnug, "Die Ausführung der Reichsgesetze durch die Länder und die Reichsaufsicht," in *Deutsche Verwaltungsgeschichte*, vol. 3: *Das Deutsche Reich bis zum Ende der Monarchie* (Stuttgart: Deutsche Verlags-Anstalt, 1984), 186–206.

62. Huber, *Deutsche Verfassungsgeschichte*, 3:806–8; Manfred Messerschmidt, *Die politische Geschichte der preussisch-deutschen Armee, Handbuch zur deutschen Militärgeschichte 1648–1939*, vol. 4, pt. 1: *Militärgeschichte im 19. Jahrhundert 1814–1890* (Munich: Bernard von Graefe, 1979), 210–13.

63. After 1911, Alsace-Lorraine gained three seats in the Bundesrat, raising the total to sixty-one.

64. Significantly, not "kaiser of Germany"—the state governments wanted to make clear that their territories did not belong to a higher monarch. See Huber, *Deutsche Verfassungsgeschichte*, 3:738–41.

65. Pflanze, *Bismarck and the Development of Germany*, 338–44; conservative dissatisfaction with Bismarck's unification is noted in Nipperdey, *Deutsche Geschichte 1866–1918*, 2:332–33; Mommsen, "Die Verfassung des Deutschen Reiches," 56–57; and idem, "Das deutsche Kaiserreich als System umgangener Entscheidungen,"

28; in general, see Kersten Rosenau, *Hegemonie und Dualismus. Preussens staatsrechtliche Stellung im Deutschen Reich* (Regensburg: S. Roderer, 1986), 39–63, 109–17.

66. Craig, *Politics of the Prussian Army*, 219–20; Messerschmidt, *Politische Geschichte*, 205–10.

67. Huber, *Deutsche Verfassungsgeschichte*, 3:825–29; Nipperdey, *Deutsche Geschichte 1866–1918*, 2:114–15; Arnold Brecht, *Federalism and Regionalism in Germany. The Division of Prussia* (New York: Oxford University Press, 1945), 17–18; and Rosenau, *Hegemonie und Dualismus*, 21–39.

68. Craig, *Politics of the Prussian Army*, 223–24.

69. Laband, *Staatsrecht*, 1:v.

70. See Max von Seydel's articles from the 1870s, repr. in *Staatsrechtliche und politische Abhandlungen* (Freiburg: J. C. B. Mohr [Paul Siebeck], 1893), 1–120; he also used Calhoun to introduce his *Commentar zur Verfassungs-Urkunde für das Deutsche Reich*, 2d ed. (Freiburg: J. C. B. Mohr [Paul Siebeck], 1897), 2–3. Justus B. Westerkamp, *Über die Reichsverfassung* (Hanover: Carl Rümpler, 1873). Albert Hänel's history of the United States up to the Civil War is in *Studien zum Deutschen Staatsrecht*, vol. 1: *Die vertragsmässigen Elemente der Deutschen Reichsverfassung*, 1–27. On the German debates over federalism in English, see Emerson, *State and Sovereignty*, 92–125 (93–96 on the U.S. example).

71. *Staatsrecht*, 1:64–65.

72. Ibid., 1:228–30.

73. Ibid., 1:68–69; Gerber, *Grundzüge*, 3–4, 4, n. 2, 46–47, n. 2, 19–22.

74. *Staatsrecht*, 1:72–75. On the notion of a nonsovereign state, see Emerson, *State and Sovereignty*, 100–105, and 53–55 on Gerber's idea of sovereignty.

75. Cf. Hugo Preuss's scathing criticism in "Zur Methode juristischer Begriffskonstruktion," *Schmollers Jahrbuch für Gesetzgebung, Verwaltung und Volkswirtschaft im Deutschen Reich* 24 (1900): 361.

76. *Staatsrecht*, 1:57, 97–102. This conception corresponded in no way to the actual alignment of power from the very beginning of the *Kaiserreich*, as Hänel notes in *Die organische Entwicklung der deutschen Reichsverfassung*, 24–30. Woodrow Wilson summarizes Laband in *The State*, 258–59. See also Emerson, *State and Sovereignty*, 105–6.

77. Seydel, *Commentar*, 2d ed., 5–6.

78. Laband, *Staatsrecht*, 1:68–69.

79. Friedrich Müller has noted how the dogma of the closed, unified legal order is related to legitimating the centralized, planning state of absolutism: *Die Einheit der Verfassung. Elemente einer Verfassungstheorie III* (Berlin: Duncker und Humblot, 1979), 92–94; idem, *Juristische Methodik*, 68–70.

80. Gerber, *Über öffentliche Rechte*, 62–66, 76–77; and *Grundzüge*, 33–35, 227–28; Pauly, *Methodenwandel*, 121, 157–68.

81. *Grundzüge,* 35ff. on specific rights, also 207-9. Pauly, *Methodenwandel,* 141, notes the addition of the *Staatswille* to Gerber's 1865 work.

82. *Staatsrecht,* 1:150-51. Specific rights often appear in Laband's work as no more than administrative directives; see, e.g., *Staatsrecht,* 3:60-65. He devotes more space to the notion of duty, esp. in 1:140-50.

83. Further elaboration of this point is in Georg Jellinek, *System der subjektiven öffentlichen Rechte,* 2d ed. (Tübingen: J. C. B. Mohr [Paul Siebeck], 1919), 42-43.

84. Boldt, *Deutsche Verfassungsgeschichte,* 2:103-4. The Prussian Landtag extended Arts. 40 and 42 in the 1850s to secure further the free exchange of property. See von Rönne, *Das Staats-Recht der preussischen Monarchie,* vol. 1, pt. 2, 81-91, 127-40; Huber, *Deutsche Verfassungsgeschichte,* 2:312-13.

85. Huber, *Deutsche Verfassungsgeschichte,* 3:104-5; he makes a similar point with respect to Art. 9 on property rights at 110-11.

86. In addition, local authorities retained rights to regulate assembly and rules prohibiting women, students, or apprentices (*Gesellen*) from becoming members of political clubs; see von Rönne, *Das Staats-Recht der preussischen Monarchie,* vol. 1, pt. 2, 209-10.

87. In general, see Ute Gerhard, *Verhältnisse und Verhinderungen. Frauenarbeit, Familie und Rechte der Frauen im 19. Jahrhundert* (Frankfurt am Main: Suhrkamp, 1978).

88. Grimm analyzes Bluntschli's postrevolutionary theory of rights in "Die Entwicklung der Grundrechtstheorie," 324. Karl Marx analyzes a similar attempt to limit rights by statute in "The Constitution of the French Republic Adopted November 4, 1848" (1851, in English original), in *Marx-Engels Collected Works,* vol. 10 (Moscow: Progress, 1978), 569-70.

89. Austin, *The Province of Jurisprudence Defined,* 212; Dicey discusses Parliament's right to suspend habeas corpus in *The Law of the Constitution,* 139-42.

90. Jacques Ellul, *Histoire des Institutions,* vol. 5: *Le XIXe siècle,* 6th ed. (Paris: Presses Universitaires de France, 1969), 318; abnegation of constitutional articles did, however, require a special assembly of both houses: Dicey, *Law of the Constitution,* 62-64.

91. Roel de Lange, "Paradoxes of European Citizenship," in *Nationalism, Racism and the Rule of Law,* ed. Peter Fitzpatrick (Aldershot: Dartmouth University Press, 1995), 97-115.

92. Huber, "Grundrechte im Bismarckschen Rechtssystem," 167-70. For the examples of the rights to a free press and to free assembly, see Huber, *Dokumente,* 2:368-78.

93. Huber, *Deutsche Verfassungsgeschichte,* 3:665-66; Boldt, *Deutsche Verfassungsgeschichte,* 2:180-81.

94. Betzold, *Materialien der Deutschen Reichs-Verfassung,* 1:401ff., esp. 431-53; and 2:896-1010 (1873), esp. 956-63; Huber, "Grundrechte," 163-64; on Catholi-

cism as a threat to liberalism, see Margaret Lavinia Anderson, "The Kulturkampf and the Course of German History," *Central European History* 19 (1986): 82-115; and Vernon L. Lidtke, "Catholics and Protestants in Nineteenth-Century Germany. A Comment," *Central European History* 19 (1986): 120-22.

95. Grimm, "Die Entwicklung der Grundrechtstheorie in der deutschen Staatsrechtslehre des 19. Jahrhunderts" (1987), repr. in *Recht und Staat der bürgerlichen Gesellschaft*, 343-44; Friedrich Müller, "Der Vorbehalt des Gesetzes" (1960), repr. in *Rechtsstaatliche Form Demokratische Politik. Beiträge zu öffentlichem Recht, Methodik, Rechts- und Staatstheorie* (Berlin: Duncker und Humblot, 1977), 15-47, esp. 17-21; Gerhard Lassar, "Administrative Jurisdiction in Germany," *Economica* 7 (1927): 179-90.

96. See, e.g., Otto Mayer, *Deutsches Verwaltungsrecht* (Leipzig: Duncker und Humblot, 1895), 104-18; and Conrad Bornhak, *Grundriss des Verwaltungsrechts in Preussen und dem Deutschen Reiche*, 3d ed. (Leipzig: Deichert, 1911), 98: "subjective rights are impossible," and 122-24 on how rights affect the administration. Mayer tempered his views in his second edition (106-16, esp. 110, n. 7), in which he opposed his theory to the police state, as exemplified in Bornhak's work. See Grimm, "Die Entwicklung der Grundrechtstheorie," 344.

97. Ulrich Scheuner, "Die Überlieferung der deutschen Staatsgerichtsbarkeit im 19. und 20. Jahrhundert," in *Bundesverfassungsgericht und Grundgesetz. Festgabe aus Anlass des 25jährigen Bestehens des Bundesverfassungsgerichts*, vol. 1, ed. L. Stark (Tübingen: J. C. B. Mohr [Paul Siebeck], 1976), 2-41; Huber, *Deutsche Verfassungsgeschichte*, 3:974-84, 1055-64.

98. Huber, "Grundrechte," 175-76.

99. Friedrich Giese, *Die Grundrechte* (Tübingen: J. C. B. Mohr [Paul Siebeck], 1905), 1.

100. Jellinek was born in Leipzig but made his career in Austria until anti-Semitism forced him to leave. See Camilla Jellinek and Josef Lukas, "Georg Jellinek. Sein Leben," in *Neue Österreichische Biographie*, vol. 7 (Vienna: Amalthea, 1931), 136-52.

101. *Die Erklärung der Menschen- und Bürgerrechte. Ein Beitrag zur modernen Verfassungsgeschichte*, 2d ed. (Leipzig: Duncker und Humblot, 1904).

102. Ibid., 26.

103. This position is made most clearly and explicitly in Karl Bergbohm, *Jurisprudenz und Rechtsphilosophie. Kritische Abhandlungen*, vol. 1 [only volume to appear]: *Einleitung—Erste Abhandlung: Das Naturrecht der Gegenwart* (Leipzig: Duncker und Humblot, 1892).

104. *System*, 8-9, 15-20; see 12-41 for Jellinek's reflections on epistemology and legal science; see also *Allgemeine Staatslehre*, 3d ed. (Berlin: O. Häring, 1914), 19-21, 50-52, and 473-74 on Gerber and the definition of sovereignty.

105. *System*, 40-41; 45-48 on *Können* and *Dürfen*; 9-10 on the possibility of pub-

lic law; 84–86 on "Asiatic despotism," in which only one human is a legal person, the absolute ruler.

106. At ibid., 71, Jellinek explicitly notes the increased rights embodied in the expanding system of administrative review. On Jellinek's discussion of administrative review and its continued relevance, see Stolleis, *Geschichte des öffentlichen Rechts*, 2:375–76.

107. Jellinek, *System*, 44; Grimm, "Die Entwicklung der Grundrechtstheorie," 344; Emerson, *State and Sovereignty*, 83–85.

108. *System*, 96–101, 71–72.

109. On Jellinek's notion of "objective" subjective rights, see Massimo la Torre, " 'Rechtsstaat' and Legal Science. The Rise and Fall of the Concept of Subjective Right," *Archiv für Rechts- und Sozialphilosophie* 76 (1990): 50–68.

110. *Staatsrecht*, 2:39–40.

111. Ibid., 2:40–41.

112. Ibid., 2:42–52. These arguments confused Laband's otherwise admiring U.S. readers. See, e.g., John W. Burgess, "Laband's Public Law of the German Empire," *Political Science Quarterly* 3 (1888): 132–35; and the review of the second edition in *Political Science Quarterly* 6 (1891): 174. Emerson notes the proximity of Laband's theory of monarchical sanction to constitutional monarchism in *State and Sovereignty*, 68–69.

113. This is not to say that Laband rejected all value-based arguments about the constitution. As Bernhard Schlink has noted, Laband used precisely such arguments as a politician in the State Council of Alsace-Lorraine: "Laband als Politiker," 563.

114. See Martin Kriele, *Theorie der Rechtsgewinnung*, 40–43, on the nonpractical nature of *Kaiserreich* constitutional theory.

115. "Die Wandlungen in der Deutschen Reichsverfassung," originally printed in *Jahrbuch der Gehe-Stiftung zu Dresden* 1 (1895): 149–86, repr. in Laband, *Abhandlungen, Beiträge, Reden und Rezensionen*, 1:574–611 (citations follow the 1895 numbering). On the *Gehe-Stiftung*, see T. Petermann, "Die Gehe-Stiftung zu Dresden in den ersten 15 Jahren ihrer Thätigkeit," in Heinrich Dietzel, *Weltwirtschaft und Volkswirtschaft, Jahrbuch der Gehe-Stiftung zu Dresden*, 5 (1900): i–xvii.

116. "Die Wandlungen in der Deutschen Reichsverfassung," 150. Viewing the constitution as a quasi-religious object had been an important part of Vormärz constitutionalism, as Paul Nolte points out in "Die badischen Verfassungsfeste im Vormärz. Liberalismus, Verfassungskultur und soziale Ordnung in den Gemeinden," in *Bürgerliche Feste. Symbolische Formen politischen Handelns im 19. Jahrhundert*, ed. Manfred Hettling and Paul Nolte (Göttingen: Vandenhoeck und Ruprecht, 1993), 63–94.

117. "Die Wandlungen in der deutschen Reichsverfassung," 161–69; Boldt, *Deutsche Verfassungsgeschichte*, 2:192–93.

118. "Die Wandlungen in der Deutschen Reichsverfassung," 169–79. Laband stressed the way these changes limited the maneuverability of the *Reich* itself—a position borne out by later experiences with growing deficits related to the Navy Bills. See Volker Berghahn, *Germany and the Approach of War in 1914*, 2d ed. (New York: St. Martin's Press, 1993), 86.

119. "Die Wandlungen in der Deutschen Reichsverfassung," 180–84.

120. Ibid., 151. The metaphor is an altered version of one used by Hugo Preuss in *Reichs- und Landesfinanzen* (Berlin: Leonhard Simon, 1894), 28–29. Throughout this essay Laband relies on the work of his "organic" opponents in state law to describe the existing state.

121. In Niklas Luhmann's phrase, the system was "normatively closed, but cognitively open"; "The Unity of the Legal System," in *Autopoietic Law: A New Approach to Law and Society*, ed. Gunther Teubner (Berlin: Walter de Gruyter, 1988), 12–35.

122. Gierke, "Labands Staatsrecht," 35; Eckart Kehr, "The Social System of Reaction in Prussia under the Puttkamer Ministry," in *Economic Interest, Militarism, and Foreign Policy: Essays in German History*, ed. Gordon Craig, trans. Grete Heinz (Berkeley: University of California Press, 1977), esp. 116: "Laband's constitutional law was attuned not only to Bismarck's police state, but even more specifically to a police state along capitalist lines." Also see Hermann Klenner, *Deutsche Rechtsphilosophie im 19. Jahrhundert* (Berlin: Akademie, 1991), 188–89.

123. See, e.g., Léon Duguit, *Law in the Modern State*, trans. Frida Laski and Harold Laski (London: Allen and Unwin, 1921), 32–39 on Hauriou, Esmein, and Barthélemy; and 28–29 on the "absolutist" notion of sovereignty in Rousseau and Laband; also see H. S. Jones, *The French State in Question: Public Law and Political Argument in the Third Republic* (New York: Cambridge University Press, 1993); Stig Strömholm, *A Short History of Legal Thinking in the West* (Stockholm: Norstedts, 1985), 278–80.

124. Introduction to *Introduction to the Study of the Law of the Constitution*. See also George Dangerfield's overstated thesis in *The Strange Death of Liberal England* (New York: Smith and Haas, 1935); and the more recent Marxist defense of his thesis: Stuart Hall and Bill Schwarz, "State and Society, 1880–1930," in *Crises in the British State 1880–1930*, ed. Mary Langan and Bill Schwarz (London: Hutchinson, 1985), 7–32.

2 The Purity of Law and Military Dictatorship

1. Stolleis, *Geschichte des öffentlichen Rechts*, 2:359–64. On Kaufmann and Smend: Stefan Korioth, "Erschütterungen des staatsrechtlichen Positivismus im ausgehenden Kaiserreich," *Archiv des öffentlichen Rechts* 117 (1992): 212–38.

2. Felix Stoerk, *Zur Methodik des öffentlichen Rechts* (Vienna: Alfred Hölder, 1885), 112; Pauly, *Methodenwandel*, 236–40.

3. On Hänel: Manfred Friedrich, *Zwischen Positivismus und materialem Verfassungsdenken. Albert Hänel und seine Bedeutung für die deutsche Staatsrechtswissenschaft* (Berlin: Duncker und Humblot, 1971). On Kohler: Wolfgang Schild, "Die Ambivalenz einer Neo-Philosophie. Zu Josef Kohlers Neuhegelianismus," in *Deutsche Rechts- und Sozialphilosophie um 1900, Archiv für Rechts- und Sozialphilosophie,* Beiheft 43, ed. Gerhard Sprenger (Stuttgart: Franz Steiner, 1991), 46–65. In general: Hermann Klenner, "Rechtsphilosophie im Deutschen Kaiserreich," in ibid., 7–17; idem, *Rechtsphilosophie im 19. Jahrhundert,* 196–208. Finally, see Stolleis's exhaustive enumeration of positions in *Geschichte des öffentlichen Rechts,* 2:344–64.

4. *Die rechtliche Natur der Staatenverträge. Ein Beitrag zur juristischen Construktion des Völkerrechts* (Vienna: Alfred Hölder, 1880), 32.

5. Georg Jellinek, *Die Lehre von den Staatenverbindungen* (Vienna: Alfred Hölder, 1882), 18–22; *System,* 8–12; *Allgemeine Staatslehre,* 476–77. See the general account in Emerson, *State and Sovereignty,* 59–68.

6. *Lehre von den Staatenverbindungen,* 16–36; *Allgemeine Staatslehre,* 10–12, 19–21. See Kurt Sontheimer, *Politische Wissenschaft und Staatsrechtslehre* (Freiburg: Rembach, 1962), 16–25; in English: Edgar Bodenheimer, *Jurisprudence* (New York: McGraw-Hill, 1940), 208–14.

7. E.g., *Die rechtliche Natur der Staatenverträge,* 57–59.

8. *Allgemeine Staatslehre,* 16–17, 51–52.

9. Ibid., 355–61.

10. See Max-Emanuel Geis, "Der Methoden- und Richtungsstreit in der Weimarer Staatslehre," *Juristische Schulung* 29 (1989): 91–92. On Jellinek as an Austrian of Jewish descent in the increasingly anti-Semitic German Empire: Stolleis, *Geschichte des öffentlichen Rechts,* 2:442; Nipperdey, *Deutsche Geschichte 1866–1918,* 1:661. Cf. Klaus Rennert, *Die "geisteswissenschaftliche Richtung" in der Staatsrechtslehre der Weimarer Republik. Untersuchungen zu Erich Kaufmann, Günther Holstein und Rudolf Smend* (Berlin: Duncker und Humblot, 1987), 55–56; and Pauly, *Methodenwandel,* 219–23, who argue that Jellinek, by considering sociology, deviated from Laband's school. In fact, Laband himself did not deny the significance of social facts, although he denied their validity within a dogmatic science of law, a position with which Jellinek was substantially in agreement.

11. Luigi Lombardi Vallauri, *Geschichte des Freirechts,* trans. Lombardi and A. S. Fouckes (Frankfurt am Main: Vittorio Klostermann, 1971); Klaus Riebschläger, *Die Freirechtsbewegung. Zur Entstehung einer soziologischen Rechtsschule* (Berlin: Duncker und Humblot, 1968); Dietmar Moench, *Die methodologischen Bestrebungen der Freirechtsbewegung auf dem Wege zur Methodenlehre der Gegenwart*

(Frankfurt am Main: Athenäum, 1971); Rainer Schröder, "Die deutsche Methodendiskussion um die Jahrhundertwende: wissenstheoretische Präzisierungsversuche oder Antworten auf den Funktionswandel von Recht und Justiz," *Rechtstheorie* 19 (1988): 323–67. In English, see Albert S. Fouckes, "On the German Free Law School (Freirechtsschule)," *Archiv für Rechts- und Sozialphilosophie* 55 (1969): 366–417; James E. Herget and Stephen Wallace, "The German Free Law Movement as the Source of American Legal Realism," *Virginia Law Review* 73 (1987): 399–455; James E. Herget, "Unearthing the Origins of a Radical Idea: The Case of Legal Indeterminacy" [with accompanying translation of Oskar von Bülow, "Gesetz und Richteramt"], *American Journal of Legal History* 39 (1995): 59–94.

12. Riebschläger, *Die Freirechtsbewegung*, 19–25.

13. Gnaeus Flavius [Kantorowicz], *Der Kampf um die Rechtswissenschaft* (Heidelberg: Carl Winter, 1906), 7. On Kantorowicz, see Karlheinz Muscheler, *Relativismus und Freiheit. Ein Versuch über Hermann Kantorowicz* (Heidelberg: C. F. Müller, 1984).

14. The word *gap*—which Bismarck had already made popular in his theory of the budget crisis—was introduced to private law in an article by Eugen Ehrlich, "Über Lücken im Recht" (1888), repr. in *Recht und Leben. Gesammelte Schriften zur Rechtstatsachenforschung und zur Freirechtslehre,* ed. M. Rehbinder (Berlin: Duncker und Humblot, 1967).

15. Max Rumpf, *Gesetz und Richter. Versuch einer Methodik der Rechtsanwendung* (Berlin: Otto Liebmann, 1906). Ehrlich's most important early articles are collected in *Recht und Leben;* see also his *Fundamental Principles of the Sociology of Law,* esp. chs. 1 and 6. Heck's basic position is in "Interessenjurisprudenz und Gesetzestreue" (1905), repr. in *Interessenjurisprudenz,* ed. Günter Ellschied and Winfried Hassemer (Darmstadt: Wissenschaftliche Buchgesellschaft, 1974), 32–35. See also Johann Edelmann, *Die Entwicklung der Interessenjurisprudenz. Eine historisch-kritische Studie über die deutsche Rechtsmethodologie vom 18. Jahrhundert bis zum Gegenwart* (Bad Homburg vor der Höhe: Max Gehlen, 1967), 82–100.

16. Okko Behrends, "Von der Freirechtsschule zum konkreten Ordnungsdenken," in *Recht und Justiz im "Dritten Reich,"* ed. Ralf Dreier and Wolfgang Sellert (Frankfurt am Main: Suhrkamp, 1989), 52–53, 57–58. Max Weber accused the latter group of seeking to aggrandize their power: *Economy and Society: An Outline of Interpretive Sociology,* ed. Guenther Roth and Claus Wittich (New York: Bedminster, 1968), 889–90. See, however, the moderating comments in Kriele, *Theorie der Rechtsgewinnung*, 63–66.

17. Lombardi, *Geschichte des Freirechts*, 65–69; Fouckes, "On the German Free Law School," 384–85; Herget and Wallace, "The German Free Law Movement," 437–39.

18. See Anschütz, "Lücken in den Verfassungs- und Verwaltungsgesetzen.

Skizze zu einem Vortrage," *Verwaltungsarchiv* 14 (1906): 315-40; Jellinek, *Allgemeine Staatslehre*, 355-58; and for an example of such thought prior to the Free Law critique, Siegfried Brie, "Zur Theorie des constitutionellen Staatsrechts," *Archiv für öffentliches Recht* 4 (1889): 24-35, cited in Jellinek.

19. Kelsen was born in 1881, Smend in 1882, Schmitt in 1888, and Heller in 1891.

20. According to Camilla Jellinek, Georg Jellinek attended Treitschke's lectures in 1870 in Heidelberg: "Georg Jellinek was so filled with enthusiasm that he had wanted to march into war as a volunteer, and he only gave in with a heavy heart when his parents put their foot down" ("Georg Jellinek," 137).

21. Stolleis, *Geschichte des öffentlichen Rechts*, 2:447-55; Emerson, *State and Sovereignty*, 155; cf. Carl Schorske, *Fin de siècle Vienna* (New York: Vintage, 1981).

22. Kelsen, *Hauptprobleme*. Although the main body of the text was reprinted verbatim in the 1923 second edition, a new foreword was added, which I refer to hereafter as the "1923 Foreword."

23. On neo-Kantianism in law, see Emerson, *State and Sovereignty*, 159-85. On the neo-Kantian philosophers, see *Neukantianismus. Texte der Marburger und der Südwestdeutscher Schule, ihrer Vorläufer und Kritiker*, ed. Hans-Ludwig Ollig (Stuttgart: Reclam, 1982), along with basic texts. In English, see Thomas Willey, *Back to Kant: The Revival of Kantianism in German Social and Historical Thought, 1860-1914* (Detroit: Wayne State University Press, 1978).

24. Jellinek, *System*, 13.

25. *Hauptprobleme*, 1923 Foreword, xvii-xviii, describes Kelsen's turn to Hermann Cohen's work; see also Kelsen's letter dated August 3, 1933, to Renato Treves, trans. into French by Giorgio Bomio, "Un inédit de Kelsen," in *Droit et Société* 7 (1987): 333-35. Chapter 4 discusses Kelsen's neo-Kantianism in more detail, with references to the literature.

26. Kelsen wrote his 1911 work explicitly as a contribution to the "neoliberal" camp (1911 Foreword, xi), a relationship worked out by Paul Silverman in "Law and Economics in Interwar Vienna. Kelsen, Mises, and the Regeneration of Austrian Liberalism" (Ph.D. diss., University of Chicago, 1984). The very "unsubstantial" nature of the Austro-Hungarian state—its lack of a unified *Volk*—may have contributed to Kelsen's abstract and formal construction of the state. See Rudolf Aladar Métall, *Hans Kelsen. Leben und Werk* (Vienna: Franz Deuticke, 1969), 42. On the concept of neoliberalism, see Wilhelm Wadl, *Liberalismus und soziale Frage in Österreich. Deutschliberale Reaktionen und Einflüsse auf die frühe österreichische Arbeiterbewegung (1867-1879)* (Vienna: Österreichische Akademie der Wissenschaften, 1987), 19-20; and John W. Boyer, "Freud, Marriage, and Late Viennese Liberalism: A Commentary from 1905," *Journal of Modern History* 50 (1978): 73-82.

27. *Hauptprobleme*, 1911 Foreword, xiii; Métall, *Hans Kelsen*, 7-17; a harsh judg-

ment of Kelsen's "traditional" approach is in Alf Ross, *Towards a Realistic Juris-prudence: A Criticism of the Dualism in Law*, trans. Annie I. Fausbøll (1946; repr., Aalen: Scientia, 1989), 40.

28. *Hauptprobleme*, 1911 Foreword, iii. Kelsen defined the reconstructed legal norm as the "hypothetical judgment on a conditioned will of the state" (ibid., 211). On the concept, see Paulson's explanatory notes to Kelsen, *Introduction to the Problems of Legal Theory*, 132-34; and Friedrich Tenzer, "Betrachtungen über Kelsens Lehre vom Rechtssatz," *Archiv des öffentlichen Rechts* 28 (1912): 325-26.

29. *Hauptprobleme*, 8.

30. Ibid., 3-11; 1911 Foreword, vi-vii.

31. *Hauptprobleme*, 1911 Foreword, iv-v, ix-x. The point constitutes a break with the neo-Kantian tradition of legal thought following Rickert and Lask, which concentrated on culture, values, and meaning (*Sinn*). See Kelsen's critique, "Rechtswissenschaft als Norm- oder als Kulturwissenschaft. Eine methodenkritische Untersuchung" (1916), in *Wiener Rechtstheoretische Schule*, 37-93.

32. *Hauptprobleme*, 11. The rejection of Kant's ethical theory was a standard motif among the neo-Kantians. See Uwe Justus Wenzel, "Recht und Moral der Vernunft. Kants Rechtslehre: Neue Literatur und neue Editionen," *Archiv für Rechts- und Sozialphilosophie* 76 (1990): 228; and Kelsen's own explicit discussion in "Un inédit de Kelsen," 334-35.

33. *Hauptprobleme*, 53-55. Kelsen also made the argument for the heteronomy of law from an argument for free will, a necessary concept for legal scholarship: ibid., 158-59, 191-92.

34. The logic of this position and its break from will-based legal positivism is brought out in Stanley L. Paulson, "Continental Normativism and Its British Counterpart: How Different Are They?" *Ratio Juris* 6 (1993): 227-44.

35. *Hauptprobleme*, 19.

36. Ibid., 133-46.

37. Ibid., 73; Silverman points out the key example of torts in Kelsen's theory in "Law and Economics," 209-15.

38. *Hauptprobleme*, 71-72; on the distinction between *Mensch* and *Person*: 122, 145-46, 518-19.

39. Ibid., 182-84, 396, 411-12, 435.

40. The conservative positivist philosopher Ernst Topitsch emphasizes this conception of ideology in his collection of Kelsen's essays, *Aufsätze zur Ideologiekritik* (Neuwied: Luchterhand, 1964). Peter Römer provides a both critical and appreciative reading in "Die Reine Rechtslehre Hans Kelsens als Ideologie und Ideologiekritik," *Politische Vierteljahresschrift* 12 (1971): 579-98. A critical interpretation of Kelsen is in Ljubomir Tadich, "Kelsen et Marx. Contribution au problème de l'idéologie dans 'la théorie pure de droit' et dans le marxisme," *Archives de Phi-*

losophie du Droit 12 (1967): 243–57. Finally, for a defense of Kelsen against his immediate post-1945 natural law critics, see Norberto Bobbio, "La teoría pura del derecho y sus críticos" (1957), trans. Mario Cerda Median, in *Hans Kelsen 1881–1973*, ed. Agustín Squella (Valparaiso: *Revista de ciencias sociales*, 1974), 299–326.

41. *Hauptprobleme*, 162–88. See the summary of the critique in Stanley L. Paulson, "Toward a Periodization of the Pure Theory of Law," 19–30. Pauly, *Methodenwandel*, 219–23, argues that Laband and Kelsen made similar methodological criticisms of Jellinek's theory of "self-limitation"; he misses the critical difference between the two. See Laband's critique of "autolimitation" on the basis of the real, existing will of the state, in his review of A. Mérignhac, *Traité de Droit public international*, in *Archiv für öffentliches Recht* 20 (1906): 302–5.

42. *Hauptprobleme*, 185–87.

43. Ibid., 99, 269–70, 630–31; 1911 Foreword, x. In later works Kelsen would argue that the public/private distinction in legal scholarship served primarily ideological purposes. See, esp., "Rechtsstaat und Staatsrecht" (1913), repr. in *Wiener Rechtstheoretische Schule*, 1525–32.

44. *Hauptprobleme*, 446–47.

45. Ibid., 245–49, 434, 511; on his later position, see 1923 Foreword, x–xii. See also Manfred Pascher, "Hermann Cohens Einfluss auf Kelsens Reine Rechtslehre," *Rechtstheorie* 23 (1992): 457–58.

46. *Hauptprobleme*, 226–27.

47. Ibid., 396–97.

48. Ibid., 40–43.

49. Ibid., 407–12, 479–80.

50. Ibid., 10. Roughly translated: "I can say: I should will, but I cannot say: I should should, which would be just as logically nonsensical as: I want to want to." See also 409, 466, 440–41.

51. Ibid., 410–11.

52. Ibid., 50–51, 247, 334. See his later self-critique: 1923 Foreword, xiv.

53. Ibid., 412–29.

54. The Austrian monarch's constitutional position after 1867 with regard to legislation and administration mirrored that of the German monarch. See Otto Stoly, *Grundriss der Österreichischen Verfassungs- und Verwaltungsgeschichte* (Innsbruck: Tyrolia, 1951), 88–89, 118–19, 122ff.

55. *Hauptprobleme*, 684.

56. Ibid., 689–90. Despite his playing down the metaphor, he employs versions of it several times to describe the monarch in ibid., 247, 684, 687, 692.

57. Ibid., 416–17, 687.

58. Ibid., 687–90. Kelsen's further argument that in practice only the minister, not the monarch, makes the truly important decisions has no bearing on the legal argument, according to Kelsen's own theoretical principles.

59. E.g., Gerber, *Grundzüge*, 77–79. Kelsen's static distinction between legislation and execution, for example, allowed him to criticize Laband's notion that some ordinances are statutes in a substantive sense as a political ploy to undermine constitutionalism. See "Zur Lehre vom Gesetz im formellen und materiellen Sinn, mit besonderer Berücksichtigung der österreichischen Verfassung" (1913), repr. in *Wiener Rechtstheoretische Schule*, 1533–43.

60. *Hauptprobleme*, 441–42, n. 1.

61. Ibid., 235–37; see also 257–58, and 15–16, 495–97, where the administration is not included on the grounds that it is practical, not theoretical.

62. Carl Schmitt, *Gesetz und Urteil. Eine Untersuchung zum Problem der Rechtspraxis* (1912; repr., Munich: C. H. Beck, 1969), 2; and Schmitt, *Der Wert des Staates und die Bedeutung des Einzelnen* (Tübingen: J. C. B. Mohr [Paul Siebeck], 1914), esp. ch. 1 ("Recht und Macht"), 31–35, in which Schmitt separates law (*Recht*) from power, as well as from will, ethics, and substantial goals (*Zwecke*). The connection between Schmitt and Kelsen was noted even before the war: Franz Weyr, review of *Wert des Staates* in *Österreichische Zeitschrift für öffentliches Recht* 1 (1914): 578–81. Hasso Hofmann asserts an essential difference between the two in *Legitimität gegen Legalität. Der Weg der politischen Philosophie Carl Schmitts* (Neuwied: Luchterhand, 1964), 44–45, n. 16; Schmitt flatly denies the relationship in *Die Diktatur. Von den Anfängen des modernen Souveränitätsgedankens bis zum proletarischen Klassenkampf*, 3d ed. (Berlin: Duncker und Humblot, 1964), xix–xx.

63. *Gesetz und Urteil*, 3, 20–21, 40–45, and elsewhere. See, especially, Schmitt's critique of legislative will as a "fiction" (26–28), which he also refers to as a "ghost" (30–32), both terms reminiscent of Kelsen. Both men turned to Vaihinger's theory of the "as if" during this period to discuss fictions and hypotheses; see Schmitt's "Juristische Fiktionen," *Deutsche Juristen-Zeitung* 18 (1913): 804–6; and Kelsen's critique of Vaihinger, "Zur Theorie der juristischen Fiktionen. Mit besonderer Berücksichtigung von Vaihingers Philosophie des Als Ob," *Vaihingers Annalen der Philosophie* 1 (1919): 630–58.

64. *Gesetz und Urteil*, 49–55.

65. Ibid., 69.

66. Ibid., 71; see also vii, 55–56, 77–79.

67. See ibid., 71–72, 116–18, where Schmitt claims to have avoided the problems of caprice and subjectivity. See also the excellent review by Felix Holdack in *Kantstudien* 17 (1912): 464–67; and Michael Stolleis, "Carl Schmitt," in Sattler, ed., *Staat und Recht*, 128. Hofmann's argument that Schmitt avoided falling back into the problem of sources (*Legitimität gegen Legalität*, 34–35) is unconvincing so long as legal predictability remains an important consideration.

68. *Gesetz und Urteil*, 49–55; see also *Wert des Staates*, 80; and Hofmann, *Legitimität gegen Legalität*, 31, 36–38.

69. *Wert des Staates*, 2–3, 52, 68; see also Helmut Rumpf, *Carl Schmitt und*

Thomas Hobbes. Ideelle Beziehungen und aktuelle Bedeutung mit einer Abhandlung über: Die Frühschriften Carl Schmitts (Berlin: Duncker und Humblot, 1972), 13–17. The formulation is reminiscent of Kelsen, *Hauptprobleme,* 511: "If the legal person of the state is only the product of the legal order, then the realization of the legal order is the only function of the state."

70. *Wert des Staates,* 73–78, 46, 53. This argument seems to me less Catholic natural law theory that we moderns cannot understand (cf. Rumpf, *Carl Schmitt und Thomas Hobbes,* 15) than an assertion—laden with unresolved problems—that the state has a kind of supernatural legitimation as such. See also Lorenz Kiefer, "Begründung, Dezision und Politische Theologie. Zu drei frühen Schriften von Carl Schmitt," *Archiv für Rechts- und Sozialphilosophie* 76 (1990): 485-89.

71. *Wert des Staates,* ch. 3.

72. On neo-Hegelianism, see Georg Lukács, *Die Zerstörung der Vernunft* (1962), repr. in *Werke,* vol. 9 (Neuwied: Luchterhand, 1974), 474–505; Emerson, *State and Sovereignty,* 186–200; and Walter Friedmann, *Legal Theory,* 5th ed. (New York: Columbia University Press, 1967), 174–76, on the connection between neo-Hegelianism and fascism. On Schmitt's highly selective appropriation of Hegel: Reinhard Mehring, *Pathetisches Denken. Carl Schmitts Denkweg am Leitfaden Hegels: Katholische Grundstellung und antimarxistische Hegelstrategie* (Berlin: Duncker und Humblot, 1989), 20, 106-10; Jean-François Kervegan, "Politik und Vernünftigkeit. Anmerkungen zum Verhältnis zwischen Carl Schmitt und Hegel," *Der Staat* 27 (1988): 371–91. John McCormick pointed out to me that the state in *Wert des Staates* is not yet the authoritarian substance that it came to be when Schmitt broke completely with neo-Kantianism. Nevertheless, by making the state a real, mediating entity, it seems that Schmitt was already moving beyond the neo-Kantian theory of the two sides.

73. Such an argument presents an ongoing theme in *Wert des Staates,* esp. 54–55, 81–83; see also Schmitt, "Die Sichtbarkeit der Kirche," in *Summa* 1 (1917), esp. 76–77; and, in the Weimar Republic, idem, *Römischer Katholizismus und politische Form* (1923; repr., Stuttgart: Klett-Cotta, 1984), 49–50.

74. Schmitt later stated that his statements on "political theology" were "assertions of a legal scholar about a systematic structural kinship, both in legal theory and legal practice, between theological and juristic concepts" (*Politische Theologie II. Die Legende von der Erledigung jeder politischen Theologie* [Berlin: Duncker und Humblot, 1970], 101, n. 1). For a short, analytical discussion of the problem, see Ernst-Wolfgang Böckenförde, "Politische Theorie und politische Theologie. Bemerkungen zu ihrem gegenseitigen Verhältnis," in *Fürst dieser Welt,* ed. Jacob Taubes (Munich: Wilhelm Fink, 1983), 16–25.

75. E.g., Erich Kaufmann's glorification of the "ethical state" as real will in *Das Wesen des Völkerrechts und die clausula rebus sic stantibus. Rechtsphilosophische Studie*

zum Rechts-, Staats- und Vertragsbegriffe (Tübingen: J. C. B. Mohr [Paul Siebeck], 1911). Reinhard Mehring comments on Schmitt's supposedly "Catholic" authoritarianism, implying that Protestantism is more worldly and liberal, in "Zu den neugesammelten Schriften und Studien Ernst-Wolfgang Böckenfördes," *Archiv des öffentlichen Rechts* 117 (1992): 449-73. A more balanced judgment, placing Schmitt on the authoritarian right wing of political Catholicism, is in Karl-Egon Lönne, "Carl Schmitt und der Katholizismus der Weimarer Republik," in *Die eigentlich katholische Verschärfung . . . Katholizismus, Theologie und Politik im Werk Carl Schmitts,* ed. Bernd Wacker (Munich: Wilhelm Fink, 1994), 11-35.

76. Martin Kitchen, *The Silent Dictatorship. The Politics of the German High Command under Hindenburg and Ludendorff, 1916-1918* (London: Croom Helm, 1976). Gerald D. Feldman, *Army, Industry and Labor in Germany, 1914-1918* (Princeton: Princeton University Press, 1966), 407-8, 499-500, suggests that the "dictatorship" (his quotation marks) was greatly limited in its actual power; Hans Fenske argues that the High Command had only a "supremacy" among a number of powers in "Die Verwaltung im Ersten Weltkrieg," *Deutsche Verwaltungsgeschichte,* vol. 3: *Das Deutsche Reich bis zum Ende der Monarchie* (Stuttgart: Deutsche Verlags-Anstalt, 1984), 875-76.

77. Albrecht Mendelssohn-Bartholdy, *The War and German Society. The Testament of a Liberal* (1937; repr., New York: Howard Fertig, 1971), esp. chs. 8-10.

78. Laband, *Staatsrecht,* 4:43-51.

79. With the exception of Bavaria; see Huber, *Deutsche Verfassungsgeschichte* 3:1044-45.

80. Schmitt, "Die Einwirkungen des Kriegszustandes auf das ordentliche strafprozessuale Verfahren," *Zeitschrift für die gesamte Strafrechtswissenschaft* 38 (1917): 786-87.

81. Prussian statute repr. in Huber, *Dokumente,* 1:414-18; see Huber, *Deutsche Verfassungsgeschichte,* 3:60-62; Hans Boldt, *Rechtsstaat und Ausnahmezustand. Eine Studie über den Belagerungszustand als Ausnahmezustand des bürgerlichen Rechtsstaates im 19. Jahrhundert* (Berlin: Duncker und Humblot, 1967), 116-18. By implication, all equivalent basic rights in the non-Prussian states were to be suspended: Huber, *Deutsche Verfassungsgeschichte,* vol. 5: *Weltkrieg, Revolution und Rechtserneuerung, 1914-1919* (Stuttgart: W. Kohlhammer, 1978), 43-44.

82. Wilhelm Haldy, *Der Belagerungszustand in Preussen* (Tübingen: J. C. B. Mohr, 1906), 62-64, 37; see also Boldt, *Rechtsstaat und Ausnahmezustand,* 136.

83. Wilhelm Deist, ed., *Militär und Innenpolitik im Weltkrieg 1914-1918,* vol. 1 (Dusseldorf: Droste, 1970), xlii and Documents 18 and 19, 35-41; Boldt, *Rechtsstaat und Ausnahmezustand,* 201-4. An example of discretion is in Heinz Kreutzer, "Der Ausnahmezustand im deutschen Verfassungsrecht," in *Der Staatsnotstand,* ed. Ernst Fraenkel (Berlin: Colloquium, 1965), 21: a military commander ordered

citizens jailed for using the words *café* and *bon-bons,* which, it was alleged, damaged public security. As Kitchen points out (*The Silent Dictatorship,* 51–54), the commanders were to be directly responsible to the kaiser, who was the (ineffective) "linchpin" of the system. See also Fenske, "Die Verwaltung im Ersten Weltkrieg," 877–78.

84. Rosenberg, "Die rechtlichen Schranken der Militärdiktatur," in *Zeitschrift für die gesamte Strafrechtswissenschaft* 37 (1916): 813, 822–25.

85. Phrase from the title of Josef Kohler's work on the state of siege and the occupation of Belgium, *Not kennt kein Gebot. Die Theorien des Notrechtes und die Ereignisse unserer Zeit* (Berlin: Walther Rothschild, 1915). This book calls into question Emerson's attempt to separate Kohler from the more authoritarian neo-Hegelians Kaufmann and Lasson (*State and Sovereignty,* 197–98).

86. "Diktatur und Belagerungszustand. Eine staatsrechtliche Studie," *Zeitschrift für die gesamte Strafrechtswissenschaft* 38 (1917): 161, n. 52. On Schmitt during the war, see Bendersky, *Carl Schmitt,* 15–16, 19; Piet Tommissen, "Bausteine zu einer wissenschaftlichen Biographie (Periode: 1888-1933)," in *Complexio Oppositorum. Über Carl Schmitt,* ed. Helmut Quaritsch (Berlin: Duncker und Humblot, 1988), 76–77; and Paul Noack, *Carl Schmitt* (Frankfurt am Main: Propyläen, 1993), 37–42, notably ignoring Schmitt's articles on dictatorship.

87. "Diktatur und Belagerungszustand," 156, all emphasized in the original.

88. E.g., George Schwab, *The Challenge of the Exception,* 14–15; Bendersky, *Carl Schmitt,* 19–20.

89. "Diktatur und Belagerungszustand," 138.

90. On the distinction, see Bodenheimer, *Jurisprudence,* 87–89.

91. Later, Schmitt was to make conceptual systems central to his "idealist" analysis of the age. See, esp., *Political Theology. Four Chapters on the Concept of Sovereignty,* trans. from the 2d (1934) ed. by George Schwab (Cambridge: MIT Press, 1985), 59–60. In other books Schmitt makes extraordinary references to the Prussian military tradition. In *Römischer Katholizismus und politische Form,* 32, he refers to the "four pillars" of traditional, truly political representation: the English House of Lords, the Prussian General Staff, the French Academy, and the Vatican—of which only the last still existed (in 1923!). See also Schmitt's 1934 essay on the Prussian constitutional conflict, *Staatsgefüge und Zusammenbruch des Zweiten Reiches,* in which Schmitt takes the side of the Prussian "*Soldatenstaat*" over against the neutral, nonpolitical, bourgeois-liberal state of law. Years later, Ernst Forsthoff, one of Schmitt's closest students, explicitly distinguished three national styles of government: French legislative power, based on the French language; English judicial power; and German administrative power: *Der Staat der Industriegesellschaft. Dargestellt am Beispiel der Bundesrepublik Deutschland* (Munich: C. H. Beck, 1971), 106–7.

92. "Diktatur und Belagerungszustand," 140–41.

93. Ibid., 152.

94. Ibid., 143.

95. Ibid., 155.

96. Ibid., 153. Cf. "Die Einwirkungen des Kriegszustandes," 783–96.

97. "Diktatur und Belagerungszustand," 139–40, 160–61.

98. Ibid., 156.

99. Ibid., 156–57.

100. Ibid., 158.

101. In a footnote, Schmitt notes the applicability of his 1912 theory of judgment to the administration (158, n. 46).

102. Ibid., 157.

103. Ibid., 159, n. 42.

104. Ibid., 157.

105. Ibid., 159.

106. Ibid., 160.

107. Ibid., 154–55, questions the importance of Art. 9, sec. b, for these reasons.

108. Employed by Schmitt in *Gesetz und Urteil,* 15. See Hofmann's remarks on the idea of a normative "bad infinity" in Hegel and Schmitt in *Legitimität gegen Legalität,* 54–55.

109. "Diktatur und Belagerungszustand," 160.

110. Ibid., 161.

111. Ibid., 156, 161.

112. Significantly, the article never discusses Napoleon III and excludes Napoleon Bonaparte from consideration as irrelevant, because absolutist (ibid., 149–50). In *Die Diktatur* as well Schmitt avoids the issue of caesarism and military dictatorship as he attempts to make dictatorship into a respectable concept for the *Rechtsstaat. Die Diktatur* also employs a set of historical examples whose importance or connection to the concrete problem of how to interpret the valid German constitution is never made clear. See Leo Wittmayer's review, *Zeitschrift für öffentliches Recht* 5 (1926): 492–95.

113. Boldt, *Rechtsstaat und Ausnahmezustand,* 205–9; but cf. Bendersky, *Carl Schmitt,* 17: Schmitt "saw no redeeming aspect to the war whatsoever."

3   The Radicalism of Constitutional Revolution

1. Craig, *Politics of the Prussian Army,* 299–341; Peter Graf Kielmansegg, *Deutschland und der Erste Weltkrieg* (Frankfurt am Main: Athenaion, 1968), 162–204, 450–51; Huber, *Deutsche Verfassungsgeschichte,* 5:73–95, 584–92; Jürgen Kocka,

Facing Total War: German Society 1914–1918, trans. Barbara Weinberger (Cambridge: Harvard University Press, 1984); Elisabeth Domansky, "Militarization and Reproduction in World War One Germany," in *Society, Culture and the State in Germany, 1870–1930,* ed. Geoff Eley (Ann Arbor: University of Michigan Press, 1996), 427–63; Boldt, *Deutsche Verfassungsgeschichte,* 2:205–16; Gerald Feldman, *Army, Industry and Labor.*

2. Hans Boldt, "Die Weimarer Reichsverfassung," in *Die Weimarer Republik 1918–1933. Politik-Wirtschaft-Gesellschaft,* ed. Karl-Dietrich Bracher, Manfred Funke, and Hans-Adolf Jacobsen (Dusseldorf: Droste, 1987), 44–47.

3. Dieter Grosser, *Vom monarchischen Konstitutionalismus zur parlamentarischen Demokratie. Die Verfassungspolitik der deutschen Parteien im letzten Jahrzehnt des Kaiserreiches* (The Hague: Nijhoff, 1980), 11, 38, 60–69; Preuss, "Die Sozialdemokratie und der Parlamentarismus" (1891) and "Volksstaat oder verkehrter Obrigkeitsstaat" (November 14, 1918), both in *Staat, Recht und Freiheit. Aus 40 Jahren deutscher Politik und Geschichte* (1926; repr., Hildesheim: Georg Olms, 1964), 144–72, 365–68; Siegfried Grassmann, *Hugo Preuss und die deutsche Selbstverwaltung* (Lübeck: Matthiesen, 1965), 9–10; Ernst Portner, *Die Verfassungspolitik der Liberalen 1919. Ein Beitrag zur Deutung der Weimarer Reichsverfassung* (Bonn: Röhrscheid, 1973), 42–43; and Willibalt Apelt, *Geschichte der Weimarer Verfassung* (Munich: Biederstein, 1946), 56. That Ebert chose a liberal rather than a Social Democrat reflects not only strategic considerations but also the paucity of serious work on constitutionalism within the s p d. See Heinrich A. Winkler, *Von der Revolution zur Stabilisierung. Arbeiter und Arbeiterbewegung in der Weimarer Republik 1918 bis 1924* (Berlin: Dietz Nachfolger, 1989), 227.

4. Apelt, *Geschichte der Weimarer Verfassung,* 56–57; Wolfgang J. Mommsen, "Editorischer Bericht" to the stenographic notes of the meeting, "Beiträge zur Verfassungsfrage anlässlich der Verhandlungen im Reichsamt des Innern vom 9. bis 12. Dezember 1918," in *Max Weber Gesamtausgabe,* pt. 1, vol. 16: *Zur Neuordnung Deutschlands. Schriften und Reden 1918–1920,* ed. Wolfgang J. Mommsen and Wolfgang Schwentker (Tübingen: J. C. B. Mohr [Paul Siebeck], 1988), 49–55.

5. A description of the writing process is in Apelt, *Geschichte der Weimarer Verfassung,* 56–124; see also Boldt, "Die Weimarer Reichsverfassung," 47–50.

6. See Thoma, "Rechtsstaatsidee und Verwaltungsrechtswissenschaft," *Jahrbuch des öffentlichen Rechts der Gegenwart* 4 (1910): 196–218, stressing primacy of statute in administrative law and opposition to nonformalist approaches.

7. On Thoma's life: Hans-Dieter Rath, *Positivismus und Demokratie. Richard Thoma 1874–1957* (Berlin: Duncker und Humblot, 1981), 19–31; Adolf Schüle, "Richard Thoma zum Gedächtnis," *Archiv des öffentlichen Rechts* 82 (1957): 153–56; Hermann Mosler, "Richard Thoma zum Gedächtnis," *Die öffentliche Verwaltung* 30 (1957): 826–28.

8. In a speech at the end of the century, for example, Anschütz viewed the Reichstag as an exception to the federalist system and deliberately excluded it from discussion: in *Bismarck und die Reichsverfassung* (Berlin: Carl Heymann, 1899), 16–17.

9. Anschütz, *Die preussische Wahlreform* (Berlin: Julius Springer, 1917); idem, *Parlament und Regierung im Deutschen Reich* (Berlin: Otto Liebmann, 1918); Ernst-Wolfgang Böckenförde, "Gerhard Anschütz" (1986), repr. in *Recht, Staat, Freiheit. Studien zur Rechtsphilosophie, Staatstheorie und Verfassungstheorie* (Frankfurt am Main: Suhrkamp, 1991), 373–75; Walter Pauly, introduction to Anschütz, *Aus meinem Leben*, ed. Walter Pauly (Frankfurt am Main: Vittorio Klostermann, 1993), xxvii–xxix.

10. Böckenförde, "Gerhard Anschütz," 375; Anschütz, *Aus meinem Leben*, 239.

11. *Handbuch des Deutschen Staatsrechts*, 2 vols., ed. Richard Thoma and Gerhard Anschütz (Tübingen: J. C. B. Mohr [Paul Siebeck], 1930–32).

12. On their relationship to the DDP, see Anschütz, *Aus meinem Leben*, 179–80; Thoma, "Gerhard Anschütz zum 80. Geburtstag," *Deutsche Rechts-Zeitschrift* 2 (1947): 26; Rath, *Demokratie und Positivismus*, 39–45; Herbert Döring, *Der Weimarer Kreis. Studien zum politischen Bewusstsein verfassungstreuer Hochschullehrer in der Weimarer Republik* (Meinenheim am Glan: Anton Hain, 1975). On legal positivism as political strategy, see Everhardt Franssen, "Positivismus als juristische Strategie," *Juristenzeitung* 24 (1969): 766–74; Peter Caldwell, "Legal Positivism and Weimar Democracy," *American Journal of Jurisprudence* 39 (1994): 273–301.

13. Anschütz's letter from 1933 explaining his position is cited in Ernst Forsthoff, "Gerhard Anschütz," *Der Staat* 6 (1967): 139.

14. Thoma retreated from state law into administrative law, which, however, is hardly as "unpolitical" a field as Rath suggests in *Demokratie und Positivismus*, 25–28.

15. *Verfassung des Deutschen Reiches* (Berlin: Georg Stilke, 1921), 25–26; 14th ed. (Berlin: Georg Stilke, 1933), 31–32.

16. *Verfassung des Deutschen Reiches*, 14th ed., 32, 37–38.

17. *Drei Leitgedanken der Weimarer Verfassung. Rede, gehalten bei der Jahresfeier der Universität Heidelberg am 22. November 1922* (Tübingen: J. C. B. Mohr [Paul Siebeck], 1923), 16, 23–24, 29–30. See also "Parlament und Regierung," 6–7, for his notion of "democracy."

18. Anschütz, *Drei Leitgedanken*, 34.

19. Ibid., 2.

20. Anschütz, *Verfassung des Deutschen Reiches*, 14th ed., 38; see also Thoma, "Das Reich als Demokratie," in *Handbuch des Deutschen Staatsrechts*, 1:187.

21. Max Weber, "Deutschlands künftige Staatsform" (1918), in *Gesammelte politische Schriften*, 5th ed. (Tübingen: J. C. B. Mohr [Paul Siebeck], 1988), 472; idem,

"The President of the Reich," in *Political Writings,* 304-8; Mommsen, *Max Weber and German Politics 1890-1920,* 2d ed., trans. Michael S. Steinberg (Chicago: University of Chicago Press, 1984), 347. This position was shared by other left-liberals (e.g., Hugo Preuss) who were influenced by the work of Robert Redslob on the British Parliament—which mistakenly viewed the British monarch as a strong state organ. See Portner, *Die Verfassungspolitik der Liberalen,* 136-38.

22. Committee discussions are in Weber, *Zur Neuordnung Deutschlands,* 56-90. Anschütz opposed direct election of the president, calling instead for a parliamentary vote to ensure the legitimacy of the representative body: "Die kommende Reichsverfassung," *Deutsche Juristen-Zeitung* 24. 3-4 (February 1, 1919): 121-22.

23. Reinhard Schiffers, *Elemente direkter Demokratie im Weimarer Regierungssystem* (Dusseldorf: Droste, 1971), 109-10; Udo Wengst, "Staatsaufbau und Verwaltungsstruktur," in *Die Weimarer Republik,* 63-64. In English, see Heneman, *The Growth of Executive Power,* 26-58.

24. Apelt, *Geschichte der Weimarer Verfassung,* 99-101; Heneman, *The Growth of Executive Power,* 46-49.

25. Anschütz, *Verfassung des Deutschen Reiches,* 14th ed., 394.

26. Apelt, *Geschichte der Weimarer Verfassung,* 188-92, 197-98.

27. For an overview of the president's rights and duties, see Otto Meissner, "Der Reichspräsident," in *Handbuch der Politik,* vol. 3, ed. Gerhard Anschütz (Berlin: Dr. Walter Rothschild, 1921), 41-44.

28. Already in the first edition of his commentary Anschütz recognized the emptiness of this prescription; see *Verfassung des Deutschen Reiches,* 79.

29. Friedrich Giese, *Deutsches Staatsrecht. Allgemeines Reichs- und Landes-Staatsrecht* (Berlin: Spaeth und Linde, 1930), 138.

30. Anschütz, *Verfassung des Deutschen Reiches,* 1st ed., 106-8; Friedrich Giese, *Die Verfassung des Deutschen Reiches vom 11. August 1919. Taschenausgabe* (Berlin: Carl Heymann, 1919), 170-75; Ulrich Scheuner, "Die Anwendung des Art. 48," 249-58; Boldt, "Die Weimarer Reichsverfassung," 51-54.

31. On the plebiscitary elements of the constitution, see Schiffers, *Elemente direkter Demokratie,* 110-17, 130-54.

32. Anschütz, *Verfassung des Deutschen Reiches,* 14th ed., 401, 403.

33. Thoma, "Die juristische Bedeutung der grundrechtlichen Sätze der Deutschen Reichsverfassung im allgemeinen," in *Die Grundrechte und Grundpflichten der Reichsverfassung. Kommentar zum zweiten Teil der Reichsverfassung,* vol. 1, ed. Hans-Carl Nipperdey (Berlin: Reimar Hobbing, 1929), 40-41; idem, "Das Reich als Demokratie," 193-94.

34. Thoma, "Die juristische Bedeutung der grundrechtlichen Sätze," 7; idem, "Der Begriff der modernen Demokratie in seinem Verhältnis zum Staatsbegriff," in *Hauptprobleme der Soziologie. Erinnerungsgabe für Max Weber,* ed. Melchior Palyi (Munich: Duncker und Humblot, 1923), 41-42.

35. Thoma, "Das Reich als Demokratie," 193.

36. Preuss, "Denkschrift zum Entwurf des allgemeinen Teils der Reichsverfassung vom 3. Januar 1919," in *Staat, Recht und Freiheit,* 370-71. On the failure of the proposals, see Preuss, *Artikel 18 der Reichsverfassung: Seine Entstehung und Bedeutung* (Berlin: Carl Heymann, 1922); Hans Herzfeld [a member of the Preuss committee], *Die Selbstverwaltung und die Weimarer Epoche* (Stuttgart: W. Kohlhammer, 1957), 18-19; Portner, *Die Verfassungspolitik der Liberalen,* 97-106; Apelt, *Geschichte der Weimarer Verfassung,* 57-64. Constitutional drafts are reproduced in Heinrich Triepel, ed., *Quellensammlung zum Deutschen Reichsstaatsrecht,* vol. 1: *Quellensammlung zum Staats-, Verwaltungs- und Völkerrecht, vornehmlich zum akademischen Gebrauch,* 5th ed. (1931; repr., Aalen: Scientia, 1987). A map showing the effect of the proposal is reproduced in Ludwig Biewer, *Reichsreformbestrebungen in der Weimarer Republik. Fragen zur Funktionalreform und zur Neugliederung im Südwesten des Deutschen Reiches* (Frankfurt am Main: Peter D. Lang, 1980), 43.

37. See Apelt, *Geschichte der Weimarer Verfassung,* 66-82, on the *Staatenausschuss;* Huber, *Deutsche Verfassungsgeschichte seit 1789,* vol. 6: *Die Weimarer Reichsverfassung* (Stuttgart: W. Kohlhammer, 1981), 374-89; Boldt, "Die Weimarer Reichsverfassung," 54-57.

38. These institutions were formally created in 1920 and 1921. Friedrich Giese, *Deutsches Staatsrecht,* 160, 184-85.

39. Anschütz, "Die kommende Reichsverfassung," 117.

40. See, e.g., Anschütz, *Das preussisch-deutsche Problem. Skizze zu einem Vortrage* (Tübingen: J. C. B. Mohr [Paul Siebeck], 1922), 12-14; and idem, "Der deutsche Föderalismus in Vergangenheit, Gegenwart und Zukunft," *VVDSRL,* 1:30-32 (1924). Anschütz was aware of the need for a reform of the German federalist system. See the appendix to the 14th edition of *Verfassung des Deutschen Reiches,* 769-70.

Here and in the following, I translate the word *Reich* as "federal government" to convey its meaning in discussions of federalism. The word *government* used in this context means not *Regierung* in the German sense, but all state organs on the level of the *Reich.*

41. Anschütz, *Verfassung des Deutschen Reiches,* 14th ed., 131-32; *Drei Leitgedanken,* 7-10.

42. This is the interpretation of Carl Schmitt, *Verfassungslehre,* 390-91; see also Hans Nawiasky, *Grundprobleme der Reichsverfassung. Erster Teil: Das Reich als Bundesstaat* (Berlin: Julius Springer, 1928), 64; Anschütz, *Verfassung des Deutschen Reiches,* 14th ed., 146-59; Oskar Altenberg, "Gebietsänderungen im Innern des Reiches nach der Verfassung des Deutschen Reiches vom 11 August 1919," *Archiv des öffentlichen Rechts* 40 (1921): 173-215; Giese, *Grundriss des neuen Reichstaatsrechts,* 24-25.

43. *Verfassung des Deutschen Reiches,* 1st ed., 62; see also 14th ed., 146-47. The

phrase omitted in the middle of the above quote concerns the one exception to the rule, the popular initiative. See also Böckenförde, "Gerhard Anschütz," 368–69.

44. Nawiasky, *Grundprobleme der Reichsverfassung*, 65. On Nawiasky, see Hans F. Zacker, "Hans Nawiasky," in *Juristen im Portrait. Verlag und Autoren in 4 Jahrzehnten. Festschrift zum 225jährigen Jubiläum des Verlages C. H. Beck* (Munich: C. H. Beck, 1988), 598–607.

45. See Anschütz's response to Nawiasky in *Verfassung des Deutschen Reichs*, 14th ed., 145–46. When Anschütz had defended the Bismarckian system in the empire, by contrast, he defended its federalist basis against the centralizing Reichstag. Cf. Richard Thoma, "Gerhard Anschütz," 26.

46. Anschütz, *Verfassung des Deutschen Reiches*, 14th ed., 269–77.

47. Nawiasky, *Grundprobleme der Reichsverfassung*, 68; Art. 13, par. 2, thus becomes a potential weapon of the state against the *Reich*.

48. *Verfassung des Deutschen Reiches*, 14th ed., 272–75; see also "Die Reichsexekution," in *Handbuch des Deutschen Staatsrechts*, 1:378–79, where Anschütz uses the same words to make his argument.

49. Anschütz himself denied that a common, higher legal institution, in Kelsen's phrase the "*Gesamtverfassung*," stood above both *Reich* and states. He explicitly referred to the State Court (Staatsgerichtshof) as an organ of the *Reich*, not a third force. See "Das System der rechtlichen Beziehungen zwischen Reich und Länder," in *Handbuch des Deutschen Staatsrechts*, 2:198.

50. *Verfassung des Deutschen Reiches*, 1st ed., 45–47; 14th ed., 101–5.

51. Kelsen, discussion in "Bundesstaatliche und gliedsstaatliche Rechtsordnung," *VVDSRL*, 6:57 (1929). Nawiasky tacitly accepted Kelsen's argument by not even discussing Art. 13, par. 1, in his *Grundprobleme der Reichsverfassung*. See also Kelsen, "Die Bundesexekution. Ein Beitrag zur Theorie und Praxis des Bundesstaates, unter besonderе Berücksichtigung der deutschen Reichs- und der österreichischen Bundesverfassung," in *Festgabe für Fritz Fleiner zum 60. Geburtstag 24. Januar 1927* (Tübingen: J. C. B. Mohr [Paul Siebeck], 1927), 180–81, and 167–71, where Kelsen admits that a failure of the Weimar Constitution to clarify the relationship between Art. 13, par. 2; Art. 19; and Art. 48, par. 1, made Anschütz's article possible from a positivist point of view.

52. Anschütz, discussion in "Bundesstaatliche und gliedsstaatliche Rechtsordnung," *VVDSRL*, 6:65.

53. Apelt, *Geschichte der Weimarer Verfassung*, 58–59; *Max Weber Gesamtausgabe*, pt. 1, vol. 16, 71; Boldt, "Die Weimarer Reichsverfassung," 57–59. Preuss's almost incidental description of the new rights in his speech to the National Assembly is reprinted as "Begründung des Entwurfs einer Verfassung für das Deutsche Reich" (1919), in *Staat, Recht und Freiheit*, 419.

54. Naumann, "Versuch volksverständlicher Grundrechte," repr. in *Werke*, vol. 2

(Cologne: Westdeutscher, 1964), 573–79. See Anschütz's account: *Verfassung des Deutschen Reiches*, 1st ed., 183–84; and Apelt, *Geschichte der Weimarer Verfassung*, 106–10.

55. Apelt, *Geschichte der Weimarer Verfassung*, 110–19.

56. Adalbert Düringer, in the National Assembly on March 3, 1919, 19th Session, in *Die Deutsche Nationalversammlung im Jahre 1919*, vol. 2, ed. Eduard Heilfron (Berlin: Norddeutsche, n.d.), 1172–73.

57. An article later stricken from the constitution stated that the basic rights would act as the measure and the limit for legislation, administration, and the judiciary. See Giese, *Die Verfassung des Deutschen Reiches*, 292–93. Anschütz, however, notes that the article still said nothing about how such norms were to be enforced, and thus actually had no meaning (*Verfassung des Deutschen Reiches*, 1st ed., 187–88).

58. Anschütz, *Verfassung des Deutschen Reiches*, 1st ed., 187–88; for an example of the style of analysis, see p. 200, where Art. 119 on marriage becomes a "negative principle" for the legislator. See also Anschütz, *Die Verfassungs-Urkunde für den preussischen Staat vom 31. Januar 1850. Ein Kommentar für Wissenschaft und Praxis* (Berlin: O. Häring, 1912), 94–95.

59. *Verfassung des Deutschen Reiches*, 1st ed., 186–87; *Die Verfassungs-Urkunde für den preussischen Staat*, 95–96.

60. *Verfassung des Deutschen Reiches*, 1st ed., 185–86; *Die Verfassungs-Urkunde für den preussischen Staat*, 96–97. Anschütz explicitly follows Jellinek in defining the subject of these rights as a "person" (*Persönlichkeit*), not a "citizen" (*Bürger*). See Jellinek, *System*, 76–80.

61. See Anschütz, *Verfassung des Deutschen Reiches*, 1st ed., 198.

62. *Verfassung des Deutschen Reiches*, 1st ed., 185, 189: "[Art. 109, par. 1,] orders equality *before* the law, not equality *of* the law"; *Die Verfassungs-Urkunde für den preussischen Staat*, 96–97.

63. *Verfassung des Deutschen Reiches*, 1st ed., 200–201; 14th ed., 508.

64. Burlage, speech of July 16, 1919 (58th sess.), *Die Deutsche Nationalversammlung*, 6:3923–24.

65. Anschütz, *Verfassung des Deutschen Reiches*, 14th ed., 563–64; Alfred Wieruzowski, "Artikel 119. Ehe, Familie, Mutterschaft," in Nipperdey, ed., *Grundrechte und Grundpflichten*, 2:72–94.

66. See the critical remarks of C. J. Klumker, "Artikel 121. Stellung der unehelichen Kinder," in Nipperdey, ed., *Grundrechte und Grundpflichten*, 2:107–8; and Renate Pore, *A Conflict of Interest. Women in German Social Democracy 1919–1933* (Westport, Conn.: Greenwood, 1981), 40–44.

67. Zietz, speeches on July 15 and 16, 1919 (57th and 58th sess.), *Die Deutsche Nationalversammlung*, 6:3812–14, 3915–22.

68. *Verfassung des Deutschen Reiches*, 14th ed., 563–64.

69. Apelt, *Geschichte der Weimarer Verfassung*, 323–29; Rudolf Morsey, *Die deutsche Zentrumspartei 1917–1923* (Dusseldorf: Droste, 1966), 208–17; on the present-day system, see Donald Kommers, *The Constitutional Jurisprudence of the Federal Republic of Germany*, 2d ed. (Durham: Duke University Press, 1997), 489–91.

70. *Verfassung des Deutschen Reiches*, 14th ed., 698.

71. Ibid., 697.

72. See Otto Kirchheimer's skeptical examination of the many opposing values among the basic rights in "Weimar—und was dann? Analyse einer Verfassung" (1930), repr. in *Politik und Verfassung* (Frankfurt am Main: Suhrkamp, 1964), 32–33; a similar point is made in Schmitt, *Verfassungslehre*, 31–35. Schmitt later argued that the rights added up to a substantive guarantee of bourgeois values: "marriage, religion, and private property": *Legalität und Legitimität*, 299–301. On Kirchheimer and Schmitt, see Scheuerman, *Between the Norm and the Exception*, 26–27.

73. Thoma, "Die juristische Bedeutung," 7–9; see also Franz Neumann, "Die soziale Bedeutung der Grundrechte in der Weimarer Verfassung" (1930), in *Wirtschaft, Staat, Demokratie. Aufsätze 1930–1954*, ed. Alfons Söllner (Frankfurt am Main: Suhrkamp, 1978), 74; and Scheuerman, *Between the Norm and the Exception*, 47–51.

74. Anschütz's famous statement, "Das Staatsrecht hört hier auf," was made as a criticism of Laband's interpretation of the Budget Law: see Anschütz and Georg Meyer, *Lehrbuch des deutschen Staatsrechts*, 7th ed. (Munich: Duncker und Humblot, 1917), 906; Forsthoff, "Gerhard Anschütz," 149.

75. Thoma, "Das richterliche Prüfungsrecht," *Archiv des öffentlichen Rechts* 43 (1922): 270. In substantial agreement, Anschütz, *Verfassung des Deutschen Reiches*, 14th ed., 369–75.

76. Thoma, "Das richterliche Prüfungsrecht," 274.

77. Ibid., 275–79. Thoma did not rule out expert review of statutes for their conformity to legislative procedures, perhaps on the lines of Kelsen's solution in the Austrian Constitution of 1920.

78. Thoma, "Grundrechte und Polizeigewalt," in *Verwaltungsrechtliche Abhandlungen. Festgabe zur Feier des fünfzigjährigen Bestehens des Preussischen Oberverwaltungsgerichts 1875–20. November 1925*, ed. Heinrich Triepel (Berlin: Carl Heymann, 1925), 217–22.

79. "Das System der subjektiven öffentlichen Rechte und Pflichten," *Handbuch des Deutschen Staatsrechts*, 2:608.

80. See, e.g., James Goldschmidt's opposition to the "democratic absolutism of the majority," in "Gesetzesdämmerung" (1924), repr. in *Zur Problematik der höchstrichterlichen Entscheidung*, ed. Gerd Roellecke (Darmstadt: Wissenschaftliche Buchgesellschaft, 1982), 76–91.

81. Thoma, "Das Reich als Demokratie," 199–200.

82. Ibid. For a parallel positivist assessment of democracy, see Hans Kelsen, *Das Problem des Parlamentarismus* (1926; repr., Darmstadt: Wissenschaftliche Buchgesellschaft, 1968); idem, "Die Entwicklung des Staatsrechts in Oesterreich seit dem Jahre 1918," in *Handbuch des Deutschen Staatsrechts*, 1:165.

83. "Das Reich als Demokratie," 195; Mosler, "Richard Thoma," 828.

84. "Das Reich als Demokratie," 187–88; "Die rechtliche Ordnung des parlamentarischen Regierungssystems," in *Handbuch des Deutschen Staatsrechts*, 1:503–11. This logic led to an affirmation of form and procedure as a way of politicizing the state, as the positivist Leo Wittmayer argues in *Reichsverfassung und Politik* (Tübingen: J. C. B. Mohr [Paul Siebeck], 1923).

85. See, e.g., the edition of Anschütz's commentary revised in 1925, after the crisis: *Die Verfassung des Deutschen Reiches*, 8th ed. (Berlin: Georg Stilke, 1928), 170–77; cf. the call for revision by Carl Schmitt and Ernst Jacobi, who sought to find substantive limits to executive decree while also claiming that the decrees could violate basic rights: "Die Diktatur des Reichspräsidenten nach Art. 48 der Reichsverfassung," *VVDSRL*, 1:63–136.

86. Anschütz, "Die kommende Reichsverfassung," 123; see also Ingeborg Maus, *Bürgerliche Rechtstheorie und Faschismus. Zur sozialen Funktion und aktuellen Wirkung der Theorie Carl Schmitts* (Munich: Wilhelm Fink, 1976), 32–33.

87. The theme of the failed return to a prewar "normality" is stressed in Richard Bessel, *Germany after the First World War* (Oxford: Clarendon, 1993).

88. Huber, *Deutsche Verfassungsgeschichte*, 7:363–64; Huber, *Dokumente*, 2d ed., 3:188.

89. Huber, *Deutsche Verfassungsgeschichte*, 7:422–25; on the Reichstag's willingness to accept these decisions and their trust in President Ebert, see Wengst, "Staatsaufbau und Verwaltungsstruktur," 72–73.

90. Michael L. Hughes, *Paying for the German Inflation* (Chapel Hill: University of North Carolina Press, 1988), 42–68; Gerald Feldman, *The Great Disorder: Politics, Economics, and Society in the German Inflation, 1914–1924* (New York: Oxford University Press, 1993), 812–19; Gertrude Lübbe-Wolff, "Safeguards of Civil and Constitutional Rights—The Debate on the Role of the *Reichsgericht*," in *German and American Constitutional Thought: Contexts, Interaction, and Historical Realities*, ed. Hermann Wellenreuther (New York: Berg, 1990), 361–63. The letter, signed by Reichsgericht president Walter Simons, originally appeared in the *Juristische Wochenschrift* on January 15, 1924, 90; repr. in Huber, *Dokumente*, 3:383–84.

91. The metaphor of legal currents is in Geis, "Der Methoden- und Richtungsstreit," 91–96.

92. Triepel, "Die Vereinigung der deutschen Staatsrechtslehrer," *Archiv des öffentlichen Rechts* 43 (1922): 349; generally, see Hollerbach, "Zu Leben und Werk Heinrich Triepels."

93. Smend, "Die Vereinigung der Deutschen Staatsrechtslehrer und der Rich-

tungsstreit," in *Festschrift für Ulrich Scheuner zum 70. Geburtstag* (Berlin: Duncker und Humblot, 1973), 576.

94. Fritz Stier-Somlo, "Die zweite Tagung der Vereinigung der deutschen Staatsrechtslehrer," *Archiv des öffentlichen Rechts* 46 (1924): 88: "Einheit, Harmonie, geistige Gemeinschaft"; idem, "Die dritte Tagung der Vereinigung der deutschen Staatsrechtslehrer," *Archiv des öffentlichen Rechts* 48 (1925): 99: summarizing "the" (singular) result; Günther Holstein, "Von Aufgaben und Zielen heutiger Staatsrechtswissenschaft. Zur Tagung der Vereinigung der deutschen Staatsrechtslehrer," *Archiv des öffentlichen Rechts* 50 (1926): 38–40, stressing the unified values of all present; Albert Hensel, "Die fünfte Tagung der Vereinigung der deutschen Staatsrechtslehrer," *Archiv des öffentlichen Rechts* 52 (1927): 97–98: claims the association has succeeded in unifying the profession; Lutz Richter, "Die sechste Tagung der Vereinigung der deutschen Staatsrechtslehrer," *Archiv des öffentlichen Rechts* 53 (1928): 443: asserts an "einheitlichen Grundzug"; and Hans Gerber, "Die siebente Tagung der Vereinigung der deutschen Staatsrechtslehrer," *Archiv des öffentlichen Rechts* 56 (1929): 253–54: "Einheit in der Vielheit." The final report by Arnold Köttgen ("Die achte Tagung der Vereinigung der deutschen Staatsrechtslehrer," *Archiv des öffentlichen Rechts* 60 [1932]: 404–31) is of a slightly different nature, since Köttgen apparently saw an alternative to the traditional system of state law in one political party, the National Socialists (431).

95. Smend, "Die Vereinigung der Deutschen Staatsrechtslehrer," 579.

96. "Wesen und Entwicklung der Staatsgerichtsbarkeit," *VVDSRL*, 5 (1929): Triepel's presentation, 2–29; Kelsen's, 30–88; discussion, 88–123. See also Ulrich Scheuner, "50 Jahre deutsche Staatsrechtswissenschaft im Spiegel der Verhandlungen der Vereinigung der Deutschen Staatsrechtslehrer. I. Die Vereinigung der Deutschen Staatsrechtslehrer in der Zeit der Weimarer Republik," *Archiv des öffentlichen Rechts* 97 (1972): 350.

97. "Wesen und Entwicklung der Staatsgerichtsbarkeit," *VVDSRL*, 5:104.

98. Ibid., 5:117.

99. The term *dual style* refers to Ernst Fraenkel's later analysis of Nazi law, based on a reading of Schmitt: *The Dual State: A Contribution to the Theory of Dictatorship*, trans. E. A. Shils, E. Loewenstein, and K. Knorr (New York: Oxford University Press, 1941).

100. "Überprüfung von Verwaltungsakten durch die ordentlichen Gerichte," *VVDSRL*, 5:207, 230.

101. Hippel, review of Wilhelm Jöckel, *Hans Kelsens rechtstheoretische Methode*, in *Juristische Wochenschrift* 60 (1931): 1175. The scare quotes around the term "*undeutsch*" are present in the original; their meaning is unclear.

102. Freiherr Marschall von Bieberstein, *Vom Kampf des Rechts gegen die Gesetze* (Stuttgart: W. Kohlhammer, 1927), 95–97; on his trial for libeling the government, see Huber, *Deutsche Verfassungsgeschichte*, 6:992.

103. Carl Bilfinger, "Verfassungsrecht als politisches Recht," *Zeitschrift für Politik* 18 (1928): 281–98; Manfred Friedrich, "Paul Laband," 204.

104. Ernst Forsthoff points out the importance of this genre in "Gerhard Anschütz," 143–45.

105. Franz Hartung, review in *Zeitschrift für die gesamte Staatswissenschaft* 87 (1929): 225, quoted in Reinhard Mehring, "Carl Schmitts Lehre von der Auflösung des Liberalismus: Das Sinngefüge der 'Verfassungslehre' als historisches Urteil," *Zeitschrift für Politik* 38 (1991): 200–201.

106. Carl Schmitt, the "man of the timely current" (Hans Mayer, *Ein Deutscher auf Widerruf. Erinnerungen,* 2 vols. [Frankfurt am Main: Suhrkamp, 1982], 1:142), was the only jurist to define clearly the concept of politics in the Republic, in *Der Begriff des Politischen. Texte von 1932 mit einem Vorwort und drei Corollarien* (Berlin: Duncker und Humblot, 1963). The concept he developed, however, was radical and "existential," and not really suited for any theory of state law; see Heinrich Triepel's comments in "Wesen und Entwicklung der Staatsgerichtsbarkeit," *VVDSRL,* 5:6–7; and Bilfinger, "Verfassungsrecht als politisches Recht," 294–95. Others had insisted that a subjective and normative—i.e., political—moment was inevitable in legal scholarship. See Rudolf Laun, "Der Staatsrechtslehrer und die Politik," *Archiv des öffentlichen Rechts* 43 (1923): 145–99; and Triepel, *Staatsrecht und Politik.* When it came down to actually defining the term *politics* concretely, however, the jurists were at a loss. Triepel, for example, could not get beyond some vague notion of high politics and the preservation of the state in his "Wesen und Entwicklung der Staatsgerichtsbarkeit."

107. See, e.g., Kaufmann, *Kritik der neukantianischen Rechtsphilosophie. Eine Betrachtung über die Beziehungen zwischen Philosophie und Rechtswissenschaft* (Tübingen: J. C. B. Mohr [Paul Siebeck], 1921), 79–80; Smend, *Verfassung und Verfassungsrecht,* 124; Heller, "Die Krise der Staatslehre" (1926), repr. in *Gesammelte Schriften,* 2:5.

108. E.g., Gerhard Lassar, "Der Schutz des öffentlichen Rechts. Die neueste Entwicklung des Gemeindeverfassungsrechts," *VVDSRL,* 2:95 (1925); Smend's critique of the "liberalizing" interpretation of basic rights as protection of minorities against the majority is in "Das Recht der freien Meinungsäusserung," *VVDSRL,* 4:47–48; Carl Schmitt, *Verfassungslehre,* 225.

109. See Schmitt's view of "authentic" basic rights as protecting the individual against the state in *Verfassungslehre,* 164–65.

110. Gerber, discussion contribution, "Verwaltungsrecht der öffentlichen Anstalt," *VVDSRL,* 6:154; Smend, "Das Recht der freien Meinungsäusserung," *VVDSRL,* 4:62; Triepel, "Wesen und Entwicklung der Staatsgerichtsbarkeit," *VVDSRL,* 5:21–22.

111. Kaufmann, discussion, "Verwaltungsrecht der öffentlichen Anstalt," *VVDSRL,* 6:151; Köttgen, in ibid., 6:105; Heller, "Der Begriff des Gesetzes in

der Reichsverfassung," in *VVDSRL*, 4:127; and Hans Mayer's reading of Laband as a monarchist, in "Krise der deutschen Staatslehre von Bismarck bis Weimar" (1931), repr. in *Karl Marx und das Elend des Geistes. Studien zur neuen deutschen Ideologie* (Miesenheim am Glan: Westkulturverlag Anton Hain, 1948), 54–55.

112. Kaufmann, discussion, "Das Recht der freien Meinungsäusserung," *VVDSRL*, 4:79-80; idem, "Gleichheit vor dem Gesetz im Sinne des Art. 109 der Reichsverfassung," *VVDSRL*, 3:15-16 (1927); Smend, "Das Recht der freien Meinungsäusserung," *VVDSRL*, 4:46-47. The problem of value relativism is discussed in Wolfram Bauer, *Wertrelativismus und Wertbestimmtheit im Kampf um die Weimarer Republik. Zur Politologie des Methodenstreites der Staatsrechtslehre* (Berlin: Duncker und Humblot, 1968). None of these positions was uncontested, of course. See, e.g., Schmitt's *Verfassungslehre*, 217, in which Kant reappears as a liberal.

113. Jellinek, "Die Schutz des öffentlichen Rechts durch ordentliche und durch Verwaltungsgerichte (Fortschritte, Rückschritte und Entwicklungstendenzen seit der Revolution)," *VVDSRL*, 2:79-80.

114. Carl Bilfinger, *Nationale Demokratie als Grundlage der Weimarer Verfassung* (Halle an der Saale: Max Niemeyer, 1929); Schmitt, *Verfassungslehre*, 102-12. Kurt Sontheimer, *Antidemokratisches Denken in der Weimarer Republik. Die politischen Ideen des deutschen Nationalismus zwischen 1918 und 1933* (Munich: Nymphenburger, 1962), examines these ideas in the larger context of Weimar antidemocratic ideologies.

115. Freiherr Marschall von Bieberstein, *Vom Kampf des Rechts gegen die Gesetze*, 13–14.

116. Schmitt, *Hüter der Verfassung* (Tübingen: J. C. B. Mohr [Paul Siebeck], 1931).

117. Günther Holstein, "Von Aufgaben und Zielen heutiger Staatsrechtswissenschaft," 26. The word *Saturiertheit*, which Bismarck had originally used to calm other states about German foreign policy intentions, is employed also in Erich Kaufmann's presentation, "Die Gleichheit vor dem Gesetz," *VVDSRL*, 3:3; see also Schmitt, *Verfassungslehre*, 55; and Hermann Heller, *Staatslehre* (1934), repr. in *Gesammelte Schriften*, 3:118.

118. The chorus in the Republic proclaiming a crisis in state law included Erich Kaufmann, *Kritik der neukantianischen Rechtsphilosophie*, preface, 1-5; Smend, *Verfassung und Verfassungsrecht* 121-23; Triepel, *Staatsrecht und Politik;* Otto Koellreutter, "Staatsrechtswissenschaft und Politik," *Deutsche Juristen-Zeitung* 33 (1928): 1221-26; Hermann Heller, "Die Krise der Staatslehre," 3-30; and Hans Mayer, "Die Krise der deutschen Staatslehre."

4 The Paradoxical Foundations of Constitutional Democracy

1. Jacques Derrida, "Declarations of Independence," *New Political Science* 15 (1986): 7–15; see also Bonnie Honig, "Declarations of Independence: Arendt and Derrida on the Problem of Founding a Republic," *American Political Science Review* 85 (1991): 97–113.

2. On Schmitt's style: Reinhard Mehring, *Pathetisches Denken*, 20–22, esp. n. 58; Holmes, *Anatomy of Antiliberalism*, 39.

3. In general, see Métall, *Hans Kelsen*, 34–37; and Erich Voegelin, "Kelsen's Pure Theory of Law," *Political Science Quarterly* 42 (1927): 268–76. On Kelsen's role in writing the 1920 Austrian Constitution, see Felix Ermacora, "Österreichische Bundesverfassung und Hans Kelsen," in *Festschrift für Hans Kelsen zum 90. Geburtstag*, ed. Adolf Merkl et al. (Vienna: Franz Deuticke, 1971), 22–54; and the following document collections: *Karl Renners Briefe aus Saint Germain und ihre rechtspolitische Folgen*, Schriftenreihe des Hans-Kelsen-Instituts, vol. 16, ed. Georg Schmitz (Vienna: Manz, 1991); *Die österreichische Bundesverfassung und Hans Kelsen. Analysen und Materialien. Zum 100. Geburtstag von Hans Kelsen*, ed. Felix Ermacora and Christiane Wirth (Vienna: Wilhelm Braumüller, 1982); *Die Entstehung der Bundesverfassung 1920*, vol. 4: *Die Sammlung der Entwürfe zur Staats- bzw. Bundesverfassung*, ed. Felix Ermacora (Vienna: Wilhelm Braumüller, 1990); and *Die Vorentwürfe Hans Kelsens für die österreichische Bundesverfassung*, Schriftenreihe des Hans-Kelsen-Instituts, vol. 6, ed. Georg Schmitz (Vienna: Manz, 1981), esp. 109–12. Robert Walter discusses the tradition of judicial review in Austria in "Die Gerichtsbarkeit," in *Das österreichische Bundes-Verfassungsgesetz und seine Entwicklung*, ed. Herbert Schambeck (Berlin: Duncker und Humblot, 1980), 443–80. In English: Klaus von Beyme, "The Genesis of Constitutional Review in Parliamentary Systems," in *Constitutional Review and Legislation: An International Comparison*, ed. Christine Landfried (Baden-Baden: Nomos, 1988), 21–38.

4. One of the major causes of the 1929 reform, which gave the president considerably more power, was a decision by Kelsen's Constitutional Court to allow the Social Democrat mayor of Vienna to annul marriages. The conservative outcry against the formal decision was directed against Kelsen in particular. See Métall, *Hans Kelsen*, 48ff.; Paul Silverman, "Law and Economics in Interwar Vienna," 690–702.

5. On the relationship between pure theory and practical politics, see Horst Dreier, *Rechtslehre, Staatssoziologie und Demokratietheorie bei Hans Kelsen* (Baden-Baden: Nomos, 1986), 249–94, with further literature. Of Kelsen's political works, see, esp., *Vom Wesen und Wert der Demokratie*, 2d ed. (Tübingen: J. C. B. Mohr [Paul Siebeck], 1929); for his connection to reformist social democracy, see "Die politische Theorie des Sozialismus," *Österreichische Rundschau* 19 (1923): 113–35;

"Marx oder Lassalle. Wandlungen in der politischen Theorie des Marxismus," *Archiv für die Geschichte des Sozialismus und der Arbeiterbewegung* 11 (1925): 261-98.

6. See Bendersky, *Carl Schmitt;* Tommissen, "Bausteine zu einer wissenschaftlichen Biographie," 71-100; and Mehring, *Carl Schmitt zur Einführung,* 33-40. Moritz Julius Bonn evaluated Schmitt in the 1920s as "brilliant" and a "genius," but afflicted with a "boundless vanity" and "intellectual waywardness," in *Wandering Scholar* (New York: John Day, 1948), 330-31; this judgment is supported by Noack, *Carl Schmitt.*

7. *Political Romanticism,* trans. from the 2d German ed. (1923) by Guy Oakes (Cambridge: MIT Press, 1986); *Die Diktatur* (1921); *Political Theology. Four Chapters on the Concept of Sovereignty,* trans. from the 2d ed. (1934) by George Schwab (Cambridge: MIT Press, 1985).

8. Ernst Rudolf Huber, "Carl Schmitt in der Rechtskrise der Weimarer Endzeit," in *Complexio Oppositorum,* 33-50; Bendersky, *Carl Schmitt,* chs. 8 and 9; Bernd Rüthers, *Carl Schmitt im Dritten Reich. Wissenschaft als Zeitgeist-Verstärkung,* 2d ed. (Munich: C. H. Beck, 1990), 57-71.

9. Schmitt's followers often avoid addressing continuities in Schmitt's thought from the critique of Weimar to the justification of Nazism, e.g., Helmut Quaritsch, *Positionen und Begriffe Carl Schmitts,* 2d ed. (Berlin: Duncker und Humblot, 1991), ch. 4, "Der Konvertit 1933-1936": "Wer zu Wölfen reden will, muss mit den Wölfen heulen." Günter Maschke, *Der Tod des Carl Schmitt. Apologie und Polemik* (Vienna: Karolinger, 1987), avoids coming to terms with Schmitt's virulent anti-Semitism and support for Hitler. See Peter Römer's critical conference report in "Tod und Verklärung Carl Schmitts," *Archiv für Rechts- und Sozialphilosophie* 76 (1990): 373-99; Stephen Holmes, "The Scourge of Liberalism," *New Republic* 199 (August 22, 1988): 31-36; Bernd Rüthers, *Entartetes Recht. Rechtslehren und Kronjuristen im Dritten Reich,* 3d ed. (Munich: DTV, 1994), which concentrates on the case of Schmitt; Mehring, *Carl Schmitt,* 101-24; and Peter Caldwell, "National Socialism and Constitutional Law: Carl Schmitt, Otto Koellreutter, and the Debate over the Nature of the Nazi State, 1933-1937," *Cardozo Law Review* 16 (1994): 399-427, with additional references.

10. This dating follows the recent work of Stanley L. Paulson, "Zur neukantianischen Dimension der Reinen Rechtslehre. Vorwort zur Kelsen-Sander Auseinandersetzung," in *Die Rolle des Neukantianismus in der Reinen Rechtslehre. Eine Debatte zwischen Sander und Kelsen,* ed. Paulson (Aalen: Scientia, 1988), 7-22; idem, preface and introduction to Kelsen, *Introduction to the Problems of Legal Theory,* v-xlii; and idem, "Toward a Periodization of the Pure Theory of Law." Important for understanding Kelsen's neo-Kantianism is his reference to Hermann Cohen in the foreword to the second edition of the *Hauptprobleme* (xvii-xviii; see, however, Kelsen's critique of Cohen as a religious thinker in "Un inédit de Kelsen,"

334–35). While Paulson ("Toward a Periodization of the Pure Theory of Law," 35–37) takes the references as a sign of critical appropriation of neo-Kantianism, Mario G. Losano ("The Periodization of Kelsen Proposed by S. L. Paulson," in *Hans Kelsen: A Diachronic Point of View*, 120) argues that Cohen served as a merely external buttress for Kelsen's theory; Paulson seems to accept the latter judgment in his later "Kelsen and the Marburg School: Reconstructive and Historical Perspectives," in *Prescriptive Formality and Normative Rationality in Modern Legal Systems. Festschrift for Robert S. Summers*, ed. Werner Krawietz, Neil MacCormick, and Georg Henrik von Wright (Berlin: Duncker und Humblot, 1994), 481–94, which stresses the influence of the Heidelberg school via Georg Simmel and Georg Jellinek. See also Manfred Paschke, "Hermann Cohens Einfluss auf Kelsens Reine Rechtslehre," 445–66; Moore, *Legal Norms and Legal Science*, 7; and Helmut Holzhey, "Die Transformation neukantianischer Theoreme in die reine Rechtslehre Kelsens," in *Hermeneutik und Strukturtheorie des Rechts, Archiv für Rechts- und Sozialphilosophie*, Beiheft 20 (Wiesbaden: Franz Steiner, 1984), 99–110. In general on neo-Kantian theories of legal epistemology, see Dreier, *Rechtslehre, Staatssoziologie und Demokratietheorie*, 57–82.

11. *Das Problem der Souveränität und die Theorie des Völkerrechts. Beiträge zu einer Reinen Rechtslehre* (Tübingen: J. C. B. Mohr [Paul Siebeck], 1920); *Der soziologische und der juristische Staatsbegriff. Kritische Untersuchungen des Verhältnisses von Staat und Recht* (Tübingen: J. C. B. Mohr [Paul Siebeck], 1922); *Allgemeine Staatslehre* (Berlin: Springer, 1925); on natural law, see, esp., "The Idea of Natural Law" (1928), trans. Peter Heath, in *Hans Kelsen. Essays in Legal and Moral Philosophy*, ed. Ota Weinberger (Dordrecht: D. Reidel, 1973), 27–60; and "Natural Law Doctrine and Legal Positivism" (1928), trans. Wolfgang Herbert Kraus, as an appendix to *General Theory of Law and State* (Cambridge: Harvard University Press, 1949), 391–446; and the English translation of the *Reine Rechtslehre*, 1st ed.: *Introduction to the Problems of Legal Theory*, trans. Bonnie Litschewski Paulson and Stanley L. Paulson.

12. See above, ch. 2, n. 28.

13. *Staatsbegriff*, 235 (emphasis in the original); see also *Allgemeine Staatslehre*, 54–55; and *Introduction to the Problems of Legal Theory*, 23–24. On the development of Kelsen's theory of the legal norm, see (among many) Dreier, *Rechtslehre, Staatssoziologie und Demokratietheorie*, 196–99; and Hendrik J. van Eikema Hommes, "The Development of Hans Kelsen's Concept of Legal Norm," in *Rechtssystem und gesellschaftliche Basis bei Hans Kelsen, Rechtstheorie*, Beiheft 5, ed. Werner Krawietz and Helmut Schelsky (Berlin: Duncker und Humblot, 1984), 159–74.

14. *Introduction to the Problems of Legal Theory*, 24; Paulson, "Zur neukantianischen Dimension der Reinen Rechtslehre," 15–22.

15. This line of thought is already present in "Rechtswissenschaft als Norm- oder als Kulturwissenschaft," 46.

16. Criticisms on this score can be found in Hermann Heller, *Die Souveränität*, 26; *Staatslehre*, 149–51; Kurt Sontheimer, *Politische Wissenschaft und Staatsrechts- lehre*, 21–23; Wolfgang Schluchter, *Entscheidung für den sozialen Rechtsstaat. Her- mann Heller und die staatstheoretische Diskussion in der Weimarer Republik* (Cologne: Kiepenheuer und Witsch, 1968), 43–52; and Christoph Müller, "Kritische Be- merkungen zur Auseinandersetzung Hermann Hellers mit Hans Kelsen," in *Der soziale Rechtsstaat. Gedächtnisschrift für Hermann Heller 1891–1933*, ed. Müller and Ilse Staff (Baden-Baden: Nomos, 1984), 693–722.

17. Kelsen's idealism is clearly apparent when he refers to the "mind-body" split during this phase of his work. See, e.g., *Staatsbegriff*, 75–76, 237–38. Kelsen calls his entire project into question at one point in his *Introduction to the Problems of Legal Theory* (32–35) when he suggests that the entire endeavor of legal scholarship might be ideological, since law might be purely and simply determined by causal factors. This remark may reflect Kelsen's pessimism as he left continental Europe to escape fascism. Note also his skepticism regarding the possibility of "freedom," or legislative autonomy of the people, in *Vom Wesen und Wert der Demokratie*, 3–13, 84–86.

18. "Juristischer Formalismus und Reine Rechtslehre," *Juristische Wochenschrift* 58 (1929): 1723–24.

19. "Natural Law Doctrine and Legal Positivism," 416.

20. *Introduction to the Problems of Legal Theory*, 18–19. Horst Dreier implies in- correctly that Kelsen's criticism was leveled mainly at conservatism, in *Rechtslehre, Staatssoziologie und Demokratietheorie*, 163, 170–74; cf. Kelsen's critique of Lenin's anarchism in "Die politische Theorie des Sozialismus," 113–35.

21. "Juristischer Formalismus und Reine Rechtslehre," 1723.

22. *Staatsbegriff*, 115–16. In general, against Jellinek, see ibid., 114–36; *Introduc- tion to the Problems of Legal Theory*, 97; *Allgemeine Staatslehre*, 6–7; and "Un inédit de Kelsen," 333. See also Paulson, "Zur neukantianischen Dimension der Reinen Rechtslehre," 13–14; idem, "Toward a Periodization of the Pure Theory of Law," 20–28.

23. "Justiz und Verwaltung" (1929), repr. in *Wiener rechtstheoretische Schule*, 1784.

24. See, e.g., *Problem der Souveränität*, 11–12; *Staatsbegriff*, 213–15; *Introduction to the Problems of Legal Theory*, 99–106; summary in *Allgemeine Staatslehre*, 16–17.

25. *Staatsbegriff*, 89–90. Explicitly on the state's "spiritual" existence, see ibid., 91. Parallel remarks are in *Introduction to the Problems of Legal Theory*, 104–5.

26. At another point Kelsen refers to "the objective validity of the normative order that we call the state. This normative validity [*Soll-Geltung*] is the specific sphere in which the state exists" ("Wesen des Staates" [1926–27], repr. in *Wiener rechtstheoretische Schule*, 1715).

27. *Allgemeine Staatslehre*, 105; *Staatsbegriff*, 86–88.

28. *Problem der Souveränität*, 12–13.

29. Heller, *Die Souveränität*, 78, 85–86.

30. See, esp., "Das Wesen des Staates," 1713–15, 1718–21; "Die Lehre von den drei Gewalten oder Funktionen des Staates" (1923–24), repr. in *Wiener rechtstheoretische Schule*, 1626; "prima causa" is discussed in *Staatsbegriff*, 84, 128–29, 223–25; *Allgemeine Staatslehre*, 102; and *Problem der Souveränität*, 5–6, 56–58. The argument in English is in "God and the State" (1922–23), in *Essays in Legal and Moral Philosophy*, 61–82.

31. I thank Stanley L. Paulson for the precise dating.

32. See *Hauptprobleme*, 1923 Foreword, xii–xvi. On Merkl: Wolf-Dietrich Grusmann, *Adolf Julius Merkl. Leben und Werk*, Schriftenreihe des Hans-Kelsen-Instituts, vol. 13 (Vienna: Manz, 1989); *Adolf J. Merkl. Werk und Wirksamkeit*, Schriftenreihe des Hans-Kelsen-Instituts, vol. 14, ed. Robert Walter (Vienna: Manz, 1990).

33. *Problem der Souveränität*, 93–94; the parallel passage is in *Staatsbegriff*, 93–94.

34. *Grundgesetz* historically referred to any set of basic laws regulating state operation and not necessarily an all-encompassing contract. See Dieter Grimm, "Der Verfassungsbegriff in historischer Entwicklung," in *Die Zukunft der Verfassung* (Frankfurt am Main: Suhrkamp, 1991), 102–3.

35. "Die Lehre von den drei Gewalten," 1634; see also *Allgemeine Staatslehre*, 249; and *Introduction to the Problems of Legal Theory*, 63–65.

36. Kelsen, *Österreichisches Staatsrecht. Ein Grundriss, entwicklungsgeschichtlich dargestellt* (Tübingen: J. C. B. Mohr [Paul Siebeck], 1923), 74–153.

37. Ibid., 78–79. The theoretical problem of this logical regression is discussed in *Introduction to the Problems of Legal Theory*, 62–63. Other examples of such breaks in legal continuity in Kelsen's text include the destruction of the Dual Monarchy in 1867 and procedures involving the monarchical edicts of 1861 and 1865, detailed in *Österreichisches Staatsrecht*, 20–22. Kelsen's characterization of any such change without legal authorization as a "revolution" is more than questionable, since it would put technical changes in constitutional monarchism on the same level as the 1918 revolution against the system itself. He provides no criteria by which a lawyer can determine which set of laws counts as valid. See Heinrich Herrfahrdt, *Revolution und Rechtswissenschaft. Untersuchungen über die juristische Erfassbarkeit von Revolutionsvorgängen und ihre Bedeutung für die allgemeine Rechtslehre* (1930; repr., Aalen: Scientia, 1970), esp. 7–9; and Margrit Kraft-Fuchs, "Kelsens Staatstheorie und die Soziologie des Staates," *Zeitschrift für öffentliches Recht* 11 (1931): 410–15.

38. See, e.g., the critique of Kant's contract theory in *Staatsbegriff*, 141–42, *Allgemeine Staatslehre*, 250–51; and "Die Lehre von den drei Gewalten," 1625–26.

39. *Problem der Souveränität*, 97–98, n. 1.

40. E.g., *Allgemeine Staatslehre*, 249; *Introduction to the Problems of Legal Theory*, 58, 63–65.

41. In this sense, and only this sense, Kelsen presented something like the "rules of recognition" theorized by H. L. A. Hart that permitted a legal actor to recognize a legally constituted authority; see Hart, *The Concept of Law*, 97–120. Note, however, that Hart rejected Kelsen's neo-Kantianism (ibid., 245–46), turning instead to what Paulson describes as "social fact." See, in general, Paulson, "Continental Normativism and Its British Counterpart."

42. "Natural Law Doctrine and Legal Positivism," 401.

43. *Problem der Souveränität*, 96.

44. *Staatsbegriff*, 83–84.

45. Ibid., 91–92.

46. Ibid., 92–93.

47. Ibid., 95–96.

48. Ibid., 97.

49. See, e.g., *Problem der Souveränität*, 96–98; *Allgemeine Staatslehre*, 18–19; and *Introduction to the Problems of Legal Theory*, 59–60. See also the explicit and polemical formulations in *Der Staat als Integration. Eine prinzipielle Auseinandersetzung* (Vienna: Julius Springer, 1930), 13–14.

50. In the Weimar Republic, see, esp., Schmitt, *Verfassungslehre*, 9–10; and Heller, *Staatslehre*, 304–5, 330–31. Similar postwar critiques are in Horst Ehmke, *Grenzen der Verfassungsänderung* (1952), repr. in *Beiträge zur Verfassungstheorie und Verfassungspolitik*, ed. Peter Häberle (Königstein: Athenäum, 1981), 37–42; Ernst Bloch, *Naturrecht und menschliche Würde* (Frankfurt am Main: Suhrkamp, 1972), 168–74; and Dreier, *Rechtslehre, Staatssoziologie und Demokratietheorie*, 55–56.

51. *Introduction to the Problems of Legal Theory*, 58.

52. *Problem der Souveränität*, v–vi, 8–9; "Natural Law Doctrine and Legal Positivism," 401. See also Dreier, *Rechtslehre, Staatssoziologie und Demokratietheorie*, 50–56; Paulson, "Zu Hermann Hellers Kritik an die Reine Rechtslehre," in *Der soziale Rechtsstaat*, 683–87.

53. "Das Wesen des Staates," 1716; see also *Problem der Souveränität*, 97n; *Staatsbegriff*, 93–95.

54. Heller, "Die Krise der Staatslehre," 23–24.

55. See, esp., the harsh critique by Alf Ross, *Towards a Realistic Jurisprudence*, 57–59, suggesting that the "normativity" thesis merely repeats the antinomy of state sovereignty found in nineteenth-century positivism. Another Kelsen student, Ota Weinberger, turned to an "institutionalist" approach that views both normative and factual cognition as necessary for legal science: Weinberger and Neil MacCormick, *An Institutional Theory of Law. New Approaches to Legal Positivism* (Dordrecht: D. Reidel, 1986), 19–20; Weinberger, "Beyond Positivism and

Natural Law," in ibid., 114; Weinberger, "The Theory of Legal Dynamics Reconsidered," *Ratio Juris* 4 (1991): 18–35. Stanley L. Paulson argues that the Kelsenian transcendental deduction, at least in the "regressive" form common to the neo-Kantians, could not exclude the possibility of nonnormative interpretations of legal phenomena—and in that form, at least, failed: introduction to Kelsen, *Introduction to the Problems of Legal Theory*, xxxviii–xli.

56. The notion of minimum and maximum correspondence is developed in *Staatsbegriff*, 92–93, 95–96; *Allgemeine Staatslehre*, 18–19; *Introduction to the Problems of Legal Theory*, 59–60.

57. "The Idea of Natural Law," 36–38; "Natural Law Doctrine and Legal Positivism," 393–94.

58. Strauss, "Notes on Carl Schmitt, *The Concept of the Political*" (1932), repr. in Heinrich Meier, *Carl Schmitt and Leo Strauss: The Hidden Dialogue*, trans. J. Harvey Lomax (Chicago: University of Chicago Press, 1995), 94–95; Meier points out (ibid., 12–14) that Strauss strengthened Schmitt's argument on this score. See also Schmitt, *Begriff des Politischen*, 26.

59. *Römischer Katholizismus und politische Form*, 22, 50. This argument is based on John McCormick's forthcoming *Against Politics as Technology: Carl Schmitt's Critique of Liberalism* (New York: Cambridge University Press, 1997); and idem, "Dangers of Mythologizing Technology and Politics: Nietzsche, Schmitt and the Antichrist," *Philosophy and Social Criticism* 21 (1995): 55–92; cf. the uncritical discussion by Klaus Kröger, "Bemerkungen zu Carl Schmitts 'Römischer Katholizismus und politische Form,'" in *Complexio Oppositorum*, 159–65.

60. On representation, see *Römischer Katholizismus und politische Form*, 31–36; and *Verfassungslehre*, 212, 209. On how Catholicism overcomes the "absolute transcendence" of "Jewish monotheism," see *Römischer Katholizismus*, 12–13. On the worldly, city-dwelling Protestants, unable to connect themselves to any soil (*Boden*), see ibid., 17–18. Another question entirely is to what extent these views were authentically "Catholic." According to the essays in *Die eigentlich katholische Verschärfung*, ed. Bernd Wacker, Schmitt represented a fairly marginal element in political Catholicism. Clearly, however, Schmitt's anti-Jewish stance is consistent throughout his work. See Raphael Gross, "Carl Schmitts 'Nomos' und die 'Juden,'" *Merkur* 47 (1993): 410–20; and his forthcoming dissertation on the topic.

61. On Schmitt's critique of Kelsen, see David Dyzenhaus, "'Now the Machine Runs Itself': Carl Schmitt on Hobbes and Kelsen," *Cardozo Law Review* 16 (1994): 10–15. How much Schmitt comprehended of Kelsen remains questionable. In *Political Theology*, 18–20, for example, he first equates the basic norm with the state, and later labels it a "mythology" (mistranslated by Schwab as "assumption").

62. See *The Crisis of Parliamentary Democracy*, trans. from the 2d ed. (1926) by Ellen Kennedy (Cambridge: MIT Press, 1985), ch. 4. See also Schmitt's many

positive references to Erich Kaufmann's political "Lebensphilosophie" in the first edition of *Politische Theologie* (Berlin: Duncker und Humblot, 1922), 14–15, 27–28; on war as the ultimate reality for the state, see *Der Begriff des Politischen*, 33.

63. *Political Theology*, 15. This quote makes reference to Kierkegaard's notion of the miraculous foundation of faith. Schmitt shifts the "exception" to the level of the superindividual state. See Karl Löwith, "Der okkasionelle Dezisionismus von Carl Schmitt" (1935), repr. in *Samtliche Schriften*, vol. 8: *Heidegger—Denker in dürftiger Zeit* (Stuttgart: J. B. Metzlersche, 1984), 32–71. Richard Wolin stresses Schmitt's decisionism and its connection to the "vitalist" tradition in "Carl Schmitt: The Conservative Revolutionary Habitus and the Aesthetics of Horror," *Political Theory* 20 (1992): 424–47; see also Jeffrey Herf, *Reactionary Modernism: Technology, Culture and Politics in Weimar and the Third Reich* (Cambridge: Cambridge University Press, 1984), esp. 44–46, 118–21.

64. Most of the criticism occurs within *Political Romanticism*. See also *Political Theology*, chs. 3 and 4, esp. 65–66: the real battle for good and evil will occur only when liberalism is cleared out of the way; the final battle will then take place between atheism and belief, anarchism and dictatorship. The present discussion concentrates on Schmitt's legal theory, not the motives for his political positions. For a theory of Schmitt's motives, see Nicolaus Sombart, *Die deutschen Männer und ihre Feinde. Carl Schmitt—ein deutsches Schicksal zwischen Männerbund und Matriarchatsmythos* (Munich: Hanser, 1991).

65. *Die Diktatur*, xii.

66. Ibid., xiv–xvi, 135, 194. See also the definition in *Verfassungslehre*, 48–49; *Political Theology*, 5. As he had in 1917, Schmitt described the concept of dictatorship using a Hegelian formulation: *Die Diktatur*, xvi.

67. *Die Diktatur*, 130.

68. Ibid., 138.

69. In several places Schmitt repeats his theory that the People is the secularized concept of God; see, esp., *Crisis*, 31–32; and *Political Theology*, 63–65.

70. *Die Diktatur*, 137.

71. But cf. Schwab, *The Challenge of the Exception*, 30–37; and Bendersky, *Carl Schmitt*, 31–33.

72. *Die Diktatur*, 142. Reinhard Mehring notes the importance of this work for Schmitt's later theory of modern democracy in *Carl Schmitt*, 38–40.

73. *Die Diktatur*, 140.

74. Ibid., 143–52, 204–5; Schmitt elaborates his limited discussion of the connection between sovereign dictatorship and proletarian class struggle in chapters 3 and 4 of *Crisis of Parliamentary Democracy*. See also Stefan Breuer, "Nationalstaat und pouvoir constituant bei Sieyes und Carl Schmitt," *Archiv für Rechts- und Sozialphilosophie* 70 (1984): 495–517.

75. Cf. Schwab, *The Challenge of the Exception*, 33–34.

76. *Verfassungslehre*, 58–60. Schmitt carefully avoids using the terms *representation* and *representative*—with all their connections to his theory of the church—to refer to the Reichstag; he uses instead the bureaucratic "*Beauftragte*." The word choice relates to Schmitt's strong suggestion that parliamentary representation is not really representation since actual argument is replaced by interest groups and lobbies (*Verfassungslehre*, 217–19).

77. *Verfassungslehre*, 44.

78. Ibid., 11–20.

79. Ibid., 75–79, 91–92, 238; against Kelsen, see 7–9, ending on p. 10 with the blunt assertion that a real will forms the basis of the constitutional system. Erich Voegelin has pointed out that many of Schmitt's points in the *Verfassungslehre* consist of assertion rather than arguments: "Die Verfassungslehre von Carl Schmitt. Versuch einer konstruktiven Analyse ihrer staatstheoretischen Prinzipien," *Zeitschrift für öffentliches Recht* 11 (1931): 93.

80. *Verfassungslehre*, 61; see also 50.

81. *Begriff des Politischen*, esp. 28–30, 33–35, 43, 50. On the concept of the political and its connection to the *Verfassungslehre*, see Ernst-Wolfgang Böckenförde, "Der Begriff des Politischen als Schlüssel zum staatsrechtlichen Werk Carl Schmitts" (1988), repr. in *Recht, Staat, Freiheit. Studien zur Rechtsphilosophie, Staatstheorie und Verfassungsgeschichte* (Frankfurt am Main: Suhrkamp, 1991), 344–66; Scheuerman, *Between the Norm and the Exception*, 17–24. Cf. McCormick, "Fear, Technology, and the State," which develops the concept of the enemy in connection with Hobbesian and technology-critical motifs.

82. A similar analysis is in Hasso Hofmann, *Legalität gegen Legitimität*, 134–41; and Maus, *Bürgerliche Rechtstheorie und Faschismus*, 121–22.

83. "Das Wesen des Staates," 1718–19; *Introduction to the Problems of Legal Theory*, 31.

84. But not from "law" itself! See, esp., Christoph Müller's critique of Friedrich Müller on this score in "Die Bekenntnispflicht der Beamten. Bemerkungen zu §35 Abs. 1 S. 2 BRRG, zugleich Anmerkungen zur Methodologie Friedrich Müllers," in *Ordnungsmacht? Über das Verhältnis von Legalität, Konsens und Herrschaft*, ed. Dieter Deiseroth, Friedhelm Hase, and Karl-Heinz Ladeur (Frankfurt am Main: Europäische Verlagsanstalt, 1981), 223–24.

85. Heller's critique is in *Souveränität*, 78, 85–86. See, esp., Kelsen's discussion contribution to "Die Gleichheit vor dem Gesetz im Sinne des Art. 109 der Reichsverfassung," in *VVDSRL*, 3:55.

86. Kelsen, in his critique of Sander ("Rechtswissenschaft und Recht," 411), makes explicit the problem of subjectivism with reference to the key differentiation between Kant's transcendental logic and Berkeley's self-enclosed "I."

87. *Verfassungslehre*, 227; on Schmitt's assumption of homogeneity, see Thomas Vesting, *Politische Einheitsbildung und technische Realisation. Über die Expansion der Technik und die Grenzen der Demokratie* (Baden-Baden: Nomos, 1990), 47–58; Ulrich K. Preuss, "Constitutional Powermaking of the New Polity: Some Deliberations on the Relations between Constituent Power and the Constitution," in *Constitutionalism, Identity, Difference, and Legitimacy: Theoretical Perspectives,* ed. Michel Rosenfeld (Durham: Duke University Press, 1994), 153–55.

88. *Verfassungslehre*, 51, 216. Schmitt's general theory of the bourgeois *Rechtsstaat* is summarized by Werner Becker, with Schmitt's approval, in "Der bürgerliche Rechtsstaat," *Die Schildgenossen* 8 (1928): 127–33; I thank Raphael Gross for this reference.

89. *Verfassungslehre*, 125–26, 200–202. A parallel discussion is in *Begriff des Politischen*, 69. On "substantial equality" and homogeneity, see *Verfassungslehre*, 226–34. Schmitt did not consider homogeneity by itself to be capable of producing political form. He privileges the mediating role of the "representative," whether *Führer* or monarch, in his critique of immanent, economic thought. See Voegelin, "Verfassungslehre von Carl Schmitt," 99–100 (on how the proletariat becomes mere formless negativity); and Günter Meuter, "Zum Begriff der Transzendenz bei Carl Schmitt," *Der Staat* 32 (1991): 486–89.

90. *Verfassungslehre*, 305–6, 41; *Crisis of Parliamentary Democracy*, 35–36. Schmitt defined the bourgeoisie vaguely, as being "educated and propertied" (e.g., *Verfassungslehre*, 308). By avoiding any substantive concept of the bourgeoisie as class, Schmitt avoided discussing his own class position. On Schmitt's "sociology," see Voegelin, "Verfassungslehre von Carl Schmitt," 96–97.

91. *Political Romanticism*, 12–13; *Verfassungslehre*, 125.

92. *Verfassungslehre*, 126 (emphasis in original).

93. *Verfassungslehre*, 163–70. This was also the Labandian tradition's usual way of understanding "subjective private rights"; e.g., Giese, *Die Grundrechte*, 44–50.

94. *Verfassungslehre*, 182–99.

95. E.g., the administrative act, in ibid., 130–31.

96. Ibid., 133.

97. Ibid., 7, 134; see also vii, 53–56.

98. Ibid., 139, 143–50. Note the use of the word *Behörde*, which implies an administrative office, not a legislative organ.

99. *Unabhängigkeit der Richter, Gleichheit vor dem Gesetz und Gewährleistung des Privateigentums nach der Weimarer Verfassung. Ein Rechtsgutachten zu den Gesetzentwürfen über die Vermögensauseinandersetzung mit den früher regierenden Fürstenhäusern* (Berlin: Walter de Gruyter, 1926), 9–11, 16–17; *Verfassungslehre*, 152. The argument I am developing here relies on Ingeborg Maus, *Bürgerliche Rechtstheorie und Faschismus*. Jerry Z. Muller's critique of Maus's reading—that she looks

only at two unrepresentative speeches given to organizations of Rhineland industrialists—fails to deal with her more basic critique of the anti-*socialist* motif throughout Schmitt's work; Schmitt was certainly willing to tolerate state intervention into the economy, but not on the terms of socialist, communist, and left-liberal political parties. Cf. Muller, *The Other God That Failed: Hans Freyer and the Deradicalization of German Conservatism* (Princeton: Princeton University Press, 1987), 211, n. 93.

100. *Unabhängigkeit der Richter*, 17–18, 20.

101. Ibid., 13–14; *Verfassungslehre*, 141–42, 151, 154–55; for further discussion, see Joachim Perels, "Die Gleichheit vor dem Gesetz," in *Grundrechte als Fundament der Demokratie*, ed. Joachim Perels (Frankfurt am Main: Suhrkamp, 1979), 69–95, esp. 71–76 on the Weimar debates.

102. *Verfassungslehre*, 18–20, 25–26; "Zehn Jahre Reichsverfassung," in *Verfassungsrechtliche Aufsätze*, 38–39.

103. Maus, *Bürgerliche Rechtstheorie und Faschismus*, 18–19.

104. Heller, "Der Begriff des Gesetzes in der Reichsverfassung," *VVDSRL*, 4:108–10.

105. *Verfassungslehre*, 144–45; see also 192, where Schmitt argues that parliament has power over the budget only "as long as the parliament limits itself to mere budgetary oversight [*Kontrolle*] and avoids directives and interventions." The similarity of Schmitt's argument to Laband's is here unmistakable, as is the similarity in political function. See Müller, "Die Bekenntnispflicht der Beamten," 239–40, n. 32.

106. *Unabhängigkeit der Richter*, 26.

107. *Verfassungslehre*, 31, 35; *Legalität und Legitimität*, 299–300.

108. On "apocryphal decisions," see *Verfassungslehre*, xii, 108, 150.

109. Maus, *Bürgerliche Rechtstheorie und Faschismus*, 57–58, 111–12; Wolfgang Luthardt, *Sozialdemokratische Verfassungstheorie in der Weimarer Republik* (Opladen: Westdeutscher, 1986). Reformist socialism made no sense to Schmitt, who could imagine only the extreme alternatives of bourgeois *Rechtsstaat* and communist revolution. Reformist socialism becomes liberalism in *Verfassungslehre*, 30–31, 225–26; reformist socialist legislation becomes Jacobin terror in *Unabhängigkeit der Richter*, 26–27.

110. "Juristischer Formalismus und reine Rechtslehre," 1723; *Introduction to the Problems of Legal Theory*, 77–89; "On the Theory of Interpretation" (1934), trans. Bonnie Litschewski Paulson and Stanley L. Paulson, *Legal Studies* 10 (1990): 127–35.

111. "Die Lehre von den drei Gewalten," 1633–34; *Introduction to the Problems of Legal Theory*, 70. In the latter, 65–67, Kelsen looks at the problem of the source of law in legislation or common law.

112. The language of the Free Law movement is adopted in *Introduction to the Problems of Legal Theory*, 81–82; explicit invocation of the movement is in "Juristischer Formalismus und reine Rechtslehre," 1726.

113. On theory of legislation, see Peter Römer, "Reine Rechtslehre und Gesetzgebungslehre," in *Rechtstheorie und Gesetzgebung. Festschrift für Robert Weimar* (Frankfurt am Main: Peter Lang, 1986), 26–27; on theory of interpretation, see Dreier, *Rechtslehre, Staatssoziologie und Demokratietheorie*, 145–55, 159–83, and pt. 5. Karl Larenz's critique of Kelsen's theory of interpretation as "empty," merely critical, is therefore correct—but misplaced. See *Methodenlehre der Rechtswissenschaft*, 5th ed. (Berlin: Springer, 1983), 69–81. For additional references and a defense of Kelsen, see Kurt Ringhofer, "Interpretation und Reine Rechtslehre. Gedanken zu einer Kritik," in *Festschrift für Hans Kelsen zum 90. Geburtstag*, ed. Adolf Merkl et al. (Vienna: Franz Deuticke, 1971), 198–210; somewhat more critical is Stanley L. Paulson, "Kelsen on Legal Interpretation," *Legal Studies* 10 (1990): 136–52.

114. "Die Diktatur des Reichspräsidenten nach Artikel 48 der Weimarer Verfassung," repr. with additional section in *Die Diktatur*, 239.

115. Ibid., 236–38.

116. Ibid., 241.

117. *Verfassungslehre*, 11.

118. "Die Diktatur des Reichspräsidenten," 242–43.

119. Ibid., 241.

120. Ibid. The Reichstag never limited presidential power according to this provision, largely because Presidents Ebert and Hindenburg resisted limitations to their powers: Bracher, *Die Auflösung der Weimar Republik*, 47–52.

121. "Die Diktatur des Reichspräsidenten," 234–35.

122. *Political Theology*, 11 (translation altered).

123. Ibid., 12 (translation altered).

124. Bracher, *Die Auflösung der Weimarer Republik*, 52–54; on the debate over Bracher's interpretation, see Stanley L. Paulson, "The Reich President and Weimar Constitutional Politics: Aspects of the Schmitt-Kelsen Dispute on the 'Guardian of the Constitution'" (paper presented at the American Political Science Association meeting, Chicago, Ill., September 1, 1995), 37–40. Hans Nawiasky makes a similar critique of the potential lack of limits to presidential powers in Schmitt's approach in "Die Auslegung des Art. 48 der Reichsverfassung," *Archiv des öffentlichen Rechts* 48 (1925): 1–55.

125. Examples of republican justification of Brüning's extraordinary measures include Richard Thoma, "Die Notstandsverordnung des Reichspräsidenten vom 26. Juli 1930," *Zeitschrift für öffentliches Recht* 11 (1931): 12–33; and, commenting on Brüning's later, more extensive measures, Gerhard Anschütz and Walter Jellinek, *Reichskredite und Diktatur. Zwei Rechtsgutachten* (Tübingen: J. C. B. Mohr

[Paul Siebeck], 1932), citing Schmitt on 22 and 24. See also Gerhard Schulz, *Zwischen Demokratie und Diktatur. Verfassungspolitik und Reichsreform in der Weimarer Republik*, vol. 3: *Von Brüning zu Hitler. Der Wandel des politischen Systems in Deutschland 1930–1933* (Berlin: Walter de Gruyter, 1992), 374–75, 792–93; Winkler, *Weimar*, 397–98. A defense of Hindenburg's use of Art. 48 during the Brüning government is in ibid., 376; and Scheuner, "Die Anwendung des Art. 48 der Weimarer Reichsverfassung," 272–81.

126. E.g., Hermann Heller, "Ziele und Grenzen einer deutschen Verfassungsreform" (1931), repr. in *Gesammelte Schriften*, 2:411–17. See Hans Mommsen, "Government without Parties: Conservative Plans for Constitutional Revision at the End of the Weimar Republic," in *Between Reform, Reaction, and Resistance: Studies in the History of German Conservatism from 1789 to 1945*, ed. Larry Eugene Jones and James Retallack (Providence: Berg, 1993), 350–51.

127. Bund zur Erneuerung des Reiches, *Die Rechte des Deutschen Reichspräsidenten nach der Reichsverfassung. Eine gemeinverständliche Darstellung* (Berlin: Bund zur Erneuerung des Reiches, 1929); idem, *Welche Rechte hat der Reichspräsident?* (Berlin: Bund zur Erneuerung des Reiches, 1931). On the monarchical intentions in Brüning's memoirs, see Karl Otmar Freiherr von Aretin, "Brünings ganz andere Rolle"; on Papen, see ch. 6.

128. "Das Reichsgericht als Hüter der Verfassung," in *Verfassungsrechtliche Aufsätze*, 69–70.

129. *Hüter der Verfassung* (Tübingen: J. C. B. Mohr [Paul Siebeck], 1931), 12–70. See the detailed critique in Kelsen, "Wer soll der Hüter der Verfassung sein?" (1931), repr. in *Wiener rechtstheoretische Schule*, 1873–1922.

130. *Der Hüter der Verfassung*, 31–33, 39n.

131. See ch. 2; and Paulson, "The Reich President and Weimar Constitutional Politics," 20–33.

132. "Wer soll der Hüter der Verfassung sein?" 1885.

133. *Hüter der Verfassung*, 42–43; "Wer soll der Hüter der Verfassung sein?" 1883, 1886–88.

134. *Hüter der Verfassung*, iii; for a historical introduction to Pufendorf's work, see Horst Denzer's afterword to Pufendorf, *Die Verfassung des deutschen Reiches*, 161–211.

135. Cited in *Verfassungslehre*, 49.

136. Pufendorf, *Die Verfassung des deutschen Reiches*, 4–5, 96–107.

137. Hegel, *Werke*, vol. 1: *Frühe Schriften*, ed. Eva Moldenhauer and Karl Markus Michel (Frankfurt am Main: Suhrkamp, 1971), 451–610.

138. *Hüter der Verfassung*, 67–68.

139. Ibid., 113–14; Hegel's discussion of the *itio in partes* is in *Die Verfassung Deutschlands*, 520–21.

140. *Hüter der Verfassung*, 110.

141. E.g., ibid., 53–54, on the notion of the constitution as contract. Schmitt's arguments against judicial decisions regarding conflicts between state and federal governments are the logical consequence of this rejection of the contract. See ibid., 55–60; and *Verfassungslehre*, 361–91. Against subjective public rights, see *Hüter der Verfassung*, 68.

142. *Hüter der Verfassung*, 71–73.

143. Ibid., 78–79. Kelsen criticizes the liberal conception of nineteenth-century state neutrality in "Wer soll der Hüter der Verfassung sein?" 1899.

144. *Hüter der Verfassung*, 82–84.

145. *Crisis of Parliamentary Democracy*, 6–7, 49–50.

146. *Hüter der Verfassung*, 89–90.

147. Ibid., 131.

148. Ibid., 100–101, 108.

149. Ibid., 131.

150. Ibid., 24–25, 145; "Das Reichsgericht als Hüter der Verfassung," 69.

151. *Hüter der Verfassung*, 136.

152. Ibid., 158–59.

153. Ibid., 91–94, 115–16.

154. See, e.g., *Legalität und Legitimität*, 266–67. The argument continued under the National Socialist regime, e.g., in "Weiterentwicklung des totalen Staates in Deutschland" (February 1933), in *Verfassungsrechtliche Aufsätze*, 359–65.

155. Harold J. Laski, *The American Presidency, an Interpretation* (New York: Harper and Brothers, 1940); on the technocrats, see William E. Akin, *Technocracy and the American Dream: The Technocratic Movement, 1900–1941* (Berkeley: University of California Press, 1977).

156. *Der Hüter der Verfassung*, 159.

157. Heller, *Souveränität*, 89–90.

158. "Wer soll der Hüter der Verfassung sein?" 1909–10.

159. Indeed, as Kelsen noted, the Austrian Constitutional Court had come under fire precisely because the president was a party to a case brought before it. See ibid., 1910–12, 1917–19; Kelsen, "Judicial Review of Legislation: A Comparative Study of the Austrian and the American Constitution," *Journal of Politics* 4 (1942): 188, with references to Art. 48 in Weimar.

160. "Wer soll der Hüter der Verfassung sein?" 1920.

161. Schmitt, *Der Hüter der Verfassung*, 158–59; Kelsen, "Wer soll der Hüter der Verfassung sein?" 1914–16.

162. See Kelsen, "Wer soll der Hüter der Verfassung sein?" 1874–75.

163. *Allgemeine Staatslehre*, 89; see also 246–48 on the "freedom" of the administration, and quotes on 402–5.

164. Laband, *Staatsrecht*, 2:44–50; see the brief summary in Christoph Gusy,

Richterliches Prüfungsrecht. Eine verfassungsgeschichtliche Untersuchung (Berlin: Duncker und Humblot, 1985), 65–68.

165. *Problem der Souveränität*, 25–26; on Saint Augustine's problem of the robber band, see *The Pure Theory of Law*, 2d ed., 48–50.

166. This continuity is stressed in Vesting, *Politische Einheitsbildung*, 44–47; Ingeborg Maus, "Zur 'Zäsur' von 1933 in der Theorie Carl Schmitts" (1969), repr. in *Rechtstheorie und politische Theorie im Industriekapitalismus*, 93–110.

167. *Introduction to the Problems of Legal Theory*, 99–101.

168. Schmitt, "Staatsethik und pluralistischer Staat," *Kantstudien* 35 (1930): 28–29.

169. Scheuerman emphasizes Schmitt's resistance to the expansion of social law through the Reichstag, and with it his fundamental opposition to Social Democracy, in *Between the Norm and the Exception*, 71–80. On the related problem of the structural change of the state in industrial society, see Thomas Vesting, "Erosionen staatlicher Herrschaft. Zum Begriff des Politischen bei Carl Schmitt," *Archiv des öffentlichen Rechts* 117 (1992): 4–45.

170. See, e.g., "Der Staatsbegriff und die Psychoanalyse" (1927), repr. in *Wiener rechtstheoretische Schule*, 212–13; on popular sovereignty as a "totemistic mask," see "Demokratie" (1927), repr. in ibid., 1762.

171. *Vom Wesen und Wert der Demokratie*, 2d ed., 26–27.

5 Constitutional Practice and the Immanence of Democratic Sovereignty

1. Francesco Gentile, "Hobbes et Kelsen. Éléments pour une lecture croisée," *Cahiers Vilfredo Pareto. Revue européenne des sciences sociales* 61 (1982): 379–92. Kelsen also stressed the role "objective" law would play in ensuring "social peace," a Hobbesian theme; see *Vom Wesen und Wert der Demokratie*, 2d ed., 66–68. Schmitt himself claimed to remain in the Hobbesian tradition. This is true, I think, as long as "Hobbesian" refers to the specifically legal aspects of Hobbes's construction of the state as sovereign, not to his politics and cultural ideas. On Schmitt's deviation from Hobbes's values of peace and individualism, see Meier, *Carl Schmitt and Leo Strauss*, 32–38; Leo Strauss, "Notes on Schmitt's *Concept of the Political*," in ibid., 99–102, 115; John McCormick, "Fear, Technology, and the State"; and Holmes, *Anatomy of Antiliberalism*, 41–42, 50–53.

2. Fuller, *The Morality of Law*; and Dworkin, *Taking Rights Seriously*, 2d ed. (Cambridge: Harvard University Press, 1978).

3. Renan is cited in Smend, *Verfassung und Verfassungsrecht*, 136; Heller, *Die Souveränität*, 104; *Staatslehre*, 261, 325.

4. Freiherr von Campenhausen, "Rudolf Smend (1882–1975)," 523–26.

5. "Integrationslehre" (1956), repr. in *Staatsrechtliche Abhandlungen*, 475; see also the "communitarian" description of integration in "Integration" (1965), repr. in *Staatsrechtliche Abhandlungen*, 486, cited in Campenhausen, "Rudolf Smend," 522–23. On the religious aspects of Smend's work, see Rennert, *Die "geisteswissenschaftliche Richtung" in der Staatslehre der Weimarer Republik*, 47, 256–57.

6. *Verfassung und Verfassungsrecht*, 274, 180–81, 212–13.

7. On the context of the "organic" break with positivism, see Korioth, "Erschütterungen des staatsrechtlichen Positivismus im ausgehenden Kaiserreich," 221–28, 234.

8. "Ungeschriebenes Verfassungsrecht im monarchischen Bundesstaat" (1916), repr. in *Staatsrechtliche Abhandlungen*, 54.

9. Kaufmann, *Studien zur Staatslehre des monarchischen Prinzipes* (Leipzig: O. Brandstetter, 1906); Smend, *Die Preussische Verfassungsurkunde im Vergleich mit der Belgischen* (Göttingen: Diederich, 1904).

10. "Ungeschriebenes Verfassungsrecht," 39–59. Manfred Friedrich emphasizes the centrality of this essay to Smend's thought in "Rudolf Smend 1882–1975," *Archiv des öffentlichen Rechts* 112 (1987): 3–5. An extended analysis is in Stefan Korioth, *Integration und Bundesstaat. Ein Beitrag zur Staats- und Verfassungslehre Rudolf Smends* (Berlin: Duncker und Humblot, 1990), 20–91.

11. "Ungeschriebenes Verfassungsrecht," 50–58.

12. Ibid., 249, citing Carl Schmitt on parliamentarianism. Smend's critique of parliamentarianism was already in print, in "Die Verschiebung der konstitutionellen Ordnung durch die Verhältniswahl" (1919) [i.e., four years before Schmitt's *Crisis of Parliamentary Democracy*], repr. in *Staatsrechtliche Abhandlungen*, 60–67.

13. *Verfassung und Verfassungsrecht*, 141, 232–33.

14. Smend and his colleague Heinrich Triepel left the party in 1930 when Hugenberg engineered its turn to open advocacy of dictatorship. See Friedrich, "Rudolf Smend," 16; and on the split in the DNVP, see Bracher, *Die Auflösung der Weimarer Republik*, 276–87.

15. Smend was aware of the methodological problems he faced in presenting the theory: *Verfassung und Verfassungsrecht*, 188–89. On the composition of the essay, see Peter Häberle, "Zum Tode von Rudolf Smend" (1975), repr. in *Verfassung als öffentlicher Prozess. Materialien zu einer Verfassungstheorie der offenen Gesellschaft* (Berlin: Duncker und Humblot, 1978), 685–87.

16. The latter is the generous interpretation of Jürgen Poeschel, *Anthropologische Voraussetzungen der Staatstheorie Rudolf Smends. Die elementaren Kategorien Leben und Leistung* (Berlin: Duncker und Humblot, 1978), 48–49.

17. Kelsen, *Der Staat als Integration*, 23. For similar critical analyses, see Hans Klinghofer, "Smends Integrationstheorie. Bemerkungen zu Smends Schrift 'Ver-

fassung und Verfassungsrecht,'" *Die Justiz* 5 (1929–30): 418–31; Fritz Stier-Somlo, "Verfassung, Verfassungsrecht," in *Handwörterbuch der Rechtswissenschaft,* vol. 6 (Berlin: Walter de Gruyter, 1929), 387–89; a more restrained critique is in Oertzen, *Die soziale Funktion des staatsrechtlichen Positivismus,* 17.

18. See the references in note 17, and Otto Koellreutter, *Integrationslehre und Reichsreform* (Tübingen: J. C. B. Mohr [Paul Siebeck], 1929), on Smend and federalism. Note also Smend's important role in Carl Bilfinger's review, "Verfassungsrecht als politisches Recht," 281–98; and the prominent place of Smend in Richard Thoma's introduction to *Handbuch des Deutschen Staatsrechts,* "Gegenstand.-Methode.-Literatur," 1:5.

19. Edgar Tatarin-Tarnheyden, review of *Verfassung und Verfassungsrecht, Juristische Wochenschrift* 57 (1928): 1028–29.

20. *Verfassung und Verfassungsrecht,* 120, 136.

21. Ibid., 129, 165–66; "Die politische Gewalt im Verfassungsstaat und das Problem der Staatsform" (1923), repr. in *Staatsrechtliche Abhandlungen,* 80. Smend borrowed the term *integration* from Spencer, although he found Spencer's thought "inorganic": *Verfassung und Verfassungsrecht,* 136–37, n. 3; see also "Die Verschiebung der konstitutionellen Ordnung durch die Verhältniswahl," 67, in which Smend argues for a "sociologically founded constitutional theory." Smend's use of the term *realer Willensverband,* the title of the section beginning p. 127 of *Verfassung und Verfassungsrecht,* is reminiscent of Gierke's organic notion of the state. Positive reference to Gierke's "methodological naïveté" is in ibid., 123–24; negative references to "mechanical" notions of sociology and psychology are at 126–30.

22. *Verfassung und Verfassungsrecht,* 136. Kelsen was Smend's main opponent. See ibid., 121–24. Kelsen, meanwhile, referred to Smend's use of the word *life* as a "true fetish cult" (*Der Staat als Integration,* 24), and even Smend's defender Poeschel noted the "ambiguity" of the term *Leben* (*Anthropologische Voraussetzungen,* 128–29). Wolfgang Schluchter views the dispute between Kelsen and Smend as the central opposition of Weimar state theory: *Entscheidung für den sozialen Rechtsstaat,* 26–89.

23. Dieter Grimm, on Smend and Schmitt, in "Die 'neue Rechtswissenschaft' —Über Funktion und Formation nationalsozialistische Jurisprudenz" (1985), repr. in *Recht und Staat der bürgerlichen Gesellschaft,* 391.

24. *Verfassung und Verfassungsrecht,* 161. Schluchter writes of a "sublation of difference" in *Entscheidung für den sozialen Rechtsstaat,* 69–71.

25. The "dialectical" formulations appear where Smend cites Litt: e.g., 131–32; immediately thereafter, he turns to the undialectical notion of the state as "community of fate" (*Schicksalgemeinschaft*) and explains how sleepers, the mentally disabled, and children are all part of the "totality of existence and lived experience" (*Wesens- und Erlebnisganzen*). Kelsen points out Smend's turn away from Litt in

Staat als Integration, 44–45. The conservative, neo-Hegelian legal theorist Karl Larenz praises Smend for abandoning Litt's dialectic in favor of a theory of the real, existing nation in *Staats- und Rechtsphilosophie der Gegenwart* (Berlin: Junker und Dünnhaupt, 1931), 99–103.

26. *Verfassung und Verfassungsrecht*, 150–52.

27. E.g., ibid., 130–35. Anatomy and physiology are mentioned in "Die Verschiebung der konstitutionellen Ordnung," 60.

28. *Verfassung und Verfassungsrecht*, 142–43. For a sense of Smend's style, note the complete sentence: "Theoretisch wirkt es [the liberal theory of the leader] sich aus in der Betrachtung der Geführten als (im physikalischen Sinne) träger Masse, auf die eine Kraft von aussen wirkt—ein mechanistisches Denken, das die notwendige Spontaneität und Produktivität auch der Geführten übersieht, die zwar zum Gruppenleben angeregt werden, aber dies Leben dann alsbald als ihr eigenes Leben, in dessen Erleben der Führer nicht alleinige Kraft und sie selbst passive Geschobene, sondern in dem sie selbst lebendig und die Führer Lebensform der sozial und geistig in ihnen lebendig und aktiv Werdenden sind."

29. Ibid., 144–46. Some of the phrases Smend employs in this section are borrowed from Thomas Mann's *Königliche Hoheit* (1909).

30. Ibid., 145, n. 12. Smend cites Marianne Weber, *Max Weber. Ein Lebensbild* (Heidelberg: Lambert Schneider, 1950), 698. The citation is actually false. Marianne Weber does not claim that her husband thought that Eastern European Jews were "by their essence" incapable of integration, but that he thought it "politically unwise" for so many Jews (not specifying those from Eastern Europe) to have played leading roles in the revolution.

31. *Verfassung und Verfassungsrecht*, 145, n. 7.

32. Ibid., 149.

33. Ibid., 159.

34. Ibid., 157. Gerhard Leibholz develops a similar argument about "plebiscitary democracy" in his Weimar work: "Die Reform des Wahlrechtes," *VVDSRL*, 7:170 (1932).

35. *Verfassung und Verfassungsrecht*, 160.

36. Ibid., 162–64.

37. Ibid., 166.

38. Ibid., 163, nn. 9, 10, 164, n. 15.

39. Ibid., 141; for further examples, see 175, 216, n. 5.

40. Fritz Borinski gives a good account of Heller's connection to youth while at the same time inexplicably arguing that he did not participate in its "cult": "Hermann Heller: Lehrer der Jugend und Vorkämpfer der freien Erwachsenenbildung," in *Der soziale Rechtsstaat*, 89–110. In general on Heller's life, see Müller, "Hermann Heller: Leben, Werk, Wirkung," 433–42. Heller's literary remains were destroyed in the Spanish Civil War.

41. Smend, "Zur Geschichte der Berliner Juristenfakultät im 20. Jahrhundert," in *Studium Berolinense,* ed. Hans Leussink, Eduard Neumann, and Georg Kotowski (Berlin: Walter de Gruyter, 1960), 124, cited in Meyer, "Hermann Heller," 81; see also Müller, "Hermann Heller: Leben, Werk, Wirkung," 438, n. 30.

42. *Sozialismus und Nation* (1925), repr. in *Gesammelte Schriften,* 1:439.

43. On Heller's reception of Marx and his idealist notion of socialism, see Ruedi Waser, *Die sozialistische Idee im Denken Hermann Hellers. Zur politischen Theorie und Praxis eines demokratischen Sozialismus* (Basel: Helbing und Lichtenhahn, 1985), 34ff. on Heller's reductive understanding of Marxism before the *Staatslehre,* 81ff. on Heller's nationalism in context. Eike Hennig accuses Heller of having a vague, ethical, "atmospheric" critique of capitalism in "Hermann Heller. Anmerkungen zum Versuch einer Synthese von Nationalismus und Sozialismus," *Neue Politische Literatur* 4 (1971): 512. But cf. Müller, "Hermann Heller: Leben, Werk, Wirkung," 443–48, which concretizes Heller's critique.

44. Gerhard Robbers, *Hermann Heller: Staat und Kultur* (Baden-Baden: Nomos, 1983), 11–12. This anecdote is cited also in Klaus Meyer, "Hermann Heller. Eine biographische Skizze" (1967), repr. in *Der soziale Rechtsstaat,* 70–71.

45. On the Hofgeismarkreis, see Franz Osterroth (a former member): "Der Hofgeismarkreis der Jungsozialisten," *Archiv für Sozialgeschichte* 4 (1964): 525–69; Dan S. White, *Lost Comrades: Socialists of the Front Generation, 1918–1945* (Cambridge: Harvard University Press, 1992), 48–51. Neither work develops the connection between the circle and the odd, far-right-far-left figure Ernst Niekisch. See Otto-Ernst Schüddekopf, *Linke Leute von rechts. Die nationalrevolutionären Minderheiten und der Kommunismus in der Weimarer Republik* (Stuttgart: W. Kohlhammer, 1960), 170–75. For the leftist critique, see the discussion among the Young Socialists repr. in *Gesammelte Schriften,* 1:553–63. A recent reiteration of the leftist criticism of Heller, unfortunately riddled with unfounded assertions and tendentious misinterpretations, is Peter Kratz, *Rechte Genossen. Neokonservatismus in der SPD* (Berlin: Elefanten Press, 1995), 228–30.

46. Meyer, "Hermann Heller," 68. A critique of "Versailler Diktat" is in *Die politischen Ideenkreise der Gegenwart* (1926), repr. in *Gesammelte Schriften,* 1:359; fear that Germany will become a white slave colony of the United States is in *Sozialismus und Nation,* 520–22; "Rechtsstaat oder Diktatur?" (1929), repr. in *Gesammelte Schriften,* 2:461; *Europa und der Faschismus,* 2d ed. (1931), repr. in *Gesammelte Schriften,* 2:470. On Europe, see *Die Souveränität,* 201; *Die politischen Ideenkreise,* 407–9; and Robbers, *Hermann Heller,* 97–99.

47. See, esp., the vitriolic public attacks on Kelsen in "Der Begriff des Gesetzes in der Reichsverfassung," *VVDSRL,* 4:176–80 (Kelsen), 201–4 (Heller); 5:113–14 (Heller), 121–23 (Kelsen).

48. *Die Souveränität,* 42–43, 84–86, 157; "Bemerkungen zur staats- und rechtstheoretischen Problematik der Gegenwart" (1929), repr. in *Gesammelte Schriften,*

2:261, 276. "Die Krise der Staatslehre," 15–24. On positivism as liberalism, see, esp., "Bemerkungen," 256; on Kelsen's "bourgeois" state theory and its proximity to "Marxist positivism," see ibid., 260–61.

49. On the state as unity of "is" and "ought": "Bemerkungen," 266–67; statist themes are developed in "Grundrechte und Grundpflichten" (1924), repr. in *Gesammelte Schriften,* 2:283–85; *Die politischen Ideenkreise,* 275–82; *Die Souveränität,* 38–41; "Bemerkungen," 253–54; and *Staatslehre,* 221–36.

50. Introduction repr. in *Gesammelte Schriften,* 1:13–20.

51. "Hegel und die deutsche Politik" (1924), repr. in *Gesammelte Schriften,* 1:244.

52. Critique of Kaufmann is in *Hegel und der nationale Machtstaatsgedanke,* 235–38; and *Staatslehre,* 329. The relevant passage is in Erich Kaufmann, *Das Wesen des Völkerrechts,* 146. Heller condemns the brutality and senselessness of modern war in *Sozialismus und Nation,* 523–24; see also Müller, "Hermann Heller: Leben, Werk, Wirkung," 436.

53. *Die Souveränität,* 141–44, 164–65: international law presupposes the sovereignty of individual states, not the international legal system; 185–86: the state is able to decide against international law since the state is a living will prior to international law; 187–89: on the right to self-preservation, using Erich Kaufmann. In this work, Heller calls Schmitt's discussion of sovereignty "exemplary," especially with respect to the search for a state "subject" endowed with "will" (88). The actual arguments, however, are usually taken from Erich Kaufmann.

54. See, esp., the debate with Adler on the state at the famous Third Conference of the Young Socialists, held April 12–13, 1925, in Jena: "Staat, Nation und Sozialdemokratie," in *Gesammelte Schriften,* 1:527–42; and Adler's speech, in ibid., 542–53, with heated discussion, 553–63.

55. Esp. "Sozialistische Aussenpolitik?" (1924), repr. in *Gesammelte Schriften,* 1:415–20. This work was written for the Hofgeismar Circle.

56. The criticisms Heller received at the 1926 conference of Young Socialists are good examples. See, esp., "Staat, Nation und Sozialdemokratie," 540, 541; and Adler's response, 552. At numerous points, participants in the discussion accused the entire Hofgeismar Circle of far-right politics. Matters were not helped by the generally favorable reception of Heller's *Souveränität* by some conservatives; for example, the far-right public lawyer Otto Koellreutter in *Archiv des öffentlichen Rechts* 52 (1928): 133–37.

57. Explicitly stated in "Staat, Nation und Sozialdemokratie," 537–38; *Sozialismus und Nation,* 480–81.

58. *Sozialismus und Nation,* 452–55; *Staatslehre,* 246–67.

59. See *Sozialismus und Nation,* 453–55.

60. The historical turn from transcendent to immanent conception of political reality is invoked in "Bemerkungen," 254.

61. *Sozialismus und Nation*, 466–68; *Die Souveränität*, 105. It is hard not to bristle when Heller refers to the *"Negerfrage"* in the United States as an "anthropological," and not a cultural problem ("Politische Demokratie und soziale Homogenität" [1928], repr. in *Gesammelte Schriften*, 2:432).

62. *Europa und der Faschismus;* Robbers, *Hermann Heller*, 16.

63. *Staatslehre*, 236–305. Franz Neumann's 1935 review points out the importance of this critical endeavor: "Zur marxistischen Staatstheorie," in *Wirtschaft, Staat, Demokratie*, 136–39.

64. "Politische Demokratie und soziale Homogenität," 427–28; *Staatslehre*, 345–46.

65. *Die Souveränität*, 125–26, 133.

66. Heller's brief discussion of Hobbes is in *Staatslehre*, 108–9 (in English, in "Political Science" [1934], repr. in *Gesammelte Schriften*, 3:62–63).

67. *Die Souveränität*, 128, 104.

68. Ibid., 102–3.

69. *Staatslehre*, 342, 361–62.

70. Ibid., 343–44, 130–42; *Die Souveränität*, 122–23. The term *Wirklichkeitswissenschaft* was borrowed from Hans Freyer; on the concept, see Muller, *The Other God That Failed*, 162–85.

71. *Die Souveränität*, 70, 107–8; *Staatslehre*, 332–35.

72. *Staatslehre*, 267.

73. *Die Souveränität*, 71–72, 107. Wolfram Bauer argues that Heller's theory of the *Rechtsgrundsätze* represents a return to natural law in *Wertrelativismus und Wertbestimmtheit*, 395–96. But note that Heller's formulation leads directly to the problem of positive law. As Kelsen noted in his discussion of natural law ("Natural Law Doctrine and Legal Positivism," 397–98), the need for legislation entails a return to the problems of positivism. See also Ilse Staff, "Staatslehre in der Weimarer Republik," in *Staatslehre in der Weimarer Republik. Hermann Heller zu ehren*, ed. Staff and Christoph Müller (Frankfurt am Main: Suhrkamp, 1985), 13–15.

74. Explicitly in *Die Souveränität*, 69, 113–14; and *Staatslehre*, 214–15, 377–79.

75. *Staatslehre*, 393; Maus, *Bürgerliche Rechtstheorie und Faschismus*, 64–66.

76. "Staat, Nation und Sozialdemokratie," 535–36; *Staatslehre*, 323–25; see the defense and elaboration of Heller's concept of the social *Rechtsstaat* in Müller, "Hermann Heller: Leben, Werk, Wirkung," 448–50.

77. Kelsen, *Der Staat als Integration*, 60–66; Klinghofer, "Smends Integrationstheorie," 426–28.

78. *Verfassung und Verfassungsrecht*, 189.

79. Ibid., 207–8. But cf. Ernst Forsthoff, who argues that Smend, like Montesquieu, recognized that the judiciary lacked its own political weight: *Lehrbuch des Verwaltungsrechts*, vol. 1: *Allgemeiner Teil*, 9th ed. (Munich: C. H. Beck, 1966), 7.

Although Smend was unsure how to conceptualize the judiciary, such a depoliticizing intention seems alien to the general thrust of his work.

80. *Verfassung und Verfassungsrecht*, 190.

81. Ibid., 190.

82. Ibid., 238–39, 262, 265–66.

83. Smend, "Das Recht der freien Meinungsäusserung," *VVDSRL*, 4:46–48. See also *Verfassung und Verfassungsrecht*, 264; Vesting, *Politische Einheitsbildung und technische Realisation*, 189–92.

84. My translation.

85. See, e.g., Anschütz, *Die Verfassung des Deutschen Reiches*, 14th ed., 550–56, with only limited concessions to the nonformalist approach.

86. "Das Recht der freien Meinungsäusserung," *VVDSRL*, 4:51–52.

87. Ibid., 53.

88. Ibid., 56–57. Note that Anschütz had come to accept a more "Smendian" position by the end of the Republic: *Verfassung des Deutschen Reiches*, 14th ed., 659.

89. "Das Recht der freien Meinungsäusserung," *VVDSRL*, 4:57–61. Smend suggested, however, that only Marxists still believed in academic progress. See ibid., 63–64.

90. Ibid., 61.

91. On Smend and the academic elite: Müller, "Hermann Heller: Leben, Werk, Wirkung."

92. Ibid., 53.

93. *Verfassung und Verfassungsrecht*, 265–66.

94. Smend seems to have assumed that a phenomenological method would reveal the "true" value system of a community. His younger follower, Günther Holstein, makes this assumption explicit in his important report on the 1926 congress: "Von Aufgaben und Zielen heutiger Staatsrechtswissenschaft," 35–36.

95. A sharp critique is in Vesting, *Politische Einheitsbildung und technische Realisation*, 63, 66–67.

96. "Das Recht der freien Meinungsäusserung," 65–66.

97. *Verfassung und Verfassungsrecht*, 211; Vesting, *Politische Einheitsbildung und technische Realisation*, 63–65.

98. Schmitt, *Verfassungslehre*, 207–8.

99. Criticism of Smend's theory from this viewpoint is in Karl Rothenbücher, "Smends *Verfassung und Verfassungsrecht*," in *Reichsverwaltungsblatt und Preussisches Verwaltungsblatt* 49 (1928): 555. See also Friedrich Müller's political and methodological critique of Smend's desire to see the constitution as a unity of values in *Die Einheit der Verfassung*, 83–84, 131–32, 146–47, 232, n. 573.

100. Smend uses the term *sovereign* several times in *Verfassung und Verfassungsrecht*, but without providing a theoretical place for it; see 139, 155, and 195–96, where it becomes something like Renan's ever-new affirmation. Rennert (*Die "geis-*

tesgeschichtliche Richtung," 234–35) suggests that Smend meant to imply popular sovereignty at these points. But the issue is not whether Smend was a "democrat," but rather why the state and no other social organization was "sovereign."

101. Against Smend: *Staatslehre*, 300. Notably, however, Heller never aimed sharp political polemics at Smend.

102. *Staatslehre*, 390–91; Robbers, *Hermann Heller*, 72–77, distinguishes eight separate definitions of constitution in these pages. See also Dian Schefold, "Hellers Ringen um den Verfassungsbegriff," in *Der soziale Rechtsstaat*, 556–64.

103. *Staatslehre*, 136–38; Schluchter, *Entscheidung für den sozialen Rechtsstaat*, 261–70.

104. *Staatslehre*, 391.

105. Ibid., 288–91. At this point in his argument, Heller begins to cite Kelsen's argument favorably that "is" and "ought" are in a constant state of tension. On the parallels between Kelsen and Heller after 1929, see Christoph Müller, "Kritische Bemerkungen," 139–43; Stanley Paulson, "Zu Hermann Hellers Kritik an die Reine Rechtslehre," 681–83. Friedrich Müller views Heller as stuck in the neo-Kantian "is-ought" distinction in *Strukturierende Rechtslehre*, 2d ed. (Berlin: Duncker und Humblot, 1994), 36–37, 81–82; cf. 73–74.

106. *Staatslehre*, 385–89. Thomas Vesting stresses the similarities and differences between Heller's notion of state evolution and Niklas Luhmann's theory of system evolution, in *Politische Einheitsbildung und technische Realisation*, 139–49.

107. *Staatslehre*, 380–82.

108. "Der Begriff des Gesetzes," *VVDSRL*, 4:98.

109. Ibid., 101–2; *Staatslehre*, 106–9.

110. "Der Begriff des Gesetzes," *VVDSRL*, 4:116.

111. Ibid., 106–15.

112. Ibid., 108.

113. Ibid., 122–23.

114. Ibid., 103.

115. Ibid., 121.

116. "Staat, Nation, Sozialdemokratie," 535–36; *Staatslehre*, 132–40; Robbers, *Hermann Heller*, 68–71; Luthardt, *Sozialdemokratische Verfassungstheorie*, 41–45.

117. "Freiheit und Form in der Reichsverfassung" (1929–30), repr. in *Gesammelte Schriften*, 2:371–77; Kennedy, "The Politics of Toleration in Late Weimar," 109–25.

118. Maus, *Bürgerliche Rechtstheorie und Faschismus*, 31–32, 42–43, 64–66; idem, "Zur Transformation des Volkssouveränitätsprinzips in der Weimarer Republic," in *Politik-Verfassung-Gesellschaft. Traditionslinien und Entwicklungsperspektiven. Otwin Massing zum 60. Geburtstag*, ed. Peter Nahamowitz and Stefan Breuer (Baden-Baden: Nomos, 1995), 113–14.

119. Kriele, *Theorie der Rechtsgewinnung*; Müller, *Juristische Methodik*. Robert

Alexy, *Theorie der Grundrechte* (Baden-Baden: Nomos, 1985), relies on the work of Dworkin rather than Smend's and Heller's.

120. Ronald Dworkin, *Life's Dominion: An Argument about Abortion, Euthanasia, and Individual Freedom* (New York: Vintage, 1993), 118–47; John H. Ely, *Democracy and Distrust: A Theory of Judicial Review* (Cambridge: Harvard University Press, 1980), esp. 58–59 against Dworkin; and Robert H. Bork, *The Tempting of America: The Political Seduction of the Law* (New York: Free Press, 1990), criticizing both Dworkin (176–77) and Ely (194–99) for deviating from the original intentions of the Founders.

121. The term *substantivist* is borrowed from Robert S. Summers, "Theory, Formality, and Practical Legal Criticism," in *Essays on the Nature of Law and Legal Realism* (Berlin: Duncker und Humblot, 1992), 154–76. Scheuerman, *Between the Norm and the Exception*, 245–48, points out some problems with a leftist turn to "substantivist" positions by juxtaposing Critical Legal Studies to arguments of the German right between the world wars.

122. *Die Verfassung des Deutschen Reichs vom 11. August 1919, Eingeleitet von Prof. Dr. R. Smend* (Berlin: Sieben Stäbe, 1929). Heller was by no means the only one to refer to *Rechtsgrundsätze* in the constitution; see, e.g., the conservative Carl Bilfinger, *Nationale Demokratie*, 17.

123. Smend, "Bürger und Bourgeois im deutschen Staatsrecht" (1933), repr. in *Staatsrechtliche Abhandlungen*, 309–25; Reinhard Mehring, "Integration und Verfassung. Zum politischen Verfassungssinn Rudolf Smends," in *Politisches Denken. Jahrbuch 1994*, ed. Volker Gerhardt, Henning Ottmann, and Martyn P. Thompson (Stuttgart: J. B. Metzler, 1995), 25–26.

124. Vesting, in *Politische Einheitsbildung und technische Realisation*, 192, argues, however, that only Smend's students gave the theory of integration a democratic turn.

125. *Preussen contra Reich* (Berlin: Dietz Nachfolger 1933), 76–78; 135–39 on preconditions for Art. 48, par. 1; 167–69.

126. Ibid., 293–94, on the substantive limits to intervention according to Art. 48, par. 2.

127. Otto Koellreutter made positive references to Heller in his failed attempt to become the "crown jurist" of the Nazis. See, e.g., *Vom Sinn und Wesen der nationalen Revolution* (Tübingen: J. C. B. Mohr [Paul Siebeck], 1933), 10, n. 1; and *Grundriss der allgemeinen Staatslehre* (Tübingen: J. C. B. Mohr [Paul Siebeck], 1933), 23–24. Use of Smend's work to defend the "national revolution" is in Ulrich Scheuner, "Die nationale Revolution. Eine staatsrechtliche Untersuchung," *Archiv des öffentlichen Rechts* 62 (1933–34): 166–220, 261–344; see also Wolfgang Kohl and Michael Stolleis, "Im Bauch des Leviathan. Zur Staats- und Verwaltungslehre im Nationalsozialismus," *Neue Juristische Wochenschrift* 41 (1988): 2852.

128. Smend, in "Integrationslehre," 480-81, criticizes his theory of integration for having ignored the formal moment of law and organization.

129. Häberle, *Verfassung als öffentlicher Prozess. Materialien zu einer Verfassungstheorie der offenen Gesellschaft* (Berlin: Duncker und Humblot, 1978).

130. Ehmke, *Grenzen der Verfassungsänderung;* " 'Staat' und 'Gesellschaft' als verfassungstheoretisches Problem," in *Staatsverfassung und Kirchenordnung. Festgabe für Rudolf Smend zum 80. Geburtstag am 15. Januar 1962,* ed. Konrad Hesse, Siegfried Reicke, and Ulrich Scheuner (Tübingen: J. C. B. Mohr [Paul Siebeck], 1962), 23-49.

6 Equality, Property, Emergency

1. Generally on institutions, see Gerhard Göhler, "Politische Institutionen und ihr Kontext. Begriffliche und konzeptionelle Überlegungen zur Theorie politischer Institutionen," in *Die Eigenart der Institution. Zum Profil politischer Institutionentheorie* (Baden-Baden: Nomos, 1994), 19-46. On the German judicial tradition, see John P. Dawson, *The Oracles of the Law* (Ann Arbor: University of Michigan Law School, 1968), 432-61. On the tradition of the *Rechtsstaat* and its transformations, see Ernst-Wolfgang Böckenförde, "Entstehung und Wandel des Rechtsstaatsbegriffs," in *Recht, Staat, Freiheit. Studien zur Rechtsphilosophie, Staatstheorie und Verfassungsgeschichte* (Frankfurt am Main: Suhrkamp, 1991), 143-69.

2. Akten der Reichskanzlei: R 43 I/1211 315-20.

3. On the place of this case in the history of U.S. institutions, see Henry J. Abraham, *The Judicial Process: An Introductory Analysis of the Courts of the United States, England, and France,* 5th ed. (New York: Oxford University Press, 1986), 320-30; Bruce Ackerman, *The Future of Liberal Revolution* (New Haven: Yale University Press, 1992), 99-100.

4. J. J. Lenoir, "Judicial Review in Germany under the Weimar Constitution," *Tulane Law Review* 14 (1940): 363-65; Johannes Mattern, *Principles of the Constitutional Jurisprudence of the German National Republic* (Baltimore: Johns Hopkins University Press, 1928), 566-67. On the creation of the Reichsgericht, see Ken Ledford, "Lawyers, Liberalism, and Procedure."

5. Dawson, *Oracles of the Law,* 446-47, 473-75, on the style of the decisions and the shift toward more details in the aftermath of the decisions on revaluation. On similar problems with writing the history of other courts, see Marc Lindner, *The Supreme Labor Court in Nazi Germany: A Jurisprudential Analysis* (Frankfurt am Main: Vittorio Klostermann, 1987), x-xi. Statistics on the Reichsgericht are in *Handbuch für das Deutsche Reich 1929,* ed. Reichsministerium des Innern (Berlin: Carl Heymann, 1929), 213-14.

6. Huber, *Deutsche Verfassungsgeschichte*, 6:546–47; Huber, *Dokumente*, 3:193–95.

7. Kommers, *Constitutional Jurisprudence of the Federal Republic of Germany*, 4–5, 8, 17–18.

8. Lübbe-Wolff, "Safeguards of Civil and Constitutional Rights," 365–72.

9. Knut Wolfgang Nörr, *Zwischen den Mühlsteinen. Eine Privatrechtsgeschichte der Weimarer Republik* (Tübingen: J. C. B. Mohr [Paul Siebeck], 1988), 57–58.

10. *Verfassung des Deutschen Reiches*, 1st ed., 185, 189.

11. Triepel, *Goldbilanzenverordnung und Vorzugsaktien*, 28.

12. Ibid., 30. For a more general discussion, see Huber, *Deutsche Verfassungsgeschichte*, 6:104–5; Hollerbach, "Heinrich Triepel," 425–26.

13. For the comparison with the United States: Triepel, *Goldbilanzenverordnung und Vorzugsaktien*, 28–29, 30–32; a defense of comparison is in "Gleichheit vor dem Gesetz," *VVDSRL*, 3:50. Walter Simons, president of the Reichgericht in the mid-1920s, took the U.S. Supreme Court as a model for German constitutional review, claiming that "more or less consciously" the founders of the Weimar Constitution had done the same (a clear overstatement): "Zum Geleit," in *Die Rechtsprechung des Staatsgerichtshofs für das Deutsche Reich und des Reichsgerichts auf Grund Artikel 13 Absatz 2 der Reichsverfassung*, vol. 1, ed. Walter Simons and Hans-Hermann Lammers (Berlin: Georg Stilke, 1929), 8–9. Gerhard Leibholz makes extensive use of the U.S. example in *Gleichheit vor dem Gesetz*.

14. At the same time, in the 1926 debate over the principle, Triepel sought to differentiate the problem of the meaning of equality before the law from the question of who would apply it, leaving the question of judicial review unresolved; see "Gleichheit vor dem Gesetz," *VVDSRL*, 3:53.

15. "Die Gleichheit vor dem Gesetz im Sinne des Art. 109 der RV," *VVDSRL*, 3:2–24.

16. Ibid., 13–18.

17. Ibid., 3.

18. Ibid., 11.

19. Ibid., 12.

20. Ibid., 23.

21. See chapter 3.

22. Triepel, *Goldbilanzenverordnung und Vorzugsaktien*, 4–6; Feldman, *The Great Disorder*, 149, 185–86, 278–79.

23. Wolff, *Reichsverfassung und Eigentum*, offprint from *Festgabe der Berliner Juristischen Fakultät für Wilhelm Kahl zum Doktorjubiläum am 19. April 1923* (Tübingen: J. C. B. Mohr [Paul Siebeck], 1923). A critique of Wolff's argument as a sudden break with the tradition is in Apelt, *Geschichte der Weimarer Verfassung*, 339–42. On the debates, see Albrecht Buschke, *Die Grundrechte der Weimarer Verfassung in der Rechtsprechung des Reichsgerichts* (Berlin: Georg Stilke, 1930), 106–7;

Helmut Rittstieg, *Eigentum als Verfassungsproblem. Zu Geschichte und Gegenwart des bürgerlichen Verfassungsstaates* (Darmstadt: Wissenschaftliche Buchgesellschaft, 1975), 258–59.

24. See, esp., Richard Epstein, *Takings: Private Property and the Power of Eminent Domain* (Cambridge: Harvard University Press, 1985).

25. Triepel, *Goldbilanzenverordnung und Vorzugsaktien*, 15–16.

26. Ibid., 18–22. Did Triepel, an expert in comparative constitutional law, have in mind when he made these formulations *Lochner* v. *New York* (1905), an important case for U.S. proponents of property rights because it forced careful consideration of the efficacy of governmental interference with property rights? Compare his examination of U.S. high court treatment of corporate and labor law in ibid., 30–31.

27. Ibid., 23.

28. Wolff, *Reichsverfassung und Eigentum*, 23–27, addresses this problem explicitly, but without providing a satisfactory theoretical foundation for drawing the line between legitimate regulation and illegitimate expropriation; see also Helmut Rittstieg, "Artikel 14/15," in *Kommentar zum Grundgesetz für die Bundesrepublik Deutschland*, 2d ed. (Neuwied: Luchterhand, 1989), 1056–57.

29. *Goldbilanzenverordnung und Vorzugsaktien*, 8–9.

30. Ibid., 1–14.

31. Heinrich Triepel, *Streitigkeiten zwischen Reich und Ländern. Beiträge zur Auslegung des Artikels 19 der Weimarer Reichsverfassung* (1923; repr., Bad Homburg von der Höhe: Hermann Gentner, 1965), 61–64, 98–101.

32. In *Streitigkeiten zwischen Reich und Ländern*, 64, 98–100, the same argument is taken to remove "political" decisions of the legislature from the jurisdiction of the courts.

33. *Entscheidungen des Reichsgerichts in Zivilsachen* [hereafter abbreviated *RGZ*], 172 vols. (Berlin: Walter de Gruyter, 1880–1945), 111:320–35.

34. Ibid., 111:323. Heinrich Stoll notes how radical the "brave step" of the court was in his comment, "Zur 3.A," *Juristische Wochenschrift* 55 (1926): 1429–30. See also Rittstieg, *Eigentum als Verfassungsproblem*, 265; Gerhard Robbers, "Die historische Entwicklung der Verfassungsgerichtsbarkeit," *Juristische Schulung* 30 (1990): 262–63; Lübbe-Wolff, "Safeguards of Civil and Constitutional Rights," 359–61.

35. *RGZ*, 111:328–30; Leibholz, "Die Gleichheit vor dem Gesetz. Ein Nachwort zur Auslegung des Art. 109 Abs. 1 RV," *Archiv des öffentlichen Rechts* 51 (1927): 27–31.

36. *RGZ*, 128:165–72.

37. Ibid., 170.

38. Notably, the Reichsgericht used virtually the same words to describe its de-

cision not to suspend a law in each case. See, e.g., decision of January 29, 1926, *RGZ*, 113:6-17, at 12-13 (revaluation ordinance's effect on joint stock corporation does not violate equality clause); decision of September 17, 1929, *RGZ*, 125:369-72, at 371-72 (Prussian law giving unmarried civil servants a supplementary salary for housing costs lower than that of married civil servants does not violate Art. 109); decision of May 27, 1932, *RGZ*, 136:211-23, at 221 (Lippe's regulation of noble mortgages is not an exceptional law that violates Art. 109); decision of November 24, 1932, *RGZ*, 139:6-12, at 11-12 (revaluation ordinance's effect on holders of government bonds does not violate the equality clause).

39. On the state of the debate at the end of the 1920s, see Fritz Stier-Somlo, "Artikel 109. Gleichheit vor dem Gesetz," in *Die Grundrechte und Grundpflichten der Deutschen*, 1:176-77.

40. Gerhard Leibholz, "Höchstrichterliche Rechtsprechung und Gleichheitssatz," *Archiv des öffentlichen Rechts* 58 (1930): 428-42, esp. 441-42.

41. Anschütz, *Die Verfassung des Deutschen Reiches*, 14th ed., 525-26; similarly, Franz Neumann, "Die soziale Bedeutung der Grundrechte in der Weimarer Verfassung," 66. A general discussion of the issue is in Wiegandt, *Norm und Wirklichkeit*, 145-46.

42. Leibholz, "Legal Philosophy and the German Constitutional Court" (1962), repr. in *Politics and Law* (Leiden: A. W. Sijthoff, 1965), 296-313.

43. The only published case in which the Reichsgericht directly opposed Triepel's arguments occurred on March 1, 1924, when the court ruled in favor of a German plaintiff seeking to avoid interest payments to a Swiss company on the basis of an emergency tax ordinance connected with revaluation, whose constitutionality Triepel had called into question (*RGZ*, 107:370-77). A political bias may well have been involved in the formalistic decision: the case fell against a foreign insurance company. Walter Schelcher asserts that by 1930, the Reichsgericht had completely adopted the Wolff-Triepel approach: "Artikel 153. Die Rechte und Pflichten aus dem Eigentum," in Nipperdey, ed., *Grundrechte und Grundpflichten*, 3:202.

44. *RGZ*, 103:200-202; Rittstieg, *Eigentum als Verfassungsproblem*, 257; on the situation in Lippe-Detmold, see Franklin C. West, *A Crisis of the Weimar Republic: A Study of the German Referendum of 20 June 1926* (Philadelphia: American Philosophical Society, 1985), 26-27.

45. Art. 153, par. 2's, limitation of the *Länder* should be considered in the context of the National Assembly's attempt to limit "wild socialization" on the local level: Apelt, *Geschichte der Weimarer Verfassung*, 111-12, 360-61; Anschütz, *Verfassung des Deutschen Reiches*, 14th ed., 709. Huber, *Deutsche Verfassungsgeschichte*, 5:1203, however, stresses Art. 153 such that the opening to the left embodied in Art. 156, which permitted socialization, is obscured.

46. *RGZ*, 103:201.

47. *RGZ*, 109:310–23.

48. Ibid., 319.

49. See, e.g., decision of June 18, 1925, *RGZ*, 111:123–34, citing Wolff (1919 expropriation of noble families by revolutionary council in Saxony-Gotha violated Art. 153 of the constitution); decision of December 8, 1925, *RGZ* 112:189–94. (Confiscation of property by local government to deal with housing shortage must compensate not only for adequate level of rent and necessary alterations but also for the effect of tenants from the lower classes on neighboring properties.)

50. *RGZ*, 116:268–74.

51. Schmitt, "Die Auflösung des Enteignungsbegriffs" (1929), repr. in *Verfassungsrechtliche Aufsätze*, 110–18; following Schmitt, Otto Kirchheimer, "Reichsgericht und Enteignung. Reichsverfassungswidrigkeit des Preussischen Fluchtliniengesetzes?" (1929–30), repr. in *Von der Weimarer Republik zum Faschismus: Die Auflösung der demokratischen Rechtsordnung*, ed. Wolfgang Luthardt (Frankfurt am Main: Suhrkamp, 1976), 83–84.

52. *RGZ*, 128: 18–34.

53. Ibid., 29–30.

54. E.g., decision of March 3, 1931, *RGZ*, 132:69–76 (overruling lower court's attempt to exclude some regulations from the concept of expropriation, the Reichsgericht grants compensation to an owner for burdens imposed by the Mecklenburg construction code). See the example of Prussian environmental law in Karl Arndt, review of Walter Jellinek, *Entschädigung für baurechtliche Eigentumsbeschränkungen*, in *Juristische Wochenschrift* 59 (1930): 789–90. See also the critical remarks in Alfons Steininger, note on *RGZ*, 128:18–34, in *Juristische Wochenschrift* 59 (1930): 2427–28, which invokes Smend in favor of a legal approach balancing rights and community needs.

55. See, e.g., decision of March 1, 1924, *RGZ*, 107:370–77, cited above; decision of January 29, 1926, *RGZ*, 113:6–17 (transformation of preferred stocks into ordinary shares on the basis of the federal ordinance of March 28, 1924, constitutes a breach of goodwill by the majority of the stockholders in a firm but does not violate Art. 153); notably, both cases explicitly took issue with Triepel.

56. Context described in Rittstieg, *Eigentum als Verfassungsproblem*, 260–62. Anschütz, *Verfassung des Deutschen Reiches*, 14th ed., 714–16, notes that the call for close review of state expropriations of royal families initially came from the government itself in response to expropriations planned in Waldeck.

57. Otto Koellreutter, "Die Auseinandersetzung mit den ehemaligen Fürstenhäusern," *Deutsche Juristen-Zeitung* 31 (1926): 109–15; his main target, however, was the Reichstag, for having failed to issue a general rule to deal with the former state monarchs.

58. West, *A Crisis of the Weimar Republic;* Huber, *Deutsche Verfassungsgeschichte,*

7:577–80, 590–93; Erich Eyck, *A History of the Weimar Republic*, 2 vols., trans. Harlan Hanson and Robert White (Cambridge: Harvard University Press, 1963), 2:62–66.

59. Schmitt, *Unabhängigkeit der Richter;* Maus, *Bürgerliche Rechtstheorie und Faschismus*, 115.

60. Decision of November 4, 1927, *RGZ*, 118:325–30 (a creditor may not receive compensation for losses incurred during the inflation that were caused by, in her estimation, poor government policy).

61. Anschütz, *Die Verfassung des Deutschen Reiches*, 14th ed., 713–14, with examples from court rulings.

62. *RGZ*, 129:146–49.

63. That the law was indeed intended to eliminate specific groups from the profession is shown in Atina Grossmann, *Reforming Sex: The German Movement for Birth Control and Abortion Reform, 1920–1950* (New York: Oxford University Press, 1995), 11.

64. Generally on the problem, see Kirchheimer, "Reichsgericht und Enteignung," 82–83.

65. A defense of the wide interpretation of Art. 153 in terms of a postliberal, "social" notion of property is in Günther Holstein, *Fideikommissauflösung und Reichsverfassung* (Berlin: Carl Heymann, 1930), 3–6; an exposition of expanded property rights as a response to changes in technology-driven capitalism is in Forsthoff, *Lehrbuch des Verwaltungsrechts*, 1:243–46; on the post-1949 notions of property rights, which both develop the wide concept of property and set social limits to its interpretation, see Kommers, *The Constitutional Jurisprudence of the Federal Republic*, 250–61.

66. See p. 4 of the explanation of his draft of a bill on compensation for expropriation, dated June 28, 1930, in Akten der Reichskanzlei R 43 I/2337 55–61; and idem, p. 3 of the revised bill, dated March 10, 1931, in Akten der Reichskanzlei R 43 I/2337 71–81. Stegerman's suggestions were part of a more general attempt by the Brüning regime to cut spending as part of a deflationary response to the depression.

67. Material on the proposed law, including statements in opposition to it from homeowners' organizations, can be found in Akten der Reichskanzlei R 43 I/2337 55–138.

68. *RGZ*, 137:183–89; admission at 188. See also Forsthoff, *Lehrbuch des Verwaltungsrechts*, 242–43, n. 3; Apelt, *Geschichte der Weimarer Verfassung*, 341–42.

69. Schelcher, "Artikel 153," 204–5; Schmitt, "Auflösung des Enteignungsbegriffs," 114–15; Buschke, *Grundrechte der Weimarer Reichsverfassung*, 105; Kirchheimer, "Reichsgericht und Enteignung," 89–90.

70. *RGZ*, 137:187.

71. See the citations in Anschütz, *Verfassung des Deutschen Reiches*, 14th ed., 280–82; Rossiter, *Constitutional Dictatorship*, 70–71; and the standard interpretation of the article in Richard Grau, "Die Diktaturgewalt des Reichspräsidenten," *Handbuch des Deutschen Staatsrechts*, 2:293–95.

72. On the concept of *Verfassungsstreitigkeiten*, see Anschütz, *Verfassung des Deutschen Reiches*, 14th ed., 161–70.

73. Printed in *RGZ*, 112:appendix, 1–12.

74. Ibid., 8–9.

75. Printed in *RGZ*, 124:appendix, 19–39. Notably, the State Court, in marked distinction to the Reichsgericht, refused to consider the legality of the decree as an act of expropriation.

76. Ibid., 36–37.

77. Printed in *RGZ*, 134:appendix, 12–26; the context of the Dietramzeller Decree is described in Schulz, *Zwischen Demokratie und Diktatur*, 3:486–90; and Gerhard Jasper, *Die gescheiterte Zähmung. Wege zur Machtergreifung Hitlers 1930–1934* (Frankfurt am Main: Suhrkamp, 1986), 76.

78. *RGZ*, 134:appendix, 21; on the logic of the special jurisdiction, see Rossiter, *Constitutional Dictatorship*, 61–62; and Grau, "Die Diktaturgewalt des Reichspräsidenten," 276–77. On the strategy of turning to the logic of "shifting jurisdictions," see Schulz, *Zwischen Demokratie und Diktatur*, 3:376–78.

79. *RGZ*, 134:appendix, 22.

80. Printed in *RGZ*, 134:appendix, 26–56.

81. Ibid., 42–46.

82. In general, see Jasper, *Die gescheiterte Zähmung*, 83–94; Dietrich Orlow, *Weimar Prussia 1925–1933: The Illusion of Strength* (Pittsburgh: University of Pittsburgh Press, 1991), 207–12; and on the change in bylaws and the elections in Prussia, Winkler, *Weimar*, 456–58.

83. Jasper, *Die gescheiterte Zähmung*, 94–96; Orlow, *Weimar Prussia 1925–1933*, 225–33, discusses the accusations of the Papen government in detail; Schulz, *Zwischen Demokratie und Diktatur*, 3:920–30, describes the action as a coup d'état.

84. A summary of the complaints is in the State Court's decision of October 25, 1932, repr. in *Preussen contra Reich*, 493–94. Henning Grund, *"Preussenschlag" und Staatsgerichtshof im Jahre 1932* (Baden-Baden: Nomos, 1976), provides a careful examination of all the legal aspects of the trial.

85. Verdict printed in *Preussen contra Reich*, 492–517.

86. For the federal government's position, see Schmitt, "Die Verfassungsmässigkeit der Bestellung eines Reichskommissars für das Land Preussen," *Deutsche Juristen-Zeitung* 37 (1932): 956; idem, in *Preussen contra Reich*, 177–81; Grund, "Preussenschlag," 91.

87. *Preussen contra Reich*, 511–13. Schmitt had argued that altering the Landtag

bylaws was the act of a political party seeking to retain power, and therefore illegitimate: "Verfassungsmässigkeit," 958.

88. Anschütz, in *Verfassung des Deutschen Reiches,* 14th ed., 782, notes that this part of the decision constituted a victory for Prussia and a judicial confirmation of his interpretation of Art. 48, par. 1. The importance of this part of the decision is noted in Grund, *"Preussenschlag,"* 103–4.

89. *Preussen contra Reich,* 513–14.

90. As Anschütz notes, in fact the State Court did "take a position": *Verfassung des Deutschen Reiches,* 14th ed., 782n.; similarly, Fritz Poetzsch-Heffter, "Staatspolitische Würdigung der Entscheidung des Staatsgerichtshofs vom 25. Oktober 1932 im Konflikte des Reiches mit Preussen," *Reich und Länder* 6 (1932): 315. See the opposite interpretation in Scheuner, "Die Anwendung des Art. 48," 282–83.

91. *Preussen contra Reich,* 514; see the defense of this account in Grund, *"Preussenschlag,"* 21–25.

92. Fritz Poetzsch-Heffter, "Der Spruch des Staatsgerichtshofes," *Deutsche Juristen-Zeitung* 37 (1932): 1377; Grund, *"Preussenschlag,"* 21–25, 130, notes that the State Court nevertheless made an important shift by even considering motives. On Papen's plans for the "new state," see Eberhard Kolb and Wolfram Pyta, "Die Staatsnotstandsplanung unter den Regierungen Papen und Schleicher," in *Die deutsche Staatskrise 1930–1933,* ed. Heinrich August Winkler (Munich: Oldenbourg, 1993), 159–63; Grimm, "Verfassungserfüllung — Verfassungsbewahrung — Verfassungsauflösung. Positionen der Staatsrechtslehre in der Staatskrise der Weimarer Republik," in ibid., 185.

93. *Preussen contra Reich,* 514–15.

94. Ibid., 515.

95. Ibid., 515–17. The argument for "absolute limits" to presidential emergency powers was already a well-developed part of legal doctrine; see, e.g., Grau, "Die Diktaturgewalt des Reichspräsidenten," 280.

96. Orlow, *Weimar Prussia 1925–1933,* 244–46.

97. On Bumke, see Ingo Müller, *Hitler's Justice: The Courts of the Third Reich,* trans. Deborah Lucas Schneider (Cambridge: Harvard University Press, 1991), 39–41. Müller's moral condemnation of Bumke's actions on the Reichsgericht during the Nazi period seeps into his judgment of Bumke in 1932 and his supposed conspiracy against the plaintiffs in the case at hand. The history of the trial and the trial records, however, provide no evidence of unfairness or arbitrariness. Grund, *"Preussenschlag,"* 150–51, on the other hand, may go too far in his unreserved defense of the decision, made without considering Bumke's politics. A more balanced judgment is in Müller, "Hermann Heller: Leben, Werk, Wirkung," 440.

98. Bracher, *Die Auflösung der Weimarer Republik,* 556–63.

99. Grund, *"Preussenschlag,"* 10.

100. Nawiasky, "Zum Leipziger Urteil," *Bayerische Verwaltungsblätter* 80 (1932): 338–45; Brecht, foreword to *Preussen contra Reich*, xii; Ernst Fraenkel's report in the republican legal journal *Die Justiz* also gives evidence of a basic respect for the decision: Hugo Sinzheimer and Ernst Fraenkel, *Die Justiz in der Weimarer Republic. Eine Chronik*, ed. Thilo Ramm (Neuwied: Luchterhand, 1968), 377, 384, 397.

101. Arnold Brecht, *Mit der Kraft des Geistes. Lebenserinnerungen.* Zweite Hälfte: 1927–1967 (Stuttgart: Deutsche Verlags-Anstalt, 1967), 229–32.

102. Anschütz, *Die Verfassung des Deutschen Reiches*, 14th ed., 780–83.

103. Triepel, "Die Entscheidung des Staatsgerichtshofs im Verfassungsstreit zwischen Preussen und dem Reiche," *Deutsche Juristen-Zeitung* 37 (1932): 1501–8. Other conservative criticisms of the decision include von Campe, "Der Prozess Preussen contra Reich im Lichte vom Rechtsstaat und Rechtsgefühl," *Deutsche Juristen-Zeitung* 37 (1932): 1384–89, stating that the State Court had not even resolved the case, that any decision would amount to "overstretching the idea of the *Rechtsstaat*," and that the courts should not review emergency actions designed to halt the dissolution of the state.

104. Triepel, *Die Staatsverfassung und die politischen Parteien* (Berlin: Otto Liebmann, 1927), 36.

105. Esp. Ernst Rudolf Huber, *Reichsgewalt und Staatsgerichtshof* (Oldenburg im Ostfriesland: Gerhard Stalling, 1932); see idem, *Deutsche Verfassungsgeschichte*, 7:1125, for a similar argument.

106. *Staat, Bewegung, Volk. Die Dreigliederung der politischen Einheit* (Hamburg: Hanseatisch, 1933), 38–39.

107. Koellreutter, *Deutsches Verfassungsrecht. Ein Grundriss*, 3d ed. (Berlin: Junker und Dünnhaupt, 1938), 181.

108. This point is made by Eyck in *History of the Weimar Republic*, 1:286–88; see 2:421–25 on the decision of October 25, 1932; Sontheimer, *Antidemokratisches Denken in der Weimarer Republik*, 91–94; Peukert, *The Weimar Republic*, 223–25. Lübbe-Wolff, "Safeguards of Civil and Constitutional Rights," 365–72, offers a balanced account of the content and political effects of the courts' change in rights doctrine.

Conclusion

1. The case for the defense was put together by Georg Gottheiner. Carl Schmitt, however, provided key arguments both for the Papen regime before the trial and as part of the defense during the trial. Ernst Rudolf Huber, "Carl Schmitt in der Rechtskrise der Weimarer Endzeit," *Complexio Oppositorum*, 33–50, views Schmitt's (and Papen's) actions in summer 1932 as a strike against both the KPD

and the Nazis, an argument that seems to ignore both Papen's aims and the dele-gitimizing effect of eliminating the caretaker s p d-Center regime in Prussia. See the discussion in ibid., 51–70. In general on the positions in the trial, see David Dyzenhaus, *Truth's Revenge: Carl Schmitt, Hans Kelsen, and Hermann Heller in Weimar* (Oxford: Clarendon, 1997).

2. Schmitt, in *Preussen contra Reich*, 39–40.

3. Ibid., 179, 311; requirement of homogeneity of *Länder* politics in the Repub-lic, 313–14.

4. Ibid., 181.

5. Nawiasky, in *Preussen contra Reich*, 329.

6. Ibid., 244.

7. Ibid., 234–35.

8. Ibid., 174.

9. Ibid., 338.

10. Anschütz, in *Preussen contra Reich*, 125–30, 161–63; and Heller, in ibid., 136–38; by contrast, Nawiasky, in ibid., 172–73, states that subjective violation of duty by a *Land* must first be ascertained before it is acted on; elsewhere, he argued ex-plicitly for a prior court ruling (*Grundprobleme der Reichsverfassung*, 68).

11. Anschütz, in *Preussen contra Reich*, 124–25; Heller, in ibid., 137–38.

12. Anschütz, in ibid., 126 (emphasis added).

13. Ibid., 125.

14. Ibid., 301–7.

15. Heller, *Preussen contra Reich*, 37–38, 76, 214, 293–94. On Heller's role in the trial, raising the political issues underlying the legal ones, see Andreas Kaiser, "Preussen *contra* Reich. Hermann Heller als Prozessgegner Carl Schmitts vor dem Staatsgerichtshof 1932," in *Der soziale Rechtsstaat*, 287–311; more generally, see David Dyzenhaus, "Hermann Heller and the Legitimacy of Legality" (paper presented at the American Political Science Association meeting, Chicago, Ill., September 1, 1995).

16. E.g., Nawiasky, in *Preussen contra Reich*, 233–34; Judge Bumke, in ibid., 252.

17. Heller's basic research even allowed him to best Schmitt in an argument on the interpretation of dictatorship before 1914, in an exchange that earned Schmitt, who falsely accused Heller and Nawiasky of poor scholarship, a sharp rebuke from Judge Bumke: *Preussen contra Reich*, 353–56; see also Bumke's later, more open re-buke of Schmitt in ibid., 469–70.

18. Heller, in *Preussen contra Reich*, 407–8; cf. the similar focus on legitimacy a few months later in Smend, "Bürger und Bourgeois."

19. Carl Schmitt's immediate recognition of the enabling act's revolutionary importance is in "Zum 21. März 1933," *Deutsche Juristen-Zeitung* 38 (1933): 453–58; see also Bendersky, *Carl Schmitt*, 199–200. Ernst Fraenkel, *The Dual State*,

3–6, puts the enabling act in the larger context of a turn to the "prerogative state" that had begun with the Emergency Decree of February 28, 1933. See also Martin Broszat, *The Hitler State: The Foundation and Development of the Internal Structure of the Third Reich,* trans. John W. Hiden (London: Longman, 1981), 80–84.

20. Friedrich Giese, the author of a standard positivist commentary on the constitution and a lawyer for Prussia in the trial, imputes this phrase to Papen and Commissar Bracht in *Preussen contra Reich,* 267; the accusation was not denied by the defense.

21. That the Papen regime removed civil servants solely because of their affiliation with the S P D became clear in the trial: Gottheiner (chief lawyer for the defense), in *Preussen contra Reich,* 164–65, 166–67; exchange between Heller and Judge Bumke, in ibid., 249–51; Arnold Brecht (chief lawyer for the plaintiff), in ibid., 261.

22. Repr. in *Nazism 1919–1945,* vol. 2: *State, Economy and Society 1933–1939. A Documentary Reader,* 5th ed., ed. J. Noakes and G. Pridham (Exeter: University of Exeter Press, 1994), 223–25.

23. Schmitt, in *Preussen contra Reich,* 321–22.

24. Repr. in *Nazism 1919–1945,* 2:250–51; Broszat, *The Hitler State,* 106–32.

25. Schmitt, *Das Reichsstatthaltergesetz,* 2d ed. (Berlin: Carl Heymann, 1934), esp. at 7, where Schmitt traces a continuity between Papen's actions of July 20, 1932, and the Nazi actions to strengthen the state; and at 23, where the irrelevance of the State Court following the new laws is noted. See also Bendersky, *Carl Schmitt,* 199–201.

26. On the legal and institutional meanings of the purge, see Otto Gritschneder, *"Der Führer hat Sie zum Tode verurteilt . . ." Hitlers "Röhm-Putsch"-Morde vor Gericht* (Munich: C. H. Beck, 1993); Bernd Rüthers, *Entartetes Recht,* 120–25; Carl Schmitt, "Der Führer schützt das Recht" (1934), repr. in *Positionen und Begriffe,* 199–203.

27. For an introduction to the broad literature on Schmitt's role in the Nazi system, see Rüthers, *Entartetes Recht;* and Caldwell, "National Socialism and Constitutional Law," 399–427.

28. Johann Hahlen, "Verfassungsreform als Problem des deutschen Wiedervereinigungsprozesses," in *Probleme des Zusammenwachsens im wiedervereinigten Deutschland,* ed. Alexander Fischer and Manfred Wilke (Berlin: Duncker und Humblot, 1994), 63–74; Robert Hettlage, "Integrationsleistungen des Rechts im Prozess der deutschen Einheit," in *Deutschland nach der Wende. Eine Zwischenbilanz,* ed. Hettlage and Karl Ley (Munich: C. H. Beck, 1995), 28–35. On the problems left unresolved by unification and the parliamentary Gemeinsame Verfassungskommission, see *Verfassungsentwicklungen in Deutschland nach der Wiedervereinigung,* ed. Eckart Klein (Berlin: Duncker und Humblot, 1994). In English

on the developments before 1993, see Peter Merkl, *German Unification in the Euro-pean Context* (University Park: Pennsylvania State University, 1993), 167–230.

29. For the positions presented on the left, see *Der Souverän auf der Nebenbühne. Essays und Zwischenrufe zur deutschen Verfassungsdiskussion,* ed. Bernd Guggen-berger and Andreas Meier (Opladen: Westdeutscher, 1994); an important formu-lation of the theoretical arguments surrounding the new constitutionalists is in Ulrich K. Preuss, *Constitutional Revolution: The Link between Constitutionalism and Progress,* trans. Deborah Lucas Schneider (Atlantic Highlands, N.J.: Humani-ties Press, 1995).

30. On the intellectual lineage of the New Right, especially its connections to Carl Schmitt and its responses to unification, see Thomas Asshener and Hans Sarkowicz, *Rechtsradikale in Deutschland. Die alte und die neue Rechte* (Munich: C. H. Beck, 1990).

31. On the crisis of the Constitutional Court after 1993, see Uwe Wesel, "Die Zweite Krise," *Die Zeit,* October 6, 1995, 7–8; Kommers, *The Constitutional Juris-prudence of the Federal Republic,* 55–57, 349–56, 472–84.

BIBLIOGRAPHY

Document Collections

Akten der Reichskanzlei, 1919–1945. Microform copies of the Bundesarchiv Koblenz holdings, housed in the Georgetown University Library, Washington, D.C.

The Democratic Tradition: Four German Constitutions. Ed. Elmar Hucko. Oxford: Berg, 1989.

Die Deutsche Nationalversammlung im Jahre 1919. 9 vols. Ed. Eduard Heilfron. Berlin: Norddeutsche, n.d.

Deutsche Verfassungen. 20th ed. Ed. Rudolf Schuster. Munich: Wilhelm Goldmann, 1992.

Dokumente zur deutschen Verfassungsgeschichte. 3 vols. Ed. Ernst Rudolf Huber. Stuttgart: W. Kohlhammer, 1961.

Entscheidungen des Reichsgerichts in Zivilsachen. 172 vols. Berlin: Walter de Gruyter, 1880–1945.

Die Entstehung der Bundesverfassung 1920. Vol. 4, *Die Sammlung der Entwürfe zur Staats- bzw. Bundesverfassung.* Ed. Felix Ermacora. Vienna: Wilhelm Braumüller, 1990.

Das Ermächtigungsgesetz vom 24. März 1933. Ed. Rudolf Morsey. Dusseldorf: Droste, 1968.

Karl Renners Briefe aus Saint Germain und ihre rechtspolitische Folgen. Ed. Georg Schmitz. Schriftenreihe des Hans-Kelsen-Instituts, vol. 16. Vienna: Manz, 1991.

Materialien der Deutschen Reichs-Verfassung. 3 vols. Ed. Ernst Betzold. Berlin: Carl Habel, 1871–73.

Militär und Innenpolitik im Weltkrieg 1914–1918. 2 vols. Ed. Wilhelm Deist. Dusseldorf: Droste, 1970.

Nazism 1919–1945. 3 vols. 5th ed. Ed. J. Noakes and G. Pridham. Exeter: University of Exeter Press, 1994.

Neukantianismus. Texte der Marburger und der Südwestdeutscher Schule, ihrer Vorläufer und Kritiker. Ed. Hans-Ludwig Ollig. Stuttgart: Reclam, 1982.

Die österreichische Bundesverfassung und Hans Kelsen. Analysen und Materialien. Zum 100. Geburtstag von Hans Kelsen. Ed. Felix Ermacora and Christine Wirth. Vienna: Wilhelm Braumüller, 1982.

Preussen contra Reich vor dem Staatsgerichtshof. Stenogrammbericht der Verhandlungen vor dem Staatsgerichtshof in Leipzig vom 10. bis 14. Oktober 1932. Berlin: Dietz Nachfolger, 1933.

Quellensammlung zum Deutschen Reichsstaatsrecht. 5th ed. Vol. 1, *Quellensammlung zum Staats-, Verwaltungs- und Völkerrecht, vornehmlich zum akademischen Gebrauch.* Ed. Heinrich Triepel. 1931. Reprint, Aalen: Scientia, 1987.

Die Rechtsprechung des Staatsgerichtshofs für das Deutsche Reich und des Reichsgerichts auf Grund Artikel 13 Absatz 2 der Reichsverfassung. Vol. 1. Ed. Walter Simons and Hans-Hermann Lammers. Berlin: Georg Stilke, 1929.

Veröffentlichungen der Vereinigung der deutschen Staatsrechtslehrer. Vols. 1–7. Berlin: Walter de Gruyter, 1924–32.

Die Vorentwürfe Hans Kelsens für die österreichische Bundesverfassung. Ed. Georg Schmitz. Scriftenreihe des Hans Kelsen-Instituts. Vol. 6. Vienna: Manz, 1981.

Sources Published before 1945

Altenberg, Oskar. "Gebietsänderungen im Innern des Reiches nach der Verfassung des Deutschen Reiches vom 11. August 1919." *Archiv des öffentlichen Rechts* 40 (1921): 173–215.

Anschütz, Gerhard. *Aus meinem Leben.* Ed. Walter Pauly. Frankfurt am Main: Vittorio Klostermann, 1993.

———. *Bismarck und die Reichsverfassung.* Berlin: Carl Heymann, 1899.

———. "Der deutsche Föderalismus in Vergangenheit, Gegenwart und Zukunft." In *VVDSRL.* Vol. 1: 11–34. Berlin: Walter de Gruyter, 1924.

———. *Die drei Leitgedanken der Weimarer Verfassung. Rede, gehalten bei der Jahresfeier der Universität Heidelberg am 22. November 1922.* Tübingen: J. C. B. Mohr (Paul Siebeck), 1923.

———. "Die kommende Reichsverfassung." *Deutsche Juristen-Zeitung* 24 (1919): 113–23.

———. "Lücken in den Verfassungs- und Verwaltungsgesetzen. Skizze zu einem Vortrage." *Verwaltungsarchiv* 14 (1906): 315–40.

———. *Parlament und Regierung im Deutschen Reich.* Berlin: Otto Liebmann, 1918.

———. *Das preussisch-deutsche Problem. Skizze zu einem Vortrage.* Tübingen: J. C. B. Mohr (Paul Siebeck), 1922.

———. *Die preussische Wahlreform.* Berlin: Julius Springer, 1917.

———. "Die Reichsexekution." In *Handbuch des Deutschen Staatsrechts.* Vol. 1, ed. Gerhard Anschütz and Richard Thoma, 377–80. Tübingen: J. C. B. Mohr (Paul Siebeck), 1930.

————. "Das System der rechtlichen Beziehungen zwischen Reich und Länder." In *Handbuch des Deutschen Staatsrechts*. Vol. 2, ed. Gerhard Anschütz and Richard Thoma, 295–300. Tübingen: J. C. B. Mohr (Paul Siebeck), 1932.

————. *Die Verfassung des Deutschen Reiches vom 11. August 1919*. 1st ed. Berlin: Georg Stilke, 1921.

————. *Die Verfassung des Deutschen Reiches vom 11. August 1919*. 8th ed. Berlin: Georg Stilke, 1928.

————. *Die Verfassung des Deutschen Reiches vom 11. August 1919*. 14th ed. Berlin: Georg Stilke, 1933.

————. *Die Verfassungs-Urkunde für den preussischen Staat vom 31. Januar 1850. Ein Kommentar für Wissenschaft und Praxis*. Berlin: O. Häring, 1912.

Anschütz, Gerhard, and Walter Jellinek. *Reichskredite und Diktatur. Zwei Rechtsgutachten*. Tübingen: J. C. B. Mohr (Paul Siebeck), 1932.

Anschütz, Gerhard, and Georg Meyer. *Lehrbuch des deutschen Staatsrechts*. 7th ed. Munich: Duncker und Humblot, 1917.

Arndt, Karl. Review of *Entschädigung für baurechtliche Eigentumsbeschränkungen*, by Walter Jellinek. *Juristische Wochenschrift* 59 (1930): 789–90.

Austin, John. *The Province of Jurisprudence Determined*. Ed. Wilfrid E. Rumble. Cambridge: Cambridge University Press, 1995.

Bergbohm, Karl. *Jurisprudenz und Rechtsphilosophie. Kritische Abhandlungen*. Vol. 1: *Einleitung. Erste Abhandlung. Das Naturrecht der Gegenwart*. Leipzig: Duncker und Humblot, 1892.

Bilfinger, Carl. *Nationale Demokratie als Grundlage der Weimarer Verfassung*. Halle an der Saale: Max Niemeyer, 1929.

————. "Verfassungsrecht als politisches Recht." *Zeitschrift für Politik* 18 (1928): 281–98.

Bismarck, Count Otto von. *Werke im Auswahl*. 9 vols. Ed. Gustav Adolf Rein et al. Stuttgart: W. Kohlhammer, 1981.

Bornhak, Conrad. *Grundriss des Verwaltungsrechts in Preussen und dem Deutschen Reiche*. 3d ed. Leipzig: Deichert, 1911.

Brie, Siegfried. "Zur Theorie des constitutionellen Staatsrechts." *Archiv für öffentliches Recht* 4 (1889): 1–61.

Bund zur Erneuerung des Reiches. *Die Rechte des Deutschen Reichspräsidenten nach der Reichsverfassung. Eine gemeinverständliche Darstellung*. Berlin: Bund zur Erneuerung des Reiches, 1929.

————. *Welche Rechte hat der Reichspräsident?* Berlin: Bund zur Erneuerung des Reiches, 1931.

Burgess, John W. "Laband's Public Law of the German Empire." *Political Science Quarterly* 3 (1888): 132–35.

————. Review of *Staatsrecht des Deutschen Reiches*, by Paul Laband, 2d ed. *Political Science Quarterly* 6 (1891): 174.

Buschke, Albrecht. *Die Grundrechte der Weimarer Verfassung in der Rechtsprechung des Reichsgerichts.* Berlin: Georg Stilke, 1930.

Campe, von. "Der Prozess Preussen contra Reich im Lichte vom Rechtsstaat und Rechtsgefühl." *Deutsche Juristen-Zeitung* 37 (1932): 1384–89.

Dicey, Albert. V. *Introduction to the Law of the Constitution.* 8th ed. 1915. Reprint, Indianapolis: The Liberty Fund, 1982.

Duguit, Léon. *Law in the Modern State.* Trans. Frida Laski and Harold Laski. London: Allen and Unwin, 1921.

Ehrlich, Eugen. *Fundamental Principles of the Sociology of Law* (1913). Trans. Walter L. Moll. Cambridge: Harvard University Press, 1936.

———. "Über Lücken im Recht" (1888). Reprinted in *Recht und Leben. Gesammelte Schriften zur Rechtstatsachenforschung und zur Freirechtslehre.* Ed. Manfred Rehbinder. Berlin: Duncker und Humblot, 1967.

Gerber, Carl Friedrich von. *Grundzüge des Deutschen Staatsrechts.* 3d ed. 1880. Reprint, Aalen: Scientia, 1969.

———. *Über öffentliche Rechte.* 1852. Reprint, Tübingen: J. C. B. Mohr (Paul Siebeck), 1913.

Gerber, Hans. "Die siebente Tagung der Vereinigung der deutschen Staatsrechtslehrer." *Archiv des öffentlichen Rechts* 56 (1929): 253–86.

Gierke, Otto von. "Labands Staatsrecht und die deutsche Rechtswissenschaft." *Schmollers Jahrbuch für Gesetzgebung, Verwaltung und Volkswirthschaft im Deutschen Reich* 7 (1883): 1–99.

Giese, Friedrich. *Deutsches Staatsrecht. Allgemeines Reichs- und Landes-Staatsrecht.* Berlin: Spaeth und Linde, 1930.

———. *Einführung in die Rechtswissenschaft.* 2d ed. Berlin: Spaeth und Linde, 1932.

———. *Die Grundrechte.* Tübingen: J. C. B. Mohr (Paul Siebeck), 1905.

———. *Die Verfassung des Deutschen Reiches vom 11. August 1919. Taschenausgabe.* Berlin: Carl Heymann, 1919.

Gneist, Rudolf von. *Gesetz und Budget. Constitutionelle Streitfragen aus der preussischen Ministerkrisis vom März 1878.* Berlin: Julius Springer, 1879.

Goldschmidt, James. "Gesetzesdämmerung" (1924). Reprinted in *Zur Problematik der höchstrichterlichen Entscheidung,* ed. Gerd Roellecke, 76–91. Darmstadt: Wissenschaftliche Buchgesellschaft, 1982.

Grau, Richard. "Die Diktaturgewalt des Reichspräsidenten." In *Handbuch des Deutschen Staatsrechts.* Vol. 2, ed. Gerhard Anschütz and Richard Thoma, 274–95. Tübingen: J. C. B. Mohr (Paul Siebeck), 1932.

Grueber, B. Erwin. *Einführung in die Rechtswissenschaft. Eine juristische Enzyklopädie und Methodologie.* Berlin: O. Häring, 1908.

Haldy, Wilhelm. *Der Belagerungszustand in Preussen.* Tübingen: J. C. B. Mohr, 1906.

Handbuch für das Deutsche Reich 1929. Ed. Reichsministerium des Innern. Berlin: Carl Heymann, 1929.

Hänel, Albert. *Studien zum Deutschen Staatsrechte*. Vol. 1, *Die vertragsmässigen Elemente der Deutschen Reichsverfassung*. Vol. 2, bk. 1, *Die organische Entwicklung der deutschen Reichsverfassung*. Leipzig: H. Haessel, 1888.

Heck, Phillip. "Interessenjurisprudenz und Gesetzestreue" (1905). Reprinted in *Interessenjurisprudenz*, ed. Günter Ellschied and Winfried Hassemer, 32–35. Darmstadt: Wissenschaftliche Buchgesellschaft, 1974.

Hegel, Georg Wilhelm Friedrich. *Die Verfassung Deutschlands* (1798–1800). Reprinted in *Werke*. Vol. 1, *Frühe Schriften*. Ed. Eva Moldenhauer and Karl Markus Michel, 451–610. Frankfurt am Main: Suhrkamp, 1971.

Heller, Hermann. "Der Begriff des Gesetzes in der Reichsverfassung." In *VVDSRL*. Vol. 4: 98–135. Berlin: Walter de Gruyter, 1928.

———. "Bemerkungen zur staats- und rechtstheoretischen Problematik der Gegenwart" (1929). Reprinted in *Gesammelte Schriften*. 2d ed. Ed. Fritz Borinski, Martin Drath, Gerhart Niemeyer, and Otto Stammer, 249–78. Tübingen: J. C. B. Mohr (Paul Siebeck), 1992.

———. *Europa und der Faschismus*. 2d ed. (1931). Reprinted in *Gesammelte Schriften*. 2d ed. Ed. Fritz Borinski, Martin Drath, Gerhart Niemeyer, and Otto Stammer, 2:463–609. Tübingen: J. C. B. Mohr (Paul Siebeck), 1992.

———. "Freiheit und Form in der Reichsverfassung" (1929–30). Reprinted in *Gesammelte Schriften*. 2d ed. Ed. Fritz Borinski, Martin Drath, Gerhart Niemeyer, and Otto Stammer, 2:371–77. Tübingen: J. C. B. Mohr (Paul Siebeck), 1992.

———. *Gesammelte Schriften*. 2d ed. 3 vols. Ed. Fritz Borinski, Martin Drath, Gerhart Niemeyer, and Otto Stammer. Tübingen: J. C. B. Mohr (Paul Siebeck), 1992.

———. "Grundrechte und Grundpflichten" (1924). Reprinted in *Gesammelte Schriften*. 2d ed. Ed. Fritz Borinski, Martin Drath, Gerhart Niemeyer, and Otto Stammer, 2:281–317. Tübingen: J. C. B. Mohr (Paul Siebeck), 1992.

———. *Hegel und der nationale Machtstaatsgedanke in Deutschland. Ein Beitrag zur politischen Geistesgeschichte* (1921). Reprinted in *Gesammelte Schriften*. 2d ed. Ed. Fritz Borinski, Martin Drath, Gerhart Niemeyer, and Otto Stammer, 1:21–240. Tübingen: J. C. B. Mohr (Paul Siebeck), 1992.

———. "Hegel und die deutsche Politik" (1924). Reprinted in *Gesammelte Schriften*. 2d ed. Ed. Fritz Borinski, Martin Drath, Gerhart Niemeyer, and Otto Stammer, 1:241–55. Tübingen: J. C. B. Mohr (Paul Siebeck), 1992.

———. "Die Krise der Staatslehre" (1926). Reprinted in *Gesammelte Schriften*. 2d ed. Ed. Fritz Borinski, Martin Drath, Gerhart Niemeyer, and Otto Stammer, 2:3–30. Tübingen: J. C. B. Mohr (Paul Siebeck), 1992.

———. "Political Science" (1934). Reprinted in *Gesammelte Schriften*. 2d ed. Ed.

Fritz Borinski, Martin Drath, Gerhart Niemeyer, and Otto Stammer, 3:45–75. Tübingen: J. C. B. Mohr (Paul Siebeck), 1992.

———. "Politische Demokratie und soziale Homogenität" (1928). Reprinted in *Gesammelte Schriften*. 2d ed. Ed. Fritz Borinski, Martin Drath, Gerhart Niemeyer, and Otto Stammer, 2:421–33. Tübingen: J. C. B. Mohr (Paul Siebeck), 1992.

———. *Die politischen Ideenkreise der Gegenwart* (1926). Reprinted in *Gesammelte Schriften*. 2d ed. Ed. Fritz Borinski, Martin Drath, Gerhart Niemeyer, and Otto Stammer, 1:267–412. Tübingen: J. C. B. Mohr (Paul Siebeck), 1992.

———. "Rechtsstaat oder Diktatur?" (1929). Reprinted in *Gesammelte Schriften*. 2d ed. Ed. Fritz Borinski, Martin Drath, Gerhart Niemeyer, and Otto Stammer, 2:443–62. Tübingen: J. C. B. Mohr (Paul Siebeck), 1992.

———. *Die Souveränität. Ein Beitrag zur Theorie des Staats- und Völkerrechts* (1927). Reprinted in *Gesammelte Schriften*. 2d ed. Ed. Fritz Borinski, Martin Drath, Gerhart Niemeyer, and Otto Stammer, 2:31–202. Tübingen: J. C. B. Mohr (Paul Siebeck), 1992.

———. *Sozialismus und Nation* (1925). Reprinted in *Gesammelte Schriften*. 2d ed. Ed. Fritz Borinski, Martin Drath, Gerhart Niemeyer, and Otto Stammer, 1:437–526. Tübingen: J. C. B. Mohr (Paul Siebeck), 1992.

———. "Sozialistische Aussenpolitik?" (1924). Reprinted in *Gesammelte Schriften*. 2d ed. Ed. Fritz Borinski, Martin Drath, Gerhart Niemeyer, and Otto Stammer, 1:415–20. Tübingen: J. C. B. Mohr (Paul Siebeck), 1992.

———. "Staat, Nation und Sozialdemokratie" (1925). Reprinted in *Gesammelte Schriften*. 2d ed. Ed. Fritz Borinski, Martin Drath, Gerhart Niemeyer, and Otto Stammer, 1:527–63. Tübingen: J. C. B. Mohr (Paul Siebeck), 1992.

———. *Staatslehre* (1934). Reprinted in *Gesammelte Schriften*. 2d ed. Ed. Fritz Borinski, Martin Drath, Gerhart Niemeyer, and Otto Stammer, 3:79–395. Tübingen: J. C. B. Mohr (Paul Siebeck), 1992.

———. "Ziele und Grenzen einer deutschen Verfassungsreform" (1931). Reprinted in *Gesammelte Schriften*. 2d ed. Ed. Fritz Borinski, Martin Drath, Gerhart Niemeyer, and Otto Stammer, 2:411–17. Tübingen: J. C. B. Mohr (Paul Siebeck), 1992.

Hensel, Albert. "Die fünfte Tagung der Vereinigung der deutschen Staatsrechtslehrer." *Archiv des öffentlichen Rechts* 52 (1927): 97–121.

Hintze, Otto. "Das monarchische Prinzip und die konstitutionelle Verfassung" (1911). Reprinted in *Gesammelte Abhandlungen*. 2d ed. Vol. 1, *Staat und Verfassung. Gesammelte Abhandlungen zur allgemeinen Verfassungsgeschichte*. Ed. Gerhard Oestreich, 359–89. Göttingen: Vandenhoeck und Ruprecht, 1962.

Hippel, Ernst von. Review of *Hans Kelsens rechtstheoretische Methode*, by Wilhelm Jöckel. *Juristische Wochenschrift* 60 (1931): 1175.

———. "Überprüfung von Verwaltungsakten durch die ordentlichen Gerichte." In *VVDSRL*. Vol. 5: 178–202. Berlin: Walter de Gruyter, 1929.

Holdack, Felix. Review of *Gesetz und Urteil*, by Carl Schmitt. *Kantstudien* 17 (1912): 464–67.

Holstein, Günther. *Fideikommissauflösung und Reichsverfassung*. Berlin: Carl Heymann, 1930.

———. "Von Aufgaben und Zielen heutiger Staatsrechtswissenschaft. Zur Tagung der Vereinigung deutscher Staatsrechtslehrer." *Archiv des öffentlichen Rechts* 50 (1926): 1–40.

Jacobi, Erwin. "Die Diktatur des Reichspräsidenten nach Art. 48 der Reichsverfassung." In *VVDSRL*. Vol. 1:105–36. Berlin: Walter de Gruyter, 1924.

Jellinek, Camilla, and Josef Lukas. "Georg Jellinek. Sein Leben." *Neue Österreichische Biographie*. Vol. 7:136–52. Vienna: Amalthea, 1931.

Jellinek, Georg. *Allgemeine Staatslehre*. 3d ed. Berlin: O. Häring, 1914.

———. "Bundesstaat und parlamentarische Regierung." In *Ausgewählte Schriften und Reden*. Vol. 2:439–47. Berlin: O. Häring, 1911.

———. *Die Erklärung der Menschen- und Bürgerrechte. Ein Beitrag zur modernen Verfassungsgeschichte*. 2d ed. Leipzig: Duncker und Humblot, 1904.

———. *Die Lehre von den Staatenverbindungen*. Vienna: Alfred Hölder, 1882.

———. *Die rechtliche Natur der Staatsverträge. Ein Beitrag zur juristischen Construktion des Völkerrechts*. Vienna: Alfred Hölder, 1880.

———. *Regierung und Parlament in Deutschland. Geschichtliche Entwickelung ihres Verhältnisses*. Leipzig: B. G. Teubner, 1909.

———. *System der subjektiven öffentlichen Rechte*. 2d ed. Tübingen: J. C. B. Mohr (Paul Siebeck), 1919.

———. "Die Verantwortlichkeit des Reichskanzlers." In *Ausgewählte Schriften und Reden*. Vol. 2:431–38. Berlin: O. Häring, 1911.

Jellinek, Walter. "Der Schutz des öffentlichen Rechts durch ordentliche und durch Verwaltungsgerichte (Fortschritte, Rückschritte und Entwicklungstendenzen seit der Revolution)." In *VVDSRL*. Vol. 2:8–80. Berlin: Walter de Gruyter, 1925.

Kantorowicz, Hermann. *Der Kampf um die Rechtswissenschaft*. Heidelberg: Carl Winter, 1906.

Kaufmann, Erich. "Die Gleichheit vor dem Gesetz im Sinne des Art. 109 der Reichsverfassung." In *VVDSRL*. Vol. 3:2–24. Berlin: Walter de Gruyter, 1927.

———. *Kritik der neukantianischen Rechtsphilosophie. Eine Betrachtung über die Beziehungen zwischen Philosophie und Rechtswissenschaft*. Tübingen: J. C. B. Mohr (Paul Siebeck), 1921.

———. *Studien zur Staatslehre des monarchischen Prinzipes*. Leipzig: O. Brandstetter, 1906.

————. *Das Wesen des Völkerrechts und die clausula rebus sic stantibus. Eine rechts-philosophische Studie zum Rechts-, Staats- und Vertragsbegriffe.* Tübingen: J. C. B. Mohr (Paul Siebeck), 1911.

Kelsen, Hans. *Allgemeine Staatslehre.* Berlin: Springer, 1925.

————. *Aufsätze zur Ideologiekritik.* Ed. Ernst Topitsch. Neuwied: Luchterhand, 1964.

————. "Die Bundesexekution. Ein Beitrag zur Theorie und Praxis des Bundes-staates, unter besondere Berücksichtigung der deutschen Reichs- und der österreichischen Bundesverfassung." In *Festgabe für Fritz Fleiner zum 60. Geburtstag 24. Januar 1927*, 127-87. Tübingen: J. C. B. Mohr (Paul Siebeck), 1927.

————. "Demokratie" (1927). Reprinted in *Die Wiener rechtstheoretische Schule*, by Hans Kelsen, Adolf Merkl, and Alfred Verdross. 2 vols. Ed. Hans Klecatsky, Rene Marcic, and Herbert Schambeck, 2:1743-1776. Vienna: Europa-Verlag, 1968.

————. "Die Entwicklung des Staatsrechts in Österreich seit dem Jahre 1918." In *Handbuch des Deutschen Staatsrechts.* Vol. 1, ed. Gerhard Anschütz and Richard Thoma, 147-65. Tübingen: J. C. B. Mohr (Paul Siebeck), 1930.

————. "God and the State" (1922-23). Reprinted in *Hans Kelsen. Essays in Legal and Moral Philosophy.* Ed. Ota Weinberger. Trans. Peter Heath, 61-82. Dor-drecht: D. Reidel, 1973.

————. *Hauptprobleme der Staatsrechtslehre entwickelt aus der Lehre vom Rechts-satze.* 1st ed. Tübingen: J. C. B. Mohr (Paul Siebeck), 1911.

————. *Hauptprobleme der Staatsrechtslehre entwickelt aus der Lehre vom Rechts-satze.* 2d ed. Tübingen: J. C. B. Mohr (Paul Siebeck), 1923.

————. "The Idea of Natural Law" (1928). Reprinted in *Hans Kelsen. Essays in Legal and Moral Philosophy.* Ed. Ota Weinberger. Trans. Peter Heath, 27-60. Dordrecht: D. Reidel, 1973.

————. "Un inédit de Kelsen concernant ses sources kantiennes." Trans. Giorgio Bomio. *Droit et Société* 7 (1987): 327-35.

————. *Introduction to the Problems of Legal Theory. A Translation of the First Edi-tion of the Reine Rechtslehre or Pure Theory of Law.* Trans. Bonnie Litschewski Paulson and Stanley L. Paulson. Oxford: Clarendon, 1992.

————. "Judicial Review of Legislation: A Comparative Study of the Austrian and the American Constitution." *Journal of Politics* 4 (1942): 183-200.

————. "Juristischer Formalismus und Reine Rechtslehre." *Juristische Wochen-schrift* 58 (1929): 1723-26.

————. "Justiz und Verwaltung" (1929). Reprinted in *Die Wiener rechtstheo-retische Schule*, by Hans Kelsen, Adolf Merkl, and Alfred Verdross. 2 vols. Ed. Hans Klecatsky, Rene Marcic, and Herbert Schambeck, 2:1781-1811. Vienna: Europa-Verlag, 1968.

———. "Die Lehre von den drei Gewalten oder Funktionen des Staates" (1923–24). Reprinted in *Die Wiener rechtstheoretische Schule,* by Hans Kelsen, Adolf Merkl, and Alfred Verdross. 2 vols. Ed. Hans Klecatsky, Rene Marcic, and Herbert Schambeck, 2:1625-60. Vienna: Europa-Verlag, 1968.

———. "Marx oder Lassalle. Wandlungen in der politischen Theorie des Marxismus." *Archiv für die Geschichte des Sozialismus und der Arbeiterbewegung* 11 (1925): 261-98.

———. "Natural Law Doctrine and Legal Positivism" (1928). Trans. Wolfgang Herbert Kraus. Reprinted in *General Theory of Law and State,* 391-446. Cambridge: Harvard University Press, 1949.

———. "On the Theory of Interpretation" (1934). Trans. Bonnie Litschewski Paulson and Stanley L. Paulson. *Legal Studies* 10 (1990): 127-35.

———. *Österreichisches Staatsrecht. Ein Grundriss, entwicklungsgeschichtlich dargestellt.* Tübingen: J. C. B. Mohr (Paul Siebeck), 1923.

———. "Die politische Theorie des Sozialismus." *Österreichische Rundschau* 19 (1923): 113-35.

———. *Das Problem der Souveränität und die Theorie des Völkerrechts. Beitrag zu einer reinen Rechtslehre.* Tübingen: J. C. B. Mohr (Paul Siebeck), 1920.

———. *Das Problem des Parlamentarismus.* 1926. Reprint, Darmstadt: Wissenschaftliche Buchgesellschaft, 1968.

———. *The Pure Theory of Law.* 2d ed. Trans. Max Knight. Berkeley: University of California Press, 1967.

———. "Rechtsstaat und Staatsrecht" (1913). Reprinted in *Die Wiener rechtstheoretische Schule,* by Hans Kelsen, Adolf Merkl, and Alfred Verdross. 2 vols. Ed. Hans Klecatsky, Rene Marcic, and Herbert Schambeck, 2:1525-32. Vienna: Europa-Verlag, 1968.

———. "Rechtswissenschaft als Norm- oder als Kulturwissenschaft. Eine methodenkritische Untersuchung" (1916). Reprinted in *Die Wiener rechtstheoretische Schule,* by Hans Kelsen, Adolf Merkl, and Alfred Verdross. 2 vols. Ed. Hans Klecatsky, Rene Marcic, and Herbert Schambeck, 1:37-93. Vienna: Europa-Verlag, 1968.

———. "Rechtswissenschaft und Recht. Erledigung eines Versuchs zur Überwindung der 'Rechtsdogmatik'" (1922). Reprinted in *Die Rolle des Neukantianismus in der Reinen Rechtslehre. Eine Debatte zwischen Sander und Kelsen,* ed. Stanley L. Paulson, 279-411. Aalen: Scientia, 1988.

———. *Der soziologische und der juristische Staatsbegriff. Kritische Untersuchungen des Verhältnisses von Staat und Recht.* Tübingen: J. C. B. Mohr (Paul Siebeck), 1922.

———. *Der Staat als Integration. Eine prinzipielle Auseinandersetzung.* Vienna: Julius Springer, 1930.

———. "Der Staatsbegriff und die Psychoanalyse" (1927). Reprinted in *Die*

Wiener rechtstheoretische Schule, by Hans Kelsen, Adolf Merkl, and Alfred Verdross. 2 vols. Ed. Hans Klecatsky, Rene Marcic, and Herbert Schambeck, 1:209–14. Vienna: Europa-Verlag, 1968.

———. *Vom Wesen und Wert der Demokratie*. 2d ed. Tübingen: J. C. B. Mohr (Paul Siebeck), 1929.

———. "Wer soll der Hüter der Verfassung sein?" (1931). Reprinted in *Die Wiener rechtstheoretische Schule*, by Hans Kelsen, Adolf Merkl, and Alfred Verdross. 2 vols. Ed. Hans Klecatsky, Rene Marcic, and Herbert Schambeck, 2:1873–1922. Vienna: Europa-Verlag, 1968.

———. "Das Wesen des Staates" (1926–27). Reprinted in *Die Wiener rechtstheoretische Schule*, by Hans Kelsen, Adolf Merkl, and Alfred Verdross. 2 vols. Ed. Hans Klecatsky, Rene Marcic, and Herbert Schambeck, 2:1713–28. Vienna: Europa-Verlag, 1968.

———. "Wesen und Entwicklung der Staatsgerichtsbarkeit." In *VVDSRL*. Vol. 5: 30–88. Berlin: Walter de Gruyter, 1929.

———. "Zur Lehre vom Gesetz im formellen und materiellen Sinn, mit besonderer Berücksichtigung der österreichischen Verfassung" (1913). Reprinted in *Die Wiener rechtstheoretische Schule*, by Hans Kelsen, Adolf Merkl, and Alfred Verdross. 2 vols. Ed. Hans Klecatsky, Rene Marcic, and Herbert Schambeck, 2:1533–43. Vienna: Europa-Verlag, 1968.

———. "Zur Theorie der juristischen Fiktionen. Mit besonderer Berücksichtigung von Vaihingers Philosophie des Als Ob." *Vaihingers Annalen der Philosophie* 1 (1919): 630–58.

Kelsen, Hans, Adolf Merkl, and Alfred Verdross. *Die Wiener rechtstheoretische Schule*. 2 vols. Ed. Hans Klecatsky, Rene Marcic, and Herbert Schambeck. Vienna: Europa-Verlag, 1968.

Kelsen, Hans, et al. *Hans Kelsen und die Rechtssoziologie. Auseinandersetzungen mit Hermann U. Kantorowicz, Eugen Ehrlich und Max Weber*. Ed. Stanley L. Paulson. Aalen: Scientia, 1992.

Kirchheimer, Otto. "Reichsgericht und Enteignung. Reichsverfassungswidrigkeit des Preussischen Fluchtliniengesetzes?" (1929–30). Reprinted in *Von der Weimarer Republik zum Faschismus: Die Auflösung der demokratischen Rechtsordnung*, ed. Wolfgang Luthardt, 77–90. Frankfurt am Main: Suhrkamp, 1976.

———. "Weimar—und was dann? Analyse einer Verfassung" (1930). Reprinted in *Politik und Verfassung*, 9–56. Frankfurt am Main: Suhrkamp, 1964.

Klinghofer, Hans. "Smends Integrationstheorie. Bemerkungen zu Smends Schrift 'Verfassung und Verfassungsrecht.'" *Die Justiz* 5 (1929–30): 418–31.

Koellreutter, Otto. "Die Auseinandersetzung mit den ehemaligen Fürstenhäusern." *Deutsche Juristen-Zeitung* 31 (1926): 109–15.

———. *Deutsches Verfassungsrecht. Ein Grundriss*. 3d ed. Berlin: Junker und Dünnhaupt, 1938.

————. *Grundriss der allgemeinen Staatslehre.* Tübingen: J. C. B. Mohr (Paul Siebeck), 1933.

————. *Integrationslehre und Reichsreform.* Tübingen: J. C. B. Mohr (Paul Siebeck), 1929.

————. Review of *Die Souveränität,* by Hermann Heller. *Archiv des öffentlichen Rechts* 52 (1928): 133–37.

————. "Staatsrechtswissenschaft und Politik." *Deutsche Juristen-Zeitung* 33 (1928): 1221–26.

————. *Vom Sinn und Wesen der nationalen Revolution.* Tübingen: J. C. B. Mohr (Paul Siebeck), 1933.

Kohler, Josef. *Not kennt kein Gebot. Die Theorien des Notrechtes und die Ereignisse unserer Zeit.* Berlin: Walther Rothschild, 1915.

Köttgen, Arnold. "Die achte Tagung der Vereinigung der deutschen Staatsrechtslehrer." *Archiv des öffentlichen Rechts* 60 (1932): 404–31.

Kraft-Fuchs, Margrit. "Kelsens Staatstheorie und die Soziologie des Staates." *Zeitschrift für öffentliches Recht* 11 (1931): 402–15.

Laband, Paul. *Das Budgetrecht nach den Bestimmungen der Preussischen Verfassungs-Urkunde unter Berücksichtigung der Verfassung des Norddeutschen Bundes.* Berlin: J. Guttentag, 1871.

————. "Der Bundesrat" (1911). Reprinted in *Der Bundesrat. Die staatsrechtliche Entwicklung des föderalen Verfassungsorgans,* ed. Dieter Wilke and Bernd Schwelte, 40–50. Darmstadt: Wissenschaftliche Buchgesellschaft, 1990.

————. *Lebenserinnerungen* (1918). Reprinted in *Abhandlungen, Beiträge, Reden und Rezensionen.* Vol. 1:1–112. Leipzig: Zentralantiquariat der DDR, 1980–83.

————. Review of *Traité de Droit public international,* by A. Mérignhac. *Archiv für öffentliches Recht* 20 (1906): 302–5.

————. *Das Staatsrecht des Deutschen Reiches.* 1st ed. 3 vols. Tübingen: H. Laupp, 1876–82.

————. *Staatsrecht des Deutschen Reiches.* 5th ed. 4 vols. 1911–13. Reprint, Aalen: Scientia, 1964.

————. "Die Wandlungen in der deutschen Reichsverfassung" (1895). Reprinted in *Abhandlungen, Beiträge, Reden und Rezensionen.* Vol. 1:574–611. Leipzig: Zentralantiquariat der DDR, 1980–83.

Landsberg, Ernst. *Geschichte der Deutschen Rechtswissenschaft.* Munich: R. Oldenbourg, 1910.

Laski, Harold J. *The American Presidency, an Interpretation.* New York: Harper and Brothers, 1940.

Lassar, Gerhard. "Administrative Jurisdiction in Germany." *Economica* 7 (1927): 179–90.

————. "Der Schutz des öffentlichen Rechts. Die neueste Entwicklung des Gemeindeverfassungsrechts." In *VVDSRL*. Vol. 2:81-105. Berlin: Walter de Gruyter, 1925.

Laun, Rudolf. "Der Staatsrechtslehrer und die Politik." *Archiv des öffentlichen Rechts* 43 (1923): 145-99.

Leibholz, Gerhard. *Die Gleichheit vor dem Gesetz. Eine Studie auf rechtsvergleichender und rechtsphilosophischer Grundlage.* Berlin: Otto Liebmann, 1925.

―――. "Die Gleichheit vor dem Gesetz. Ein Nachwort zur Auslegung des Art. 109 Abs. 1 RV." *Archiv des öffentlichen Rechts* 51 (1927): 1-36.

―――. "Höchstrichterliche Rechtsprechung und Gleichheitssatz." *Archiv des öffentlichen Rechts* 58 (1930): 428-42.

―――. "Legal Philosophy and the German Constitutional Court" (1962). Reprinted in *Politics and Law*, 296-301. Leiden: A. W. Sijthoff, 1965.

―――. "Die Reform des Wahlrechtes." In *VVDSRL*. Vol. 7:159-90. Berlin: Walter de Gruyter, 1932.

Löwith, Karl. "Der okkasionelle Dezisionismus von Carl Schmitt" (1935). Reprinted in *Sämtliche Schriften*. Vol. 8, *Heidegger—Denker in dürftiger Zeit*, ed. Klaus Stichweh and Marc B. de Launay, 32-71. Stuttgart: J. B. Metzlersche, 1984.

Marschall von Bieberstein, Freiherr Adolf Hans. *Vom Kampf des Rechts gegen die Gesetze. Akademische Rede zum Gedächtnis der Reichsgründung gehalten am 17. Januar 1925 in der Aula der Albrecht-Ludwigs-Universität.* Stuttgart: W. Kohlhammer, 1927.

Marx, Karl. "The Constitution of the French Republic Adopted November 4, 1848" (1851, English original). Reprinted in *Marx-Engels Collected Works*. Vol. 10:567-80. Moscow: Progress, 1978.

Mattern, Johannes. *Principles of the Constitutional Jurisprudence of the German National Republic.* Baltimore: Johns Hopkins University Press, 1928.

Mayer, Otto. *Deutsches Verwaltungsrecht.* Leipzig: Duncker und Humblot, 1895.

Meissner, Otto Heinrich. "Bundesrat, Bundeskanzler und Bundeskanzleramt (1867-1871)" (1943). Reprinted in *Moderne deutsche Verfassungsgeschichte (1815-1918)*, ed. Ernst-Wolfgang Böckenförde, 76-94. Cologne: Kiepenheuer und Witsch, 1972.

―――. "Der Reichspräsident." In *Handbuch der Politik*. Vol. 3, ed. Gerhard Anschütz, 41-44. Berlin: Walter Rothschild, 1921.

Mendelssohn-Bartholdy, Albrecht. *The War and German Society. The Testament of a Liberal.* 1937. Reprint, New York: Howard Fertig, 1971.

Naumann, Friedrich. "Versuch volksverständlicher Grundrechte." In *Werke*. Vol. 2:573-79. Cologne: Westdeutscher, 1964.

Nawiasky, Hans. "Die Auslegung des Art. 48 der Reichsverfassung." *Archiv des öffentlichen Rechts* 48 (1925): 1-55.

————. "Die Gleichheit vor dem Gesetz im Sinne des Art. 109 der Reichsverfassung." In *VVDSRL*. Vol. 3:25–43. Berlin: Walter de Gruyter, 1927.

————. *Grundprobleme der Reichsverfassung. Erster Teil. Das Reich als Bundesstaat.* Berlin: Julius Springer, 1928.

————. "Zum Leipziger Urteil." *Bayerische Verwaltungsblätter* 80 (1932): 338–45.

Neumann, Franz. "Die soziale Bedeutung der Grundrechte in der Weimarer Verfassung" (1931). Reprinted in *Wirtschaft, Staat, Demokratie. Aufsätze 1930–1954*, ed. Alfons Söllner, 57–75. Frankfurt am Main: Suhrkamp, 1978.

————. "Zur marxistischen Staatstheorie" (1935). Reprinted in *Wirtschaft, Staat, Demokratie. Aufsätze 1930–1954*, ed. Alfons Söllner, 134–43. Frankfurt am Main: Suhrkamp, 1978.

Poetzsch-Heffter, Fritz. "Der Spruch des Staatsgerichtshofes." *Deutsche Juristen-Zeitung* 37 (1932): 1373–78.

————. "Staatspolitische Würdigung der Entscheidung des Staatsgerichtshofs vom 25. Oktober 1932 im Konflikte des Reiches mit Preussen." *Reich und Länder* 6 (1932): 309–16.

Pözl, Joseph von. Review of *Staatsrecht des Deutschen Reiches*, by Paul Laband. *Kritische Vierteljahresschrift für Gesetzgebung und Rechtswissenschaft* 13 (1871): 567–75.

Preuss, Hugo. *Artikel 18 der Reichsverfassung: Seine Entstehung und Bedeutung.* Berlin: Carl Heymann, 1922.

————. "Begründung des Entwurfs einer Verfassung für das Deutsche Reich" (1919). Reprinted in *Staat, Recht und Freiheit. Aus 40 Jahren deutscher Politik und Geschichte*, 394–421. 1926. Reprint, Hildesheim: Georg Olms, 1964.

————. "Denkschrift zum Entwurf des allgemeinen Teils der Reichsverfassung vom 3. Januar 1919." In *Staat, Recht und Freiheit. Aus 40 Jahren deutscher Politik und Geschichte*, 368–79. 1926. Reprint, Hildesheim: Georg Olms, 1964.

————. "Die organische Bedeutung der Art. 15 und 17 der Reichsverfassung." *Zeitschrift für die gesamte Staatswissenschaft* 45 (1889): 420–49.

————. *Reichs- und Landesfinanzen.* Berlin: Leonhard Simion, 1894.

————. "Die Sozialdemokratie und der Parlamentarismus" (1891). Reprinted in *Staat, Recht und Freiheit. Aus 40 Jahren deutscher Politik und Geschichte*, 144–72. 1926. Reprint, Hildesheim: Georg Olms, 1964.

————. "Volksstaat oder verkehrter Obrigkeitsstaat" (1918). Reprinted in *Staat, Recht und Freiheit. Aus 40 Jahren deutscher Politik und Geschichte*, 365–68. 1926. Reprint, Hildesheim: Georg Olms, 1964.

————. "Zur Methode juristischer Begriffskonstruktion." *Schmollers Jahrbuch für Gesetzgebung, Verwaltung und Volkswirtschaft im Deutschen Reich* 24 (1900): 359–72.

Pufendorf, Samuel. *Die Verfassung des deutschen Reiches.* Ed. and trans. Horst Denzer. Stuttgart: Reclam, 1985.

Richter, Lutz. "Die sechste Tagung der Vereinigung der deutschen Staatsrechts-lehrer." *Archiv des öffentlichen Rechts* 53 (1928): 441-59.

Rönne, Ludwig von. *Das Staats-Recht der preussischen Monarchie.* Leipzig: Brock-haus, 1870.

Rosenberg, Werner. "Die rechtlichen Schranken der Militärdiktatur." *Zeitschrift für die gesamte Strafrechtswissenschaft* 37 (1916): 808-25.

Rothenbücher, Karl. "Smends *Verfassung und Verfassungsrecht.*" *Reichsverwaltungs-blatt und Preussisches Verwaltungsblatt* 49 (1928): 554-55.

Rumpf, Max. *Gesetz und Richter. Versuch einer Methodik der Rechtsanwendung.* Ber-lin: Otto Liebmann, 1906.

Schelcher, Walter. "Artikel 153. Die Rechte und Pflichten aus dem Eigentum." In *Die Grundrechte und Grundpflichten der Reichsverfassung. Kommentar zum zweiten Teil der Reichsverfassung.* Vol. 3, ed. Hans-Carl Nipperdey, 196-249. Berlin: Reimar Hobbing, 1930.

Schmitt, Carl. "Die Auflösung des Enteignungsbegriffs" (1929). Reprinted in *Ver-fassungsrechtliche Aufsätze aus den Jahren 1924-1954. Materialien zu einer Verfas-sungslehre.* 2d ed., 110-18. Berlin: Duncker und Humblot, 1973.

———. *Der Begriff des Politischen. Texte von 1932 mit einem Vorwort und drei Corol-larien.* Berlin: Duncker und Humblot, 1963.

———. *The Crisis of Parliamentary Democracy.* 2d ed. 1926. Trans. Ellen Kennedy. Cambridge: MIT Press, 1985.

———. "Die Diktatur des Reichspräsidenten nach Art. 48 der Reichsverfassung." In *VVDSRL.* Vol. 1:63-104. Berlin: Walter de Gruyter, 1924.

———. "Diktatur und Belagerungszustand. Eine staatsrechtliche Studie." *Zeit-schrift für die gesamte Strafrechtswissenschaft* 38 (1917): 138-61.

———. *Die Diktatur. Von den Anfängen des modernen Souveränitätsgedankens bis zum proletarischen Klassenkampf.* 3d ed. Berlin: Duncker und Humblot, 1964.

———. "Die Einwirkungen des Kriegszustandes auf das ordentliche strafprozes-suale Verfahren." *Zeitschrift für die gesamte Strafrechtswissenschaft* 38 (1917): 783-97.

———. "Der Führer schützt das Recht" (1934). Reprinted in *Positionen und Begriffe im Kampf mit Weimar-Genf-Versailles, 1923-1939,* 199-203. Hamburg: Hanseatisch, 1940.

———. *Gesetz und Urteil. Eine Untersuchung zum Problem der Rechtspraxis.* 1912. Reprint, Munich: C. H. Beck, 1969.

———. *Hüter der Verfassung.* Tübingen: J. C. B. Mohr (Paul Siebeck), 1931.

———. "Juristische Fiktionen." *Deutsche Juristen-Zeitung* 18 (1913): 804-6.

———. *Legalität und Legitimität* (1932). Reprinted in *Verfassungsrechtliche Aufsätze aus den Jahren 1924-1954. Materialien zu einer Verfassungslehre.* 2d ed., 262-350. Berlin: Duncker und Humblot, 1973.

———. *Political Romanticism.* 2d ed. 1923. Trans. Guy Oakes. Cambridge: MIT Press, 1986.

———. *Political Theology. Four Chapters on the Concept of Sovereignty.* 2d ed. 1934. Trans. George Schwab. Cambridge: MIT Press, 1985.

———. *Politische Theologie. Vier Kapitel zur Lehre von der Souveränität.* Berlin: Duncker und Humblot, 1922.

———. *Politische Theologie II. Die Legende von der Erledigung jeder politischen Theologie.* Berlin: Duncker und Humblot, 1970.

———. "Das Reichsgericht als Hüter der Verfassung" (1929). Reprinted in *Verfassungsrechtliche Aufsätze aus den Jahren 1924–1954. Materialien zu einer Verfassungslehre.* 2d ed., 63–109. Berlin: Duncker und Humblot, 1973.

———. *Das Reichsstatthaltergesetz.* 2d ed. Berlin: Carl Heymann, 1934.

———. *Römischer Katholizismus und politische Form.* 1923. Reprint, Stuttgart: Klett-Cotta, 1984.

———. "Die Sichtbarkeit der Kirche." *Summa* 1.2 (1917): 71–80.

———. *Staat, Bewegung, Volk. Die Dreigliederung der politischen Einheit.* Hamburg: Hanseatisch, 1933.

———. "Staatsethik und pluralistischer Staat." *Kantstudien* 35 (1930): 28–42.

———. *Staatsgefüge und Zusammenbruch des Zweiten Reiches. Der Sieg des Bürgers über den Soldaten.* Hamburg: Hanseatisch, 1934.

———. *Unabhängigkeit der Richter, Gleichheit vor dem Gesetz und Gewährleistung des Privateigentums nach der Weimarer Verfassung. Ein Rechtsgutachten zu den Gesetzentwürfen über die Vermögensauseinandersetzung mit den früher regierenden Fürstenhäusern.* Berlin: Walter de Gruyter, 1926.

———. *Verfassungslehre.* 6th ed. Berlin: Duncker und Humblot, 1983.

———. "Die Verfassungsmässigkeit der Bestellung eines Reichskommissars für das Land Preussen." *Deutsche Juristen-Zeitung* 37 (1932): 953–58.

———. "Weiterentwicklung des totalen Staates in Deutschland" (February 1933). Reprinted in *Verfassungsrechtliche Aufsätze aus den Jahren 1924–1954. Materialien zu einer Verfassungslehre.* 2d ed., 359–65. Berlin: Duncker und Humblot, 1973.

———. *Der Wert des Staates und die Bedeutung des Einzelnen.* Tübingen: J. C. B. Mohr (Paul Siebeck), 1914.

———. "Zehn Jahre Reichsverfassung" (1929). Reprinted in *Verfassungsrechtliche Aufsätze aus den Jahren 1924–1954. Materialien zu einer Verfassungslehre.* 2d ed., 34–40. Berlin: Duncker und Humblot, 1973.

———. "Zum 21. März 1933." *Deutsche Juristen-Zeitung* 38 (1933): 453–58.

Schmitt, Carl, and Werner Becker. "Der bürgerliche Rechtsstaat." *Die Schildgenossen* 8 (1928): 127–33.

Seydel, Max von. *Commentar zur Verfassungs-Urkunde für das Deutsche Reich.* 2d ed. Freiburg: J. C. B. Mohr (Paul Siebeck), 1897.

————. *Staatsrechtliche und politische Abhandlungen*. Freiburg: J. C. B. Mohr (Paul Siebeck), 1893.

Simons, Walter. "Zum Geleit." In *Die Rechtsprechung des Staatsgerichtshofs für das Deutsche Reich und des Reichsgerichts auf Grund Artikel 13 Absatz 2 der Reichsverfassung*. Vol. 1, ed. Walter Simons and Hans-Hermann Lammers, 7-15. Berlin: Georg Stilke, 1929.

Sinzheimer, Hugo, and Ernst Fraenkel. *Die Justiz in der Weimarer Republic. Eine Chronik*. Ed. Thilo Ramm. Neuwied: Luchterhand, 1968.

Smend, Rudolf. "Bürger und Bourgeois im deutschen Staatsrecht" (1933). Reprinted in *Staatsrechtliche Abhandlungen und andere Aufsätze*. 3d ed., 309-25. Berlin: Duncker und Humblot, 1994.

————. "Integration" (1965). Reprinted in *Staatsrechtliche Abhandlungen und andere Aufsätze*. 3d ed., 482-86. Berlin: Duncker und Humblot, 1994.

————. "Integrationslehre" (1956). Reprinted in *Staatsrechtliche Abhandlungen und andere Aufsätze*. 3d ed., 475-81. Berlin: Duncker und Humblot, 1994.

————. "Die politische Gewalt im Verfassungsstaat und das Problem der Staatsform" (1923). Reprinted in *Staatsrechtliche Abhandlungen und andere Aufsätze*. 3d ed., 68-88. Berlin: Duncker und Humblot, 1994.

————. *Die Preussische Verfassungsurkunde im Vergleich mit der Belgischen*. Göttingen: Diederich, 1904.

————. "Das Recht der freien Meinungsäusserung." In *VVDSRL*. Vol. 4:44-74. Berlin: Walter de Gruyter, 1928.

————. "Ungeschriebenes Verfassungsrecht im monarchischen Bundesstaat" (1916). Reprinted in *Staatsrechtliche Abhandlungen und andere Aufsätze*. 3d ed., 29-59. Berlin: Duncker und Humblot, 1994.

————. "Die Vereinigung der Deutschen Staatsrechtslehrer und der Richtungsstreit." In *Festschrift für Ulrich Scheuner zum 70. Geburtstag*, 575-89. Berlin: Duncker und Humblot, 1973.

————. *Die Verfassung des Deutschen Reichs vom 11. August 1919, Eingeleitet von Prof. Dr. R. Smend*. Berlin: Sieben Stäbe, 1929.

————. *Verfassung und Verfassungsrecht* (1928). Reprinted in *Staatsrechtliche Abhandlungen und andere Aufsätze*. 3d ed., 119-276. Berlin: Duncker und Humblot, 1994.

————. "Die Verschiebung der konstitutionellen Ordnung durch die Verhältniswahl" (1919). Reprinted in *Staatsrechtliche Abhandlungen und andere Aufsätze*. 3d ed., 60-67. Berlin: Duncker und Humblot, 1994.

Steininger, Alfons. Comment on decision of the *Reichsgericht* of February 28, 1930, printed in *Entscheidungen des Reichsgerichts in Zivilsachen*, 128:18-34. *Juristische Wochenschrift* 59 (1930): 2427-28.

Stier-Somlo, Fritz. "Artikel 109. Gleichheit vor dem Gesetz." In *Die Grund-*

rechte und Grundpflichten der Reichsverfassung. Kommentar zum zweiten Teil der Reichsverfassung. Vol. 1, ed. Hans-Carl Nipperdey, 158–218. Berlin: Reimar Hobbing, 1929.

———. "Die dritte Tagung der Vereinigung der deutschen Staatsrechtslehrer." *Archiv des öffentlichen Rechts* 48 (1925): 98–109.

———. "Verfassung, Verfassungsrecht." In *Handwörterbuch der Rechtswissenschaft.* Vol. 6:387–95. Berlin: Walter de Gruyter, 1929.

———. "Die Zweite Tagung der Vereinigung der deutschen Staatsrechtslehrer." *Archiv des öffentlichen Rechts* 46 (1924): 88–105.

Stoerk, Felix. *Zur Methodik des öffentlichen Rechts.* Vienna: Alfred Hölder, 1885.

Stoll, Heinrich. "Zur 3.A." *Juristische Wochenschrift* 55 (1926): 1429–30.

Tatarin-Tarnheyden, Edgar. Review of *Verfassung und Verfassungsrecht,* by Rudolf Smend. *Juristische Wochenschrift* 57 (1928): 1028–29.

Tenzer, Friedrich. "Betrachtungen über Kelsens Lehre vom Rechtssatz." *Archiv des öffentlichen Rechts* 28 (1912): 325–44.

Thoma, Richard. "Der Begriff der modernen Demokratie in seinem Verhältnis zum Staatsbegriff." In *Hauptprobleme der Soziologie. Erinnerungsgabe für Max Weber,* ed. Melchior Palyi, 37–64. Munich: Duncker und Humblot, 1923.

———. "Gegenstand.-Methode.-Literatur." In *Handbuch des Deutschen Staatsrechts.* Vol. 1, ed. Gerhard Anschütz and Richard Thoma, 1–13. Tübingen: J. C. B. Mohr (Paul Siebeck), 1930.

———. "Gerhard Anschütz zum 80. Geburtstag." *Deutsche Rechts-Zeitschrift* 2 (1947): 25–27.

———. "Grundrechte und Polizeigewalt." In *Festgabe zur Feier des fünfzigjährigen Bestehens des Preussischen Oberverwaltungsgerichts 1875–20. November 1925,* ed. Heinrich Triepel, 183–223. Berlin: Carl Heymann, 1925.

———. "Die juristische Bedeutung der grundrechtlichen Sätze der Deutschen Reichsverfassung im allgemeinen." In *Die Grundrechte und Grundpflichten der Reichsverfassung. Kommentar zum zweiten Teil der Reichsverfassung.* Vol. 1, ed. Hans-Carl Nipperdey, 1–53. Berlin: Reimar Hobbing, 1929.

———. "Die Notstandsverordnung des Reichspräsidenten vom 26. Juli 1930." *Zeitschrift für öffentliches Recht* 11 (1931): 12–33.

———. "Die rechtliche Ordnung des parlamentarischen Regierungssystems." In *Handbuch des Deutschen Staatsrechts.* Vol. 1, ed. Gerhard Anschütz and Richard Thoma, 503–11. Tübingen: J. C. B. Mohr (Paul Siebeck), 1930.

———. "Rechtsstaatsidee und Verwaltungsrechtswissenschaft." *Jahrbuch des öffentlichen Rechts der Gegenwart* 4 (1910): 196–218.

———. "Das Reich als Demokratie." In *Handbuch des deutschen Staatsrechts.* Vol. 1, ed. Gerhard Anschütz and Richard Thoma, 186–200. Tübingen: J. C. B. Mohr (Paul Siebeck), 1930.

———. "Das richterliche Prüfungsrecht." *Archiv des öffentlichen Rechts* 43 (1922): 267–86.

———. "Das System der subjektiven öffentlichen Rechte und Pflichten." *Handbuch des Deutschen Staatsrechts.* Vol. 2, ed. Gerhard Anschütz and Richard Thoma, 606–23. Tübingen: J. C. B. Mohr (Paul Siebeck), 1932.

Triepel, Heinrich. "Die Entscheidung des Staatsgerichtshofs im Verfassungsstreit zwischen Preussen und dem Reiche." *Deutsche Juristen-Zeitung* 37 (1932): 1501–8.

———. *Goldbilanzenverordnung und Vorzugsaktien. Zur Frage der Rechtsgültigkeit der über sogenannte schuldverschreibungsähnliche Aktien in den Durchführungsbestimmungen zur Goldbilanzen-Verordnung enthaltenen Vorschriften.* Berlin: Walter de Gruyter, 1924.

———. *Staatsrecht und Politik.* Berlin: Walter de Gruyter, 1927.

———. *Die Staatsverfassung und die politischen Parteien.* Berlin: Otto Liebmann, 1927.

———. *Streitigkeiten zwischen Reich und Ländern. Beiträge zur Auslegung des Artikels 19 der Weimarer Reichsverfassung.* 1923. Reprint, Bad Homburg von der Höhe: Hermann Gentner, 1965.

———. "Die Vereinigung der deutschen Staatsrechtslehrer." *Archiv des öffentlichen Rechts* 43 (1922): 349–51.

———. "Wesen und Entwicklung der Staatsgerichtsbarkeit." In *VVDSRL.* Vol. 5:2–29. Berlin: Walter de Gruyter, 1929.

Voegelin, Eric. "Kelsen's Pure Theory of Law." *Political Science Quarterly* 42 (1927): 268–76.

———. "Die Verfassungslehre von Carl Schmitt. Versuch einer konstruktiven Analyse ihrer staatstheoretischen Prinzipien." *Zeitschrift für öffentliches Recht* 11 (1931): 89–109.

Weber, Marianne. *Max Weber. Ein Lebensbild.* Heidelberg: Lambert Schneider, 1950.

Weber, Max. "Beiträge zur Verfassungsfrage anlässlich der Verhandlungen im Reichsamt des Innern vom 9. bis 12. Dezember 1918." In *Max Weber Gesamtausgabe.* Pt. 1, vol. 16, *Zur Neuordnung Deutschlands. Schriften und Reden 1918–1920.* Ed. Wolfgang Mommsen and Wolfgang Schwentker, 49–90. Tübingen: J. C. B. Mohr (Paul Siebeck), 1988.

———. "Deutschlands künftige Staatsform" (1918). In *Gesammelte politische Schriften.* 5th ed., ed. Johannes Winckelmann, 448–83. Tübingen: J. C. B. Mohr (Paul Siebeck), 1988.

———. *Economy and Society. An Outline of Interpretive Sociology.* Trans. Günther Roth and Claus Wittich. New York: Bedminster, 1968.

———. "Parliament and Government in Germany" (1918). In *Political Writings.*

Ed. Peter Lassman and Ronald Speirs, 130–271. Cambridge: Cambridge University Press, 1994.

———. "The President of the Reich." In *Political Writings*. Ed. Peter Lassman and Ronald Speirs, 304–8. Cambridge: Cambridge University Press, 1994.

Westerkamp, Justus B. *Über die Reichsverfassung*. Hanover: Carl Rümpler, 1873.

Weyr, Franz. Review of *Wert des Staates und Bedeutung des Einzelnen*, by Carl Schmitt. *Österreichische Zeitschrift für öffentliches Recht* 1 (1914): 578–81.

Wieruzowski, Alfred. "Artikel 119. Ehe, Familie, Mutterschaft." In *Die Grundrechte und Grundpflichten der Reichsverfassung. Kommentar zum zweiten Teil der Reichsverfassung*. Vol. 2, ed. Hans-Carl Nipperdey, 72–94. Berlin: Reimar Hobbing, 1929.

Wilson, Woodrow. *The State. Elements of Historical and Practical Politics*. 2d ed. Boston: D. C. Heath, 1903.

Wittmayer, Leo. *Reichsverfassung und Politik*. Tübingen: J. C. B. Mohr (Paul Siebeck), 1923.

———. Review of *Die Diktatur*, by Carl Schmitt. *Zeitschrift für öffentliches Recht* 5 (1926): 492–95.

Wolff, Martin. *Reichsverfassung und Eigentum*. Offprint from *Festgabe der Berliner Juristischen Fakultät für Wilhelm Kahl zum Doktorjubiläum am 19. April 1923*. Tübingen: J. C. B. Mohr (Paul Siebeck), 1923.

Sources Published after 1945

Abraham, Henry J. *The Judicial Process: An Introductory Analysis of the Courts of the United States, England, and France*. 5th ed. New York: Oxford University Press, 1986.

Ackerman, Bruce. *The Future of Liberal Revolution*. New Haven: Yale University Press, 1992.

———. *We the People*. Vol. 1, *Foundations*. Cambridge: Harvard University Press, 1991.

Akin, William E. *Technocracy and the American Dream: The Technocratic Movement, 1900–1941*. Berkeley: University of California Press, 1977.

Alexy, Robert. *Theorie der Grundrechte*. Baden-Baden: Nomos, 1985.

Anderson, Margaret Lavinia. "The Kulturkampf and the Course of German History." *Central European History* 19 (1986): 82–115.

Apelt, Willibalt. *Geschichte der Weimarer Verfassung*. Munich: Biederstein, 1946.

Aretin, Karl Otmar Freiherr von. "Brünings ganz andere Rolle." *Frankfurter Hefte* 26 (1971): 931–939.

Asshener, Thomas, and Hans Sarkowicz. *Rechtsradikale in Deutschland. Die alte und die neue Rechte*. Munich: C. H. Beck, 1990.

Aufricht, Hans. "The Theory of Pure Law in Historical Perspective." In *Law,*

State, and International Legal Order. Essays in Honor of Hans Kelsen, ed. Salo Engel, 29–41. Knoxville: University of Tennessee Press, 1964.

Badura, Peter. *Staatsrecht. Systematische Erläuterung des Grundgesetzes für die Bundesrepublik Deutschland.* Munich: C. H. Beck, 1986.

Bärsch, Claus-Ekkehard. "Der Gerber-Laband'sche Positivismus." In *Staat und Recht. Die deutsche Staatslehre im 19. und 20. Jahrhundert,* ed. Martin J. Sattler, 43–71. Munich: List, 1972.

Bauer, Wolfram. *Wertrelativismus und Wertbestimmtheit im Kampf um die Weimarer Republik. Zur Politologie des Methodenstreites der Staatsrechtslehre.* Berlin: Duncker und Humblot, 1968.

Behrends, Okko. "Von der Freirechtsschule zum konkreten Ordnungsdenken." In *Recht und Justiz im "Dritten Reich,"* ed. Ralf Dreier and Wolfgang Sellert, 34–79. Frankfurt am Main: Suhrkamp, 1989.

Bendersky, Joseph W. *Carl Schmitt: Theorist for the Reich.* Princeton: Princeton University Press, 1983.

Berghahn, Volker. *Germany and the Approach of War in 1914.* 2d ed. New York: St. Martin's Press, 1993.

Bessel, Richard. *Germany after the First World War.* Oxford: Clarendon, 1993.

Beyer, Wilhelm Raimund. "Paul Laband: ein Pionier des öffentlichen Rechts." *Neue Juristische Wochenschrift* 41 (1988): 2227–28.

Beyme, Klaus von. "The Genesis of Constitutional Review in Parliamentary Systems." In *Constitutional Review and Legislation. An International Comparison,* ed. Christine Landfried, 21–38. Baden-Baden: Nomos, 1988.

Bickel, Alexander. *The Least Dangerous Branch: The Supreme Court at the Bar of Politics.* 2d ed. New Haven: Yale University Press, 1986.

Biewer, Ludwig. *Reichsreformbestrebungen in der Weimarer Republik. Fragen zur Funktionalreform und zur Neugliederung im Südwesten des Deutschen Reiches.* Frankfurt am Main: Peter D. Lang, 1980.

Bloch, Ernst. *Naturrecht und menschliche Würde.* Frankfurt am Main: Suhrkamp, 1972.

Bobbio, Norberto. "La teoría pura del derecho y sus críticos" (1957), trans. Mario Cerda Median. Reprinted in *Hans Kelsen 1881–1973,* ed. Agustín Squella, 299–326. Valparaiso: *Revista de ciencias sociales,* 1974.

Bodenheimer, Edgar. *Jurisprudence.* New York: McGraw-Hill, 1940.

Böckenförde, Ernst-Wolfgang. "Der Begriff des Politischen als Schlüssel zum staatsrechtlichen Werk Carl Schmitts" (1988). Reprinted in *Recht, Staat, Freiheit. Studien zur Rechtsphilosophie, Staatstheorie und Verfassungsgeschichte,* 344–66. Frankfurt am Main: Suhrkamp, 1991.

———. "Entstehung und Wandel des Rechtsstaatsbegriffs" (1969). Reprinted in *Recht, Staat, Freiheit. Studien zur Rechtsphilosophie, Staatstheorie und Verfassungsgeschichte,* 143–69. Frankfurt am Main: Suhrkamp, 1991.

————. "Gerhard Anschütz" (1986). Reprinted in *Recht, Staat, Freiheit. Studien zur Rechtsphilosophie, Staatstheorie und Verfassungsgeschichte*, 367–78. Frankfurt am Main: Suhrkamp, 1991.

————. "The German Type of Constitutional Monarchy in the Nineteenth Century" (1967). Reprinted in *State, Society and Liberty. Studies in Political Theory and Constitutional Law*. Trans. J. A. Underwood, 87–114. New York: Berg, 1991.

————. *Gesetz und gesetzgebende Gewalt. Von den Anfängen der deutschen Staatsrechtslehre bis zur Höhe des staatsrechtlichen Positivismus*. Berlin: Duncker und Humblot, 1958.

————. "Politische Theorie und politische Theologie. Bemerkungen zu ihrem gegenseitigen Verhältnis." In *Der Fürst dieser Welt. Carl Schmitt und die Folgen*, ed. Jacob Taubes, 16–25. Munich: W. Fink, 1983.

————. "The School of Historical Jurisprudence and the Problem of the Historicity of Law" (1965). Reprinted in *State, Society and Liberty. Studies in Political Theory and Constitutional Law*. Trans. J. A. Underwood, 1–25. New York: Berg, 1991.

Boldt, Hans. *Deutsche Verfassungsgeschichte: Politische Strukturen und ihr Wandel*. Vol. 1, *Von den Anfängen bis zum Ende des älteren deutschen Reiches*. Munich: DTV, 1984. Vol. 2, *Von 1806 bis zur Gegenwart*. Munich: DTV, 1990.

————. "Deutscher Konstitutionalismus und Bismarckreich." In *Das Kaiserliche Deutschland. Politik und Gesellschaft, 1870–1918*, ed. Michael Stürmer, 119–42. Dusseldorf: Droste, 1970.

————. *Einführung in die Verfassungsgeschichte. Zwei Abhandlungen zu ihrer Methode und Geschichte*. Dusseldorf: Droste, 1984.

————. *Rechtsstaat und Ausnahmezustand. Eine Studie über den Belagerungszustand als Ausnahmezustand des bürgerlichen Rechtsstaates im 19. Jahrhundert*. Berlin: Duncker und Humblot, 1967.

————. "Verfassungskonflikt und Verfassungshistorie. Eine Auseinandersetzung mit Ernst Rudolf Huber." In *Probleme des Konstitutionalismus im 19. Jahrhundert. Der Staat*, Beiheft 1, ed. Ernst-Wolfgang Böckenförde, 75–102. Berlin: Duncker und Humblot, 1975.

————. "Die Weimarer Reichsverfassung." In *Die Weimarer Republik 1918–1933. Politik-Wirtschaft-Gesellschaft*, ed. Karl-Dietrich Bracher, Manfred Funke, and Hans-Adolf Jacobsen, 44–62. Dusseldorf: Droste, 1987.

Bonn, Moritz Julius. *Wandering Scholar*. New York: John Day, 1948.

Borinski, Fritz. "Hermann Heller: Lehrer der Jugend und Vorkämpfer der freien Erwachsenenbildung." In *Der soziale Rechtsstaat. Gedächtnisschrift für Hermann Heller 1891–1933*, ed. Christoph Müller and Ilse Staff, 89–110. Baden-Baden: Nomos, 1984.

Bork, Robert H. *The Tempting of America: The Political Seduction of the Law*. New York: Free Press, 1990.

Boyer, John W. "Freud, Marriage, and Late Viennese Liberalism: A Commentary from 1905." *Journal of Modern History* 50 (1978): 72-102.

Bracher, Karl Dietrich. *Auflösung der Weimar Republik. Eine Studie zum Problem des Machtverfalls in der Demokratie.* 5th ed. Dusseldorf: Droste, 1984.

———. *The German Dictatorship: The Origins, Structure, and Effects of National Socialism.* Trans. Jean Steinberg. New York: Praeger, 1970.

Brecht, Arnold. *Federalism and Regionalism in Germany. The Division of Prussia.* New York: Oxford University Press, 1945.

———. *Mit der Kraft des Geistes. Lebenserinnerungen. Zweite Hälfte 1927-1967.* Stuttgart: Deutsche Verlags-Anstalt, 1967.

Breuer, Stefan. "Nationalstaat und poivoir constituant bei Sieyes und Carl Schmitt." *Archiv für Rechts- und Sozialphilosophie* 70 (1984): 495-517.

Broszat, Martin. *The Hitler State: The Foundation and Development of the Internal Structure of the Third Reich.* Trans. John W. Hiden. London: Longman, 1981.

Butz, Otto. *Modern German Political Theory.* Garden City, N.Y.: Doubleday, 1955.

Caldwell, Peter. "Legal Positivism and Weimar Democracy." *American Journal of Jurisprudence* 39 (1994): 273-301.

———. "National Socialism and Constitutional Law: Carl Schmitt, Otto Koell-reutter, and the Debate over the Nature of the Nazi State, 1933-1937." *Cardozo Law Review* 16 (1994): 399-427.

Corwin, Edward S. *The Constitution and What It Means Today.* 14th ed. Rev. Harold W. Chase and Craig R. Ducat. Princeton: Princeton University Press, 1978.

Craig, Gordon. *The Politics of the Prussian Army, 1640-1945.* London: Oxford University Press, 1955.

Dangerfield, *The Strange Death of Liberal England.* New York: Smith and Haas, 1935.

Dawson, John P. *The Oracles of the Law.* Ann Arbor: University of Michigan Law School, 1968.

de Lange, Roel. "Paradoxes of European Citizenship." In *Nationalism, Racism and the Rule of Law,* ed. Peter Fitzpatrick, 97-115. Aldershot: Dartmouth University Press, 1995.

Derrida, Jacques. "Declarations of Independence." *New Political Science* 15 (1986): 7-15.

Domansky, Elisabeth. "Militarization and Reproduction in World War One Germany." In *Society, Culture and the State in Germany, 1870-1930,* ed. Geoff Eley, 427-63. Ann Arbor: University of Michigan Press, 1996.

Döring, Herbert. *Der Weimarer Kreis. Studien zum politischen Bewusstsein verfassungstreuer Hochschullehrer in der Weimarer Republik.* Meinenheim am Glan: Anton Hain, 1975.

Dreier, Horst. *Rechtslehre, Staatssoziologie und Demokratietheorie bei Hans Kelsen.* Baden-Baden: Nomos, 1986.

Dworkin, Ronald. *Life's Dominion: An Argument about Abortion, Euthanasia, and Individual Freedom.* New York: Vintage, 1993.

———. *Taking Rights Seriously.* 2d ed. Cambridge: Harvard University Press, 1978.

Dyzenhaus, David. "Hermann Heller and the Legitimacy of Legality." Paper presented at the American Political Science Association annual meeting, Chicago, Ill., September 1, 1995.

———. " 'Now the Machine Runs Itself': Carl Schmitt on Hobbes and Kelsen." *Cardozo Law Review* 16 (1994): 1-19.

———. *Truth's Revenge: Carl Schmitt, Hans Kelsen, and Hermann Heller in Weimar.* New York: Clarendon, 1997.

Edelmann, Johann. *Die Entwicklung der Interessenjurisprudenz. Eine historisch-kritische Studie über die deutsche Rechtsmethodologie vom 18. Jahrhundert bis zum Gegenwart.* Bad Homburg von der Höhe: Max Gehlen, 1967.

Ehmke, Horst. *Grenzen der Verfassungsänderung* (1952). In *Beiträge zur Verfassungstheorie und Verfassungspolitik.* Ed. Peter Häberle, 21-141. Königstein: Athenäum, 1981.

———. " 'Staat' und 'Gesellschaft' als verfassungstheoretisches Problem." In *Staatsverfassung und Kirchenordnung. Festgabe für Rudolf Smend zum 80. Geburtstag am 15. Januar 1962,* ed. Konrad Hesse, Siegfried Reicke, and Ulrich Scheuner, 23-49. Tübingen: J. C. B. Mohr (Paul Siebeck), 1962.

Eikema Hommes, Hendrik J. van. "The Development of Hans Kelsen's Concept of Legal Norm." In *Rechtssystem und gesellschaftliche Basis bei Hans Kelsen. Rechtstheorie,* Beiheft 5, ed. Werner Krawietz and Helmut Schelsky, 159-74. Berlin: Duncker und Humblot, 1984.

Ellul, Jacques. *Histoire des Institutions.* Vol. 5, *Le XIXe siècle.* 6th ed. Paris: Presses Universitaires de France, 1969.

Ely, John Hart. *Democracy and Distrust: A Theory of Judicial Review.* Cambridge: Harvard University Press, 1980.

Emerson, Rupert. *State and Sovereignty in Modern Germany.* New Haven: Yale University Press, 1928.

Epstein, Richard A. "Property, Speech, and the Politics of Distrust." In *The Bill of Rights in the Modern State,* ed. Geoffrey R. Stone, Richard A. Epstein, and Cass Sunstein, 41-89. Chicago: University of Chicago Press, 1992.

———. *Takings: Private Property and the Power of Eminent Domain.* Cambridge: Harvard University Press, 1985.

Ermacora, Felix. "Österreichische Bundesverfassung und Hans Kelsen." In *Festschrift für Hans Kelsen zum 90. Geburtstag,* ed. Adolf Merkl et al., 22-54. Vienna: Franz Deuticke, 1971.

Eyck, Erich. *A History of the Weimar Republic.* 2 vols. Trans. Harlan Hanson and Robert White. Cambridge: Harvard University Press, 1963.

Fehrenbach, Elisabeth. "Reich." In *Geschichtliche Grundbegriffe. Historisches Lexikon zur politisch-sozialen Sprache in Deutschland.* Vol. 5, ed. Otto Brunner et al., 423–508. Stuttgart: Klett-Cotta, 1984.

―――. *Verfassungsstaat und Nationsbildung 1815–1871.* Munich: Oldenbourg, 1992.

―――. *Wandlungen des deutschen Kaisergedankens 1871–1918.* Munich: Oldenbourg, 1969.

Feldman, Gerald D. *Army, Industry and Labor in Germany, 1914–1918.* Princeton: Princeton University Press, 1966.

―――. *The Great Disorder: Politics, Economics, and Society in the German Inflation, 1914–1924.* New York: Oxford University Press, 1993.

Fenske, Hans. "Die Verwaltung im Ersten Weltkrieg." *Deutsche Verwaltungsgeschichte.* Vol. 3, *Das Deutsche Reich bis zum Ende der Monarchie,* 866–908. Stuttgart: Deutsche Verlags-Anstalt, 1984.

Forsthoff, Ernst. "Gerhard Anschütz." *Der Staat* 6 (1967): 139–50.

―――. *Lehrbuch des Verwaltungsrechts.* Vol. 1: *Allgemeiner Teil.* 9th ed. Munich: C. H. Beck, 1966.

―――. *Der Staat der Industriegesellschaft. Dargestellt am Beispiel der Bundesrepublik Deutschland.* Munich: C. H. Beck, 1971.

Fouckes, Albert S. "On the German Free Law School (Freirechtsschule)." *Archiv für Rechts- und Sozialphilosophie* 55 (1969): 366–417.

Fraenkel, Ernst. *The Dual State: A Contribution to the Theory of Dictatorship.* Trans. E. A. Shils, E. Loewenstein, and K. Knorr. New York: Oxford University Press, 1941.

―――. "Der Ruhreisenstreik 1928–1929 in historisch-politischer Sicht." In *Staat, Wirtschaft und Politik in der Weimarer Republik. Festschrift für Heinrich Brüning,* ed. Ferdinand A. Hermens and Theodor Schieder, 97–117. Berlin: Duncker und Humblot, 1967.

Franssen, Everhardt. "Positivismus als juristische Strategie." *Juristen-Zeitung* 24 (1969): 766–74.

Freiherr von Campenhausen, Axel. "Rudolf Smend (1882–1975). Integration in zerrissener Zeit." In *Rechtswissenschaft in Göttingen. Göttinger Juristen aus 250 Jahren,* ed. Fritz Loos, 510–27. Göttingen: Vandenhoeck und Ruprecht, 1987.

Friedmann, Lawrence M. *Law and Society: An Introduction.* Englewood Cliffs, N.J.: Prentice-Hall, 1977.

Friedmann, Wolfgang. *Legal Theory.* 5th ed. New York: Columbia University Press, 1967.

Friedrich, Manfred. "Der Methoden- und Richtungsstreit. Zur Grundlagendiskussion der Weimarer Staatsrechtslehre." *Archiv des öffentlichen Rechts* 102 (1977): 161–209.

―――. "Paul Laband und die Staatsrechtswissenschaft seiner Zeit." *Archiv des öffentlichen Rechts* 111 (1986): 197–218.

―――. "Rudolf Smend 1882–1975." *Archiv des öffentlichen Rechts* 112 (1987): 1–26.

―――. *Zwischen Positivismus und materialem Verfassungsdenken. Albert Hänel und seine Bedeutung für die deutsche Staatsrechtswissenschaft.* Berlin: Duncker und Humblot, 1971.

Fröhling, Ortrun. "Labands Staatsbegriff. Die anorganische Staatsperson als Konstruktionsmittel der deutschen konstitutionellen Staatslehre." Ph.D. diss., Universität Marburg, 1967.

Fromme, Friedrich Karl. *Von der Weimarer Verfassung zum Bonner Grundgesetz. Die verfassungspolitischen Folgerungen des Parlamentarischen Rates aus Weimarer Republik und nationalsozialistischer Diktatur.* Tübingen: J. C. B. Mohr (Paul Siebeck), 1960.

Fuller, Lon L. *The Morality of Law.* Rev. ed. New Haven: Yale University Press, 1969.

Gall, Lothar. *Bismarck: The White Revolutionary.* Vol. 1, *1851–1871.* Trans. J. A. Underwood. London: Allen and Unwin, 1986.

Geis, Max-Emanuel. "Der Methoden- und Richtungsstreit in der Weimarer Rechtslehre." *Juristische Schulung* 29 (1989): 91–96.

Gentile, Francesco. "Hobbes et Kelsen. Éléments pour une lecture croisée." *Cahiers Vilfredo Pareto. Revue européenne des sciences sociales* 61 (1982): 379–92.

Gerhard, Ute. *Verhältnisse und Verhinderungen. Frauenarbeit, Familie und Rechte der Frauen im 19. Jahrhundert.* Frankfurt am Main: Suhrkamp, 1978.

Gilissen, John. "La constitution belge de 1831: ses sources, son influence." *Res Publica* 10 (1968): 107–41.

Göhler, Gerhard. "Politische Institutionen und ihr Kontext. Begriffliche und konzeptionelle Überlegungen zur Theorie politischer Institutionen." In *Die Eigenart der Institution. Zum Profil politischer Institutionentheorie,* ed. Gerhard Göhler, 19–46. Baden-Baden: Nomos, 1994.

Gooch, R. K. *Parliamentary Government in France: Revolutionary Origins, 1789–1791.* Ithaca: Cornell University Press, 1960.

Gottfried, Paul Edward. *Carl Schmitt: Politics and Theory.* New York: Greenwood, 1990.

Grassmann, Siegfried. *Hugo Preuss und die deutsche Selbstverwaltung.* Lübeck: Matthiesen, 1965.

Grebing, Helga. *Der deutsche Sonderweg in Europa 1806–1945. Eine Kritik.* Stuttgart: W. Kohlhammer, 1986.

Grimm, Dieter. *Deutsche Verfassungsgeschichte 1776–1866. Vom Beginn des modernen Verfassungsstaats bis zur Auflösung des Deutschen Bundes.* Frankfurt am Main: Suhrkamp, 1988.

―――. "Die Entwicklung der Grundrechtstheorie in der deutschen Staatsrechtslehre des 19. Jahrhunderts" (1987). Reprinted in *Recht und Staat der bürgerlichen Gesellschaft*, 308–46. Frankfurt am Main: Suhrkamp, 1987.

———. "Methode als Machtfaktor" (1982). Reprinted in *Recht und Staat der bürgerlichen Gesellschaft*, 347–72. Frankfurt am Main: Suhrkamp, 1987.

———. "Die 'neue Rechtswissenschaft'—Über Funktion und Formation nationalsozialistische Jurisprudenz" (1985). Reprinted in *Recht und Staat der bürgerlichen Gesellschaft*, 373–95. Frankfurt am Main: Suhrkamp, 1987.

———. "Der Verfassungsbegriff in historischer Entwicklung" (1990). Reprinted in *Die Zukunft der Verfassung*, 101–55. Frankfurt am Main: Suhrkamp, 1991.

———. "Verfassungserfüllung—Verfassungsbewahrung—Verfassungsauflösung. Positionen der Staatsrechtslehre in der Staatskrise der Weimarer Republik." In *Die deutsche Staatskrise 1930–1933. Handlungsspielräume und Alternativen*, ed. Heinrich August Winkler with Elisabeth Muller-Luckner, 183–99. Munich: Oldenbourg, 1993.

———. "Der Wandel der Staatsaufgaben und die Krise des Rechtsstaats" (1990). Reprinted in *Die Zukunft der Verfassung*, 159–75. Frankfurt am Main: Suhrkamp, 1991.

Gritschneder, Otto. *"Der Führer hat Sie zum Tode verurteilt . . ." Hitlers "Röhm-Putsch"-Morde vor Gericht*. Munich: C. H. Beck, 1993.

Gross, Raphael. "Carl Schmitts 'Nomos' und die 'Juden.'" *Merkur* 47 (1993): 410–20.

Grosser, Dieter. *Vom monarchischen Konstitutionalismus zur parlamentarischen Demokratie. Die Verfassungspolitik der deutschen Parteien im letzten Jahrzehnt des Kaiserreiches*. The Hague: Nijhoff, 1980.

Grossmann, Atina. *Reforming Sex: The German Movement for Birth Control and Abortion Reform, 1920–1950*. New York: Oxford University Press, 1995.

Grund, Henning. *"Preussenschlag" und Staatsgerichtshof im Jahre 1932*. Baden-Baden: Nomos, 1976.

Grusmann, Wolf-Dietrich. *Adolf Julius Merkl. Leben und Werk*. Schriftenreihe des Hans-Kelsen-Instituts, vol. 13. Vienna: Manz, 1989.

Guggenberger, Bernd, and Andreas Meier, eds. *Der Souverän auf der Nebenbühne. Essays und Zwischenrufe zur deutschen Verfassungsdiskussion*. Opladen: Westdeutscher, 1994.

Gusy, Christoph. *Richterliches Prüfungsrecht. Eine verfassungsgeschichtliche Untersuchung*. Berlin: Duncker und Humblot, 1985.

Häberle, Peter. "Zum Tode von Rudolf Smend" (1975). Reprinted in *Verfassung als öffentlicher Prozess. Materialien zu einer Verfassungstheorie der offenen Gesellschaft*, 685–87. Berlin: Duncker und Humblot, 1978.

Hahlen, Johann. "Verfassungsreform als Problem des deutschen Wiedervereinigungsprozesses." In *Probleme des Zusammenwachsens im wiedervereinigten*

Deutschland, ed. Alexander Fischer and Manfred Wilke, 63–74. Berlin: Duncker und Humblot, 1994.

Hall, Stuart, and Bill Schwarz. "State and Society, 1880–1930." In *Crises in the British State 1880–1930,* ed. Mary Langan and Bill Schwarz, 7–32. London: Hutchinson, 1985.

Hart, H. L. A. *The Concept of Law.* London: Oxford University Press, 1961.

Heckart, Beverly. *From Bassermann to Bebel: The Grand Bloc's Quest for Reform in the Kaiserreich, 1900–1914.* New Haven: Yale University Press, 1974.

Heneman, Harlow James. *The Growth of Executive Power in Germany: A Study of the German Presidency.* Minneapolis: Voyageur, 1934.

Hennig, Eike. "Hermann Heller. Anmerkungen einer Synthese von Nationalismus und Sozialismus." *Neue Politische Literatur* 4 (1971): 507–19.

Herberger, Maximilian. "Logik und Dogmatik bei Paul Laband. Zur Praxis der sog. juristischen Methode im 'Staatsrecht des Deutschen Reiches.'" In *Wissenschaft und Recht der Verwaltung seit dem Ancien Regime. Europäische Ansichten,* ed. Erk Volkmar Heyen, 91–104. Frankfurt am Main: Vittorio Klostermann, 1984.

Herf, Jeffrey. *Reactionary Modernism: Technology, Culture and Politics in Weimar and the Third Reich.* Cambridge: Cambridge University Press, 1984.

Herget, James E. "Unearthing the Origins of a Radical Idea: The Case of Legal Indeterminacy." [Includes translation of Oskar von Bülow, "Gesetz und Richteramt."] *American Journal of Legal History* 39 (1995): 59–94.

Herget, James E., and Stephen Wallace. "The German Free Law Movement as the Source of American Legal Realism." *Virginia Law Review* 73 (1987): 399–455.

Herrfahrdt, Heinrich. *Revolution und Rechtswissenschaft. Untersuchungen über die juristische Erfassbarkeit von Revolutionsvorgängen und ihre Bedeutung für die allgemeine Rechtslehre.* 1930. Reprint, Aalen: Scientia, 1970.

Herzfeld, Hans. *Die Selbstverwaltung und die Weimarer Epoche.* Stuttgart: W. Kohlhammer, 1957.

Hesse, Konrad. *Grundzüge des Verfassungsrechts der Bundesrepublik Deutschland.* 18th ed. Heidelberg: C. F. Müller, 1991.

Hettlage, Robert. "Integrationsleistungen des Rechts im Prozess der deutschen Einheit." In *Deutschland nach der Wende. Eine Zwischenbilanz,* ed. Robert Hettlage and Karl Ley, 28–35. Munich: C. H. Beck, 1995.

Heyen, Erk Volkmar. "Die Anfangsjahre des 'Archivs für öffentliches Recht.' Programmatischer Anspruch und redaktioneller Alltag im Wettbewerb." In *Wissenschaft und Recht der Verwaltung seit dem Ancien Regime. Europäische Ansichten,* ed. Erk Volkmar Heyen, 347–73. Frankfurt am Main: Vittorio Klostermann, 1984.

Hofmann, Hasso. *Legitimität gegen Legalität. Der Weg der politischen Philosophie Carl Schmitts.* Neuwied: Luchterhand, 1964.

———. "Das Problem der cäsaristischen Legitimität im Bismarckreich" (1977). Reprinted in *Recht-Politik-Verfassung. Studien zur Geschichte der politischen Philosophie*, 181–205. Frankfurt am Main: Alfred Metzner, 1986.

Hollerbach, Alexander. "Zu Leben und Werk Heinrich Triepels." *Archiv des öffentlichen Rechts* 91 (1966): 417–41.

Holmes, Stephen. *The Anatomy of Antiliberalism*. Cambridge: Harvard University Press, 1993.

———. "The Scourge of Liberalism." *New Republic* 199 (August 22, 1988): 31–36.

Holzhey, Helmut. "Die Transformation neukantianischer Theoreme in die reine Rechtslehre." In *Hermeneutik und Strukturtheorie des Rechts. Archiv für Rechts- und Sozialphilosophie*, Beiheft 20, 99–110. Wiesbaden: Franz Steiner, 1984.

Honig, Bonnie. "Declarations of Independence: Arendt and Derrida on the Problem of Founding a Republic." *American Political Science Review* 85 (1991): 97–113.

Huber, Ernst Rudolf. "Bismarck und der Verfassungsstaat" (1964). Reprinted in *Nationalstaat und Verfassungsstaat. Studien zur Geschichte der modernen Staatsidee*, 188–223. Stuttgart: W. Kohlhammer, 1965.

———. "Carl Schmitt in der Rechtskrise der Weimarer Endzeit." In *Complexio Oppositorum. Über Carl Schmitt*, ed. Helmut Quaritsch, 33–50. Berlin: Duncker und Humblot, 1988.

———. *Deutsche Verfassungsgeschichte seit 1789*. Vol. 2, *Der Kampf um Einheit und Freiheit 1830 bis 1850*. 3d ed. Stuttgart: W. Kohlhammer, 1988. Vol. 3, *Bismarck und das Reich*. 3d ed. Stuttgart: W. Kohlhammer, 1988. Vol. 4, *Struktur und Krisen des Kaiserreichs*. Stuttgart: W. Kohlhammer, 1969. Vol. 5, *Weltkrieg, Revolution und Rechtserneuerung, 1914–1919*. Stuttgart: W. Kohlhammer, 1978. Vol. 6, *Die Weimarer Reichsverfassung*. Stuttgart: W. Kohlhammer, 1981. Vol. 7, *Ausbau, Schutz und Untergang der Weimarer Republik*. Stuttgart: W. Kohlhammer, 1984.

———. "Grundrechte im Bismarckschen Rechtssystem." In *Festschrift für Ulrich Scheuner zum 70. Geburtstag*, ed. Horst Ehmke et al., 163–81. Berlin: Duncker und Humblot, 1973.

———. *Reichsgewalt und Staatsgerichtshof*. Oldenburg im Ostfriesland: Gerhard Stalling, 1932.

Hughes, Michael L. *Paying for the German Inflation*. Chapel Hill: University of North Carolina Press, 1988.

Jasper, Gerhard. *Die gescheiterte Zähmung. Wege zur Machtergreifung Hitlers 1930–1934*. Frankfurt am Main: Suhrkamp, 1986.

John, Michael. *Politics and the Law in Late Nineteenth-Century Germany. The Origins of the Civil Code*. Oxford: Clarendon, 1989.

Jones, H. S. *The French State in Question: Public Law and Political Argument in the Third Republic*. New York: Cambridge University Press, 1993.

Kaiser, Andreas. "Preussen *contra* Reich. Hermann Heller als Prozessgegner Carl Schmitts vor dem Staatsgerichtshof 1932." In *Der soziale Rechtsstaat. Gedächtnisschrift für Hermann Heller 1891–1933*, ed. Christoph Müller and Ilse Staff, 287–311. Baden-Baden: Nomos, 1984.

Kehr, Eckart. *Economic Interest, Militarism, and Foreign Policy: Essays in German History*. Ed. Gordon Craig. Trans. Grete Heinz. Berkeley: University of California Press, 1977.

Kennedy, Ellen. "The Politics of Toleration in Late Weimar: Hermann Heller's Analysis of Fascism and Political Culture." *History of Political Thought* 5 (1984): 109–25.

Kervegan, Jean-François. "Politik und Vernünftigkeit. Anmerkungen zum Verhältnis zwischen Carl Schmitt und Hegel." *Der Staat* 27 (1988): 371–91.

Kiefer, Lorenz. "Begründung, Dezision und Politische Theologie. Zu drei frühen Schriften von Carl Schmitt." *Archiv für Rechts- und Sozialphilosophie* 76 (1990): 479–99.

Kielmansegg, Peter Graf. *Deutschland und der Erste Weltkrieg*. Frankfurt am Main: Athenaion, 1968.

Kitchen, Martin. *The Silent Dictatorship. The Politics of the German High Command under Hindenburg and Ludendorff, 1916–1918*. London: Croom Helm, 1976.

Klein, Eckart, ed. *Verfassungsentwicklungen in Deutschland nach der Wiedervereinigung*. Berlin: Duncker und Humblot, 1994.

Klenner, Hermann. *Deutsche Rechtsphilosophie im 19. Jahrhundert*. Berlin: Akademie, 1991.

———. "Rechtsphilosophie im Deutschen Kaiserreich." In *Deutsche Rechts- und Sozialphilosophie um 1900. Archiv für Rechts- und Sozialphilosophie*, Beiheft 43, ed. Gerhard Sprenger, 7–17. Stuttgart: Franz Steiner, 1991.

Klumker, C. J. "Artikel 121. Stellung der unehelichen Kinder." In *Die Grundrechte und Grundpflichten der Reichsverfassung. Kommentar zum zweiten Teil der Reichsverfassung*. Vol. 2, ed. Hans-Carl Nipperdey, 107–28. Berlin: Reimar Hobbing, 1929.

Kocka, Jürgen. *Facing Total War: German Society 1914–1918*. Trans. Barbara Weinberger. Cambridge: Harvard University Press, 1984.

Kohl, Wolfgang, and Michael Stolleis. "Im Bauch des Leviathan. Zur Staats- und Verwaltungslehre im Nationalsozialismus." *Neue Juristische Wochenschrift* 41 (1988): 2849–56.

Kolb, Eberhard, and Wolfram Pyta. "Die Staatsnotstandsplanung unter den Regierungen Papen und Schleicher." In *Die deutsche Staatskrise 1930–1933. Handlungsspielräume und Alternativen*, ed. Heinrich August Winkler with Elisabeth Muller-Luckner, 155–81. Munich: Oldenbourg, 1993.

Kommers, Donald. *The Constitutional Jurisprudence of the Federal Republic of Germany*. 2d ed. Durham: Duke University Press, 1997.

Korioth, Stefan. "Erschütterungen des staatsrechtlichen Positivismus im ausgehenden Kaiserreich." *Archiv des öffentlichen Rechts* 117 (1992): 212–38.

———. *Integration und Bundesstaat. Ein Beitrag zur Staats- und Verfassungslehre Rudolf Smends.* Berlin: Duncker und Humblot, 1990.

Kratz, Peter. *Rechte Genossen. Neokonservatismus in der SPD.* Berlin: Elefanten Press, 1995.

Kraus, Hans-Christof. "Ursprung und Genese der 'Lückentheorie' im preussischen Verfassungskonflikt." *Der Staat* 14 (1990): 209–34.

Kreutzer, Heinz. "Der Ausnahmezustand im deutschen Verfassungsrecht." In *Der Staatsnotstand. Vorträge gehalten im Sommersemester 1964*, ed. Ernst Fraenkel, 9–38. Berlin: Colloquium, 1965.

Kriele, Martin. *Theorie der Rechtsgewinnung entwickelt am Problem der Verfassungsinterpretation.* 2d ed. Berlin: Duncker und Humblot, 1976.

Kröger, Klaus. "Bemerkungen zu Carl Schmitts 'Römischer Katholizismus und politische Form.'" In *Complexio Oppositorum. Über Carl Schmitt*, ed. Helmut Quaritsch, 159–65. Berlin: Duncker und Humblot, 1988.

Landecker, Werner S. "Smend's Theory of Integration." *Social Forces* 29 (1950): 39–48.

Larenz, Karl. *Methodenlehre der Rechtswissenschaft.* 5th ed. Berlin: Springer, 1983.

———. *Staats- und Rechtsphilosophie der Gegenwart.* Berlin: Junker und Dünnhaupt, 1931.

La Torre, Massimo. "'Rechtsstaat' and Legal Science. The Rise and Fall of the Concept of Subjective Right." *Archiv für Rechts- und Sozialphilosophie* 76 (1990): 50–68.

Ledford, Ken. "Lawyers, Liberalism, and Procedure: The German Imperial Justice Laws of 1877–1879." *Central European History* 26 (1993): 165–93.

Lenoir, J. J. "Judicial Review in Germany under the Weimar Constitution." *Tulane Law Review* 14 (1940): 361–83.

Lidtke, Vernon L. "Catholics and Politics in Nineteenth-Century Germany. A Comment." *Central European History* 19 (1986): 116–22.

Lindner, Marc. *The Supreme Labor Court in Nazi Germany: A Jurisprudential Analysis.* Frankfurt am Main: Vittorio Klostermann, 1987.

Lombardi Vallauri, Luigi. *Geschichte des Freirechts.* Trans. Lombardi and A. S. Fouckes. Frankfurt am Main: Vittorio Klostermann, 1971.

Lönne, Karl-Egon. "Carl Schmitt und der Katholizismus der Weimarer Republik." In *Die eigentlich katholische Verschärfung. . . . Katholizismus, Theologie und Politik im Werk Carl Schmitts*, ed. Bernd Wacker, 11–35. Munich: Wilhelm Fink, 1994.

Losano, Mario G. "The Periodization of Kelsen Proposed by S. L. Paulson." In *Hans Kelsen's Legal Theory: A Diachronic Point of View*, ed. Letizia Gianformaggio, 111–21. Turin: G. Giappichli, 1990.

Lübbe-Wolff, Gertrude. "Safeguards of Civil and Constitutional Rights—The Debate on the Role of the *Reichsgericht*." In *German and American Constitutional Thought: Contexts, Interaction, and Historical Realities,* ed. Hermann Wellenreuther, 353–72. New York: Berg, 1990.

Luhmann, Niklas. *Rechtssoziologie.* 3d ed. Opladen: Westdeutscher, 1987.

———. "The Unity of the Legal System." In *Autopoietic Law: A New Approach to Law and Society,* ed. Gunther Teubner, 12–35. Berlin: Walter de Gruyter, 1988.

Lukács, Georg. *Die Zerstörung der Vernunft* (1960). Reprinted in *Werke.* Vol. 9. Neuwied: Luchterhand, 1974.

Luthardt, Wolfgang. *Sozialdemokratische Verfassungstheorie in der Weimarer Republik.* Opladen: Westdeutscher, 1986.

Mallmann, Walter. "Laband." In *Staatslexikon. Recht-Wirtschaft-Gesellschaft.* 6th ed. Vol. 5: 203–7. Freiburg: Herder, 1960.

Maschke, Günter. *Der Tod des Carl Schmitt. Apologie und Polemik.* Vienna: Karolinger, 1987.

Maus, Ingeborg. *Bürgerliche Rechtstheorie und Faschismus. Zur sozialen Funktion und aktuellen Wirkung der Theorie Carl Schmitts.* Munich: Wilhelm Fink, 1976.

———. "Plädoyer für eine rechtsgebietsspezifische Methodologie oder: wider den Imperialismus in der juristischen Methodendiskussion." *Kritische Vierteljahresschrift für Gesetzgebung und Rechtswissenschaft* 74 (1991): 107–22.

———. "Zur Transformation des Volkssouveränitätsprinzips in der Weimarer Republic." In *Politik-Verfassung-Gesellschaft. Traditionslinien und Entwicklungsperspektiven. Otwin Massing zum 60. Geburtstag,* ed. Peter Nahamowitz and Stefan Breuer, 107–23. Baden-Baden: Nomos, 1995.

———. "Zur 'Zäsur' von 1933 in der Theorie Carl Schmitts" (1969). Reprinted in *Rechtstheorie und politische Theorie im Industriekapitalismus,* 93–110. Munich: Wilhelm Fink, 1986.

Mayer, Hans. *Ein Deutscher auf Widerruf. Erinnerungen.* 2 vols. Frankfurt am Main: Suhrkamp, 1982.

———. "Die Krise der deutschen Staatslehre von Bismarck bis Weimar" (1931). Reprinted in *Karl Marx und das Elend des Geistes. Studien zur neuen deutschen Ideologie,* 48–75. Miesenheim am Glan: Westkulturverlag Anton Hain, 1948.

McCormick, John. *Against Politics as Technology: Carl Schmitt's Critique of Liberalism.* New York: Cambridge University Press, 1997.

———. "Dangers of Mythologizing Technology and Politics: Nietzsche, Schmitt and the Antichrist." *Philosophy and Social Criticism* 21 (1995): 55–92.

———. "Fear, Technology and the State: Carl Schmitt, Leo Strauss and the Revival of Hobbes in Weimar and National Socialist Germany." *Political Theory* 22 (1994): 619–52.

Mehring, Reinhard. *Carl Schmitt zur Einführung.* Hamburg: Junius, 1992.

———. "Carl Schmitts Lehre von der Auflösung des Liberalismus: Das Sinngefüge der 'Verfassungslehre' als historisches Urteil." *Zeitschrift für Politik* 38 (1991): 200-216.

————. "Integration und Verfassung. Zum politischen Verfassungssinn Rudolf Smends." In *Politisches Denken. Jahrbuch 1994,* ed. Volker Gerhardt, Henning Ottmann, and Martyn P. Thompson, 19-35. Stuttgart: J. B. Metzler, 1995.

————. *Pathetisches Denken. Carl Schmitts Denkweg am Leitfaden Hegels: Katholische Grundstellung und antimarxistische Hegelstrategie.* Berlin: Duncker und Humblot, 1989.

————. "Zu den neugesammelten Schriften und Studien Ernst-Wolfgang Böckenfördes." *Archiv des öffentlichen Rechts* 117 (1992): 449-73.

Meier, Heinrich. *Carl Schmitt and Leo Strauss: The Hidden Dialogue.* Trans. J. Harvey Lomax. Chicago: University of Chicago Press, 1995.

Merkl, Peter. *German Unification in the European Context.* University Park: Pennsylvania State University, 1993.

Messerschmidt, Manfred. *Die politische Geschichte der preussisch-deutschen Armee. Handbuch zur deutschen Militärgeschichte 1648-1939.* Vol. 4, pt. 1, *Militärgeschichte im 19. Jahrhundert 1814-1890.* Munich: Bernard von Graefe, 1979.

Métall, Rudolf Aladar. *Hans Kelsen. Leben und Werk.* Vienna: Franz Deuticke, 1969.

Meuter, Günter. "Zum Begriff der Transzendenz bei Carl Schmitt." *Der Staat* 32 (1991): 483-512.

Meyer, Klaus. "Hermann Heller. Eine biographische Skizze." In *Der soziale Rechtsstaat, Gedächtnisschrift für Hermann Heller,* ed. Christoph Müller and Ilse Staff, 65-87. Baden-Baden: Nomos, 1984.

Mommsen, Hans. "Government without Parties: Conservative Plans for Constitutional Revision at the End of the Weimar Republic." In *Between Reform, Reaction, and Resistance: Studies in the History of German Conservatism from 1789 to 1945,* ed. Larry E. Jones and James Retallack, 347-73. Providence: Berg, 1993.

Mommsen, Wolfgang J. "Das deutsche Kaiserreich als System umgangener Entscheidungen" (1978). Reprinted in *Der autoritäre Nationalstaat. Verfassung, Gesellschaft und Kultur im deutschen Kaiserreich,* 11-38. Frankfurt am Main: Fischer, 1990.

————. *Max Weber and German Politics 1890-1920.* 2d ed. Trans. Michael S. Steinberg. Chicago: University of Chicago Press, 1984.

————. "Die Verfassung des Deutschen Reiches von 1871 als dilatorischer Herrschaftskompromiss" (1983). Reprinted in *Der autoritäre Nationalstaat. Verfassung, Gesellschaft und Kultur im deutschen Kaiserreich,* 39-65. Frankfurt am Main: Fischer, 1990.

Moore, Ronald. *Legal Norms and Legal Science. A Critical Study of Kelsen's Pure Theory of Law.* Honolulu: University of Hawaii Press, 1978.

Morsey, Rudolf. *Die deutsche Zentrumspartei 1917–1923.* Dusseldorf: Droste, 1966.

Mosler, Hermann. "Richard Thoma zum Gedächtnis." *Die öffentliche Verwaltung* 30 (1957): 826–28.

Mouffe, Chantal. "Pluralism and Modern Democracy: Around Carl Schmitt." *New Formations* 14 (1991): 1–16.

Müller, Christoph. "Die Bekenntnispflicht der Beamten. Bemerkungen zu §35 Abs. 1 S. 2 BRRG, zugleich Anmerkungen zur Methodologie Friedrich Müllers." In *Ordnungsmacht? Über das Verhältnis von Legalität, Konsens und Herrschaft,* ed. Dieter Deiseroth, Friedhelm Hase, and Karl-Heinz Ladeur, 211–44. Frankfurt am Main: Europäische Verlagsanstalt, 1981.

———. "Hermann Heller: Leben, Werk, Wirkung." In Heller, *Gesammelte Schriften.* 2d ed. Ed. Fritz Borinski, Martin Drath, Gerhart Niemeyer, and Otto Stammer, 3:429–76. Tübingen: J. C. B. Mohr (Paul Siebeck), 1992.

———. "Kritische Bemerkungen zur Auseinandersetzung Hermann Hellers mit Hans Kelsen." In *Der soziale Rechtsstaat. Gedächtnisschrift für Hermann Heller 1891–1933,* ed. Christoph Müller and Ilse Staff, 693–722. Baden-Baden: Nomos, 1984.

Müller, Frank. *Die "Brüning Papers." Der letzte Zentrumskanzler im Spiegel seiner Selbstzeugnisse.* Frankfurt am Main: Peter Lang, 1993.

Müller, Friedrich. *Die Einheit der Verfassung. Elemente einer Verfassungstheorie III.* Berlin: Duncker und Humblot, 1979.

———. *Juristische Methodik.* 3d ed. Berlin: Duncker und Humblot, 1989.

———. "Der Vorbehalt des Gesetzes" (1960). Reprinted in *Rechtsstaatliche Form Demokratische Politik. Beiträge zu öffentlichem Recht, Methodik, Rechts- und Staatstheorie,* 15–47. Berlin: Duncker und Humblot, 1977.

———. *Strukturierende Rechtslehre.* 2d ed. Berlin: Duncker und Humblot, 1994.

Müller, Ingo. *Hitler's Justice: The Courts of the Third Reich.* Cambridge: Harvard University Press, 1991.

Muller, Jerry Z. *The Other God That Failed: Hans Freyer and the Deradicalization of German Conservatism.* Princeton: Princeton University Press, 1987.

Muscheler, Karlheinz. *Relativismus und Freiheit. Ein Versuch über Hermann Kantorowicz.* Heidelberg: C. F. Müller, 1984.

Mussgnug, Reinhard. "Die Ausführung der Reichsgesetze durch die Länder und die Reichsaufsicht." In *Deutsche Verwaltungsgeschichte.* Vol. 3, *Das Deutsche Reich bis zum Ende der Monarchie,* 186–206. Stuttgart: Deutsche Verlags-Anstalt, 1984.

Nipperdey, Thomas. *Deutsche Geschichte 1800–1866: Bürgerwelt und starker Staat.* Munich: C. H. Beck, 1983.

———. *Deutsche Geschichte 1866–1918.* Vol. 1, *Arbeitswelt und Bürgergeist.* Munich: C. H. Beck, 1990.

————. *Deutsche Geschichte 1866–1918.* Vol. 2, *Machtstaat vor der Demokratie.* Munich: C. H. Beck, 1990.

Noack, Paul. *Carl Schmitt.* Frankfurt am Main: Propyläen, 1993.

Nolte, Paul. "Die badischen Verfassungsfeste im Vormärz. Liberalismus, Verfassungskultur und soziale Ordnung in den Gemeinden." In *Bürgerliche Feste. Symbolische Formen politischen Handelns im 19. Jahrhundert,* ed. Manfred Hettling and Paul Nolte, 63–94. Göttingen: Vandenhoeck und Ruprecht, 1993.

Nörr, Knut Wolfgang. *Zwischen den Mühlsteinen. Eine Privatrechtsgeschichte der Weimarer Republik.* Tübingen: J. C. B. Mohr (Paul Siebeck), 1988.

Oertzen, Peter von. *Die politische Funktion des staatsrechtlichen Positivismus. Eine wissenssoziologische Studie über die Entstehung des formalistischen Positivismus in der deutschen Staatsrechtswissenschaft.* Ed. Dieter Sterzel. Frankfurt am Main: Suhrkamp, 1974.

Orlow, Dietrich. *Weimar Prussia 1925–1933: The Illusion of Strength.* Pittsburgh: University of Pittsburgh Press, 1991.

Osterroth, Franz. "Der Hofgeismarkreis der Jungsozialisten." *Archiv für Sozialgeschichte* 4 (1964): 525–69.

Ott, Walter. *Der Rechtspositivismus. Kritische Würdigung auf der Grundlage eines juristischen Pragmatismus.* Berlin: Duncker und Humblot, 1976.

Pascher, Manfred. "Hermann Cohens Einfluss auf Kelsens Reine Rechtslehre." *Rechtstheorie* 23 (1992): 445–66.

Paulson, Stanley L. "Continental Normativism and Its British Counterpart: How Different Are They?" *Ratio Juris* 6 (1993): 227–44.

————. Introduction to *Introduction to the Problems of Legal Theory. A Translation of the First Edition of the Reine Rechtslehre or Pure Theory of Law,* by Hans Kelsen. Trans. Bonnie Litschewski Paulson and Stanley L. Paulson, v–xlii. Oxford: Clarendon, 1992.

————. "Kelsen and the Marburg School: Reconstructive and Historical Perspectives." In *Prescriptive Formality and Normative Rationality in Modern Legal Systems. Festschrift for Robert S. Summers,* ed. Werner Krawietz, Neil MacCormick, and Georg Henrik von Wright, 481–94. Berlin: Duncker und Humblot, 1994.

————. "Kelsen on Legal Interpretation." *Legal Studies* 10 (1990): 136–52.

————. "The Reich President and Weimar Constitutional Politics: Aspects of the Schmitt-Kelsen Dispute on the 'Guardian of the Constitution.'" Paper presented at the American Political Science Association annual meeting, Chicago, Ill., September 1, 1995.

————. "Toward a Periodization of the Pure Theory of Law." In *Hans Kelsen's Legal Theory: A Diachronic Point of View,* ed. Letizia Gianformaggio, 11–48. Turin: G. Giappichelli, 1990.

————. "Zu Hermann Hellers Kritik an die Reine Rechtslehre." In *Der soziale*

Rechtsstaat. Gedächtnisschrift für Hermann Heller, 1891–1934, ed. Christoph Müller and Ilse Staff, 679-92. Baden-Baden: Nomos, 1984.

—————. "Zur neukantianischen Dimension der Reinen Rechtslehre. Vorwort zur Kelsen-Sander Auseinandersetzung." Introduction to *Die Rolle des Neukantianismus in der Reinen Rechtslehre,* ed. Stanley L. Paulson, 7-22. Aalen: Scientia, 1988.

Pauly, Walter. *Der Methodenwandel im deutschen Spätkonstitutionalismus. Ein Beitrag zu Entwicklung und Gestalt der Wissenschaft vom öffentlichen Recht in 19. Jahrhundert.* Tübingen: J. C. B. Mohr (Paul Siebeck), 1993.

Perels, Joachim. "Gleichheit vor dem Gesetz." In *Grundrechte als Fundament der Demokratie,* ed. Joachim Perels, 69-95. Frankfurt am Main: Suhrkamp, 1979.

Petermann, T. "Die Gehe-Stiftung zu Dresden in den ersten 15 Jahren ihrer Thätigkeit." In *Weltwirtschaft und Volkswirtschaft, Jahrbuch der Gehe-Stiftung zu Dresden.* Vol. 5, ed. Heinrich Dietzel, i-xvii. Dresden: von Zahn und Jaensch, 1900.

Peukert, Detlev. *The Weimar Republic: The Crisis of Classical Modernity.* Trans. Richard Deveson. New York: Hill and Wang, 1992.

Pflanze, Otto. *Bismarck and the Development of Germany. The Period of Unification, 1815–1871.* Princeton: Princeton University Press, 1963.

Poeschel, Jürgen. *Anthropologische Voraussetzungen der Staatstheorie Rudolf Smends. Die elementaren Kategorien Leben und Leistung.* Berlin: Duncker und Humblot, 1978.

Pore, Renate. *A Conflict of Interest. Women in German Social Democracy 1919–1933.* Westport, Conn.: Greenwood, 1981.

Portner, Ernst. *Die Verfassungspolitik der Liberalen 1919. Ein Beitrag zur Deutung der Weimarer Reichsverfassung.* Bonn: Röhrscheid, 1973.

Preuss, Ulrich K. "Constitutional Powermaking of the New Polity: Some Deliberations on the Relations between Constituent Power and the Constitution." In *Constitutionalism, Identity, Difference, and Legitimacy: Theoretical Perspectives,* ed. Michel Rosenfeld, 143-64. Durham: Duke University Press, 1994.

—————. *Constitutional Revolution: The Link between Constitutionalism and Progress.* Trans. Deborah Lucas Schneider. Atlantic Highlands, N.J.: Humanities Press, 1995.

Quaritsch, Helmut. *Positionen und Begriffe Carl Schmitts.* 2d ed. Berlin: Duncker und Humblot, 1991.

Rath, Hans-Dieter. *Positivismus und Demokratie. Richard Thoma, 1874–1957.* Berlin: Duncker und Humblot, 1981.

Rennert, Klaus. *Die "geisteswissenschaftliche Richtung" in der Staatsrechtslehre der Weimarer Republik. Untersuchungen zu Erich Kaufmann, Günther Holstein und Rudolf Smend.* Berlin: Duncker und Humblot, 1987.

Riebschläger, Klaus. *Die Freirechtsbewegung. Zur Entstehung einer soziologischen Rechtsschule.* Berlin: Duncker und Humblot, 1968.

Ringhofer, Kurt. "Interpretation und Reine Rechtslehre. Gedanken zu einer Kritik." In *Festschrift für Hans Kelsen zum 90. Geburtstag,* ed. Adolf Merkl et al., 198–210. Vienna: Franz Deuticke, 1971.

Rittstieg, Helmut. "Artikel 14/15." In *Kommentar zum Grundgesetz für die Bundesrepublik Deutschland.* 2d ed., ed. Richard Bäumlin et al., 1046–1145. Neuwied: Luchterhand, 1989.

———. *Eigentum als Verfassungsproblem. Zu Geschichte und Gegenwart des bürgerlichen Verfassungsstaates.* Darmstadt: Wissenschaftliche Buchgesellschaft, 1975.

Robbers, Gerhard. *Hermann Heller: Staat und Kultur.* Baden-Baden: Nomos, 1983.

———. "Die historische Entwicklung der Verfassungsgerichtsbarkeit." *Juristische Schulung* 30 (1990): 257–63.

Rogers, Lindsay, Sanford Schwarz, and Nicholas S. Kaltchas. "German Political Institutions II. Article 48." *Political Science Quarterly* 47 (1932): 583–94.

Römer, Peter. "Die Reine Rechtslehre Hans Kelsens als Ideologie und Ideologiekritik." *Politische Vierteljahresschrift* 12 (1971): 579–98.

———. "Reine Rechtslehre und Gesetzgebungslehre." In *Rechtstheorie und Gesetzgebung. Festschrift für Robert Weimar,* 25–36. Frankfurt am Main: Peter Lang, 1986.

———. "Tod und Verklärung des Carl Schmitt." *Archiv für Rechts- und Sozialphilosophie* 76 (1990): 373–99.

Rosenau, Kersten. *Hegemonie und Dualismus. Preussens staatsrechtliche Stellung im Deutschen Reich.* Regensburg: S. Roderer, 1986.

Ross, Alf. *Towards a Realistic Jurisprudence: A Criticism of the Dualism in Law.* Trans. Annie I. Fausbøll. 1946. Reprint, Aalen: Scientia, 1989.

Rossiter, Clinton L. *Constitutional Dictatorship: Crisis Government in the Modern Democracies.* Princeton: Princeton University Press, 1948.

Rumpf, Helmut. *Carl Schmitt und Thomas Hobbes. Ideelle Beziehungen und aktuelle Bedeutung mit einer Abhandlung über Die Frühschriften Carl Schmitts.* Berlin: Duncker und Humblot, 1972.

Rüthers, Bernd. *Carl Schmitt im Dritten Reich. Wissenschaft als Zeitgeist-Verstärkung.* 2d ed. Munich: C. H. Beck, 1990.

———. *Entartetes Recht. Rechtslehren und Kronjuristen im Dritten Reich.* 3d ed. Munich: DTV, 1994.

Schefold, Dian. "Hellers Ringen um den Verfassungsbegriff." In *Der soziale Rechtsstaat. Gedächtnisschrift für Hermann Heller 1891–1933,* ed. Christoph Müller and Ilse Staff, 555–72. Baden-Baden: Nomos, 1984.

Scheuerman, William P. *Between the Norm and the Exception: The Frankfurt School and the Rule of Law.* Cambridge: MIT Press, 1994.

Scheuner, Ulrich. "Die Anwendung des Art. 48 der Weimarer Reichsverfassung unter den Präsidentschaften von Ebert und Hindenburg." In *Staat, Wirtschaft und Politik in der Weimarer Republik. Festschrift für Heinrich Brüning,* ed. Ferdinand A. Hermens and Theodor Schieder, 249–86. Berlin: Duncker und Humblot, 1967.

———. "50 Jahre deutsche Staatsrechtswissenschaft im Spiegel der Verhandlungen der Vereinigung der Deutschen Staatsrechtslehrer. I. Die Vereinigung der Deutschen Staatsrechtslehrer in der Zeit der Weimarer Republik." *Archiv des öffentlichen Rechts* 97 (1972): 349–74.

———. "Die nationale Revolution. Eine staatsrechtliche Untersuchung." *Archiv des öffentlichen Rechts* 62 (1933–34): 166–220, 261–344.

———. "Die rechtliche Tragweite der Grundrechte in der deutschen Verfassungsentwicklung des 19. Jahrhunderts." In *Festschrift für Ernst Rudolf Huber,* ed. Ernst Forsthoff, 139–65. Göttingen: Otto Schwarz, 1973.

———. "Die Überlieferung der deutschen Staatsgerichtsbarkeit im 19. und 20. Jahrhundert." In *Bundesverfassungsgericht und Grundgesetz. Festgabe aus Anlass des 25jährigen Bestehens des Bundesverfassungsgerichts.* Vol. 1, ed. Christian Stark, 2–41. Tübingen: J. C. B. Mohr (Paul Siebeck), 1976.

Schiffers, Reinhard. *Elemente direkter Demokratie im Weimarer Regierungssystem.* Dusseldorf: Droste, 1971.

Schild, Wolfgang. "Die Ambivalenz einer Neo-Philosophie. Zu Josef Kohlers Neuhegelianismus." In *Deutsche Rechts- und Sozialphilosophie um 1900. Archiv für Rechts- und Sozialphilosophie,* Beiheft 43, ed. Gerhard Sprenger, 46–65. Stuttgart: Franz Steiner, 1991.

Schlink, Bernhard. "Laband als Politiker." *Der Staat* 31 (1992): 553–69.

———. "Why Carl Schmitt?" *Rechtshistorisches Journal* 10 (1991): 160–76.

Schluchter, Wolfgang. *Entscheidung für den sozialen Rechtsstaat. Hermann Heller und die staatstheoretische Diskussion in der Weimarer Republik.* Cologne: Kiepenheuer und Witsch, 1968.

Schorske, Carl E. *Fin de siècle Vienna.* New York: Vintage, 1981.

Schröder, Rainer. "Die deutsche Methodendiskussion um die Jahrhundertwende: wissenstheoretische Präzisierungsversuche oder Antworten auf den Funktionswandel von Recht und Justiz." *Rechtstheorie* 19 (1988): 323–67.

Schüddekopf, Otto-Ernst. *Linke Leute von rechts. Die nationalrevolutionären Minderheiten und der Kommunismus in der Weimarer Republik.* Stuttgart: W. Kohlhammer, 1960.

Schüle, Adolf. "Richard Thoma zum Gedächtnis." *Archiv des öffentlichen Rechts* 82 (1957): 153–56.

Schulz, Gerhard. *Zwischen Demokratie und Diktatur. Verfassungspolitik und Reichsreform in der Weimarer Republik.* Vol. 3, *Von Brüning zu Hitler. Der Wandel des politischen Systems in Deutschland 1930–1933.* Berlin: Walter de Gruyter, 1992.

Schulze, Hagen. *Weimar. Deutschland 1917–1933.* 4th ed. Berlin: Severin und Siedler, 1994.

Schwab, George. *The Challenge of the Exception: An Introduction to the Political Ideas of Carl Schmitt between 1921 and 1936.* Berlin: Duncker und Humblot, 1970.

Siemann, Wolfram. *Gesellschaft im Aufbruch. Deutschland 1849–1871.* Frankfurt am Main: Suhrkamp, 1990.

Silverman, Paul. "Law and Economics in Interwar Vienna. Kelsen, Mises, and the Regeneration of Austrian Liberalism." Ph.D. diss., University of Chicago, 1984.

Sombart, Nicolaus. *Die deutschen Männer und ihre Feinde. Carl Schmitt—ein deutsches Schicksal zwischen Männerbund und Matriarchatsmythos.* Munich: Hanser, 1991.

Sontheimer, Kurt. *Antidemokratisches Denken in der Weimarer Republik. Die politischen Ideen des deutschen Nationalismus zwischen 1918 und 1933.* 3d ed. Munich: DTV, 1992.

———. *Politische Wissenschaft und Staatsrechtslehre.* Freiburg: Rembach, 1962.

Staff, Ilse. "Staatslehre in der Weimarer Republik." In *Staatslehre in der Weimarer Republik. Hermann Heller zu ehren,* ed. Ilse Staff and Christoph Müller, 7–23. Frankfurt am Main: Suhrkamp, 1985.

Stein, Ekkehard. *Staatsrecht.* 9th ed. Tübingen: J. C. B. Mohr (Paul Siebeck), 1984.

Stolleis, Michael. "Carl Schmitt." In *Staat und Recht. Die deutsche Staatslehre im 19. und 20. Jahrhundert,* ed. Martin J. Sattler, 123–46. Munich: List, 1972.

———. *Geschichte des öffentlichen Rechts in Deutschland.* Vol. 2, *Staatsrechtslehre und Verwaltungswissenschaft 1800–1914.* Munich: C. H. Beck, 1992.

Stoly, Otto. *Grundriss der Österreichischen Verfassungs- und Verwaltungsgeschichte.* Innsbruck: Tyrolia, 1951.

Strömholm, Stig. *A Short History of Legal Thinking in the West.* Stockholm: Norstedts, 1985.

Summers, Robert S. "Theory, Formality, and Practical Legal Criticism." In *Essays on the Nature of Law and Legal Realism,* 154–76. Berlin: Duncker und Humblot, 1992.

Tadich, Ljubomir. "Kelsen et Marx. Contribution au problème de l'idéologie dans 'la théorie pure de droit' et dans le marxisme." *Archives de Philosophie du Droit* 12 (1967): 243–57.

Tommissen, Piet. "Bausteine zu einer wissenschaftlichen Biographie (Periode: 1888-1933)." In *Complexio Oppositorum. Über Carl Schmitt,* ed. Helmut Quaritsch, 71–100. Berlin: Duncker und Humblot, 1988.

Tumanov, W. A. *Contemporary Bourgeois Legal Thought: A Marxist Evaluation of the Basic Concepts.* Moscow: Progress, 1974.

Vesting, Thomas. "Aporien des rechtswissenschaftlichen Formalismus: Hermann

Hellers Kritik an der Reinen Rechtslehre." *Archiv für Rechts- und Sozialphiloso-phie* 77 (1991): 348–73.

———. "Erosionen staatlicher Herrschaft. Zum Begriff des Politischen bei Carl Schmitt." *Archiv des öffentlichen Rechts* 117 (1992): 4–45.

———. *Politische Einheitsbildung und technische Realisation. Über die Expansion der Technik und die Grenzen der Demokratie.* Baden-Baden: Nomos, 1990.

Wadl, Wilhelm. *Liberalismus und soziale Frage in Österreich. Deutsch-liberale Reak-tionen und Einflüsse auf die frühe österreichische Arbeiterbewegung (1867–1879).* Vienna: Österreichische Akademie der Wissenschaften, 1987.

Walter, Robert, ed. *Adolf J. Merkl. Werk und Wirksamkeit.* Schriftenreihe des Hans-Kelsen-Instituts, vol. 14. Vienna: Manz, 1990.

———. "Die Gerichtsbarkeit." In *Das österreichische Bundes-Verfassungsgesetz und seine Entwicklung,* ed. Herbert Schambeck, 443–80. Berlin: Duncker und Humblot, 1980.

Waser, Ruedi. *Die sozialistische Idee im Denken Hermann Hellers. Zur politischen Theorie und Praxis eines demokratischen Sozialismus.* Basel: Helbing und Lichtenhahn, 1985.

Wehler, Hans-Ulrich. *The German Empire 1871–1918.* Trans. Kim Traynor. Leamington Spa: Berg, 1985.

Weinberger, Ota. "The Theory of Legal Dynamics Reconsidered." *Ratio Juris* 4 (1991): 18–35.

Weinberger, Ota, and Neil MacCormick. *An Institutional Theory of Law. New Approaches to Legal Positivism.* Dordrecht: D. Reidel, 1986.

Wengst, Udo. "Staatsaufbau und Verwaltungsstruktur." In *Die Weimarer Republik 1918–1933. Politik-Wirtschaft-Gesellschaft,* ed. Karl-Dietrich Bracher, Manfred Funke, and Hans-Adolf Jacobsen, 63–77. Dusseldorf: Droste, 1987.

Wenzel, Uwe Justus. "Recht und Moral der Vernunft. Kants Rechtslehre: Neue Literatur und neue Editionen." *Archiv für Rechts- und Sozialphilosophie* 76 (1990): 227–43.

Wesel, Uwe. "Die Zweite Krise." *Die Zeit,* October 6, 1995, 7–8.

West, Franklin C. *A Crisis of the Weimar Republic: A Study of the German Referen-dum of 20 June 1926.* Philadelphia: American Philosophical Society, 1985.

White, Dan S. *Lost Comrades: Socialists of the Front Generation, 1918–1945.* Cambridge: Harvard University Press, 1992.

Wiegandt, Manfred H. *Norm und Wirklichkeit. Gerhard Leibholz (1901–1982). Leben, Werk und Richteramt.* Baden-Baden: Nomos, 1995.

Wilhelm, Walter. *Zur juristischen Methodenlehre im 19. Jahrhundert. Die Herkunft der Methode Paul Labands aus der Privatrechtswissenschaft.* Frankfurt am Main: Vittorio Klostermann, 1958.

Willey, Thomas. *Back to Kant: The Revival of Kantianism in German Social and Historical Thought, 1860–1914.* Detroit: Wayne State University Press, 1978.

Winkler, Heinrich August. "Unternehmer und Wirtschaftsdemokratie in der Weimarer Republik." In *Probleme der Demokratie Heute. Politische Vierteljahrsschrift*, Sonderheft 2 (1970): 308–22.

———. *Von der Revolution zur Stabilisierung. Arbeiter und Arbeiterbewegung in der Weimarer Republik 1918 bis 1924*. Berlin: Dietz Nachfolger, 1989.

———. *Weimar 1919–1933. Die Geschichte der ersten deutschen Demokratie*. Munich: C. H. Beck, 1993.

Wolin, Richard. "Carl Schmitt: The Conservative Revolutionary Habitus and the Aesthetics of Horror." *Political Theory* 20 (1992): 424–47.

Zacker, Hans F. "Hans Nawiasky." In *Juristen im Portrait. Verlag und Autoren in 4 Jahrzehnten. Festschrift zum 225jährigen Jubiläum des Verlages C. H. Beck*, 598–607. Munich: C. H. Beck, 1988.

INDEX

Peter Caldwell is Assistant Professor of History

at Rice University

Library of Congress Cataloging-in-Publication Data

Caldwell, Peter C.
Popular sovereignty and the crisis of German constitutional law : the theory &
practice of Weimar constitutionalism / Peter C. Caldwell.
p.   cm.
Includes bibliographical references and index.
ISBN 0-8223-1979-9 (alk. paper). — ISBN 0-8223-1988-8 (pbk. : alk. paper)
1. Constitutional history—Germany.   2. Constitutional law—Germany—
Philosophy—History.   3. Constituent power—Germany—History.
4. Germany—Politics and government—1918-1933.   I. Title.
KK4710.C35   1997
342.43—dc21   97-17282